The common good is an idea whose meaning has been debated since classical times. For Christians, a crucial question concerns the common good's relationship with the Kingdom of God. In *The Kingdom of God and the Common Good*, Dylan Pahman has penned a systematic analysis of this topic from an Orthodox Christian standpoint that brings together a thorough grounding in theology with a strong grasp of history as well as the social sciences of economics and politics. Readers will discover that the Orthodox Tradition provides powerful guidance into how our anticipation of the Kingdom of God can help us realize the common good in this world while avoiding the errors of utopianism and resignation. All Christians, whatever their confession, will see the common good in a new light after reading this book.

—Samuel Gregg, Friedrich Hayek Chair in Economics and Economic
History, American Institute for Economic Research

*The Kingdom of God and the Common Good* is a superb blend of history, theology, and social science. Pahman dispels the notion that concern for man's economy of goods blinds us to God's economy of salvation. In doing so, he offers a compelling vision of how faith and economics can work in harmony to promote both spiritual and societal flourishing.

—Alexander William Salter, PhD, Georgie G. Snyder Professor of
Economics, Rawls College of Business, Texas Tech University

Dylan Pahman's *The Kingdom of God and the Common Good* is a thoughtful and timely exploration of Christian social thought, offering a rich Orthodox perspective on human dignity, neighborly love, and our pursuit of the common good. Drawing from Scripture, history, and insights across Christian traditions, Pahman shows how the Orthodox vision uniquely deepens our understanding of what it means to be persons created in the image of God. I found the book deeply engaging—both intellectually and spiritually—prompting reflection on how we love our neighbors and care for the poor. It's a book I am grateful for and eager to share.

—Simon Scionka, Filmmaker, *Sacred Alaska* and *Poverty, Inc.*

What do St. John Chrysostom, *The Lego Movie*, Shakespeare, and the band Radiohead have in common? They're all featured in Dylan Pahman's fast-paced but thorough introduction to Christian social thought. The Bible, Church Tradition, and modern economics meet here to give us the principles that guide us in our stickiest political theology questions. Unlike most of what we'll come across here in the West, Pahman shows that the Orthodox Tradition includes contributions that might unravel some of our greatest frustrations around politics and economics.

—Rachel Ferguson, Director of the Free Enterprise Center at Concordia University Chicago

While religion and economics have been recognized as two of the great driving forces of human action, their interrelationship and interdependence remain underappreciated and underexamined. Dylan Pahman has become one of the world's leading scholars of not only the history of economics and theology but also of the need to properly integrate them for an authentic and responsible social ethic today. *The Kingdom of God and the Common Good* stands as a signal contribution to this ongoing work and will reward the careful reader with knowledge and wisdom. Orthodoxy has much to teach other Christian confessions, and Pahman is helping to make the riches of that Tradition accessible not only to others but, just as importantly, to Orthodox believers as well.

—Dr. Jordan J. Ballor, Executive Director, First Liberty's Center for Religion, Culture & Democracy

As Orthodoxy takes hold in the West, it must offer its distinctive social thought to fellow Christians and the world. The Church needs scholars to guide us through Orthodox thought and teach us how to apply those teachings to real-world institutions. In this book, Dylan Pahman emerges as precisely such a guide. This essential work will bless those seeking to engage contemporary social questions from an Orthodox perspective.

—Kevin Vallier, Professor of Philosophy, Institute of American Constitutional Thought and Leadership, University of Toledo

# THE KINGDOM
# *of* GOD *and the*
# COMMON GOOD

*Orthodox Christian Social Thought*

DYLAN PAHMAN

ANCIENT FAITH PUBLISHING
CHESTERTON, INDIANA

Published by:
Ancient Faith Publishing
A Division of Ancient Faith Ministries
1050 Broadway, Suite 6
Chesterton, IN 46304

Unless otherwise noted, Scripture quotations are taken from the New King James Version, © 1979, 1980, 1982 by Thomas Nelson, Inc. Used by permission.

Cover art: detail, Novgorod Marketplace, Appolinari Mikhaylovich Vasnetsov, early 20th century; State Museum of History, Moscow. HIP / Art Resource, NY.

Cover design: Amber Schley Iragui.

ISBN: 978-1-955890-80-9

Library of Congress Control Number: 2025941887

# Contents

# Contents

# Abbreviations

# Acknowledgments

THIS BOOK BEGAN AS A series of essays for Fr. Daniel Greeson's *Every Thought Captive* blog at Ancient Faith Ministries. About half of the chapters were first published there, and I'm grateful for Fr. Greeson's support and feedback, as well as for the responses of readers.

John Pinheiro, director of research for my employer, the Acton Institute for the Study of Religion and Liberty, has supported this endeavor, allowing me to forgo other research in order to finish this book on time. I'm thankful to him and to Acton, where I've been privileged to write this book as part of my job.

The Russell Kirk Center for Cultural Renewal further blessed me with a Wilbur Fellowship in August of 2024, during which I was able to research and write four of the chapters on modern economics, as well as to summarize and present those chapters in small seminars where those present offered helpful commentary.

My colleague Daniel Hugger read over the chapter titled "Middle Eastern Melkites" and even interviewed me about it for one of our podcasts at the Acton Institute. Indeed, I greatly benefited from my many conversations with him about each chapter as I wrote it. Samuel Gregg also read this chapter and offered encouraging comments. Additionally, Samuel Noble directed me to excellent resources on Arab Orthodoxy, and I'm thankful to Marcus Shera for his feedback on the chapter "Scholastic Economics."

Erik Matson read the chapter "Adam Smith" and helped guide its revision. James Otteson reviewed the table there (Table 27.1), which is based on his own summarizing of Smith's social science, and he offered feedback so that I could be confident of its accuracy, and Alexander Salter provided challenging comments on the chapter titled "The Marginal Revolution."

My colleague Vladimir Snurenco helpfully checked over the chapters "The Economics of Crisis" and "The Great Divergence," offering his expertise as an economist and from his upbringing in Moldova. Father Gregory Jensen offered his guidance for the chapter "How Should We Think Socially?" Joseph Steineger steered me clear of philosophical imprecision in my chapter "Sophia."

John Pinheiro looked over the chapter "Sobornost'," offering comparative commentary from his Roman Catholic perspective. Gabe Martini helpfully read the chapter "Liturgical Theology," and Fr. Lucas Christensen answered questions I had on the topic. Father Alexis Torrance shared his perspective on the social ethos document written in response to the Council of Crete and reviewed in chapter 37.

All these reviewers caught and corrected many errors, taking time out of their own schedules, for which, again, I'm grateful. Any remaining errors are my own.

I'm also thankful for the support of my family—my wife Kelly and our four children—and for my church family at Holy Trinity in Grand Rapids.

I'd also like to thank Ancient Faith for believing in this book and for their help in marketing and editing it, especially my editor Marci Johnson. And, of course, I'm deeply thankful to anyone who takes time out of his or her life to read and discuss *The Kingdom of God and the Common Good* in the years to come—including you.

Glory to God for all things!

# Foreword

I F THE KINGDOM OF HEAVEN is truly at hand, what does it mean to live as a subject of that Kingdom? And what does it mean to live as a citizen of our Lord's Land, not just our particular nation or polity?

When I was growing up in the Orthodox Church, I heard a lot about private disciplines like prayer and fasting. I knew I was supposed to attend liturgical services, abstain from certain foods during specified periods, and avoid unhealthy conduct (lying, boasting, and so on). But my identity as an Orthodox Christian felt consistently *private* in that it was a sliver of myself that only applied in certain contexts.

Was I an Orthodox Christian when I picked my college major? When I was at work? When I was at the store?

For most of my young life, I honestly didn't know how to answer those questions. I knew that I was supposed to get good grades, get a good job, and become successful (both in the sense of social prestige and material comfort).

And I was well on my way. After studying history at Yale University, I went to the Fordham University School of Law and began practicing at a Wall Street firm. I had a plan for my life, one that would help me acquire both wealth and power (I had dreams of one day running for office).

But certain experiences led me to question those desires. I began to realize my own unworthiness and brokenness and started to wonder: How could I possibly hope to lead and "fix" my city, state, or country when my own heart was in shambles?

After seminary, I spent a decade in youth and young adult ministry where questions about how we navigate the world in the light of Christ were always top of mind. These questions—which I wish I had been asked in my formative years—inspired a video series my team and I used to produce, *Be the Bee*, which attempted to share what it meant to seek (and find) Christ in all things, every day. We also produced a podcast, *Pop Culture Coffee Hour*, that modeled what it meant to wrestle with contemporary art and media as an Orthodox Christian: to seek (and find) Christ in movies, TV shows, books, and music.

We undertook that work because we knew how important it was for young people—still finding their footing and wrestling with questions of identity—to learn how to think and act as Orthodox Christians. Yet it quickly became clear that it's not just young people who need this guidance: People of any age need to see what it's like to live as citizens of the Lord's Kingdom, to live in the full light of the Gospel rather than confine that light to a sliver of their attention and a piece of their larger identity.

As the executive director of FOCUS North America (a pan-Orthodox ministry that brings together Orthodox Christians and community partners to see and serve Christ in our neighbor), I now work to lead a ministry that offers a variety of services across the United States. But FOCUS is not just a nonprofit. As an affiliate of the Assembly of Canonical Bishops, it's a ministry of the Church in America. And our task isn't simply to feed and house people but to inspire Orthodox Christians to join in this vital work.

As you might expect, that presents challenges. People cannot help but be shaped by the ideas and assumptions of the wider culture. We Orthodox Christians who live in the United States, for example, are shaped by American attitudes and beliefs; we may believe the Faith of our forefathers, but we believe differently than they did. Perhaps we've internalized dichotomies between the "deserving" and "undeserving" poor, for example, despite the counsel of St. John Chrysostom that "need alone is the poor man's worthiness." Or maybe we've internalized an individualistic way of approaching the world, which has led to a rise in loneliness and disconnection in our country. And we've probably internalized a consumerist ethos that seeks fulfillment in material acquisition, even if we have to step over Lazarus at our gate to grab the brass ring.

That's why I'm grateful to Dylan for his efforts in drafting this book. Much of this work offers an overview of important ideas, from Christian social thought to modern economics. By arming the reader with this important context, Dylan then challenges us to begin thinking deeply about how we navigate the world as Orthodox Christians: How do we live ascetically in a culture built around the attainment of comfort, for example?

I'm particularly grateful that Dylan isn't too prescriptive in his approach. As he observes in his epilogue, he's offering us a vision of the Kingdom rather than a particular policy platform—just like how, when my team and I produced *Pop Culture Coffee Hour*, we weren't trying to tell people what to think about particular works of art. We were, rather, trying to demonstrate the importance of wrestling with the culture in which we're embedded while retaining a Christ-centered curiosity. I see Dylan's work as a similar model, which the Church needs: We need to think deeply about questions of wealth and poverty, about the structure of political and economic systems, about the nature of our personal relationship with money and our vision of "the good life."

As with any good book, I earnestly hope that the ideas Dylan explores and the questions he asks stay with you—that you don't just mull them over on a walk but discuss them with family over dinner, with friends at coffee hour fellowship, even with a stranger at the gym.

And if I happen to be in your city to support an existing FOCUS Center or work on the development of a new one, perhaps we can explore these ideas together.

—Steven Christoforou
Executive Director, FOCUS North America
March 6, 2025

# Blessed Is the Kingdom

T HIS BOOK IS ABOUT THREE things: the Kingdom of God, the common good, and Orthodox Christian social thought. Along the way, it
will touch on a wide range of topics, but these things—particularly the last
one—remain the heart of the book. This introduction aims to orient my readers for what follows. While we will encounter many surprising details I uncovered in my research for these chapters, I firmly believe that the primary goal
and contents of a book should not be a mystery to readers. If by the end readers have a better understanding of Orthodox Christian social thought, I will
consider the book a success.

## *Christian Social Thought: The Church, the*
## *Kingdom, and the Common Good*

JESUS BEGAN HIS MINISTRY BY proclaiming, "The time is fulfilled, and
the kingdom of God is at hand. Repent, and believe in the gospel" (Mark 1:15).
He taught His disciples to pray, "Your kingdom come. / Your will be done /
On earth as it is in heaven" (Matt. 6:10). And He taught St. Nicodemus that
"unless one is born of water and the Spirit," i.e., baptized, "he cannot enter
the kingdom of God" (John 3:5). Through these instances and many others,
Jesus taught us that the Kingdom of God is wherever His reign prevails. And
through His life, death, and Resurrection, Christ brought to us communion
with God and each other and established His Church, which according to

1

Vladimir Soloviev, "binds . . . together" the world and the Kingdom of God. Indeed, we could even say that the Church is the world becoming the Kingdom of God—not identical with either but "intermediary between the two."[1]

As Fr. Alexander Schmemann put it, "The proper function of the 'leitourgia' "—i.e., liturgy, then—"has always been to *bring together*, within one symbol, the three levels of the Christian faith and life: the Church, the world, and the Kingdom; that the Church herself is thus the sacrament in which the broken, yet still 'symbolical,' life of 'this world' is brought, in Christ and by Christ, into the dimension of the Kingdom of God, becoming itself the sacrament of the 'world to come.' "[2] In her mediatorial role between heaven and earth, the Church proclaims the Gospel of Christ's Kingdom, beginning every Divine Liturgy with the proclamation, "Blessed is the Kingdom!" But she also seeks the common good of the kingdoms and communities of this world, whose leaders and actors she commemorates in various litanies. Therefore, our "Blessed is the Kingdom!" should lead us to bless the various kingdoms in which we reside, which means not only repeating the words of the litanies but showing our care for the common good through our actions.

We see many examples of this in Scripture. For one, Jesus often showed His desire to care for the common good by healing the sick and visiting the outcast—doing both, for example, when He healed ten lepers, one of whom was a Samaritan, an outcast in Jewish society (see Luke 17:11–19). He taught His disciples to do the same (see Luke 9:1–6). He acknowledged the authority of Caesar while pointing to the greater authority of God (see Matt. 22:21), showing us that acknowledging God does not require us to reject earthly kingdoms. In the Old Testament, through the prophet Jeremiah, God showed His care for the common good when He commanded His people to seek peace even for their enemies: "Seek the peace of the city where I have caused

---

1   Vladimir Solovyov, *The Justification of the Good*, rev. ed., ed. Boris Jakim, trans. Natalie A. Duddington (Eerdmans, 2005), 371, emphasis original. The Russian surname "Soloviev" can be transliterated in several ways in English. I use the spelling "Soloviev" in the body of this text because that was his own preference. On which, see Vladimir Wozniuk, "Vladimir S. Soloviev: Moral Philosopher of Unity," *Journal of Markets & Morality* 16, no. 1 (Spring 2013): 323–329.

2   Alexander Schmemann, *For the Life of the World: Sacraments and Orthodoxy*, rev. and expanded ed. (SVS Press, 1979), 151, emphasis original.

you to be carried away captive, and pray to the LORD for it; for in its peace you will have peace" (Jer. 29:7). Saint Constantine confirmed this concept when he prayed, "My own desire is, for the common good of the world and the advantage of all mankind, that thy people should enjoy a life of peace and undisturbed concord. Let those, therefore, who still delight in error, be made welcome to the same degree of peace and tranquillity [sic] which they have who believe."[3]

Thus, citizenship in God's Kingdom should make us *more* concerned with the common good of even secular society. As St. John Chrysostom said, "How may we become imitators of Christ? By acting in everything for the common good, and not merely seeking our own. . . . In truth, a man (really) seeks his own good when he looks to that of his neighbor."[4] The common good, then, consists of the health and flourishing of *both ourselves and our communities*, from families and friendships, to workplaces and social clubs, to cities, nations, and the whole world. And caring for the common good is, of course, about love. As St. Nicholas Cabasilas taught, God himself is "the common good of all" and "man goes beyond his nature and becomes like God" when he does not "love [his] own gain alone, but consider[s] [himself] rewarded by the triumph of others"[5] through love. How we care for the common good by loving, in particular, our poor and marginalized neighbors is what Christian social thought is all about. And Christian social thought does not cover every important aspect of morality but focuses specifically on the economic aspect of our lives.

We can learn from other Christian traditions that have developed principles and teachings of their own social thought for our very peculiar modern economies in the last 150 years. And of course, the Bible, common to all Christians, is also full of commandments about wealth and poverty, rich and poor. The Orthodox Church, in her mediatorial role between the Kingdom of God and the common good, has two thousand years of social thought, too. And in our modern era, we can and should learn even from the one specialized

---

3    Eusebius of Caesarea, *The Life of Constantine*, 2.56, in NPNF² 1:513.

4    John Chrysostom, *Homilies of St. John Chrysostom on the Gospel of St. John*, 15, in NPNF¹ 14:52.

5    Nicholas Cabasilas, *The Life in Christ*, trans. Carmino J. de Catazanaro (SVS Press, 1974), 210–211.

science that exists to figure out how best to improve the material and social conditions of our neighbors: economics.

## The Plan of This Book

ACCORDINGLY, THIS BOOK HAS FIVE parts:

Part 1 sets the stage for *modern* Christian social thought and surveys some basic teachings of other Christian traditions. While we confess in the Creed that the Orthodox Church is the "one, holy, Catholic, and Apostolic Church" of Jesus Christ, we nevertheless should know what other Christians have done and what common ground might exist to help us think and work together. "For he who is not against us," says Christ, "is on our side" (Mark 9:40).

Part 2 surveys the Bible, building a biblical theology of wealth and poverty in the context of our salvation through the Gospel. The Bible is the most precious aspect of Holy Tradition, and we cannot hope to understand the latter without a decent grasp of the former. The Liturgy of the Catechumens precedes the Liturgy of the Faithful in the Divine Liturgy for this reason. Every Orthodox Christian must hear the Holy Scriptures before receiving Holy Communion. As St. Paul commanded, "Let the word of Christ dwell in you richly in all wisdom, teaching and admonishing one another in psalms and hymns and spiritual songs, singing with grace in your hearts to the Lord" (Col. 3:16).

Part 3 surveys Church history in order to more fully ground Orthodox social thought in Holy Tradition. From martyrs to monks to Church Fathers, theologians, and philosophers, we have our own deep well of living water to contribute to broader conversations about Christian social thought today. As an author and researcher, I firmly believe that all Orthodox reflection on the issues of our times must take account of the contributions of those who went before us. "Every scribe instructed concerning the kingdom of heaven," said Jesus, "is like a householder who brings out of his treasure things new and old" (Matt. 13:52). We cannot just say, "New problems require new ideas," when "there is nothing new under the sun" (Eccl. 1:9).

Conversely, Part 4 surveys the history of economics in order to help us incorporate its genuinely new insights for understanding our world today.

Human nature has not changed. People still need to love God and their neighbors. People still struggle with the same sins. But our world has changed, particularly its economies. We need not only the "old" things, but "new" things as well. And we'll see that the history of economics contains many stories, insights, principles, and examples to help us more prudently "remember the poor" (Gal. 2:10) in our contemporary contexts.

Last, Part 5 surveys more recent Orthodox social thought. In particular, I look at insights from the controversial teachings of Fr. Sergei Bulgakov and Fr. Pavel Florensky on divine wisdom or "Sophia." Then, I examine the contributions of S. L. Frank and St. Maria Skobtsova regarding the concept of *sobornost'* and the imitation of the Mother of God. Next, I sketch out economic implications of liturgical theology via Fr. Alexander Schmemann and Paul Evdokimov. Last, I survey and evaluate recent Church documents that touch on wealth, poverty, markets, business, economic development, and globalization. As an epilogue, I end with an invitation to see the many ways we all can contribute—and already are contributing—to Orthodox social thought in action for both the Kingdom of God and the common good today.

While the topics I explore in this book may be new and intimidating for some readers, I've kept the chapters short—each about the length of a long blog post. So folks should be able to read one chapter a day, for example. And as much as possible, I've written them so that readers could even skip around without too much confusion. Most chapters begin with a "hook" drawn from my admittedly limited and dated grasp of pop culture as an aging millennial dad, or else from history—something familiar, silly, or interesting—so that my readers aren't just bombarded with technical terms from the start. I always write out names of important figures fully in their first occurrence in each chapter, so readers won't need to wonder which "Smith" or whomever I mean. And each of the five parts ends with a summary and discussion questions.

I want this book to start conversations in parishes, classrooms, ministries, even businesses. I want it to get people excited about living our Orthodox Faith in our world today. Asking forgiveness for any ways I may fall short of that goal, this book is my "widow's mite," offered in gratitude for the grace God has given me to read, think, and write about these topics as my career. I've been blessed to write it. I hope others will be blessed to read it.

PART I

# Modern Christian Social Thought

CHAPTER I

# What Is Modern Christian Social Thought?

I N "YORKTOWN," THE CLIMAX TO the first half of the hit Broadway musical *Hamilton*, the victory marking the end of the American Revolution concludes with the refrain "the world turned upside down"[1]—an apt description of the birth of the first modern, liberal, democratic republic that has survived to the present. A decade later, a very different liberal and democratic revolution in France would upend the established political and social order all throughout Europe and beyond.

At the same time, beginning with the automation of the textile industry in the second half of the eighteenth century and the publication of Adam Smith's *Wealth of Nations* in 1776, the Industrial Revolution brought about equally radical social and economic change, pushing the poor in the nineteenth century from traditional life in the rural countryside to the promise of the better life made available through urban mass production . . . and to a reality of hardship that often fell far short of that promise. While in the long run their economic fortunes frequently did improve, it often came at the cost of uprootedness from family, exposure to an abundance of new hazards of factory work and urban life, and inadequate social safety nets.

In response, some longed for a return to the *ancien régime*, the old order of Christian monarchy variously disrupted, transformed, or abandoned in the

---

1    Lin-Manuel Miranda, "Yorktown (The World Turned Upside Down)," track 20 on *Hamilton: An American Musical* (Original Broadway Cast Recording), Atlantic Records, 2015, compact disc.

new age of social change. Others sought to extend the right to vote to the working classes so that they would have greater self-determination in these new democratic orders. Some worked to organize laborers to negotiate better contracts and working conditions. And some sought radical, even violent, revolution to further upend the social order in favor of the working poor—the seeds of the Communist revolutions that would tragically sweep across Central Asia and Eastern Europe in the twentieth century. While we face additional and unique challenges today, in the previous two centuries the world—through revolutions, two World Wars, the collapse of colonial empires, and the fall of the Soviet Union—has indeed "turned upside down."

## *The Social Question*

THE PLIGHT OF THE WORKING poor in the nineteenth century came to be called the "Social Question," and by the end of that century Christian pastors and intellectuals across the world refused to remain silent. Neither did they pine away for a bygone social order that could never realistically be recovered in the age of modern democracy, industry, and science. In addition to an increase in charitable work during that century, the publication of two major works in 1891 marked a significant turn in Christian engagement with this multifaceted problem of the industrial era: Pope Leo XIII's encyclical *Rerum Novarum* (literally, "On the New Things") and the Dutch Neo-Calvinist Abraham Kuyper's address to the First Christian Social Congress in the Netherlands "The Social Question and the Christian Religion."[2]

In the Orthodox world, we see a similar response in Vladimir Soloviev's 1897 work *The Justification of the Good*. Furthermore, Fr. Georges Florovsky even noted, "'Social Christianity' was the basic and favorite theme of the whole religious thinking in Russia in the course of the last century [i.e., the nineteenth], and the same thought colored also the whole literature of the same period."[3]

---

2    Both can be found in Jordan J. Ballor, ed., *Makers of Modern Christian Social Thought: Leo XIII and Abraham Kuyper on the Social Question* (Acton Institute, 2016).

3    Georges Florovsky, "The Social Problem in the Eastern Orthodox Church," in *Christianity and Culture*, vol. 2, The Collected Works of Georges Florovsky (Nordland Publishing Company, 1974), 136.

Indeed, an ecumenical movement of "social Christianity" can be observed across the world at this time, variously emphasizing: 1) the duty of Christian care for the poor and marginalized; 2) the pluriform nature of social life that cannot be reduced to politics; and 3) an insistence that, despite their importance, the material needs of the body ought never to distract us from the spiritual needs of the soul, or vice versa. Salvation of the whole person means that one cannot displace the other. As Soloviev put it, "It is written that man does not live by bread *alone*, but it is not written that he lives without bread."[4]

## Modern Christian Social Thought

WHILE CHRISTIANS HAVE CONCERNED THEMSELVES with care for the poor and marginalized since the ministry of Christ Himself, and have since the New Testament developed a body of moral teaching that can be classified as "Christian social thought," it is the unique application of that teaching to the new challenges of the present that constitutes *modern* Christian social thought. While members of the Orthodox Church contributed to this effort from the beginning, Orthodox reflection on these issues largely collapsed in the wake of the militantly atheist, Soviet overthrow of traditionally Orthodox social orders in the twentieth century.

Roman Catholics today can boast a vast body of modern Christian social thought spanning more than a century, often promulgated and developed through further papal encyclicals since the time of Leo XIII, which in several cases commemorated the anniversary of *Rerum Novarum*. Various Protestants, too, including Neo-Calvinists building upon the legacy of Kuyper, but also with contributions from other traditions such as the Lutheran Dietrich Bonhoeffer, have continued to develop a nuanced body of moral reflection on modern society to guide their adherents in applying the timeless mandates of the "faith . . . once for all delivered to the saints" (Jude 1:3) to cultures and contexts two thousand years removed from the first reception of Holy Tradition. And American Protestant Christianity has a long legacy of a "Social Gospel" that deserves our attention as well.

---

4    Vladimir Solovyov, *The Justification of the Good*, rev. ed., ed. Boris Jakim, trans. Natalie A. Duddington (Eerdmans, 2005), 394–395, emphasis original.

That we Orthodox believe both Roman Catholics and Protestants to have only retained that faith in a distorted form should not prevent us from inquiring into areas of common cause with them, just as our Lord gave His followers the example of a Samaritan (Luke 10:25–37)—a heretic by Jewish standards—as the fulfillment of the command to "love your neighbor as yourself" (Lev. 19:18). So, too, if the Church Fathers could find inspiration from pagan philosophers, how much more ought we to build upon the good efforts of our fellow Christians? Indeed, we cannot identify our own distinctly Orthodox contributions to this necessary and ongoing discussion unless we first familiarize ourselves with the work of other Christian traditions, moral philosophers, social theorists, and even economists.

Doing so has been the major focus of my academic work for more than a decade now, and I hope that this book, beginning with this survey of other Christian traditions in Part 1, will facilitate more nuanced and faithful Orthodox reflection on how best to embody that "faith . . . once for all delivered to the saints"—the Gospel of a Kingdom "not of this world" (John 18:36) and yet "for the life of the world" (John 6:51), a gospel we believe to be uniquely preserved in the Orthodox Church today.

# CHAPTER 2

# Roman Catholic Social Thought

I N AN EPISODE OF *THE Twilight Zone* in 1962,[1] aliens known as Kanamits make first contact with Earth, claiming that they come in peace. They offer advanced technology that eliminates famine, disease, and war. When they go, they leave behind a book written in their undecipherable alien language. Naturally, cryptographers get to work decoding it, led by scientist Michael Chambers (Lloyd Bochner).

While some respond with skepticism toward the Kanamits' mission, their technology works. A new era of peace and prosperity sweeps across the globe. To seal the deal, Patty (Susan Cummings), a member of the cryptography team, successfully translates the title of the alien book: *To Serve Man*. It seems they did come in peace after all!

The Kanamits return and offer humans expeditions to their home planet, which they claim to be a paradise. Swept up in the optimistic fervor, even Michael Chambers chooses to go. However, as he's about to board the Kanamits' flying saucer, Patty comes racing to stop him. He's on the spaceship's stairs. She's held back by Kanamit security, and so she cries out the horror she discovered: "The rest of the book, it's . . . it's a cookbook!" Just then the stairs retract, and Chambers, despite his struggle to escape, ends the episode

---

1    *The Twilight Zone*, season 3, episode 24, "To Serve Man," written by Rod Sterling, directed by Richard L. Bare, featuring Lloyd Bochner, Richard Kiel, and Susan Cummings, aired March 2, 1962, on CBS.

13

a prisoner aboard an alien cattle car, on the menu for an extraterrestrial Thanksgiving.

In a way, Roman Catholic social thought began with Pope Leo XIII (1810–1903) crying out like Patty, "It's a cookbook!" What worried Leo was a revolutionary fervor sweeping across the working classes of Europe. The socialists promised to cure all of society's ills, but the pope feared their medicine would be worse than the malady.

## Pope Leo XIII

IN HIS 1891 ENCYCLICAL RERUM Novarum—on the topic of the "new things" or "revolutionary change" of the industrial era—Leo began the modern Roman Catholic social encyclical tradition by accepting some of the terms and critiques of revolutionary socialism while rejecting the overall worldview and answers it proposed. The subtitle of the work is "Rights and Duties of Capital and Labor," and it uses the terms "capital" and "labor" throughout to indicate socioeconomic classes, as did Marxist analysis, not to indicate factors of production, as does mainstream economic science. The pope furthermore warned that "to misuse men as though they were things in the pursuit of gain . . . is truly shameful and inhuman."[2]

A socialist at the time would likely agree with that, but for Leo this principle led to drastically different conclusions—an extended defense of private property and a rejection of class conflict, metaphysical materialism, and violent revolution. For Leo, all persons—rich and poor, employer and employee—"are children of the same common Father, who is God" and "each and all are redeemed and made sons of God, by Jesus Christ."[3] "Eating the rich" may sound just to the desperate, but the pope insisted there was a better way. The most important solution to the condition of the working classes, to Leo, was Jesus Christ.

---

2    Leo XIII, *Rerum Novarum*, encyclical letter,, May 15, 1891, §20, https://www.vatican .va/content/leo-xiii/en/encyclicals/documents/hf_l-xiii_enc_15051891_rerum -novarum.html.

3    Leo XIII, *Rerum Novarum*, §25.

Furthermore, his conclusion also addressed the human person's social nature—all the ways in which we need each other—and the fact that "it is not good that man should be alone," which means we all have a duty to be "a helper" to one another (Gen. 2:18). Thus, Catholic workers' unions and mutual aid societies, which in some cases included rich and poor alike, had a primary role to play. State assistance should be reserved only for where the fruits of labor and Christian charity proved inadequate. So, too, the family, as the most fundamental social institution, has rights and duties over/against the state and for society.

## *Natural Law and Human Dignity*

CATHOLIC SOCIAL TEACHING GROUNDS THOSE rights and duties in natural law, "the law written in [our] hearts" (Rom. 2:15) and attested by our conscience, by which all people recognize the truth of the basic morality of the Ten Commandments and the cardinal virtues (courage, temperance, justice, and prudence). *What* we are by nature dictates *how* we ought to treat one another. The fact that God made us the apex of His creation such that no irrational animal but only another human person could be "comparable" to us, enjoins on us a "primordial moral requirement of loving and respecting the person as an end and never as a mere means,"[4] as Pope John Paul II put it, from the womb to natural death.

From this centrality of human dignity, the Roman Catholic tradition derives three fundamental social principles: the common good, subsidiarity, and solidarity.

The Roman Catholic account of the common good is fairly standard: It is the social dimension and goal of morality—all those conditions necessary for a full and flourishing life. We might say that the common good is another name for social justice. While it can be traced as far back as Aristotle, its appropriation by and development in Christian theological reflection, most

---

4    John Paul II, *Veritatis Splendor*, encyclical letter, August 6, 1993, §48, https://www
     .vatican.va/content/john-paul-ii/en/encyclicals/documents/hf_jp-ii_enc_06081993
     _veritatis-splendor.html.

prominently by the Western, medieval saint Thomas Aquinas, grounds the Roman Catholic conception.

Subsidiarity, as Pope Pius XI outlined it in 1931, dictates that "the more perfectly a graduated order is kept among the various associations [of society] . . . the happier and more prosperous the condition of the State."[5] Think again of the Catholic workers' unions and mutual aid societies. The more churches and associations of private citizens can do to help one another, the more resources the state has to allocate to more pressing problems. To be clear, the state has a *positive* duty to offer help (*subsidium*) where needed but also a *negative* duty to refrain or withdraw when its involvement would interfere with the successful functioning of the various associations of civil society.

Lastly, there is both a de facto and a moral dimension to solidarity. Our lives are interconnected in manifold ways, which is all the more apparent to us in the rapid globalization of the Information Age today. This interdependence is an undeniable fact, but for it to be a moral reality, we must overcome the "structures of sin" that impede our true communion, and in this sense, "It is a virtue directed *par excellence* to the *common good*,"[6] as the *Compendium* of Rome's social teaching puts it.

These principles come together to promote the values of truth, freedom, justice, and love in a nuanced and careful critique of, and dialogue with, what has become a perennial "spirit of revolutionary change,"[7] to quote the opening words of *Rerum Novarum*. From the Industrial Revolution, to the rise and fall of fascism and Communism, to the sexual revolution, to climate change, to the financial crisis of the last decade, these principles have allowed Roman Catholic clergy and laity to, at their best, creatively and faithfully respond with love and prudence to the unique challenges of each passing era.

---

5    Pius XI, *Quadragesimo Anno*, encyclical letter,, May 15, 1931, §80, https://www.vatican
     .va/content/pius-xi/en/encyclicals/documents/hf_p-xi_enc_19310515_quadragesimo
     -anno.html.

6    Pontifical Council for Justice and Peace, *Compendium of the Social Doctrine of the
     Church* (Reprint April 2005), §193, https://www.vatican.va/roman_curia/pontifical
     _councils/justpeace/documents/rc_pc_justpeace_doc_20060526_compendio-dott
     -soc_en.html.

7    Leo XIII, *Rerum Novarum*, §1.

## An Orthodox Assessment

IN SHARING THE DOCTRINE OF humanity as the image of God, and even much of the philosophical development on display in Roman Catholic social thought, including natural law, Orthodox Christians who hope to apply their faith to the social crises of our era—from poverty to racial injustice to climate change and more—would certainly benefit from deeper engagement with this tradition.

That said, I also think seeing what Rome has accomplished sheds light on what we Orthodox might uniquely contribute. As just one example, Orthodox theological anthropology features a much stronger emphasis on the need for asceticism for true communion with God and our neighbors. Though Roman Catholics have their own venerable ascetic tradition, references to asceticism are almost entirely absent from their social teaching. This neglect seems to me a major oversight, as all Christians are expected to pray, fast, and give alms. Additionally, organized asceticism in the institution of monasticism has historically had an immensely positive social impact in the founding of hospitals, orphanages, and schools; the adoption of new technologies; the economic development of nations; the expansion of international trade; the invention of international banking; the cultivation of spiritual practices and teaching; the spread of the Gospel through evangelism; and so on, in both the East and the West. Surely, we Orthodox should at least have something to say about that, and thus I conclude with a challenge to any readers so inspired: "The harvest truly is plentiful, but the laborers are few" (Matt. 9:37).

CHAPTER 3

# Lutheran Social Thought

IN 1987, ROCK STAR, SEX symbol, and later literal symbol Prince released a song replete with apocalyptic overtones: "Sign o' the Times."[1] The events of the year provided a powerful backdrop—the AIDS crisis ("In France, a skinny man died of a big disease with a little name"); gang violence, drug addiction, natural disasters ("Hurricane Annie ripped the ceiling off a church and killed everyone inside"); desperate poverty and inequality ("A sister killed her baby 'cause she couldn't afford to feed it / And yet we're sending people to the moon"); the Cold War; and the Space Shuttle Challenger explosion ("It's silly, no? / When a rocket ship explodes and everybody still wants to fly").

Yet in a short documentary on the song,[2] commentators expressed bewilderment at Prince's conclusion: "Sign o' the times mess with your mind / Hurry before it's too late / Let's fall in love, get married, have a baby / We'll call him Nate / If it's a boy." The song spends three and a half minutes cataloging all the ways the world is falling apart through tragedy, injustice, and evil, and Prince ends it with an exhortation to embrace family life. What gives?

---

1  Prince, "Sign o' the Times," track 1 on *Sign o' the Times*, Paisley Park; Warner Bros., 1987.
2  *The New York Times*, "How Prince Wrote 'Sign o' the Times' | Diary of a Song," posted December 3, 2020, YouTube video, 9:48, https://youtu.be/tLe7FdaldBo?si=7XzjdIjmLaGSzbol.

While in his last fifteen years Prince actually became a Jehovah's Witness,[3] I think "Sign o' the Times" embodies one of the core convictions of Lutheran social thought. A saying attributed to Martin Luther, but that more likely comes from the German Confessing Church (*Bekennende Kirche*) that resisted the Nazis in the 1930s and '40s, captures this conviction: "If I knew the world was to end tomorrow, I would still plant an apple tree today."[4] The statement may not come from Luther, but it represents a more palatable presentation of the Protestant Reformer's infamous exhortation to his more mild-mannered friend Philip Melanchthon: "Sin boldly."[5]

## Martin Luther

THE IDEA BEHIND LUTHER'S EXHORTATION is this: The world has fallen into sin. Rather than deny that reality, admit that you are a sinner and only capable of doing good by the grace of Jesus Christ. Despite Luther's character-istically bombastic rhetoric, it is actually an exhortation *to do good*, whatever "sign o' the times" may reside in our world lying in darkness. Hence, he con-cludes that we ought to "pray boldly,"[6] knowing ourselves to be sinners. It is an ethic flowing from the central Reformation doctrine of justification by faith.

While there are significant differences between an Orthodox understand-ing of salvation and certain core Protestant commitments, one must acknowl-edge that Luther, among others, explicitly rejected libertinism. He insisted that even though, by his account, "righteousness does not consist in works," nevertheless, "works neither can nor ought to be wanting" from the Christian life.[7] All need Christ, and through faith the sinner receives Christ's righteous-ness, which bears good fruit. Additionally, bemoaning the clericalism of his

---

3    Claire Hoffman, "Prince's Life as a Jehovah's Witness: His Complicated and Ever-Evolving Faith," *Billboard*, April 28, 2016, https://www.billboard.com/music/features/prince-jehovahs-witness-life-7348538/.

4    Scott H. Hendrix, *Martin Luther: A Very Short Introduction* (Oxford University Press, 2010), 90.

5    Martin Luther, Letter to Melanchthon, August 1, 1521, in *Luther's Works: Letters I*, trans. and ed. Gottfried G. Krodel (Fortress Press, 1963), 48:282.

6    Luther, Letter to Melanchthon, 48:282.

7    Martin Luther, *Christian Liberty*, trans. W. A. Lambert (Fortress Press, 1957), 36.

day, he argued that "Christians are all kings and priests"[8] in Christ, expanding the idea of vocation to all walks of life.

Regarding the sacred character of everyday work, with direct application to the "social question" of how best to serve the poor today, Luther wrote: "This is what makes caring for the body a Christian work, that through its health and comfort we may be able to work, to acquire, and lay by funds with which to aid those who are in need."[9] So for Luther, one works and cares for oneself in order to make some profit and acquire some property with which to care for others. As Lutheran theologian Gene Edward Veith put it, for Luther "the purpose of every vocation is to love and serve our neighbors."[10]

## Nineteenth-Century Lutheran Social Thought

MOVING INTO THE NINETEENTH CENTURY, Lutherans were able to respond to the challenges of industrialization and democratic revolution by building upon Luther's doctrine of vocation. They had already, on the basis of natural law,[11] applied their idea of secular vocations to develop a social theory that distinguished between three creational "estates" of church, state, and family. The German pastor and theologian Adolf von Harless (1806–1879), for example, taught, "The systematic organism which also lies at the base of political communities and their order, manifests itself in the variety of the objects of earthly vocations; and their exercise is no thing of human devising, but the result of the will of the Creator."[12] Thus, for von Harless, God created a structure to human social life that people are called to discover and cultivate for the sake of their own flourishing.

As for the unique role of the church, von Harless wrote later in his *System of Christian Ethics*: "The true spirit of the church of Christ and its members

---

8   Luther, *Christian Liberty*, 20.
9   Luther, 28.
10  Gene Edward Veith, *Working for Our Neighbor: A Lutheran Primer on Vocation, Economics, and Ordinary Life* (Christian's Library Press, 2016), 13.
11  See, e.g., Niels Hemmingsen, *On the Law of Nature: A Demonstrative Method*, trans. E. J. Hutchinson (Christian's Library Press, 2018).
12  Gottlieb Christoph Adolf von Harless, *The System of Christian Ethics*, 6th ed., trans. A. W. Morrison, rev. William Findlay (T & T Clark, 1868), 399.

recognises all the relations of human life and society . . . in preserving intact and sanctifying their mutual alternate relations, as the sphere of the sovereignty of that Lord to whom also the individual Christian, from baptism onwards, is bound as a member in faith, and in whom he has to exert himself in every one of these spheres of life."[13] Thus, he says, the Christian approaches secular vocations with a baptized vision, working to counteract the effects of sin and restore each area of life to its proper order on the basis of its own "limits," "fundamental principles," and "mutual . . . relations" under the sovereignty of Jesus Christ.

Von Harless, however, does not elaborate much on what these details are beyond the categories of church, state, and family. The Danish Lutheran theologian and bishop of Zealand, Hans Lassen Martensen (1808–1884), did. For Martensen, our social life consists of innumerable "spheres," including not just church, state, and family but "factory work," education, and even music, among others.[14] Unfortunately, he still seems to imagine that a person's vocation will ultimately be limited to a single sphere, and that each person (more accurately, each man) should be educated for the single sphere in which he finds his vocation. However, Martensen's broad social vision gave him an ability to speak to the concerns of the dynamically changing economic circumstances of common people in his day, and he ultimately endorsed a kind of Christian socialism he termed "ethic socialism," distinguishing it from utopian and revolutionary socialism. He supported labor organization and even the creation of a labor code, drafted by workers themselves, to provide guidelines for equitable working conditions and advice to policymakers, similar to how chambers of commerce work today.[15] While well-known in his time, Martensen's work has largely been neglected since the rise to popularity in the twentieth century of his former student, Søren Kierkegaard, who criticized Martensen as a symbol of inauthenticity and Hegelianism in the Church of Denmark.

---

13   Von Harless, *System of Christian Ethics*, 480.
14   See, e.g., Hans Lassen Martensen, *Christian Ethics: Social Ethics*, trans. Sophia Taylor (T&T Clark, 1899), 99, 145.
15   Martensen, *Christian Ethics: Social Ethics*, 165.

## Dietrich Bonhoeffer

FOR A BETTER-KNOWN LUTHERAN THEOLOGIAN, we can round out this chapter by moving on to the twentieth century and the German Confessing Church responsible for the apocryphal saying about the apple tree. Once again, we see how the Lutheran understanding of vocation fits into a broader theology of society in the work of Dietrich Bonhoeffer (1906–1945). Bonhoeffer's times were far more apocalyptic than Prince's, and the hypocrisy he saw makes Kierkegaard's criticisms of Martensen seem tame. Bonhoeffer witnessed vast swaths of Christians fall captive to fascism and anti-Semitic conspiracy theories that led to one of the largest mass murders in human history. Indeed, the Nazis promoted Martin Luther's own violent antisemitism.

By contrast, Bonhoeffer and others like him put the Protestant ideal of *semper reformanda* ("always reforming") above further perpetuating this darkest legacy of the first Reformer. Today, nearly all Lutheran churches and organizations not only reject antisemitism but explicitly disavow Luther's anti-Semitic works. In hindsight, the German Confessing Church won the war, even if they lost the battle in their own day, which in some cases cost them their very lives. In fact, Bonhoeffer was arrested for his involvement in the Abwehr resistance and executed at Flossenbürg concentration camp just two weeks before Allied forces liberated it.

Following the Lutheran rejection of a strict sacred and secular divide, Bonhoeffer argued in his *Ethics*—his unfinished magnum opus—that in Christ the world, despite all its darkness, has been reconciled to God. Thus, "A world existing on its own, withdrawn from the law of Christ, falls prey to the severing of all bonds and to arbitrariness. A Christianity that withdraws from the world falls prey to unnaturalness, irrationality, triumphalism, and arbitrariness."[16] Adding to the Lutheran doctrines of the three creational estates, this reconciliation finds expression in *four* divine mandates: "*work* [elsewhere 'culture'], *marriage, government, and church.*"[17] Bonhoeffer uses the term *mandate*

---

16  Dietrich Bonhoeffer, *Ethics*, in *Dietrich Bonhoeffer Works*, trans. Reinhard Krauss, Charles C. West, and Douglas W. Stott, vol. 6 (Fortress Press, 2005), 61.

17  Bonhoeffer, *Ethics*, 68, emphasis original.

to indicate "their character as divinely imposed tasks."[18] It concerns what these institutions ought to *do*.

In particular, work fulfills the command "to tend and keep" (Gen. 2:15) the Garden of Eden. "After the fall," he continues, "work remains a mandate of divine discipline and grace."[19] It is the mandate of *production* through all forms of creative work.

Marriage and the family must fulfill the mandate of *procreation*, "where children not only are born but also are educated into obedience to Jesus Christ. As procreators and educators, parents are commissioned by God to be representatives of God for the children. Just as in work new values are created, in marriage new persons are created to serve Jesus Christ."[20] Through work, we create new things from the world for its care, our well-being, and God's glory. Through the family, we create and form new people who will, in turn, contribute their own work to the mandate of production.

Government must fulfill the mandate of *preservation and protection* of work and marriage, since it "presupposes" both as pre-state institutions. "Government itself cannot produce life or values. . . . Government maintains what is created in the order that it was given." Furthermore, it "protects" the order God established "by establishing justice in acknowledgement of the divine mandates and by enforcing justice with the power of the sword."[21] So the mandate of government is to provide and enforce a just legal structure that enables the flourishing of work and marriage.

Lastly, the church is "concerned . . . with the eternal salvation of the world." Far from a matter of mere private faith, the church participates in all other mandates to the extent that individual Christians participate in them: "The Christian is at the same time worker, spouse, and citizen."[22] Bonhoeffer concludes that "here . . . everything finally flows into the reality of the body of Jesus Christ, in whom God and human being became one."[23]

---

18   Bonhoeffer, 68–69.
19   Bonhoeffer, 70.
20   Bonhoeffer, 71.
21   Bonhoeffer, 72.
22   Bonhoeffer, 73.
23   Bonhoeffer, 74.

### *An Orthodox Assessment*

WHAT CAN WE ORTHODOX LEARN from Lutheran social thought? For one thing, despite our theological differences I find it admirable that Lutherans, especially in the case of Bonhoeffer, put Jesus Christ clearly in the center. Christ is the Savior of all the world from all evil—every Christian should believe this. But finding a framework of action by which to carefully bring the Gospel into dialogue with modern societies and problems is not easy to do well. Luther's doctrine of vocation, von Harless's and Martensen's organic understanding of society and social spheres, and Bonhoeffer's four divine mandates offer an outline that could serve as a foundation for more faithful reflection and fruitful ministry.

By way of criticism, I have at least two:

First, we have seen in the last chapter that Orthodox asceticism may have something to offer that Roman Catholic social thought has overlooked. In Lutheranism, sixteenth-century polemics against monastic abuses often led to an unfortunate disparagement of all asceticism, even though many Lutherans still may promote prayer, fasting, and almsgiving. In general, Lutherans are not simply silent about asceticism but often hostile and uncharitable toward it, even Bonhoeffer,[24] which raises serious questions about ecumenical dialogue and cooperation.

Second, though the difference may be partly semantic, I have often found Bonhoeffer in particular to come close to, but fall short of, what the Fathers would say concerning the reconciliation between God and humanity in Jesus Christ. For example, he writes, "Human beings become human because God became human. But human beings do not become God."[25] Contrast this statement with St. Athanasius the Great, who wrote that the Son of God "was made man that we might be made God."[26]

Both agree that the Incarnation means the re-creation of humanity in the image of God, but St. Athanasius is able to theologize boldly (if I may)

---

24  See, e.g., Dietrich Bonhoeffer, *The Cost of Discipleship*, rev. ed., trans. R. H. Fuller (Macmillan, 1959).

25  Bonhoeffer, *Ethics*, 96.

26  Athanasius, *On the Incarnation of the Word*, 54.3, in *NPNF*[2] 4:65.

because an Orthodox understanding of salvation as deification (*theosis*) has more to say than can be said within the limits of a Lutheran framework. That said, Lutherans and others deserve credit for showing us that being able to say more about God ought to empower us to say more about the world He so loves and sent His Son to save. For the time being, however, we must continue to review the contributions of other Christian traditions.

CHAPTER 4

# Neo-Calvinist Social Thought

W HO SAID IT? "THE MAN of faith acts, not as one endowed with free will, but as a beast that is led by the will of God." Martin Luther? John Calvin? No, the answer is St. Peter of Damascus, from the *Philokalia*. He goes on to pray, "Do what Thou wilt to Thy creature; for I believe that, being good, Thou bestowest blessings on me, even if I do not recognize that they are for my benefit."[1] Total acceptance of all one endures in this life as the will of God is a recurring theme in Orthodox spirituality.

I bring this commonality up not to draw a false equivalency—St. Peter was neither a Lutheran nor a Calvinist; that would be anachronistic at best. And his statement should not be taken as a denial of free will. Rather, I know some readers, due to their personal experiences, may balk at the idea that we Orthodox have anything to learn from Calvinists of any kind.[2] That objection often

---

1    Peter of Damaskos, *A Treasury of Divine Knowledge*, in *The Philokalia*, trans. and ed. G. E. H. Palmer, Philip Sherrard, and Kallistos Ware, vol. 3 (Faber and Faber, 1984), 163.

2    Some might also think of the tragic tale of Cyril Lucaris, sometime Patriarch of Alexandria and later of Constantinople, who produced a Calvinist-inspired *Confession* that was rejected by the Orthodox Church at the 1672 Synod of Jerusalem. For the Greek and Latin texts of Patriarch Dositheus of Jerusalem's own *Confession*, written in response to Lucaris and produced by that Synod, see *The Confession of Dositheus, or the Eighteen Decrees of the Synod of Jerusalem*, in *The Creeds of Christendom*, ed. Philip Schaff, vol. 2 (Harper & Brothers, 1919), 401–444. If one wishes for a detailed list of how precisely Calvinism and Orthodoxy are incompatible, this *Confession* is a helpful resource. See also Peter Mogila, *The Orthodox Confession of the Eastern Church. A. D. 1643*, in *The Creeds of Christendom*, vol. 2, 275–400. Mogila's catechism (which is what this *Confession*

26

focuses on a certain, distinctly American Calvinist understanding of the sovereignty of God over all things. True, all Calvinists share this emphasis, but not all of them deny the reality of free will or reduce it to psychological determinism or "compatibilism." Indeed, in my limited expertise, that vein of Calvinism seems to originate with the American Puritan Jonathan Edwards, who though influential in the United States is rarely cited by Calvinists abroad.[3]

Neo-Calvinism originates abroad, specifically in the Netherlands, with the Dutch theologian, statesman, educator, and editorialist Abraham Kuyper. Nevertheless, over the past few decades this tradition's expansive social vision has found new life across the globe, even outside of Reformed churches. Thus, any Orthodox contribution to modern Christian social thought requires some familiarity with Neo-Calvinist social thought as well.

## Abraham Kuyper

IN 1891, THE SAME YEAR as Pope Leo XIII's encyclical *Rerum Novarum*, Kuyper gave a speech on "The Social Question and the Christian Religion" at the first Christian Social Congress in Amsterdam, organized by the (Protestant) Dutch Workers Association Patrimonium and Kuyper's own political party. Like Leo, Kuyper was both sympathetic to socialists' critiques of the social order and their concern for the working classes while also critical of socialist principles and solutions. Indeed, his party, the first modern political party in the Netherlands, was named the Anti-Revolutionary Party for their opposition to the French Revolution and its rallying cry, *Ni Dieu, ni maître!* ("No God, no master!"). The liberal principles of the Revolution—fraternity, equality, and liberty—were taken up again in 1848, first in Paris and then all across Europe, in the name of both democracy and socialism. This French liberalism, and the socialism that grew out of it and in response to it, had reshaped many Western societies by Kuyper's time, including the

---

is) was first accepted at the 1643 Synod of Jassy and then later at the 1672 Synod of Jerusalem.

3   On Edwards and free will, see Richard A. Muller, "Jonathan Edwards and the Absence of Free Choice: A Parting of Ways in the Reformed Tradition," *Jonathan Edwards Studies* 1, no. 1 (2001): 3–22.

Netherlands. "Socialism is in the air," said Kuyper. "The social wind, which can at any moment turn into a storm, is swelling the sails of the ship of state. And it may safely be said that the social question has become *the* question, the burning life-question at the close of this century."[4]

Kuyper agreed with the socialist defense of "the rights of community and the organic nature of society"[5] as well as their opposition to laissez-faire capitalism. But he went on to reject the largely atheistic and materialistic bases of socialism in his day—making exception for Christian socialists such as F. D. Maurice and Hans Lassen Martensen—claiming that "people who do not believe in God to whose eternal ordinances we are to submit, and who do not attach much importance in the life of nations to historical development that never permits its intrinsic law of life to be violated with impunity—such people look upon the entire structure of contemporary society as nothing but a product of human convention."[6] Kuyper saw atheistic socialism as a mere logical extension of the French Revolution. In opposition to both, he believed that God, sovereign over all history, has a plan even for our social life, which is gradually revealed and developed over time. Thus, historical social institutions should not be too rashly dismissed or dismantled.

Nevertheless, Kuyper was no European-style conservative either. He didn't advocate a return to medieval or early modern theocratic monarchy but instead forged a unique path forward in the pluralistic, constitutional monarchy of his time. Calvinist Christians, he believed, needed their own "architectonic critique"[7] of society to counter the socialists'. Kuyper rejected the socialists' godless worldview governed by a materialist and deterministic social-historical dialectic. A dialectic is a process that unfolds according to its own internal logic. For socialists, that was the conflict between social classes. Instead of this, Kuyper insisted on a world where, as he put it in his speech at the opening of the Free University of Amsterdam, "there is not a square inch

---

4  Abraham Kuyper, "The Social Question and the Christian Religion," trans. Harry Van Dyke, in *On Business & Economics*, ed. Peter S. Heslam, Jordan J. Ballor, and Melvin Flikkema, Abraham Kuyper Collected Works in Public Theology (Lexham Press; Acton Institute, 2021), 205.

5  Kuyper, "The Social Question," 205.

6  Kuyper, 206.

7  See, e.g., Kuyper, 201.

in the whole domain of our human existence over which Christ, who is Sovereign over *all*, does not cry: 'Mine!' "[8]

## Common Grace and Sphere Sovereignty

EXPANDING ON THE THOUGHT OF John Calvin and other Reformed Protestants, Kuyper developed a doctrine known as "common grace"—a shorthand for all the ways, beyond His providential care for creation, God preserves humanity from the full effects of sin and death this side of Paradise. This grace, to Kuyper, is distinct from "particular grace," that grace specific to the eternal salvation of souls. Hence, while the latter is unique to Christians, the former can be found in every human community and society. This distinction enabled Kuyper to affirm a pluralistic order, and the insights of even secular science, while still maintaining his distinctive Calvinist convictions.

Kuyper further developed his own alternative historical dialectic—"sphere sovereignty"—in ways that echo and expand the insights of the Lutherans Adolf von Harless and Hans Lassen Martensen, both of whose work he knew.[9] For Kuyper, our social and even intellectual lives consist of spheres or circles, each with their own principles, domains, and boundaries. Kuyper did not content himself with speaking in broad terms of family, church, state, and culture—though his younger contemporary Herman Bavinck (1854–1921) did identify these as "primary spheres."[10] All of these are spheres of life to Kuyper, but there are many more: art, science, ethics, cities, nations, peoples, industry, philanthropy, labor, hunting, and invention are each listed as spheres at one point or another across Kuyper's works. Each has independent authority over its own domain, but all must be subordinate to God, who alone has absolute authority.

---

8   Abraham Kuyper, "Sphere Sovereignty," trans. Harry Van Dyke, in *On Charity & Justice*, ed. Matthew J. Tuininga, Jordan J. Ballor, and Melvin Flikkema, Abraham Kuyper Collected Works in Public Theology (Lexham Press; Acton Institute, 2022), 141.

9   Dylan Pahman, "Going Abroad in the German Academy: Abraham Kuyper as Continental Philosopher," *Calvin Theological Journal* 58, no. 1 (April 2023): 3–28.

10  Herman Bavinck, "The Kingdom of God, the Highest Good," trans. Nelson Kloosterman, *The Bavinck Review* 2 (2011): 133–170. Brock and Sutanto even refer to these as "meta-spheres." See Cory C. Brock and N. Gray Sutanto, *Neo-Calvinism: A Theological Introduction* (Lexham Academic, 2022), 272.

Sphere sovereignty becomes dialectical in Kuyper's concern for history. Whence a sphere came tells us something about its present structure and direction, to use the Neo-Calvinist Albert Wolters's terminology.[11] Over time, as more spheres of life differentiate themselves from one another, existing in themselves with their own God-given authority, they must resist the temptation to exist *for* themselves rather than for God—an expression of sin in the social order that Kuyper termed "the antithesis." Thus, for Kuyper something like "art for art's sake" is mistaken not because all art should be church art but rather because art should, through common grace, glorify God in all of life. Sphere sovereignty is an open and theistic dialectic as opposed to the Marxists' deterministic and atheistic one.

Consistent with Neo-Calvinist pluralism, Bavinck even countered the Marxist dichotomy of bourgeois vs. proletariat, noting: "Within society, there is not only an aristocratic class, but also an academic class, a merchant class, a manufacturing class, a middle class, a retail class, a skilled laboring class, and a laboring class. Among each of those classes there is . . . endless movement. . . . The misery of society is not that classes exist . . . [but] that people . . . contrary to all reality, [are] divided into two classes, in terms of which only outward property, apart from all enterprise, serves as the measure."[12] Bavinck's Neo-Calvinist worldview helps him appreciate the complex nature of social life and economic struggle. With sound principles, he is able to be less judgmental and more sympathetic to all people of all vocations. And most importantly, his analysis is at once both theological and realist, avoiding the errors of materialism, reductionism, and envy.

However, Kuyper and Bavinck believed human society does need government, too. The state, to Kuyper, has both the exalted status of the "sphere of spheres" as well as a distinctly "mechanical" nature, lacking the organic nature of other spheres of life.[13] The state exists to check the power of sin, but apart from sin there would be no need for human government. Its duty is to mediate

---

11  Albert M. Wolters, *Creation Regained: Biblical Basics for a Reformational Worldview*, 2nd ed. (Eerdmans, 2005).

12  Herman Bavinck, *The Christian Family* (Christian's Library Press, 2012), 126.

13  Kuyper changed his view on the state, speaking of it as organic in his early work but later shifting to a purely mechanical conception in his later work. Compare Abraham Kuyper, *Our Program*, trans. and ed. Harry Van Dyke, ed. Jordan J. Ballor and Melvin Flikkema,

conflicts between spheres—such as business and labor—and to step in only on a provisional basis if a sphere fails in its calling. Thus, where philanthropy, for example, proves insufficient to ameliorate human hardship, the state has a duty to provide what is lacking. Nevertheless, he warned Christians that "the holy art of 'giving for Jesus' sake' [see 2 Cor. 4:11] should become much more developed among us Christians. All poverty relief by the state, never forget, always leaves a blot on the honor of your Savior."[14]

## Neo-Calvinism and the Social Question

AS FOR HOW BEST TO advance the conditions of the working poor, Kuyper supported Patrimonium, the Dutch Protestant labor organization. Patrimonium was more than a union, however; it provided insurance and spiritual care in addition to collective bargaining, and it allowed employers as well as workers to become members, cultivating solidarity across social classes. Kuyper even, similar to Martensen, endorsed the idea of a "labor code," written by workers and recommended to the state via a "chamber of labor."[15] For Kuyper, this proposition followed from the principle of sphere sovereignty: "The realm of labor is a world of its own and best suited to be the judge of its own interests."[16] Yet Kuyper was far more democratic than Martensen, working to expand suffrage in the Netherlands to heads of blue-collar households, which massively increased the franchise and eventually propelled him to the office of prime minister from 1901–1905, under a coalition government between his party and the Roman Catholic party.[17] In this democratic advocacy, he was motivated by the example of Christ, who aligned Himself with the poor, teaching, "Foxes have holes and birds of the air have nests, but the Son of Man has nowhere to lay his head" (Luke 9:58).

---

Abraham Kuyper Collected Works in Public Theology (Lexham; Acton Institute, 2015 [1881]) with *Lectures on Calvinism* (Eerdmans, 1931 [1898]).

14  Kuyper, "The Social Question," 228.
15  Kuyper, *Our Program*, 159.
16  Kuyper, 166.
17  See, e.g., Abraham Kuyper, "Christ and the Needy," trans. Herbert Donald Morton, in *On Charity & Justice*, 1–44.

Kuyper also gained popular appeal by fighting for school choice, so that instead of funding only secular liberal schools with taxes, the state would provide funding regardless of creed or income so that families would better be able to "train up a child in the way he should go" (Prov. 22:6). This legacy continues in the Netherlands and many other European nations to this day. Nor was Kuyper content with improving only primary and secondary education. He founded the Free University—"free" because it was an institution of its own sphere (science), distinct from church and state—in which scholars would be free to conduct their studies on the basis of their own principles: in Kuyper's case, Calvinist ones.

Writing in a time where only an elite few (mostly men) ever attended institutions of higher education, Kuyper nevertheless saw the social vocation of those who did: "*Scola* is . . . that distinctive sphere of society which indeed centers on the university yet pervades the country with young men who thirst after knowledge and with men of learning who illumine our towns and villages like bright stars."[18] Thus, having a university education gives one a responsibility to the communities in which one lives. Kuyper even extended this educational vocation to his journalism, editing two newspapers and writing eight editorials a week. As his biographer James Bratt noted, "For many it provided a post-elementary school education, a sustained induction into politics, culture, and social affairs."[19]

## *An Orthodox Assessment*

MUCH MORE COULD BE SAID about Kuyper and other Neo-Calvinists, but this summary is good enough. What might we Orthodox have to contribute?

First, as I opened this chapter, belief in the absolute sovereignty of God is not the sole property of Calvinists. Furthermore, far from fatalism, Kuyper's sphere sovereignty has the virtue of adaptability—"there are in life all kinds of

---

18    Abraham Kuyper, "Scholarship: Two Convocation Addresses—The Secret of Genuine Study," trans. Harry Van Dyke, in *On Education*, ed. Jordan J. Ballor and Melvin Flikkema, Abraham Kuyper Collected Works in Public Theology (Lexham; Acton Institute, 2019), 100.

19    James D. Bratt, *Abraham Kuyper: Modern Calvinist, Christian Democrat* (Eerdmans, 2013), 83.

spheres as numerous as constellations in the heavens,"[20] he claimed. His social vision transcends his own time, context, and theological tradition,[21] and it is uniquely suited to principled engagement with our pluralistic societies today. Could it be adapted to Orthodox principles? What would those principles be?

Second, to explore just one criticism, I'm unsure whether the Calvinist distinction between "common" and "particular" grace makes sense from an Orthodox point of view. The difference may only be semantic, but isn't all grace at least potentially salvific, even sacramental? No one would dispute that Orthodoxy is more sacramental than Calvinism, and I would submit that the outlook of Fr. Schmemann, for example,[22] may provide a better reference point for us, going beyond our role as God's stewards to more vividly serving as God's priests in all of life. Perhaps that's even something that Calvinists and other Protestants, who famously affirm a "priesthood of all believers," could learn from us.

---

20   Kuyper, "Sphere Sovereignty," 120.

21   We've already seen something like Kuyper's worldview foreshadowed in Lutheranism in the previous chapter. And I know at least one scholar who identifies as a "Roman Catholic Kuyperian." See Eduardo Echeverria, "Do You Have to Be a Calvinist to be a Kuyperian? In Memoriam John H. Kok," *Pro Rege* 49, no. 3 (2021): 15.

22   See Alexander Schmemann, *For the Life of the World: Sacraments and Orthodoxy*, rev. and expanded ed. (SVS Press, 1979), discussed in chapter 36 of this book.

CHAPTER 5

# The Social Gospel

MANY AMERICAN HIGH SCHOOL STUDENTS in my generation shared the experience of having to read selections from Upton Sinclair's 1906 novel *The Jungle*. The book describes the tragic story of Lithuanian immigrants working under harrowing conditions in Chicago's meat processing industry. Sinclair hoped it would serve as a sort of tract for socialism—the book even ends with the protagonist having a conversion experience at a political meeting, becoming a socialist, and then spreading the good news to his mother-in-law.

This era was an age of social reforms, often supported not only by socialist activists like Sinclair but concerned Christians seeking to spread what came to be termed the "Social Gospel." *The Jungle* serves as a window into the social problems these Christian activists sought to remedy in the United States at the beginning of the twentieth century.

To cite just one example, the novel begins with a poor but joyous Lithuanian wedding reception. The first glimpse of the factory worker's plight comes in the image of a couple, Jadvyga and Mikolas, swaying on the dance floor. "This is the fifth year, now, that Jadvyga has been engaged to Mikolas, and her heart is sick,"[1] Sinclair writes. Why? Mikolas's father is an alcoholic, and there is no other man to support his large family. Struggling to provide and save for

---

1    Upton Sinclair, *The Jungle* (Doubleday, Page & Company, 1906), 12.

34

his and Jadvyga's wedding, he labors on piecework as a "beef-boner," which Sinclair tells us "is a dangerous trade." He continues, "Your hands are slippery, and your knife is slippery, and you are toiling like mad, when somebody happens to speak to you, or you strike a bone. . . . Twice now; within the last three years, Mikolas has been lying at home with blood poisoning. . . . The last time, too, he lost his job. . . . There are learned people who can tell you out of the statistics that beef-boners make forty cents an hour, but, perhaps, these people have never looked into a beef-boner's hands."[2]

While the immediate response to Sinclair's book came in the form of food safety legislation, the Social Gospel represents a longstanding movement that speaks to even deeper wells of compassion in the public's heart than Sinclair perceived.

In contrast to Roman Catholic, Lutheran, and Neo-Calvinist social thought, the Social Gospel reflects American religious pluralism, transcending denominational boundaries and even the poles of "conservative" and "liberal" theology. That said, I will here focus on two of the most well-known figures of the movement: Washington Gladden and Walter Rauschenbusch. Both were theological liberals in their time, but Gladden was a Congregationalist and Rauschenbusch a Baptist.

## *Washington Gladden*

IN HIS WORK AS A pastor, Gladden became familiar with the rising movement of organized labor, which he actively supported. Yet his perspective offers an admirable balance too often missing in narratives of the time: "I knew these employers, many of them, to be men of humane and generous purposes; I knew many of the workingmen, and was in entire sympathy with their condition; and I witnessed with sorrow and alarm the widening of the breach between these classes."[3] He believed that all social relations should be governed by "the law of Christ" to "love your neighbor as yourself" (Lev. 19:18),

---

2  Sinclair, *The Jungle*, 12–13.
3  Washington Gladden, *Recollections* (Houghton Mifflin Company; The University Press Cambridge, 1909), 294–295.

which he took to imply both service to others and self-care. He also sought to ground his economic ethics in economic science, favoring the German historical school that had also influenced Abraham Kuyper.[4]

Seeing the growing enmity between employers and factory workers, Gladden asked the question, "Is It Peace or War?" in an 1886 speech. He noted how the incomes of many professions had increased during the Industrial Revolution, including clergy, doctors, lawyers, teachers, accountants, and artists: "A large share of the national income falls into the hands of such persons,"[5] he admitted. Welfare was on the rise, but not equally so— industrial workers' wages did not evince a proportional increase, and their working conditions required improvement. He argued that, to the extent employers had colluded to influence legislation in their favor, employees were more than justified in organizing for their interests as well. However, he rightly warned, "Surely the world is not enriched by warfare; it is impoverished."[6] Continued conflict would undermine the interests of both capital and labor. Like St. Paul, he argued for "a more excellent way" (1 Cor. 12:31), i.e., love.

For Gladden, this love meant shorter work days, profit sharing, nationalization of utilities, ending child labor, and the use of arbitrage instead of boycotts by organized labor. One may disagree with his practical recommendations, but Gladden's balanced, nonpolemical application of the simple biblical basis of love for one's neighbor is admirable. Nevertheless, it is fair to say that he lacked theological sophistication. The same cannot be said for his younger contemporary Walter Rauschenbusch.

---

4    On Kuyper and the German historical school of economics, see Joost Hengstmengel, "The Amateur Economist: Abraham Kuyper and Economics," *Journal of Economics, Theology and Religion* 1, no. 2 (2021): 137–158. Unfortunately, I will not be able to survey the distinctives and varieties of the German historical school in this book. Prominent figures of this school include Wilhelm Georg Friedrich Roscher and Gustav von Schmoller, who emphasized the importance of historical over/against theoretical approaches to economic analysis.

5    Washington Gladden, "Is It Peace or War?" in *Applied Christianity: Moral Aspects of Social Questions* (Houghton Mifflin Company; The University Press Cambridge, 1897), 117.

6    Gladden, "Is It Peace or War?" 112.

## *Walter Rauschenbusch*

RAUSCHENBUSCH WITNESSED THE WORKERS' STRUGGLE during his time as a pastor in New York's Hell's Kitchen. Like Gladden, his social interests were broad. He supported Prohibition, as did Gladden. Rauschenbusch was also a committed passivist and opposed all violence and war. His economic perspective was likely more Georgist[7] and socialist than Gladden's, and generally less economically informed, but his theological vision was far more expansive. Indeed, in his 1917 book *A Theology for the Social Gospel*, he sought to provide a unifying theology for the movement.

Despite his theological liberalism, Rauschenbusch really did try to offer a theology to unite a wide variety of perspectives, including theological "conservatives" (from a Protestant point of view). It is fair to say that he didn't succeed in that ecumenical goal, but he did inspire many during and after his time, most notably Martin Luther King Jr., despite Rauschenbusch's own fashionable racism.[8]

For Rauschenbusch, the Social Gospel found its biblical justification in the Kingdom of God, which was central to Jesus' preaching but, he believed, too often sidelined in church history. One need not share his assessment to agree that neglect of social ministry and confusion concerning God's Kingdom are potential dangers for all Christians in every age. Nevertheless, his work is profoundly marked by his time and context.

At its best, his understanding of the Kingdom of God involves a Protestant version of the Roman Catholic principle of solidarity. He argued that the world needs salvation not only from individual sin but from sinful social structures, and to that end he sought to recast classic Christian doctrines, such as sin, eschatology, and atonement, with an eye toward addressing the social problems of his day. As Rauschenbusch put it, "It requires no legal fiction of

---

7   The term *Georgist* refers to followers of the American economist Henry George, most famous for his support for a "single tax" or "land tax" and his moral advocacy for the working poor. See Henry George, *Progress and Poverty: An Inquiry into the Cause of Industrial Depressions and of Increase of Want with Increase of Wealth—The Remedy* (D. Appleton and Company, 1881).

8   On Rauschenbusch's racism, see Christopher H. Evans, *The Kingdom Is Always but Coming: A Life of Walter Rauschenbusch* (Eerdmans, 2006), 254–256.

imputation to explain that 'he was wounded for our transgressions, he was crushed for our iniquities.' Solidarity explains it."[9] While he is too dismissive of other explanations, there is no reason why more than one can't be true.

For example, his social atonement theology can still be insightful. He lists several such social causes of the Crucifixion: 1) "The most persistent force which pushed Jesus toward death . . . was religious bigotry."[10] 2) "A second evil which contributed to kill him was the combination of graft and political power."[11] 3) "A third historic evil is the corruption of justice."[12] 4) "A fourth . . . was the mob spirit and mob action."[13] 5) "The fifth . . . was militarism."[14] And 6) "The last . . . is class contempt."[15] He summarizes, "Jesus bore these sins in no legal or artificial sense, but in their impact on his own body and soul. . . . They were not only the sins of Caiaphas, Pilate, or Judas, but the social sin of all mankind, to which all who ever lived have contributed, and under which all who ever lived have suffered."[16]

Christ did suffer all these things for our salvation (*willingly*, we should add). That He did not suffer *only* these things does not make them any less important. All people have a familial bond under God as "our Father," and redeemed through Christ's bearing of these social sins, Christians have a responsibility in the present to work to undo them and embody the prayer, "Your kingdom come. / Your will be done / On earth as it is in heaven" (Matt. 6:9–10).

## An Orthodox Assessment

WHILE BOTH GLADDEN AND RAUSCHENBUSCH have lessons to teach us, at least from their examples if not their theology, at his worst, Rauschenbusch in particular seems to simply equate the Kingdom of God, salvation, and social

---

9    Walter Rauschenbusch, *A Theology for the Social Gospel* (The MacMillan Company, 1918), 248.
10   Rauschenbusch, *A Theology for the Social Gospel*, 248.
11   Rauschenbusch, 250.
12   Rauschenbusch, 252.
13   Rauschenbusch, 254.
14   Rauschenbusch, 255.
15   Rauschenbusch, 256.
16   Rauschenbusch, 258.

justice with a naive form of direct democracy: "The fundamental step of repentance and conversion for professions and organizations is to give up monopoly power and the incomes derived from legalized extortion, and to come under the law of service, content with a fair income for honest work." These are fair points as far as they go, but he continues: "The corresponding step in the case of governments and political oligarchies, both in monarchies and in capitalistic semi-democracies, is to submit to real democracy. Therewith they step out of the Kingdom of Evil into the Kingdom of God."[17] I'm a supporter of democracy, too, but there are good and bad forms of it. Even where it has been an earthly good, I'm uncomfortable with so flatly equating democracy and the Kingdom of God.

Despite Rauschenbusch's protests to the contrary, his version of the Social Gospel comes off as too utopian today. We Orthodox would do well to temper our own aspirations with the caution of Abba Poemen, one of the desert Fathers: "If a man makes a new heaven and a new earth, he still cannot be safe from temptation."[18] In his defense, Rauschenbusch didn't advocate for static perfection but for continued progress, which is actually quite Orthodox. Saint Gregory of Nyssa even defined spiritual perfection as an unending process.[19] But when applied to society, where our work directly and indirectly affects the lives of others, we also ought to be wary of unintended consequences.

No element of the Social Gospel Movement more clearly illustrates this disregard for unintended consequences than the many, like Gladden and Rauschenbusch, who supported Prohibition. The goal was noble: Reduce drunkenness and alcoholism, which would in turn decrease domestic abuse and the number of broken families. While there may have been minor successes in that regard, the resulting black market for alcohol and the outbreak of organized crime far outweighed any benefits. There are limits to the state's power to improve the social order that many failed to see.

---

17   Rauschenbusch, 117.
18   *Sayings of the Desert Fathers,* in *Western Asceticism,* ed. Owen Chadwick, vol. 12, The Library of Christian Classics (The Westminster Press, 1958), 135.
19   Gregory of Nyssa, *The Life of Moses,* trans. Abraham J. Malherbe and Everett Ferguson (Paulist Press, 1978), 31.

Nevertheless, Rauschenbusch's goal of providing a theology for the Social Gospel, and the broader movement's humanitarian work, are commendable. Could we Orthodox provide a better "theology for the social gospel" today? If so, on what basis?

Having sampled various approaches of other traditions to modern Christian social thought, we can now explore the many and rich resources in Holy Tradition for engaging with modern economies and economics for that end today.

# Part 1 Summary and Discussion Questions

## *Summary*

Modern Christian social thought began with the "Social Question," the plight of the working classes during the industrialization of the nineteenth century. Christians sought guidance from their various traditions in order to provide theologically informed principles for loving their neighbors in our modern economies.

Roman Catholic social thought focuses on the equal and inviolable human dignity of all people, created in the image of God. It grounds its teaching in natural law and further distinguishes between the common good, subsidiarity, and solidarity. The good of communities and societies depends on respect for human dignity in terms of the autonomy of individuals and communities—including workers' associations—in solidarity with all who suffer.

Lutherans draw upon Scripture and natural law to distinguish between three creational "estates": family, church, and state. Some also acknowledge a plurality of spheres of social life, and Dietrich Bonhoeffer expanded the concept of three estates into four "mandates," adding work or culture to the other three. Each person's individual vocation, as well as the centrality of the Cross, form common Lutheran emphases as well.

Neo-Calvinists emphasize the sovereignty of Christ over all creation, God's common grace in all of life, and the historical dialectic of sphere sovereignty, by which new social spheres emerge as God's decree unfolds throughout history. They also emphasize the reality of sin in the danger of the antithesis—when various spheres come to exist for their own sake rather than for the glory of God. Historically, Neo-Calvinists also affirm natural law and have their own tradition of organized labor.

The American Social Gospel tradition sought to spread God's love through tangible social action. Though theologically diverse, Social Gospelers agreed on the imminence of the Kingdom of God, support for labor unions, pacifism, and the prohibition of alcohol. Their influence included the eighteenth amendment to the US Constitution prohibiting alcohol (repealed by the twenty-first). Furthermore, many leaders of the Civil Rights Movement, including Martin Luther King Jr., cited the Social Gospel as an influence behind their work to end the race-based segregation of Jim Crow laws in the American South.

## *Discussion Questions*

- What is modern Christian social thought? Having read these chapters, how would you summarize it?
- What principle of Roman Catholic social thought resonated most with you? How would you relate it to Orthodoxy? Was there any aspect that you think clashes with Orthodoxy?
- How would you compare Lutheran social thought to Roman Catholic? What makes the two most distinct from one another? How does Lutheran social thought connect or clash with Orthodoxy?
- What makes Neo-Calvinist social thought most distinctive from the Roman Catholic and Lutheran perspectives? What common ground does it share with them? What can Orthodox Christians learn from Neo-Calvinism? What might Neo-Calvinists learn from us?
- What lessons can Orthodox social thought glean from the successes, struggles, and failures of the American Social Gospel tradition? How might the work and theology of Washington Gladden or Walter Rauschenbusch be adapted to Orthodoxy?

# PART 2

# The Bible

# CHAPTER 6

# What Is Biblical Theology?

G ROWING UP EVANGELICAL (I'M A convert to Orthodoxy), I sang a lot of songs about the Bible. In principle, there's nothing wrong with that— the Bible is great! (Turns out, we Orthodox have one, too.) However, upon reflection as a Greek Orthodox adult, not all of these songs hold up. In particular, consider the first verse of "The B-I-B-L-E": "Oh! The B-I-B-L-E, / Yes, that's the book for me. / I stand alone on the word of God, / The B-I-B-L-E!"[1]

The phrase "I stand alone" is probably a reference to the famous words Martin Luther likely never said at the Diet of Worms: "Here I stand. I can do no other." In any case, I'm glad to say that as Orthodox Christians we do not "stand alone." When we consult the "word of God," we read it with the Church.

Having reviewed a few other Christian traditions' contributions in Part 1, it's time to dig into some of the many resources at our disposal within our Orthodox Tradition, starting with Holy Scripture, i.e., the "B-I-B-L-E."

## Orthodox Biblical Theology

IN MY NEXT SEVERAL CHAPTERS I will explore what Scripture, read within the Church, can teach us about our social relations in general and our duties to the poor among us in particular. The goal will be to construct what some Protestants might refer to as a "biblical theology" for modern Orthodox

---

1   Authorship unknown.

Christian social thought. That is, rather than proceeding systematically by theological topic, I will attempt to trace themes and principles as they come to the fore throughout our current biblical canon, in the course of the biblical story, with reference to our contemporary question of how best to serve the poor in the modern world.

Being Orthodox, I do not intend to "stand alone," but rather to follow the rule of St. Vincent of Lérins: "universality, antiquity, consent." He explains: "We shall follow universality if we confess that one faith to be true, which the whole Church throughout the world confesses; antiquity, if we in no wise depart from those interpretations which it is manifest were notoriously held by our holy ancestors and fathers; consent, in like manner, if in antiquity itself we adhere to the consentient definitions and determinations of all, or at the least of almost all priests and doctors."[2]

There is, in fact, a social principle already present in our method of reading Scripture: We owe a debt to those who came before us, who gave their lives to pass on the Faith—and the Bible—to us. Indeed, it is from the Church that we get the Bible. Christians, including Orthodox Christians among themselves, have disagreed across times and regions as to specifically which books should be included in the Bible, but what has remained constant is the Faith by which those books were interpreted and believed to be inspired by God. Every Sunday, in fact, we confess in the Creed that the Holy Spirit "spoke through the prophets." And in the Church's Liturgy and lectionary we see preference given to some books, and kinds of books, over others.

## The Plan for Part 2

IN ORDER TO DIVIDE MY task into several concise chapters, I have chosen to follow a few historical divisions of the biblical books. For the Old Testament, I will examine the Law, Prophets, and Writings. The triplet of Law, Prophets, and Psalms occurs among the Fathers with relative frequency. Writings, borrowed from Jewish tradition but also found in the Fathers, is simply a broader category than Psalms, which may sometimes have been used as a synecdoche

---

2    Vincent of Lérins, *The Commonitory*, 2.6, in *NPNF*[2] 11:132.

for the Writings. The Law is the Torah or Pentateuch, the first five books of the Bible. The Prophets, for my purposes here at least, include not only those books named for specific prophets, such as Isaiah, but also the narratives of God's work among His people from the conquest of Canaan to the revolt of the Maccabees. Last, the Writings include the more poetic and philosophical books, such as Psalms, Proverbs, and Ecclesiastes. More specific categorizations are possible, but these terms will suit our needs well enough.

Notice that during Great Lent our lectionary features one book from each of these categories for the weekday readings: Genesis (Law), Isaiah (Prophets), and Proverbs (Writings). So, once again, there is some Orthodox precedent for these divisions. In addition to these prescribed readings, our Liturgy itself is adorned with Old Testament quotations, and whole psalms are often recited in the course of Matins and Vespers.

For the New Testament, I will look at the Gospel (in three parts) and the Apostles, which of course we hear readings from every Divine Liturgy. However, while we sit for the Apostles reading, we stand for the Gospel, coat it in gold, and regularly venerate it. Obviously, Matthew, Mark, Luke, and John hold a special place among the Scriptures as they contain the life and teachings of our Lord and God and Savior Jesus Christ.

Finally, there is one additional category worth mentioning, which for lack of a better term I will call Apocrypha. This word has taken on a negative meaning over time, usually indicating books falsely claimed to be divinely inspired. However, the word simply means "hidden," and in fact some of our Old Testament bonus books (as I, a former Protestant, lovingly call them) are sometimes referred to with this term. In any case, there are books and parts of books that we do not read liturgically and in some cases that the laity are even discouraged from reading. In particular, I'm thinking of the Apocalypse (Revelation) of St. John, the Song of Songs, and a few others. These could all be lumped in with the previous five divisions, but I expect I wouldn't talk about them at all in that case.

While I have no intention of dwelling on the more obscure passages of our biblical Apocrypha, it also would be an error to assume that these books have nothing to say regarding our social relations. Apocalypse, for example, is actually a genre, not just a book, of which there are more than one in the Bible (the book of Zechariah and parts of Daniel and Ezekiel, for example). As visions of the redemption of God's people and the Final Judgment are common in this genre, and as Christ tells us we will be judged especially for our treatment of "the least of these" among us (see Matt. 25:31–46), I don't think we can just skip these texts altogether.

## Why We Need the Bible

THE FACT IS, IF WE aren't consulting Scripture we're probably "doing" theology wrong. But the real question is not whether we use the Bible but whether we do so well or poorly. By following the narratives and themes of the Scriptures, guided by the Church, we guard against "prooftexting," i.e., grabbing quotes from the Bible out of context to serve our own purposes. And, just like when we read any other book, we need to pay attention to context and grammar and literary devices and whatnot. As for the more spiritual level of meaning to the texts—which certainly exists—I will defer to the Fathers if and when recourse to that is necessary.

Lastly, we should always keep in mind the warning of St. Moses the Ethiopian: "The loss you incur by being irritated outweighs the gain of fasting; dislike of your brother cannot be counterbalanced by reading the Bible."[3] Rather, concerning both ascetic disciplines and meditation on the Scriptures, "all are subordinate means to your chief aim, which is purity of heart, or charity [i.e., love], and we ought never to allow them to take precedence [over love]."[4] Asceticism and the Bible are given to us so that we can grow in love. Our "chief aim" is love for both our neighbors and strangers, for both friends and enemies, for both those in high social positions and the "least of these" among us.

Hopefully these next chapters will serve as a solid foundation for then moving forward throughout the history of salvation to see how the Church proved the Scriptures to be "profitable for doctrine, for reproof, for

---

3    John Cassian, *Conferences* 1.7, in *Western Asceticism*, ed. Owen Chadwick, vol. 12, The Library of Christian Classics (The Westminster Press, 1958), 198–199.

4    Cassian, *Conferences*, 199.

correction, for instruction in righteousness, that the man of God may be complete, thoroughly equipped for every good work" (2 Tim. 3:16–17)— mercy for the poor and the marginalized not least of all. To that end, Part 2 will explore the biblical basis of foundational social principles and insti- tutions, as well as their application to works of justice and mercy. These will help us begin to form a theological worldview for Orthodox Christian social thought today.

CHAPTER 7

# The Law

A FEW YEARS AGO, I ran across an amusing meme on social media that went like this: Moses comes down from Mt. Sinai carrying the two stone tablets engraved by the finger of God with the Ten Commandments, and a thought bubble comes from the crowd below, saying, "Whew! Glad my name's not 'Thou.'"

When we think of the Law of Moses, we often think of just the "Thou shalt nots" and forget the story in which they come about. But the Law is actually the first five books of the Bible: Genesis, Exodus, Leviticus, Numbers, and Deuteronomy. Genesis and the first half of Exodus are almost entirely narratives, as is every other section of Numbers, which alternates between laws and stories throughout. Most of Deuteronomy (as the name, meaning "second law," implies) is an extended repetition of the Law in the form of Moses's farewell speech to the people. And there is poetry interspersed throughout many of these books as well.

So while the laws are important, in order to understand how the "Thou" of "Thou shalt not" actually *does* apply to us and our social and economic life, we need to know the story of the Law, which begins with, well, the beginning.

## The Start of the Story

"IN THE BEGINNING," SO THE story goes, "God created the heavens and the earth" (Gen. 1:1). After creating, naming, and distinguishing all things within creation and pronouncing them "good" over a series of six days, God then creates humanity and calls His creation "very good" (1:31). Unlike similar stories from the Ancient Near East, humankind is made to "have dominion" over creation "in the image" of the one God (Gen. 1:27–28), rather than to work as slaves of the lesser gods of a vast pantheon. As St. Athenagoras of Athens put it, "Nothing that is endowed with reason and judgment has been created . . . for the use of another, whether greater or less than itself, but for the sake of the life and continuance of the being itself so created."[1] In short: God makes humanity free, with inviolable dignity.

Then God rests from His work on the seventh day, after which we find the first of a recurring theme in Genesis: "These are the generations," it reads, but not of people, rather, "of the heavens and the earth" (Gen. 2:4 NRSVCE). Here we encounter another, more detailed narrative of humanity's creation, where Adam is a microcosm whose body is made from the earth and whose spirit is breathed into him from heaven by God, as St. Irenaeus, St. Gregory the Theologian, and St. Maximus the Confessor, among others, all affirm.[2] He is made "to till the ground" (2:5) and "tend and keep" (2:15) the Lord's Garden, where "it is not good that man should be alone" but, rather, where we are all created, like Eve, to be "a helper" (2:20) to one another in these tasks. As microcosms, we are meant to extend the dominion of heaven over the earth, both within us and without.

Only here, in this context, do we encounter our first law, a fast: "Of the tree of the knowledge of good and evil you shall not eat" (Gen. 2:17).[3] Long story short, through the temptation of the Serpent, Adam and Eve decide asceticism isn't important, disregard God's law, and face dire consequences: their eventual deaths and a curse upon the earth, their labor, and their relations to

---

1   Athenagoras of Athens, *On the Resurrection of the Dead*, 12, in *ANF* 2:155. Scholars disagree over whether St. Athenagoras of Athens really wrote this work, but either way it is an authentic Christian text from the same period of Church history.

2   Irenaeus of Lyons, *Against Heresies*, 3.22, in *ANF* 1:454; Gregory Nazianzen, "Oration 38: On the Theophany, or Birthday of Christ," 11, in *NPNF²* 7:348; Maximus the Confessor, "Ambiguum 7," in *The Cosmic Mystery of Jesus Christ*, trans. Paul M. Blowers and Robert Louis Wilken (SVS Press, 2003), 68; Alexander Treiger, trans., "The Noetic Paradise," in *The Orthodox Church in the Arab World, 700–1700: An Anthology of Sources*, eds. Samuel Noble and Alexander Treiger (Northern Illinois University Press, 2014), 190–191.

3   See Alexander Schmemann, *Great Lent: Journey to Pascha* (SVS Press, 2001), 93.

each other and creation. Asceticism is the proper way to use our freedom to live in right relation to God's creation.

Thankfully, despite the Fall, God also gives Adam and Eve a promise of salvation. He says to the Serpent, "I will put enmity / Between you and the woman, / And between your seed and her seed; / He shall bruise your head, / And you shall bruise his heel" (Gen. 3:15). Things quickly get ugly: Adam and Eve's oldest son, Cain, murders their second son, Abel, out of envy. Ten generations later, the evil of humankind reaches its nadir in the story of the Flood, after which God makes a covenant with all the earth and blesses humanity and gives them additional laws. Then begins the origins of Israel, starting with their ancestors Abraham, Isaac, and Jacob, all of whom enter into a covenant with the Lord, dedicating themselves to Him in order to carry on the promised blessing for all people: the seed of the woman who will crush the head of the Serpent—a reminder, even at the beginning, of the centrality of Jesus Christ for our worldview.

## *The Exodus*

GENERATIONS LATER, WE GET TO Exodus. The people of Israel have grown numerous, as the Lord promised, but the Egyptians feared them and have enslaved them. Under the leadership of Moses, God frees His people through the Passover.

When they are safe in the desert, Jethro, Moses's father-in-law, seeing how everyone in Israel comes to Moses all day with their problems, gives Moses some good advice: "The thing that you do is not good. Both you and these people who are with you will surely wear yourselves out. For this thing is too much for you; you are not able to perform it by yourself" (Ex. 18:17–18). Instead, Jethro tells Moses to follow the principle of subsidiarity: "Select from all the people able men, such as fear God, men of truth, hating covetousness; and place such over them to be rulers of thousands, rulers of hundreds, rulers of fifties, and rulers of tens. . . . Then it will be that every great matter they shall bring to you, but every small matter they themselves shall judge. So it will be easier for you" (Ex. 18:21–22). Later, the tribe of Levi—i.e., the Levites— would even be designated priests in place of each family's firstborn sons.

After delegating responsibility this way, Moses finally leads Israel to Sinai, where he ascends the mountain and God makes a covenant with Israel and gives them the Ten Commandments, which begins with these words: "I am the LORD your God, who brought you out of the land of Egypt, out of the house of bondage" (Ex. 20:2). The most emblematic commandments in the Law begin with this story of liberation. And while Israel has been freed, just as in the Garden, freedom entails responsibility. The Lord demands their exclusive worship and tells them not to murder, lie, steal, or commit adultery. He commands them to observe the Sabbath day, in which every member of the household, including even slaves and animals, gets a day off of work to attend to spiritual things.

## *Natural Law*

YET THESE COMMANDS, ESPECIALLY THOSE dealing with human relations, are not considered by the Fathers to originate at Sinai but to be written, first of all, into our human nature, as Father Stanley Harakas thoroughly demonstrated in his book *Toward a Transfigured Life*. Here he shows that the idea of a natural moral law is part of the *consensus patrum*, East as much as West,[4] and while there may be some differences between Eastern and Western perspectives, we all agree that God has given value and meaning to our lives, and that some actions work against that value and meaning and are correctly regarded as sinful and wrong by our conscience, if we haven't shut our hearts to its voice within us. As St. Tikhon of Zadonsk put it, "The Law of God and conscience mutually agree and are appointed for the same end, that is our blessedness, whence even pagans, enlightened by philosophical teaching wrote many useful precepts. This comes from nothing other than conscience or natural law illumined by much labor and instruction."[5]

The upshot of natural law is that it helps us sort out the relationship between the many commandments in the Law and our lives as Christians.

---

4   Stanley S. Harakas, *Toward Transfigured Life: The* Theoria *of Eastern Orthodox Ethics* (Light and Life Publishing, 1983); *Living the Faith: The* Praxis *of Eastern Orthodox Ethics* (Light and Life Publishing, 1992).

5   Tikhon of Zadonsk, *Journey to Heaven*, trans. George D. Lardas (Holy Trinity Monastery, 1991), 21.

While the Ten Commandments aren't too hard to apply to our lives, the Law contains commands about dietary rules, Sabbaths, ritual cleanliness, animal sacrifices, and many other things that fit the context of a tribal, Bronze Age people much better than our lives today. According to Abba Serenus in the *Conferences* of St. John Cassian, "The severe restrictions of the law of Moses were added as the executor and vindicator of this (earlier [natural] law) and to use the expressions of Scripture, as its helper, that through fear of immediate punishment men might be kept from altogether losing the good of natural knowledge."[6] The Law was given for a specific people to be their civil law, in order to help them conform their lives more closely to universal natural law.

Civil law, however, is not the same as natural law. In the Law, the Lord condescended to Israel's weaknesses. As St. John Chrysostom noted, God "did not draw them to the highest kind of conversation, but allowed them to enjoy wealth, and did not forbid having several wives, and to gratify anger in a just cause, and to make use of luxury within bounds. And so great was this condescension, that the written Law even required less than the law of nature."[7] So also, Theodore Abu Qurrah claimed that through the Law and the Prophets God gave the people imperfect teachings, commandments, and rewards due to their weakness and the corruption of the world in their times, for the sake of ultimately drawing them to what is perfect.[8] Nevertheless, "the law is holy" (Rom. 7:12) and was meant to distinguish God's people from the nations as bearers of His promise, such that the Fathers regard even many ceremonial laws and rituals, such as the Passover, to be types that found their fulfillment in Jesus Christ.

## *The Eighth Commandment*

FURTHERMORE, THE LAW STILL STANDS as a witness to what it looks like to apply the natural law to a specific people and polity, even if many details differ from our lives today. We can see in the commandments

---

6    John Cassian, *Conferences*, 8.23, in NPNF² 11:384.

7    John Chrysostom, *Homilies on Romans*, 13, in NPNF¹ 11:431.

8    "Theodore Abu Qurra," trans. John C. Lamoreaux, in *The Orthodox Church in the Arab World, 700–1700: An Anthology of Sources*, eds. Samuel Noble and Alexander Treiger (Northern Illinois University Press, 2014), 88.

principles that transcend that specific context. For example—to stick to our topic of Christian social thought—what exactly does "you shall not steal" (Ex. 20:15) look like?

A more specific version appears in Leviticus: "You shall not steal, nor deal falsely, nor lie to one another. . . . You shall not cheat your neighbor, nor rob him. The wages of him who is hired shall not remain with you all night until morning. . . . You shall not be partial to the poor, nor honor the person of the mighty. In righteousness you shall judge your neighbor" (19:11, 13, 15). The principle: God's prohibition against stealing includes all dishonest dealings. Most of us wait a week or two for our paycheck, but in the agrarian world of subsistence living in ancient Israel, workers needed to be paid every day. Even holding due payment too long, whatever constitutes "too long" in a given context, violates the commandment. So also, all people deserve justice in the courts. Preferential legal treatment undermines justice and opens the door to all sorts of theft. This expansive understanding of "you shall not steal" is essential for any Christian approach to our economic life.

The Law continues to expand on its application of this underlying principle: "The stranger who dwells among you shall be to you as one born among you, and you shall love him as yourself. . . . You shall do no injustice in judgment, in measurement of length, weight, or volume. You shall have honest scales, honest weights, an honest ephah, and an honest hin" (Lev. 19:34–36). Immigrants who joined the people of Israel were not to be treated differently, which reflects the universal nature of the principle: Respect for property applies to every human being. One must not disguise any defective goods in an exchange, and the currency used must be stable to ensure that no one gets cheated. We may not use an "ephah" or "hin," but that principle is still something we can and should apply to our economic lives today.

## Witnesses in the Promised Land

AFTER MANY SUCH APPLICATIONS, EXPLANATIONS, and punishments for transgressions (see Numbers), the story of the Law concludes where it began: "I call heaven and earth as witnesses today against you, that I have set before you life and death, blessing and cursing; therefore choose life, that both you and your descendants may live" (Deut. 30:19). At the brink of entering the Promised Land and transitioning from a nomadic life to a kingdom, heaven and earth look on as the Lord gives his people a free choice between life and blessing with Him or death and a curse without Him—not just for their own good but for all the nations of the world: "The peoples . . . will hear all these statutes, and say, 'Surely this great nation is a wise and understanding people.' For what great nation is there . . . that has such statutes and righteous judgments as are in all this law which I set before you this day?" (4:6–8).

As for how Israel did in living out that vocation of faithfulness to the Law and what we as Orthodox Christians can learn from their example, we will explore that in my next chapter on the Prophets.

CHAPTER 8

# The Prophets

O NE MIGHT THINK THAT AFTER the Lord Himself freed the Israel-
ites from Egyptian slavery and gave them the Law, conquering Canaan
would be a cakewalk. Despite some clear warning signs in Numbers, by the
end of Deuteronomy things feel a bit like that song from *The Lego Movie*:
"Everything Is Awesome."[1] What could go wrong? Well . . . everything.

Sure, the story of Israel from Joshua to the Maccabees isn't *entirely* awful.
But anyone who reads through that narrative feels the weight of disappoint-
ment by the end. The reality is more like that song from *The Lego Movie 2*:
"Everything's Not Awesome." It begins as a pessimistic parody of the original, in which Batman (Will Arnett) recommends the somber music of Elliott
Smith when the spaceman Benny (Charlie Day) claims to finally "get" the
experimental alternative rock band Radiohead due to the unfortunate turn of
the story.[2] The song ends by comically rallying for a more measured, realistic
optimism, which, to circle back to the Bible, is about all God's people could
have had left by the end of the Old Covenant.

---

1    Teagan and Sara (ft. The Lonely Island), "Everything Is Awesome," track 1 on *The Lego
     Movie* (Original Motion Picture Soundtrack), WaterTower Music, 2014.
2    Beatriz, Ben Schwartz, Alison Brie, Noel Fielding, Charlie Day, Nick Offerman,
     Will Arnett, Elizabeth Banks, Chris Pratt, and Richard Ayoade, "Everything's Not
     Awesome," track 7 on *The Lego Movie 2: The Second Part* (Original Motion Picture
     Soundtrack), WaterTower Music, 2019.

## *What Went Wrong?*

UNDER THE LEADERSHIP OF JOSHUA, Moses' successor, Israel makes great strides in conquering the Promised Land. But they soon face oppression from without and turmoil from within. In our Orthodox Bible, we can find a short summary in Judith:

> God dried up the Red Sea before them. . . . They drove out all the people of the desert . . . and crossing over the Jordan they took possession of all the hill country. They drove out before them the Canaanites, the Perizzites, the Jebusites, the Shechemites, and all the Gergesites, and lived there a long time.
>
> As long as they did not sin against their God they prospered, for the God who hates iniquity is with them. But when they departed from the way he had prescribed for them, they were utterly defeated in many battles and were led away captive to a foreign land. The temple of their God was razed to the ground, and their towns were occupied by their enemies. [But they] returned to their God, and [came] back from the places where they were scattered, and have occupied Jerusalem, where their sanctuary is. (Jdt. 5:13–19, NRSVCE)

Thus, because God's people failed to follow the Law, they were exiled from the Promised Land. They only returned to God after a long, sad journey.

Despite claiming to be about Nebuchadnezzar and/or the Assyrians, most scholars agree Judith was written at a later time, perhaps drawing upon a real-life story of a Jewish victory over the Hellenistic Seleucid Empire during the third century BC. The Seleucids fought with Ptolemaic Egypt over Palestine for a century, finally obtaining control of it around 200, only to be defeated by the Jews in the Maccabean Revolt starting in 166. The Maccabees, a century later, would be conquered by the Roman Republic, which soon after became the Roman Empire, setting the stage for the time of Christ with that tragic backdrop: God's people failing to keep His Law, over and over again.

How did Israel's story come to this end? Judith tells us: "As long as they did not sin against their God they prospered. . . . But when they departed from the way he had prescribed for them, they were utterly defeated." The death of Joshua left a leadership vacuum. "In those days there was no king in Israel;

everyone did what was right in his own eyes" (Judg. 17:6). The people fell into the following cycle: They would forsake the Lord and His Law, fall victim to foreign oppressors, then cry out for redemption. God would then raise up a "judge" to save them. Even though the judges were chosen by God, we again see that everything's not awesome: Most of the judges violated the Law themselves. Samson, the Hebrew Hercules, may be the most infamous in this regard, but he wasn't alone. Gideon, for example, immediately led the people back into idolatry after freeing them.

The implied solution to this turmoil is that if "in those days Israel had no king," then having a king would make everything awesome again. The story even culminates in Ruth, King David's great-great-grandmother, indicating that the author of both books was likely an apologist for the Davidic dynasty. But when we examine how Israel became a kingdom, the contrast between this ideal and the reality couldn't be sharper. Through this sacred history, the Prophets teach us of both the need for good government and the dangers of political power. Orthodox social thought must incorporate both.

## *The Kingdoms*

SINCE THROUGHOUT JUDGES THE PEOPLE continually descended into apostasy and conflict without a king, eventually they cried out, "Make us a king to judge us like all the nations" (1 Kingdoms/1 Sam. 8:5). So in the books of Kingdoms (1–2 Samuel / 1–2 Kings), we see another figure like Moses or Joshua, a mighty leader who serves as prophet, priest, and ruler: Samuel, who was faithful to the Lord all his life. Despite providing guidelines for a king in Deuteronomy, indicating that the idea of a king wasn't against the Law, the Lord consoles Samuel in his grief when the people want a king to lead them, saying, "They have not rejected you, but they have rejected Me, that I should not reign over them" (8:7). How exactly did they reject God? Because they didn't just request a king but one "like all the nations." God made them holy, His peculiar people, but Israel asked to be like everyone else. Thus, while granting their request for a king, the Lord instructs Samuel to warn them that their king would conscript their sons and take their daughters into his household service; he would take the best of their produce and livestock in taxes;

and "[they] will cry out in that day because of [their] king whom [they] have chosen for [themselves], and the LORD will not hear [them] in that day" (8:18). Their king would be a great economic burden.

Nevertheless, like the story of Joseph in Genesis, what the people intended for evil, God used for good. The role of the Lord's anointed one (Messiah, Christ) becomes divided between several persons, offices, and social spheres: the king and the state, the priests and the Temple, and the prophets among the people. As head of the state, the king should rule in justice and not lead the people into idolatry. The priests must faithfully administer the rites, sacrifices, and ceremonies commanded by the Law. And the prophets . . . well, their job came about when everything wasn't awesome with the other two. Here we see an outline of three social estates or spheres: the state, religion, and the rest of society.

It wasn't all bad. God made a covenant with David that a descendant of his would someday rule Israel forever. But in the meantime, David's grandson Rehoboam laid so heavy an economic burden upon the people that the kingdom split in two: The northern ten tribes formed the kingdom of Israel, with its capital in Samaria. These tribes intermarried with the surrounding people and became known as the Samaritans. The remaining tribes in the south continued the line of David in Judah, with its capital in Jerusalem (the Jews). The economic burden divided God's people into two kingdoms, with the ten northern tribes essentially supporting a revolution. So, too, we should remember today that radical ideas flourish when the common good suffers.

## From Kingdoms to Exile and Back Again

WE SEE IN THE DIFFERENTIATION of Temple, state, family life, and the synagogue something like the progressive development of spheres in Neo-Calvinist social thought. And Christ Himself, though our perfect priest, king, and prophet, would come as a rabbi, a teacher of this new social institution, thus sanctifying the new social sphere of education while also perhaps teaching us not to be too rigid in our social categories in general. So, too, we shouldn't rigidly limit the role of prophet to those books that bear prophets' names. Perhaps the most famous prophet, Elias (Elijah), has no book named for him. Rather, we find the works of Elias in 3 Kingdoms (1 Kings), in particular how he preached against King Ahab and Queen Jezebel of Israel, who turned the people to worship Baal (among other gods) and who notoriously slaughtered Naboth, a poor man, to acquire his property (see 3 Kingdoms/1 Kings 21). Despite all the other evil they committed, this act of murder to violate the property rights of the poor became emblematic of their wickedness.

The prophets preached against impiety, to be sure, but they never separated that mission from the plight of the impoverished, and we shouldn't separate the two today. Through Isaiah, for example, the Lord reprimanded His people in the times of Ahaz and Hezekiah of Judah (and perhaps later). "'Why have we fasted,' they say, 'and You have not seen? / Why have we afflicted our souls, and You take no notice?'" The Lord responds:

In fact, in the day of your fast you find pleasure,
And exploit all your laborers. . . .
Is this not the fast that I have chosen:
To loose the bonds of wickedness,
To undo the heavy burdens,
To let the oppressed go free,
And that you break every yoke?
Is it not to share your bread with the hungry,
And that you bring to your house the poor who are cast out;
When you see the naked, that you cover him,
And not hide yourself from your own flesh? (Is. 58:3, 6–7)

This passage in particular rebukes those who fasted but neglected almsgiving.

The point: Asceticism is social as well as personal. The Lord reminds us that fasting shouldn't just benefit ourselves but should free up resources to help the needy. He expects His people to give their workers time off, feed the hungry, clothe the naked, free prisoners, welcome the homeless, and care for their kindred. Their seeming piety is not enough. The Lord "desire[s] mercy and not sacrifice," as the prophet Hosea put it (6:6). And so even at their best—even when knowledge of the Lord had spread so far that Elisaie (Elisha), Elias's successor, healed the leprosy of the Syrian commander Namaan (4 Kingdoms/2 Kin. 5:1–19) and Jonah preached to Nineveh—Israel and Judah fell gravely short of their calling.

## *The Meek Inherit the Land*

BY THE END OF THE Prophets, the Hasmonean dynasty—the name for the Jewish kingdom the Maccabees established—ruled a Hellenized Judea, complete with gymnasiums as centers of Greek culture and education. While the Maccabees fought for the people's right to follow the Law, their descendants declared themselves kings without Davidic lineage, and some also acted as priests. Thus, the anointed offices of prophet, priest, and king came together again, but their dynasty lacked legitimacy. Despite fighting for and adhering to Jewish religion, they came to be culturally Hellenized themselves. Their downfall to the Romans, though considered tragic, also fit with the pattern of God using foreign powers to judge His people.

Yet the people by this time held on to the hope—delivered to them through countless prophets scorned and martyred in their times—of a true Messiah or Christ, from the line of David, who would usher in that day when "Many nations shall come and say, / 'Come, and let us go up to the mountain of the LORD. . . .' For out of Zion the law shall go forth, / And the word of the LORD from Jerusalem." (Mic. 4:2) And what would happen in that day? The meek would inherit the land: "I will make the lame a remnant, / And the outcast a strong nation; / So the LORD will reign over them in Mount Zion / From now on, even forever. (4:7) The Lord asks rhetorically, "Is there no king in your midst?" (4:9) and consoles them with the assurance that their suffering is not in vain but rather the birth pangs of their redemption.

Before we get to the surprising manifestation of that promise in our Lord Jesus Christ—when as St. Ephraim the Syrian put it, "The prophets' sweet salt is to-day sprinkled among the Gentiles"[3]—we will continue these chapters on biblical theology by first examining the social thought of what St. Jerome noted the Jews in his day called *Hagiographa* ("holy writings").[4] These are the more poetic and philosophical books that echo themes of the Law and the Prophets while developing a distinct tradition of wisdom and prayer for everyday life still relevant to Orthodox social thought today.

---

3    Ephrem the Syrian, *Hymns on the Nativity*, 1, in *NPNF²* 13:226.
4    See Jerome, "Preface to Daniel," in *NPNF²* 6:493.

# CHAPTER 9

# The Writings

AMERICAN WRITER KURT VONNEGUT'S NOVEL *Slaughterhouse-Five* tells the story of the Allied bombing of Dresden during World War II, which Vonnegut, held by the Nazis there as a prisoner of war, survived. Thousands of civilians died, and the Nazis made POWs like Vonnegut bury or burn the bodies before the Russians liberated the city. In an interview with *The Paris Review*, Vonnegut reflected on his success as a writer in relation to Dresden: "The raid didn't shorten the war by half a second, didn't weaken a German defense or attack anywhere, didn't free a single person from a death camp. Only one person benefited—not two or five or ten. Just one." The interviewer asked, "And who was that?" Vonnegut replied, "Me. I got three dollars for each person killed. Imagine that."[1]

One might get the mistaken impression from reading the Prophets that divine justice works according to some kind of cosmic karma. When Israel sinned, they were punished. When they cried out for redemption, God saved them and punished those who oppressed them. When they were faithful to Him, they prospered. And so on. But that wouldn't explain Dresden to Vonnegut: This impression would be mistaken because it does not take account of individual persons. Indeed, many prophets suffered unjustly and received no earthly redemption: "They were stoned, they were sawn in two, were tempted,

---

1  George Plimpton, David Hayman, David Michaelis, and Richard Rhodes, "Kurt Vonnegut: The Art of Fiction No. 64," *The Paris Review* 69 (Spring 1977), https://www.theparisreview.org/interviews/3605/the-art-of-fiction-no-64-kurt-vonnegut.

were slain by the sword. They wandered about in sheepskins and goatskins, being destitute, afflicted, tormented—of whom the world was not worthy" (Heb. 11:37–38). And often the wicked prospered for generations before any faced the Lord's retribution.

The Old Testament Writings—those more poetic and philosophical books, often written by or attributed to King David or his wise son Solomon—more pronouncedly prevent us from jumping to that karmic conclusion by adding a personal, existential, and deeply theological perspective. Relevant to Orthodox Christian social thought, they confront us with profound injustice and inequality, calling us to raise our vision beyond our earthly horizons while exhorting us to economic prudence. They point us to that divine Wisdom through which nature was made and the Law was given, and by which we have access to the unsearchable, unfathomable, and unknowable God. While in the Law we find God's plan for Israel, and in the Prophets we see how well (or poorly) they lived according to the Law, the Writings offer another perspective, at once more mystical and practical.

## The Wisdom of Job

ON THE ONE HAND, THE Writings differ from the Law in their focus on practical, heuristic, natural law instruction. For example: "It is honorable to refrain from strife, but every fool is quick to quarrel" (Prov. 20:3). This saying is just good advice. It immediately resonates with our conscience, and our reason confirms the wisdom in it, because God has created our human nature with innate meaning, value, and purpose. Proverbs like this one are matters of natural law, not special instructions for a particular people like some commands of the Law of Moses.

On the other hand, the Writings differ from the Prophets in their philosophical and existential character. The clearest example of this character comes to us in the book of Job—an ancient dialogue on the problem of suffering. Job, we are told, was a rich and righteous man, apparently living in the time of Abraham, i.e., before Israel or the Mosaic Law. Satan, wishing to insult the Lord, claims that if Job lost all his wealth, his family, and his health, he would surely curse the Lord. The Lord disagrees but allows it all to happen.

But Job persists in his faith, stoically asking, "Shall we receive the good at the hand of God, and not receive the bad?" (Job 2:10)

Job's friends come to comfort him, but they all quickly reveal that they think God works through karma. If Job suffers, they reason, it must be because he sinned. Thus, they remind him of the justice and power of God and urge him to repent. But the assumption that all those who suffer deserve it, presumes unobtainable knowledge of God. Health and wealth are not measures of a person's righteousness. Job does not fall into this error, nor does he, as Satan contended, ever curse God. But he also thinks God would vindicate him in this life, even, perhaps, that God owes him that much. This claim, too, presumes more than any human can know, and God doesn't owe us anything.

The Lord rebukes Job's friends for their karmic thinking and Job for his presumption that God owed him an explanation. True, then God restores Job's health and grants him greater wealth and a larger family than he had before. But the Lord gave Job something greater than all that. Job had known *about* God—"I had heard of you by the hearing of the ear"—but through encountering the Lord in His transcendent glory, Job met God firsthand—"but now my eye sees you"—through what Dionysius the Areopagite called the "unknowing" of true Wisdom.[2] Similarly, St. Maximus noted, "The scriptural Word knows of two kinds of knowledge of divine things. On the one hand, there is relative knowledge, rooted only in reason and ideas, and lacking in the kind of experiential perception of what one knows through active engagement; such relative knowledge is what we use to order our affairs in our present life. On the other hand, there is that truly authentic knowledge, gained only by actual experience, apart from reason and ideas, which provides a total perception of the known object through a participation . . . by grace."[3] We cannot make sense of inequality, injustice, and tragedy without this personal knowledge of God.

---

2    Dionysius the Areopagite, *On the Divine Names*, 7.3, in *Dionysius the Areopagite: On the Divine Names and the Mystical Theology,* trans. C. E. Rolt (Kessinger Publishing Company, 1991), 152.

3    Maximus the Confessor, "Ad Thalassium 60," in *On the Cosmic Mystery of Jesus Christ,* trans. Paul M. Blowers and Robert Louis Wilken (SVS Press, 2003), 126.

THE KINGDOM OF GOD AND THE COMMON GOOD

When it comes to our knowledge of God—or of persons in general—nothing compares to the knowledge of encounter, "gained only by actual experience." This corresponds to the Fathers' distinction between nature or essence and "energies" (*energia*) or natural activity. As St. Basil the Great put it, "I at the same time both know and do not know Timothy. . . . I know him according to his form and other properties; but I am ignorant of his essence."[4] So, too, with God. We know and experience and even cooperate with God's activity in the world, but even that can never give us comprehensive knowledge of God's essence. Our conceptual knowledge—"relative knowledge" of "reason and ideas"—cannot ever fathom the divine depths, and trying to put God in a box in that way will only misrepresent Him and distort our understanding of good or ill fortune in this life, as did Job and his friends.

By contrast, St. Ambrose of Milan discerned the following lesson from Job's encounter with God: "Therefore the blessedness of individuals must not be estimated at the value of their known wealth, but according to the voice of their conscience within them. For this, as a true and uncorrupted judge of punishments and rewards, decides between the deserts of the innocent and the guilty."[5] This lesson, once again, calls to mind the natural law through his appeal to conscience. But it also touches on something higher still: the source of nature itself, the Wisdom of God. Some Fathers call it the "spiritual law," and St. Augustine called it the "eternal law," which "is the divine order or will of God, which requires the preservation of natural order, and forbids the breach of it."[6] Knowledge of this divine Wisdom keeps us from being misled by worldly "wisdom" that sees wealth and material success as all that matters.

## The Wisdom of Creation

THE WRITINGS OFTEN PERSONIFY WISDOM, a grammatically feminine word in Hebrew and Greek, as God's handmaid in creation. "From the beginning, before there was ever an earth," she says, "I was there" (Prov. 8:23, 27). God "poured her out upon all his works" (Ecclesiasticus 1:9, NRSVCE). So

---

4   Basil the Great, Letter 235, in *NPNF*[2] 8:275.
5   Ambrose of Milan, *On the Duties of the Clergy*, 1.12.44, in *NPNF*[2] 10:8.
6   Augustine of Hippo, *Reply to Faustus the Manichæan*, 22.27, in *NPNF*[1] 4:283.

also, "She is a reflection of eternal light, / a spotless mirror of the working of God, / and an image of his goodness" (Wisdom 7:26, NRSVCE). Thus, "The heavens declare the glory of God" (Ps. 19/18:1), and at the creation of the world, Wisdom was there, "delighting in the human race" (Prov. 8:31 NRSVCE).

The Law taught us that not only were we created after the image of God, but we are also microcosms of creation. Like the heavens and the earth, we bear the imprint of this divine Wisdom that "cannot be purchased for gold" (Job 28:15) on our being. In exploring the depths of nature, we see the marks of divine Wisdom through which the world came to be, according to which God sustains it and for which He created it.

Wisdom, then, can be found anywhere, from the heights of heaven to the most mundane occupations and labors of this life. "I know," says the Preacher, "that every man should eat and drink and enjoy the good of all his labor— it is the gift of God" (Eccl. 3:12–13). It even extends to what we do with the fruits of our labor. Indeed, the Psalms, Proverbs, Ecclesiasticus, and Wisdom of Solomon suffer no shortage of sayings about riches and poverty, often how the wise tend to prosper but folly leads to ruin. At the same time, they also acknowledge the dangers of both material success and privation: "Give me neither poverty nor riches— / Feed me with the food allotted to me; / Lest I be full and deny You, / And say, 'Who is the LORD?' / Or lest I be poor and steal, / And profane the name of my God" (Prov. 30:8–9). One learns that "almsgiving atones for sin" (Ecclesiasticus 3:30, NRSVCE). But Wisdom warns, "Assist your neighbor to the best of your ability, / but be careful not to fall yourself" (Ecclesiasticus 29:20, NRSVCE). So too, the righteous person "does not put out his money at usury, / Nor does he take a bribe against the innocent" (Ps. 15/14:5). Divine Wisdom permeates our economic life—in our work, our stewardship, our giving, even our lending. It must, therefore, play a role in Orthodox social thought today.

## *The Need for Wisdom*

YET WISDOM ALSO REMAINS ELUSIVE: "But where shall wisdom be found?" asks Job. "And where is the place of understanding? / Mortals do not know the way to it, / and it is not found in the land of the living" (Job 28:12–13,

NRSVCE). We can catch glimpses of Wisdom in the world and even, through Scripture's higher, spiritual level of meaning, in the Law of Moses. We also see its reflection in human nature, but through the Psalmist the Lord humbles us like Job: "I said, 'You are gods, / And all of you are children of the Most High. / But you shall die like men, / And fall like one of the princes'" (Ps. 82/81:6–7). We must hold this elusiveness in tension with Wisdom's revelatory quality. Orthodox social thought must always be humble.

Through the ascetic practice of memento mori (meditation on our mortality), Wisdom directs our attention to the transitory aspect of material life, the inestimable value of virtue, the hope of the Resurrection, and the justice of God at the Day of Judgment. We see our deep need for God, and in the Psalms we find words to pray for every occasion. Saint Athanasius the Great even encouraged others, as the Church has done in her liturgical tradition, to make the prayers of the Psalter their own.[7] The Psalms are the Church's first prayer book, and in them we find wisdom for every circumstance we may face, even in our very different social contexts today.

Nevertheless, while individual men and women of old found consolation in their sorrows and fellowship with God through what wisdom and virtue they could obtain, humanity's problem is not just personal but social and, ultimately, cosmic: We all, together—and, through us, the heavens and the earth—need salvation from sin, death, corruption, and the devil. We need more than knowledge *of* Wisdom; we need true *communion* with it, the "tree of life"—that which we lost in Eden—"to those who take hold of her" (Prov. 3:18). In my next chapters on the Gospels, we will see that hope first fully realized in our Lord Jesus Christ.

---

7   See Athanasius of Alexandria, A Letter of Athanasius Our Holy Father, Archbishop of Alexandria, to Marcellinus on the Interpretation of the Psalms, 11, in *Athanasius: The Life of Anthony and the Letter to Marcellinus,* trans. Robert C. Gregg (Paulist Press, 1980), 110.

# CHAPTER 10

# Prologue to the Gospel

WHEN PEOPLE TODAY WANT TO share their thoughts about a recent TV show or movie, they often say "spoiler alert" to warn others that, if they haven't seen it yet, important plot elements, twists and turns and surprises, may be spoiled by the ensuing discussion. This trend is a recent phenomenon. William Shakespeare, for one, apparently had no concern for dramatic surprise, at least not in his prologue to *Romeo and Juliet*: "A pair of star-cross'd lovers take their life; / Whose misadventur'd piteous overthrows / Doth with their death bury their parents' strife."[1] Imagine if M. Night Shyamalan began *The Sixth Sense* with a narrator saying (spoiler alert), "By the way, Bruce Willis is a ghost." Yet Shakespeare wants you to get one thing straight from the start of his famous play: Romeo and Juliet are going to kill themselves in the end and as a result finally bring their families together.

For Christians, the biblical story, from the Law through the Prophets and other Old Testament Writings, culminates in the Gospel. The four books that bear that title, Matthew, Mark, Luke, and John, all emphasize that the end should have been clear from the beginning: Jesus is the promised Christ, the "Seed" of the woman who will crush the head of the Serpent (Gen. 3:15).

---

1   William Shakespeare, *Romeo and Juliet* (CBC Enterprises/Les Enterprises Radio Canada, 1985), 7.

## *The Gospel of the Logos*

ACCORDINGLY, ST. JOHN THE THEOLOGIAN begins the prologue to his Gospel with, well, the beginning: "In the beginning was the Logos" (John 1:1, my translation). The what?

The Greek word *logos* has a wide range of meanings. It can mean simply "word," as it is often translated, or "saying." But by the first century AD, it had a refined, philosophical meaning as well, indicating the divine reason or ordering principle by which the universe holds together and obeys set laws. Saint John masterfully combines these two, drawing upon the Creation account of Genesis 1 in which God speaks the world into being: "All things came to be through it" (John 1:3, my translation)—the Word or Logos that "is God" (John 1:1)—"and apart from it nothing that exists came to be" (John 1:3, my translation). So, too, the concept perfectly translates the Hebrew idea of divine Wisdom personified, through which God created and sustains the world and through which our economic life carries eternal significance.

Saint Augustine even claimed to have encountered all these ideas in the "books of the Platonists."[2] Yet, while there is much to learn from this worldly wisdom, he acknowledged that it has its limits: "But that 'the Word was made flesh, and dwelt among us' [John 1:14], I read not there,"[3] says St. Augustine. Indeed, though foreshadowed in the Law and the Prophets and even Greek philosophy, in Jesus Christ the Gospel proclaims something new to all people: "For the law was given through Moses, but grace and truth came through Jesus Christ" (John 1:17). And just as the Law contained guidance about wealth, poverty, property, and care for the poor, the Gospel sheds greater light on these dimensions of our lives as well.

## *Not the Gospel of Caesar*

BUT WHAT IS THE GOSPEL? For that matter, what is *a* gospel?

One early occurrence of the word "gospel" (*evangelion*) sheds some light on what our Evangelists intended. A late first-century BC inscription explains that

---

2     Augustine of Hippo, *The Confessions of Saint Augustine*, trans. Edward B. Pusey (Logos Research Systems, Inc., 1999), 7.9, 88.

3     Augustine, *Confessions*, 7.9, 88.

all calendars would henceforth begin with the nativity of Caesar Augustus. The gospel of Caesar was the good news of the kingdom of "a savior" and "god" who "would end war and order all things,"[4] bringing peace and hope to the world forever . . . in particular by keeping the Parthians from conquering Roman lands and brutally suppressing all civil unrest. The Gospel of Jesus Christ is superficially similar in the first part but importantly different in the second part. That is, it is also the good news of a Savior, the Son of God, "of [whose] kingdom there will be no end" (Luke 1:33), who brings an end to all hostilities, order to all things, peace and hope . . . by submitting to the Cross, suffering the death of a criminal—ridiculed, abandoned, naked, and alone—yet rising again to new life, victorious over death, corruption, the devil, and sin. In this sense, the Kingdom of God is profoundly different from the kingdoms of this world.

Both Matthew and Luke begin by tracing Jesus' own kingly lineage. Despite this royal pedigree, however, Jesus' earthly family had no king's fortune to sustain them. We know they were poor because when his parents brought the offering for Jesus' circumcision to the Temple in Jerusalem, in accordance with the Law they offered "[a] pair of turtledoves or two young pigeons" (Luke 2:24), which was only allowed if the mother "is not able to bring a lamb" (Lev. 12:8). It is possible, indeed likely, that they couldn't afford one. Craftsmen like St. Joseph would have been among the lower socioeconomic strata of Roman society, living at or perhaps only slightly above subsistence.[5] Through the Incarnation, Jesus teaches us about poverty from firsthand experience. As St. Paul wrote, "Though He was rich, yet for your sakes He became poor" (2 Cor. 8:9).

## The Forerunner to the Gospel

MEANWHILE, THE FIRST STORY IN the Gospels of Mark and John (also found later in Matthew and Luke) begins with St. John the Forerunner.

---

4    Reproduced in Craig A. Evans, "Mark's Incipit and the Priene Calendar Inscription: From Jewish Gospel to Greco-Roman Gospel," *Journal of Greco-Roman Christianity and Judaism* 1 (2000): 69. Evans highlights even more parallels with reference to the Gospel of St. Mark in particular.

5    Helen Rhee, "The Social, Economic, and Theological World of Early Christianity," in *Loving the Poor, Saving the Rich: Wealth, Poverty and Early Christian Formation* (Baker Academic, 2012), 1–48.

71

Through the prophet Malachi, the Lord emphasized the momentous nature of John's mission, describing him as a new Elias (Elijah) who will prepare the way of the Lord and "turn / The hearts of the fathers to the children, / And the hearts of the children to their fathers" (Mal. 4:5–6). How did John do that? He told those who came to him to be baptized and taught them: "He who has two tunics, let him give to him who has none; and he who has food, let him do likewise" (Luke 3:11). To the tax collectors, he instructed, "Collect no more than what is appointed for you" (3:13). To soldiers, he said, "Do not intimidate anyone or accuse falsely, and be content with your wages" (3:14).

According to John, the judgment of God is at hand, and what does the Forerunner tell the people to do? Repent, be baptized, clothe the naked, feed the hungry, do not defraud others, do not pressure or slander anyone, and be content with what you have. This practical, economic morality, too, is part of the prologue to the Gospel, the essential orientation needed to understand the whole story. The Logos of God, through which the world was made, has taken on flesh for our salvation. Those who wish to receive Him and avoid being "thrown into the fire" (Luke 3:9) ought to be baptized and reform their lives, including the economic sphere of life, each in his or her own vocation.

And when Jesus came to John to be baptized, John saw the Holy Spirit descend upon Him as a dove. This event not only reveals the Holy Trinity—the Father speaking from heaven, the Son standing in the water, and the Spirit as a dove—but Christ's specifically social mission: "The Spirit of the LORD GOD [was] upon" Jesus, "Because He . . . anointed [him] / To preach the gospel to the poor" (Is. 61:1; Luke 4:18). In the next chapter, I will further explore that "gospel to the poor" and then examine with the Fathers of the Church some principles by which it relates to and fulfills the Law and the Prophets.

CHAPTER 11

# Good News to the Poor

I N *TILL WE HAVE FACES*, C. S. Lewis's retelling of the myth of Cupid and Psyche, one scene vividly captures a recurring phenomenon in the Gospels. As Lewis tells it, Orual, the story's narrator and half-sister of the beautiful Psyche, believes the people of her kingdom to have killed her sister in order to placate the jealous wrath of the goddess Ungit. Unable to stop them, she searches for Psyche after it's too late. But rather than finding her sister dead, Orual discovers her alive. Psyche claims to now live in the palace of a god, and she offers Orual "honeycakes" and a "cup" of "wine," cupping water in her hands, and Orual accepts. However, it becomes clear that the two sisters' perspectives differ sharply: "Wine? What wine? What are you talking about?" says Orual at one point, wishing to put aside what—despite one haunting glimpse of the divine palace—she believes to be a playful charade. In disbelief, Psyche asks, "You mean you saw no cup? tasted no wine? . . . Aiai! . . . so this is what he meant. You can't see it. You can't feel it. For you, it is not there at all."[1]

Similarly, many people who hoped to see God's Kingdom were blind to it. The "gospel to the poor" (Is. 61:1; Luke 4:18) is also the Gospel of the Kingdom of God, which Jews in the time of Christ hoped the Messiah would finally inaugurate, but they thought it would be an earthly kingdom, a kingdom they could *see*. This confusion is understandable. King David reigned over a *visible* kingdom, after all. After the Jews returned from exile, they lived half a

---

1    C. S. Lewis, *Till We Have Faces: A Myth Retold* (Harcourt, Inc., 1956), 119–120.

millennium in the Promised Land with a rebuilt Temple but no Davidic king-dom. When would God's Kingdom finally come?

Yet Jesus preached a radically different message: "The kingdom of God does not come with observation; nor will they say, 'Look here!' or 'there!' For indeed, the kingdom of God is within you" (Luke 17:20–21, my transla-tion). He continues to warn them to be patient in awaiting His return: "The days will come when you will desire to see one of the days of the Son of Man, and you will not see it. And they will say to you, 'Look here!' or 'Look there!' Do not go after them or follow them" (Luke 17:22–23). The Kingdom of God is not one of worldly glory or prosperity. Rather, "Blessed are you poor, / For yours is the kingdom of God" (Luke 6:20). We cannot see the Kingdom unless we can see our own poverty before God in solidarity with the poor among us.

## Not the Gospel of the Zealots

THE SAME LORD WHO FULFILLED His promise to return the people from exile also promised that someday a king would rule Israel—and all nations—from the throne of his father David. By the time of Christ, a movement of nationalist Zealots even rose up, first occasioned by the very census that brought the Theotokos and St. Joseph to Bethlehem. They viewed the Romans as illegitimate and Roman taxes as theft. Their founder, Judas of Galilee, led an ill-fated revolt.[2] He and his followers are referenced in the Acts of the Apos-tles among other failed Messianic movements that the Pharisee Gamaliel compares to the early Church, cautioning others that "if this plan or this work is of men, it will come to nothing; but if it is of God, you cannot overthrow it—lest you even be found to fight against God" (Acts 5:38–39).

Thanks in no small part to the witness of St. John the Forerunner at His Baptism, Jesus quickly gained a reputation for being the promised Messiah. He taught the Law with wisdom and authority. Moreover, He healed the sick

---

2    For more on Judas and the Zealots, see Flavius Josephus, *Antiquities of the Jews*, 18.1, in *Josephus: The Complete Works*, trans. William Whiston (Kregel Publications, 1960), 376–377.

and exorcised demons. And He prophetically exposed the hypocrisy of the Sadducees (the rich, priestly elite), the Pharisees (the more rigorist rabbis), and the scribes and lawyers (academics like me).

Yet some things didn't add up. One of His disciples, St. Simon, was "called the Zealot" (Luke 6:15), but another, St. Matthew, was a tax collector (Matt. 9:9)! When asked whether it was "lawful to pay taxes to Caesar" (Matt. 22:17), Jesus answered, "Render to Caesar the things that are Caesar's, and to God the things that are God's" (Mark 12:17). Judas the Galilean would have answered, "No!" to the question of whether one should pay taxes to Caesar. Jesus was no Zealot, and His Kingdom cannot be found in radical religious nationalism. But what did Jesus mean by the Kingdom of God or heaven?

## *Seeing the Kingdom*

INSTEAD OF JUST TELLING PEOPLE what He means, Jesus speaks in cryptic parables, saying the Kingdom is like a shepherd, a coin, an unjust judge, a Samaritan, ten virgins, and many other things. He even tells His disciples that He speaks in parables precisely so that "seeing they"—the people—"do not see" (Matt. 13:13; see Is. 6:9). In one instance, when Jesus opens the eyes of a man born blind—whom everyone wrongly believed deserved his blindness as a matter of karmic justice—He tells the man, "For judgment I have come into this world, that those who do not see may see, and that those who see may be made blind" (John 9:39).

Yet Jesus begins His preaching by saying, "Repent, for the kingdom of heaven is at hand" (Matt. 4:17). He tells his apostles to preach the same (Matt. 10:7), and instructs them to pray, "Your kingdom come" (Matt. 6:10). If the long-awaited Kingdom is so close . . . where is it? Why can't anyone see it? If Jesus is truly the promised Christ, when does the revolution start? Even just before His Ascension, some of His disciples still ask, "Lord, will You at this time restore the kingdom to Israel?" Jesus evasively responds, "It is not for you to know times or seasons which the Father has put in His own authority. But—" (Acts 1:6–7). Well, now I'm getting ahead of myself. . . .

How is the Gospel of Jesus Christ, of this Kingdom that is neither "here" nor "there" and "not of this world" (John 18:36), yet is somehow both "within you" and "at hand," also the "gospel to the poor"? The light of the Fathers can help us see.

Saint Jerome, St. Augustine, and St. Ambrose see the parable of the "good Samaritan" (Luke 10:25–37), perhaps the quintessential image of mercy for the poor, as an image of the salvation of all humanity through Jesus Christ.[3] The man who descended from Jerusalem to Jericho is all of us, fallen from Paradise into death and sin through the violence of the robber, the devil. Stripped naked of our proper dignity and left for dead, the Law proves impotent to save us: The priest and the Levite, afraid of violating its ceremonial rules, fail to fulfill the command to "love your neighbor" (Lev. 19:18), passing by on the other side of the road. But the Samaritan, Christ (thought a heretic of illegitimate birth by rival rabbis), tends to our wounds with oil and wine and brings us upon His beast (His flesh, according to St. Augustine) to the inn, the Church, to recover under the care of the innkeeper, the apostles, and await His return. Thus, we are all poor and need mercy. Hence, our most common prayer: "Lord, have mercy."

Seeing our universal spiritual poverty is essential to seeing the Kingdom, as the first of the Beatitudes, according to St. Matthew, says, "Blessed are the poor in spirit, / For theirs is the kingdom of heaven" (Matt. 5:3). And St. Luke adds a grave warning: "But woe to you who are rich, / For you have received your consolation" (Luke 6:24).

## Can We Rich Be Saved?

MANY MISREAD THESE PASSAGES AND fall into a false dualism, thinking wealth to be intrinsically evil and material poverty automatically good. This view fits better with those ancient Gnostic heretics like Marcion, who taught that the material world was evil. By contrast, the Fathers, building upon the Stoics, consistently rejected this ethical dualism.

Saint John Chrysostom, St. John Cassian, and St. Gregory the Theologian all affirm that only virtue is good and sin evil—all else, including wealth and

---

3   See, respectively, Jerome, *Letter 108: To Eustochium*, in NPNF[2] 6:195–212; Augustine of Hippo, "Psalm 126," in *Expositions on the Psalms*, in NPNF[1] 8:603–606; Ambrose of Milan, *Concerning Repentance*, 1.11, in NPNF[2] 10:337–338.

poverty, are only good or evil depending on their use.[4] Saint Basil the Great likewise instructs, "Health and sickness, riches and poverty, credit and discredit . . . are not . . . naturally good, but, in so far as in any way they make life's current flow more easily, in each case the former is to be preferred."[5] Clement of Alexandria taught the same and pointedly asked, "If no one had anything, what room would be left among men for giving?"[6] Pope St. Leo the Great further considers the social dimension: "Wealth, after its kind and regarded as a means, is good and is of the greatest advantage to human society, when it is in the hands of the benevolent and open-handed."[7] And Metropolitan St. Filaret of Moscow asks in his *Catechism*, "Can the rich, too, be poor in spirit?" To which he answers, "Doubtless they can: if they consider that visible riches are corruptible and soon pass away, and can never compensate for the want of spiritual goods."[8]

We all suffer the poverty of death and sin, but we all may be "poor in spirit" through grace, humility, detachment, and mercy. That said, we shouldn't take lightly the many warnings in the Scriptures and the Writings of the Fathers about the dangers of material wealth. Material poverty, rightly "used," reveals to us our poverty before God and our need for salvation. Through faith, it can help us see the Kingdom of heaven. Material wealth, though capable of alleviating some struggles of this life, can blind us to the Kingdom through its comforts and, switching metaphors, choke the seeds of faith (see Matt. 13:22).

Given that many more of us today than in the ancient world enjoy the comforts of relative wealth, we all ought to ask with the disciples, "Who then can be saved?" (Matt. 19:25) But unlike the rich young ruler who despaired for his soul, we should also take comfort in the Lord's response: "With men this is impossible, but with God all things are possible" (19:26). God becomes man. A Virgin gives birth. The blind see. Death is put to death. Those born once can

---

4     See, respectively, John Chrysostom, *Against Publishing the Errors of the Brethren*, 2, in *NPNF*[1] 9:236; John Cassian, *Conferences*, 21.14, in *NPNF*[2] 11:508–509; Gregory Nazianzen, *Orations*, 2.22, in *NPNF*[2] 7:209.

5     Basil of Caesarea, *Letters*, 236.7, in *NPNF*[2] 8:278.

6     Clement of Alexandria, *Who Is the Rich Man That Shall Be Saved?*, 13, in *ANF* 2:594.

7     Leo the Great, *Sermons*, 10.1, in *NPNF*[2] 12:120.

8     Philaret of Moscow, *The Longer Catechism of the Orthodox, Catholic, Eastern Church*, in *The Creeds of Christendom with a History and Critical Notes*, trans. R. W. Blackmore, ed. Philip Schaff, vol. 2 (Harper & Brothers, 1889), 514.

be "born again" (John 3:3). Even we rich can be saved if we see our true poverty before God and prudently use our resources for mercy.

In the next chapter, I will continue to explore how the Gospel both fulfills and differs from the Law, teaching us to "be merciful, just as your Father also is merciful" (Luke 6:36), even to "be perfect, just as your Father in heaven is perfect" (Matt. 5:48).

# CHAPTER 12

# The Perfection of the Gospel

H AVING WORKED AS AN AUTHOR and editor for over a decade now, I strongly doubt that a technically perfect journal, magazine, or book exists (not even this one!). "Don't let the perfect be the enemy of the good"— so the saying goes. Look hard enough and you will find a grammatical slip, misalignment, misspelling, or misprint. In this sense, perfection paralyzes those who adopt it as their standard. Perfectionism doesn't publish.

Without contradicting that advice, the Gospel challenges us to consider its seeming opposite: "Don't let the good be the enemy of the perfect." The Old Covenant was good. The New Covenant is perfect. For our social thought to be truly *Christian*, it must go beyond the Law to the perfection of the Gospel.

## *The Good and the Perfect*

FOR EXAMPLE, TO COMMEMORATE THEIR Exodus from Egypt, the people of Israel celebrated the Feast of Tabernacles: "You shall dwell in booths for seven days . . . that your generations may know that I made the children of Israel dwell in booths when I brought them out of the land of Egypt" (Lev. 23:42–43). In the Exodus, Moses brought the people to Mt. Horeb, which he ascended, receiving the Ten Commandments and instructions for the Tabernacle, in which the presence of the Lord traveled with the people, who dwelt in tabernacles in the desert. When Moses emerged from the cloud of God's presence, his face shone with the reflection of divine glory. The Feast of Tabernacles commemorated this.

Compare that to the Transfiguration (Matt. 17:1–8; Mark 9:2–8; Luke 9:28–36). Saint Peter, St. James, and St. John accompany Jesus, the Logos of God that "tabernacled in us" (*eskenosen en emin*—John 1:14), to the top of Mt. Tabor, where His face shines like the sun and a bright cloud descends upon them. There Moses, the giver of the Law, and Elias (Elijah), the most famous of the prophets, appear and discuss with Jesus His forthcoming "exodus" (*exodon*—Luke 9:31). Saint Peter, overwhelmed by this revelation, suggests that everyone observe the ceremony the Law prescribed: "Master, it is good for us to be here; and let us make three tabernacles: one for you, one for Moses, and one for Elijah" (Luke 9:33). In response, the voice of the Father thunders out, "This is My beloved Son. Hear him!" (Luke 9:35)

How should Orthodox Christians understand the relationship between the Law and Prophets, and the Gospel? "This is My beloved Son. Hear him!" Moses and the Prophets are good. Jesus is perfect—but he did not come "to destroy the Law or the Prophets. [He] did not come to destroy but to fulfill" (Matt. 5:17). What's the difference? There are, at least, six: transformation, supersession, transnationality, clarification, natural law, and perfection. We should take all of these into account as we incorporate both the Law and the Gospel into Orthodox social thought.

## Six Differences

FIRST, THE GOSPEL FULFILLS AND goes beyond the Law and the Prophets by divine Wisdom becoming incarnate in Jesus Christ, who teaches the way of salvation, dies, and rises again victorious over death, the devil, and sin—just as the Law and the Prophets promised. As such, many Old Covenant ceremonies are *transformed* in the New: The Feast of Tabernacles becomes the Feast of the Transfiguration. The Hebrew Passover becomes the Christian Pascha. And so on.

Second, other ceremonies were not destroyed but *superseded* by the new reality of the Incarnation. When a child grows into an adult, that person isn't destroyed, though they are a child no longer. Thus the perfect Body and Blood of Christ, and our participation in them through the Eucharist, supersedes the sacrifices of the Law. As Agathon of Homs put it, "When Christ . . . came and sacrificed Himself for us who believe in Him, redeeming us from the law of sin, He instituted for us a new law which neither decreases nor changes and which tribulations of time cannot abolish. He purified us from [animal] sacrifices, blood, burned hair, wool, and bones."[1] So also, dietary rules and other taboos meant to distinguish God's people from other nations are superseded in Christ's Church, which includes all nations.

God chose Israel not only as His own special people but also in order to bless all nations. Thus, Christ rebukes the people for cluttering up with commerce the outer court of the Temple, the only place Gentiles could come to worship.[2] "Is it not written," Jesus asks, " 'My house shall be called a house of prayer for all nations'? But you have made it a 'den of thieves' " (Mark 11:17; see Is. 56:6–8; Jer. 7:11). Commerce *per se* isn't bad—people needed animals for sacrifices and to change their Roman currency for the Temple coin—but commerce that filled the outer court robbed the nations of their place in the Lord's House.

Thus, third, the Gospel *transcends nationality.* The civil provisions of the Law that governed a particular polity—Israel, and later Judah—no longer apply. As Fr. Georges Florovsky noted, "Christianity entered the historical scene as a Society or Community, as a new social order or even a new social dimension, i.e. as the Church."[3] Studying the Law's civil provisions can help us understand how God's moral laws were applied to a specific polity in a specific historical context, but they require further study to apply to our contexts today.

Fourth, in some cases Jesus refuted not the Law itself but misinterpretations of it. For example, he *clarified,* "The Sabbath was made for man, and not man for the Sabbath" (Mark 2:27), emphasizing that the Sabbath prohibition

---

1   "Agathon of Homs," in *The Orthodox Church in the Arab World, 700–1700: An Anthology of Sources,* eds. Alexander Treiger and Samuel Noble (Northern Illinois University Press, 2014), 210–211.

2   Flavius Josephus, *The Wars of the Jews,* in *Josephus: The Complete Works,* trans. William Whiston (Kregel Publications, 1960), 846–850.

3   Georges Florovsky, "Faith and Culture," in *Christianity and Culture,* vol. 2, The Collected Works of Georges Florovsky (Nordland Publishing Company, 1974), 26.

of economic labor does not prohibit *good works*. While we Orthodox still honor the Sabbath by relaxing the work of fasting on Saturdays during Lent,[4] the Sabbath has also been superseded by the Lord's Day, Sunday, when Christ, after resting from the labor of His Passion, rose from the dead "after the Sabbath, as the first day of the week began to dawn" (Matt. 28:1).

Fifth, to the extent that the Law of Moses simply made explicit the *natural law* that God "implanted within [us] from the beginning,"[5] as St. John Chrysostom put it, it still applies today. Impiety, murder, theft, adultery, dishonesty, and covetousness remain sins not only against God and our neighbors but against our very nature as human beings.

Sixth, the Gospel shows that the Law in this sense should be the beginning, the minimal standard, for our lives in Christ. Thus, when the rich young ruler says, "all these things I have kept from my youth," "Jesus, looking at him, loved him" (Mark 10:20–21), then challenged him to go beyond the Law: "If you want to be perfect, go, sell what you have and give to the poor, and you will have treasure in heaven; and come, follow Me" (Matt. 19:21). Saint Ambrose even draws a distinction from this passage between "ordinary" and "perfect" duties,[6] and St. John Cassian builds on it similarly as well.[7] This distinction also makes sense of the teaching of St. Isaac the Syrian that the truly merciful person must be "above justice": "surpassing justice by mercy, wreathing for himself the crown not of the just under the law, but of the perfect under the new covenant."[8] Justice is a good way of loving our neighbors. Mercy is *perfect*.

## A Personal Perfection

IN ADDITION TO ORDINARY, UNIVERSAL morality, each of us has his or her own calling from Christ, who embodies the personal nature of divine

---

4    On the Sabbath during Lent, see Alexander Schmemann, *Great Lent: Journey to Pascha* (SVS Press, 1990), 67–73.
5    John Chrysostom, *Homilies on the Statues to the People of Antioch*, 12.9, in NPNF[1] 9:421.
6    Ambrose of Milan, *On the Duties of the Clergy*, 1.11, in NPNF[2] 10:7.
7    John Cassian, *Conferences*, 21.5, in NPNF[2] 11:504–505.
8    Isaac the Syrian, "Treatise IV," in *Mystic Treatises by Isaac of Nineveh*, trans. A. J. Wensinck (Koninklijke Akademie Van Wetenschappen, 1923), 30.

Wisdom in the biblical Writings. Christ called the rich young man to total material renunciation. But as Clement of Alexandria points out, "He bids Zaccheus and Matthew, the rich tax-gathers, to entertain Him hospitably. And He does not bid them to part with their property, but . . . He subjoins, 'To-day salvation has come to this house.'"[9] So also, St. Cyril of Jerusalem exhorted his catechumens, "Hast thou been put in trust with riches? Dispense them well. Hast thou been entrusted with the word of teaching? Be a good steward thereof. Canst thou attach the souls of the hearers? Do this diligently. There are many doors of good stewardship."[10]

The perfection of the Gospel, then, goes beyond the Law, but in this life that looks different for each person (this is the biblical foundation for the Lutheran doctrine of vocation). For example, parents must have some income and property to provide for their children, whereas the rich young ruler had no such obligations. Thus, trying to depersonalize the Gospel in this life confuses it with the Law and undermines it. For example, the Lord even said that some "have made themselves eunuchs for the kingdom of heaven's sake," meaning those who embrace celibacy, not literal castration.[11] But he adds, "He who is able to accept it, let him accept it" (Matt. 19:12), acknowledging that not all are "able to accept it." If, instead, someone tried to mandate celibacy for everyone, it would be tyranny, not the Gospel. So also the renunciation of property.

That said, all people *are* called to chastity and not just in the outward sense of the Law. "You have heard that it was said to those of old, 'You shall not commit adultery,'" says Jesus. "But I say to you that whoever looks at a woman to lust for her has already committed adultery with her in his heart" (Matt. 5:27–28). The Gospel calls everyone to the higher standard of purity of heart. So also with detachment, generosity, and mercy. The difference between monasticism and the everyday asceticism of all Christians is a matter of degree, not kind. We should not, on the one hand, expect everyone to live the radical vocation of monks. Any monk will tell you it's not for everyone. But on the other hand,

---

9   Clement of Alexandria, *Who Is the Rich Man That Shall Be Saved?*, 13, in ANF 2:594–595.

10  Cyril of Jerusalem, *Catechetical Lectures*, 15.26, in NPNF[2] 7:112.

11  Likely in reference to those such as Origen of Alexandria, known for his "rash act" in taking this saying of Christ too literally, Canon 1 of the Council of Nicaea I prohibits castration. See *The First Ecumenical Council: The First Council of Nicea*, Canon 1, in NPNF[2] 14:8.

asceticism is for everyone, and we can all learn from the example of monastic ways to more perfectly relate to our material resources and serve our neighbors. We can't all take vows of poverty, but we can be content with enough to meet our needs and share whatever we have beyond that. We all, whether in the world or in monasteries, are walking the same path of perfection.

## The Process of Perfection

INDEED, ST. GREGORY OF NYSSA clarified that spiritual perfection is an unending process, a journey, rather than a static state: "The person who looks at a cubit or the number ten knows that its perfection consists in the fact that it has both beginning and end. In the case of virtue . . . its one limit of perfection is the fact that it has no limit."[12] Our everyday asceticism, even in the mundane concerns of our jobs, our families, and our other communities, is quite literally eternal life.

As created beings, perfection is a continuum, not a binary proposition for us. We become by grace what God is by nature, but we never fully "arrive." Many Fathers, such as St. Gregory of Nyssa, St. John Climacus, and St. Nicholas Cabasilas,[13] even identify three "different stages of perfection," as Abba Chæremon put it in St. John Cassian's *Conferences*: "We are called by the Lord from high things to still higher in such a way that he who has become blessed and perfect in the fear of God; going . . . from fear to hope, is summoned in the end to that still more blessed stage, which, is love."[14]

They identified these states with images taken from the social life of the time: the slave, the steward, and the son or child of God. The slave obeys out of fear of punishment, barely surpassing the Law and fulfilling the requirements of natural justice. The servant or steward goes beyond this fear, adding prudence to justice, obeying out of hope for reward. But the mature heir and child

---

12   Gregory of Nyssa, *The Life of Moses*, trans. Abraham J. Malherbe and Everett Ferguson (Paulist Press, 1978), 31.

13   See, respectively, Gregory of Nyssa, *The Life of Moses*, 137; John Climacus, *The Ladder of Divine Ascent*, trans. Colm Luibheid and Norman Russell (Paulist Press, 1982), 76; Nicholas Cabasilas, *The Life in Christ*, trans. Carmino J. de Catazanaro (SVS Press, 1974), 224.

14   John Cassian, *Conferences*, 11.12, in *NPNF²* 11:420.

(or friend) of God obeys simply out of love for the Father in perfect mercy, as Christ demonstrated for us even with His last breath from the Cross: "It is perfected" (*tetelestai*—John 19:30, my translation). The Old Testament Writings taught us that "fear of the LORD is the beginning of wisdom" (Ps. 111/110:10), but fear is not the end: "Greater love has no one than this, than to lay down one's life for his friends" (John 15:13). Such is the perfect love of the Gospel, which is not limited to individuals but ought to permeate our own social contexts today.

On our better days, we manage some foretaste of the "heavenly bliss"[15] that love contains. Many other times, however, we struggle even to fear God as we ought. But by the "grace and truth" that "came through Jesus Christ" (John 1:17), we make progress, however imperfect, along that narrow and difficult "way which leads to life" (Matt. 7:14) in the Church. In my next chapter on the Apostles, we will begin to see the transformative mission of that new and heavenly polity, both for the Kingdom of God and the common good.

---

15    Gregory Nazianzen, *Orations*, 2.22, in NPNF[2] 7:209.

CHAPTER 13

# The Apostles

W HEN I WAS GROWING UP, my mother tried to enforce age-
appropriate entertainment consumption for me. However, she did
make exceptions, one such being legal dramas based on John Grisham novels
like *The Client*. It was released in 1994, which means I probably didn't first see
it on VHS until 1995, when I was eleven years old, just like the lead witness at
the center of the story, Mark Sway (Brad Renfro).

After Mark witnesses the confession and suicide of a mob lawyer, ambitious
prosecutor Roy Foltrigg (Tommy Lee Jones) wants Mark to give an account of
what he saw and heard. Mark worries for his and his family's safety and seeks
a lawyer of his own in Regina Love (Susan Sarandon). *The Client* stands on its
effectiveness as a moral drama, challenging assumptions about our justice system for the sake of a higher justice, in this case for the rights of eyewitnesses,
no matter their age or economic status, to withhold their evidence until their
safety can be ensured.

## *Witnesses to the Resurrection*

THE CONTRAST BETWEEN OUR LEGAL norms and expectations and
those of the ancient world, Rome in particular, could not be sharper. The latter comes to full relief in the Apostles (Acts and the Epistles), in which the
legal rights and procedures for Roman citizens play a major role. Apostles like
St. Peter were eyewitnesses to the risen Christ, and that mattered for refuting

Docetism, the heretical belief that Jesus wasn't really an incarnate, flesh-and-blood human being, but only *seemed* to be. But eyewitness testimony wasn't an essential part of being a witness in ancient Rome. The ideal Roman witness was a person of proven character who could vouch for the trustworthiness of the accused, not necessarily an eyewitness who could make sense of empirical evidence.[1]

It is this kind of witness—character witnesses, not eyewitnesses—that Christ told His disciples they would be for him, when He said at His Ascension, "You shall receive power when the Holy Spirit has come upon you; and you shall be witnesses to Me in Jerusalem, and in all Judea and Samaria, and to the end of the earth" (Acts 1:8). And at Pentecost, St. Peter, "ready to give a defense . . . for the hope that is in [him]" (1 Pet. 3:15), proclaimed to the crowd, "Repent, and let every one of you be baptized in the name of Jesus Christ for the remission of sins; and you shall receive the gift of the Holy Spirit" (Acts 2:38). To repent is to change one's ways and perspective. What, then, did St. Peter hope they would reconsider? "This Jesus God has raised up, of which we are all witnesses" (Acts 2:32). Eyewitnesses, yes, but more importantly those who could testify to Christ's faithfulness.

All Christians, in our lives and even our deaths, are called out of the world to be witnesses to Christ's Resurrection, our faith being "the evidence of things not seen" (Heb. 11:1) and "the victory that has overcome the world" (1 John 5:4). The world continually puts Christ on trial in the members of His Church, his "cloud of witnesses" (Heb. 12:1). The devil, whose name literally means "accuser," represents death and prosecutes the case against the Resurrection. But we are not alone. The Holy Spirit acts as the defense attorney (*parakletos*—John 15:26). And we, "justified by faith" (Rom. 5:1), testify to the trustworthiness of Christ and the grace of the Resurrection through our love, ascetically dying and rising daily with Him and for our neighbors.

Thus, writes St. Luke, "Now all who believed were together, and had all things in common, and sold their possessions and goods, and divided them

---

1 Anthony Harvey, Richard Finn, and Michael Smart, "Christian Martyrdom: History and Interpretation," in *Witness to Faith? Martyrdom in Christianity and Islam*, ed. Brian Wicker (Ashgate, 2006), 33–48.

among all, as anyone had need" (Acts 2:44–45). Even whole communities may be called to complete material renunciation—or near complete. Members of the Church still owned houses, however, breaking "bread from house to house" (Acts 2:46), becoming "one bread and one body" (1 Cor. 10:17) through the Eucharist. The point is that these first Christians were willing to give up anything to meet anybody's needs, not that they literally owned no private property. It was sacramental love, not an impersonal economic system, as St. Paul would later warn, "Though I bestow all my goods to feed the poor . . . but have not love, it profits me nothing" (1 Cor. 13:3).

## From Saul to Paul

FURTHERMORE, THE STORY OF THE early Church does not end with the first Christians sharing "all things in common" in Acts 2. As the Church grew, unequal distribution of alms for Judean and Hellenistic widows required an expansion of her clerical hierarchy in the institution of deacons (Acts 6). Saint Stephen, foremost among the first seven, also became the Church's first martyr (*martys*—the same word as "witness") when a crowd, under the supervision of one Saul of Tarsus, stoned him to death for his testament to the Resurrection: "Look! I see the heavens opened and the Son of Man standing at the right hand of God!" (Acts 7:56)

This same Saul inadvertently fulfilled Christ's words that the first disciples would be His witnesses in "all Judea and Samaria" (Acts 1:8). Saint Luke records that "those who were scattered" there by him "went everywhere preaching the word" (Acts 8:4). But Christ wasn't done with Saul. From a blinding light, He spoke to him on the road to Damascus, saying, "Saul, Saul, why are you persecuting Me?" (Acts 9:4) In Damascus, Jesus called upon St. Ananias, who was understandably hesitant to help Saul and restore his sight. Yet Christ reassured him that Saul was "a chosen vessel of Mine to bear My name before Gentiles, kings, and the children of Israel" (Acts 9:15).

Saul, whom we know as St. Paul, was no lost cause. Though he "saw no one" (Acts 9:8), he was Christ's star witness "to the end of the earth" (Acts 1:8). Saint Gregory the Theologian perfectly captures his transformation: "If [the Holy Spirit] takes possession . . . of zealous persecutors, he changes the current of their zeal, and makes them Pauls instead of Sauls, and as full of piety as he found them of wickedness."[2]

Saint Paul's witness began by submitting to the Church and waiting for the Holy Spirit. In Syrian Antioch, in the midst of Liturgy (*leitourgounton*) and fasting the Spirit commanded the Church to "separate to Me Barnabas and Saul for the work to which I have called them" (Acts 13:2)—to preach the Gospel in Asia Minor. Throughout the region, some in the synagogues accepted the Gospel, but others agitated against St. Paul, driving him to preach to the Gentiles instead.

Returning to Syrian Antioch, some Christians from Judea arrived, claiming, "Unless you are circumcised according to the custom of Moses, you cannot be saved" (Acts 15:1). Saint Paul and St. Barnabas objected, as St. Paul would later write, "In Christ Jesus neither circumcision nor uncircumcision avails anything, but faith working through love" (Gal. 5:6), showing that while the Law was good, the Gospel is perfect. So they took their dispute to St. Peter and St. James in Jerusalem, where the first-ever Church council settled the matter. They composed an encyclical to "the Gentiles in Antioch, Syria, and Cilicia" (Acts 15:23), ruling that Christians do not need to "be circumcised and keep the law" (Acts 15:24) but only to "abstain from things offered to idols, from blood, from things strangled, and from sexual immorality" (Acts 15:29). Who better to deliver this letter than St. Paul?

After doing so in Antioch, St. Paul revisited the Church in Asia Minor and later traveled to Corinth, where we learn of his custom to work as a tentmaker. As he said to the Ephesian elders on his way back to Jerusalem, "You yourselves know that these hands have provided for my necessities, and for those who were with me. I have shown you in every way, by laboring like this, that you must support the weak. And remember the words of the Lord Jesus, that He said, 'It is more blessed to give than to receive'" (Acts 20:34–35). How was St. Paul able to give? When the revenue from his trade exceeded his expenses, i.e., when he made a profit. Thus, he was able to provide not only for his own "necessities" but "for those who were with [him]," and he exhorted the Ephesians to do the same.

2    Gregory Nazianzen, *Orations*, 41.14, in *NPNF*[2] 7:384.

Saint Paul's exhortation came in this context: "The Holy Spirit testifies in every city, saying that chains and tribulations await me [in Jerusalem]. But none of these things move me; nor do I count my life dear to myself, so that I may finish my race with joy, and the ministry which I received from the Lord Jesus, to testify to the gospel of the grace of God" (Acts 20:23–24). Just as at Pentecost, St. Paul's martyric witness entails material mercy as well.

## From Jerusalem to Rome

WHEN ST. PAUL ARRIVED BEARING alms in Jerusalem, Jewish authorities incited the Romans to arrest him. But before the soldiers could flog him, he objected, "Is it lawful for you to scourge a man who is a Roman, and uncondemned?" (Acts 22:25) It wasn't,[3] and the revelation that he was a Roman citizen whose rights they had nearly violated terrified them. Roman civil rights were regarded as the privilege of citizens, not universal rights. Yet despite his teaching that "our citizenship is in heaven" (Phil. 3:20), St. Paul used his Roman citizenship for the Gospel. The Kingdom of God is greater than Caesar, but Caesar got some things right, like due process and transparency (see Acts 16:37), even if only for citizens.

After St. Paul's nephew uncovered a plot to assassinate him, the Romans transferred him to Caesarea, where he eloquently testified to the Resurrection and taught about "righteousness, self-control, and the judgment to come" (Acts 24:25). However, when his trial stalled, he appealed to Caesar and went to Rome, where the Jews hadn't heard of him and brought no charges against him. Meanwhile, his preaching received mixed reviews, once again prompting St. Paul to emphasize the transnational nature of the Gospel: "Let it be known to you that the salvation of God has been sent to the Gentiles, and they will hear it!" (Acts 28:28).

The rest of the story must be pieced together from the Epistles and Tradition. Saint Paul wrote many of the Apostolic Epistles throughout his missionary journeys, which continued after the end of Acts. However, possibly the earliest Epistle is from St. James, who comforted poor Christians oppressed by

---

3    Titus Livius (Livy), *The History of Rome*, trans. George Baker, vol. 1 (Jones & Co., 1830), 10.9, 344–345.

the rich and "scattered abroad" like the "twelve tribes" of Israel in exile (James 1:1), before he was martyred in Jerusalem.[4] Saint Peter also wrote "to the pilgrims of the Dispersion in Pontus, Galatia, Cappadocia, Asia, and Bithynia" (1 Pet. 1:1), like St. James employing the motif of exile for our relation to the world, before he, too, faced martyrdom by Nero in Rome with St. Paul.[5] Their letters teach even more about wealth and poverty, the Church, the world, the family, and the state, all themes we will explore further in later chapters.

As for the other major author of the Apostles, St. John the Theologian, his witness goes beyond his Gospel and Epistles to the Apocalypse of Jesus Christ (Revelation) and a category of Scriptures that, though regarded as canonical, remain Apocrypha in the sense of being "hidden" from public reading in the Orthodox Church. These more mystical texts have as much to say about the present as the future, including our economic life together, and they fittingly conclude our examination of the Bible in my next chapter.

---

4     On the martyrdom of St. James, see Eusebius of Caesarea, *Ecclesiastical History*, 2.23, in *NPNF*[2] 1:125–128.

5     On the martyrdoms of St. Peter and St. Paul, see Eusebius, *Ecclesiastical History*, 2.25, in *NPNF*[2] 1:128–130.

CHAPTER 14

# Biblical Apocrypha

A LL THROUGHOUT HISTORY, SOME HAVE thought Revelation to be a secret code all about them and their time. These misinterpretations presume that a true understanding ultimately *eliminates* uncertainty and ignorance about the future. Better interpretations instead view it as an aid to *living with* uncertainty today. In the words of St. Dionysius: "I do not reject what I cannot comprehend, but rather wonder because I do not understand it."[1] Ignorance and terror are the point. So are patient faithfulness and wonder. Uncertainty touches every aspect of life, including our economic lives, and the biblical Apocrypha teach us how to wait for our Lord in that uncertainty, doing what good we can in the present.

The term *apocrypha* sometimes has a negative meaning. Saint Athanasius referred to "apocryphal writings" that "are an invention of heretics."[2] So also, some Protestants came to refer to our Old Testament bonus books as apocrypha as well. But for my purposes, Apocrypha is simply a term of convenience for those books of the Bible not often read in the Orthodox Church. Not only that, but I do not just refer to them as "apocalyptic," because I think it is helpful to include the Song of Songs, which though not an apocalypse is far more than a sappy love poem. Biblical Apocrypha is the "weird stuff" of Scripture, best understood through the lens of Pope St. Gregory the Great (Dialogos):

---

1 Eusebius of Caesarea, *Ecclesiastical History*, 7.25.4, in *NPNF*[2] 1:309.
2 Athanasius of Alexandria, *Festal Letters*, 39.7, in *NPNF*[2] 4:552.

92

"A divine discourse . . . communicated to the frigid, sluggish soul by means of enigmas [that] secretly teaches such a soul the love that it does not know by means of what it knows."[3]

## True Riches

Let's start with Revelation then. Edith M. Humphrey adds some helpful perspective in her series of essays: It isn't just a book about the end of the world. Rather, "it comprises the whole of time, which is in God's hands."[4] Its real title is "The Apocalypse [literally, 'unveiling'] of Jesus Christ" (Rev. 1:1, my translation). It is from Him and chiefly *about Him*. It only tells us about the Church, the world, and history as they relate to Him in all His heavenly, crucified-resurrected-and-ascended glory.

Saint John (the Theologian, presumably), like the prophets Zechariah, Daniel, and Ezekiel, serves a common apocalyptic role as narrator of the book. Through a celestial mediator, he witnesses divine visions for the sake of comforting God's suffering people. Indeed, while Jesus is the source and focus, St. John addresses Revelation "to the seven churches which are in Asia" (Rev. 1:4) that suffered under Roman persecution "towards the end of Domitian's reign," at least according to St. Irenaeus.[5] So right from the start, we ought to caution ourselves before applying it to our own time and context.

Each of these seven churches receives a letter from Christ Himself, following, as Humphrey notes, the same pattern: "An address reminding them of His character . . . ; a confirmation of their strengths; a warning and call to repentance where necessary; a closing command . . . ; and finally a promise."[6]

---

3   Gregory the Great, *Commentary on the Song of Songs*, 1, trans. Cassian DelCogliano, OCSO (Spencer, MA, n. d.), retrieved from http://www.lectio-divina.org/images /patristics/Commentary%20on%20the%20Song%20of%20Songs%20by%20Gregory %20the%20Great.pdf. A fragmentary text; I know of no other published translation.

4   Edith M. Humphrey, "Lighting Up the Apocalypse 4: Our Times Are in His Hands," March 12, 2021, https://edithmhumphrey.com/2021/03/12/lighting-up-the-apocalypse -4-our-times-are-in-his-hands/.

5   Irenaeus of Lyons, *Against Heresies*, 5.30.3, in *ANF* 1:560.

6   Edith M. Humphrey, "Lighting Up the Apocalypse 5: One for All, and All for One," March 26, 2021, https://edithmhumphrey.com/2021/03/26/lighting-up-the-apocalypse -5-one-for-all-and-all-for-one/.

Regarding social thought, the warning to Laodicea ought to catch our attention: "Because you say, 'I am rich, have become wealthy, and have need of nothing'—and do not know that you are wretched, miserable, poor, blind, and naked—I counsel you to buy from Me gold refined in the fire, that you may be rich" (Rev. 3:17–18).

Our definitions of riches and wealth need to be transfigured in Christ's Kingdom: Our true riches are righteous perseverance, apart from which we are "wretched, miserable, poor, blind, and naked" no matter our socioeconomic status. Material wealth can be used for good, but it cannot of itself purchase the greatest treasure of all: "If a man would give for love / All the wealth of his house, / It would be utterly despised" (Song 8:7). How do we make that love "happen," then? We don't: "Do not stir up nor awaken love / Until it pleases" (Song 3:5). We must wait patiently, like a bride anticipating her betrothed, until the grace of Christ our Bridegroom comes to us. Yet, paradoxically, *waiting* is something: "When the church sighs," wrote St. Gregory Dialogos, "when the church, as it were, seeks its absent spouse—it suddenly beholds him as present."[7]

## Waiting for the Bridegroom

THIS SEEKING WE DO—AND SEE in every biblical vision of heaven—through liturgy. Some say liturgy means "the work of the people," but that isn't quite right. In ancient Greece and Rome, *leitourgia* signified a "public work" of the wealthy, primarily financing services like education and theater. Thus, we refer to our eucharistic service as the "Divine Liturgy." It is as much God's economy *for us* as it is our work for God or each other. Liturgy teaches us "not [to] stir up nor awaken love" on our own time but to wait on God.

Waiting as Christ's unwedded and virgin bride—the Theotokos being our prime, unique example—also means patient faithfulness, which requires rejecting illegitimate suitors. "As you have heard that the Antichrist is coming," wrote St. John, "even now many antichrists have come" (1 John 2:18). Notice the time, "now," and the plural, "antichrists." The word means a

---

7    Gregory the Great, *Commentary on the Song of Songs*, 13

fraudulent messiah, anyone who "does not confess that Jesus Christ has come in the flesh" (1 John 4:3), demanding the love and loyalty proper to Christ and His Kingdom for themselves.

While, yes, we do think "*the* Antichrist is coming," we risk missing the message if we overfocus on the future. Saint John refers to an evil city (likely Rome) as "Babylon," suggesting that, like Babylon, we've seen this city before (and will again). Jesus spoke of an "abomination of desolation" (Matt. 24:15) from Daniel—which referred to Antiochus IV offering sacrifices to Zeus in the Lord's Temple—as an event in "the end" that "will come" (Matt. 24:14). So also, famines, wars, and even plagues throughout history should have a deeper meaning to Christians. The light of Christ reveals our world as saturated with iconographic symbolism, directing us ascetically to endure present trials and watch with bated breath for our Bridegroom's return at the final resurrection.

Thus, we can learn about the present from the end, and the end from the present, including for our economic lives. The Antichrist, the beast from the abyss, St. John tells us, institutes impious obstacles to commerce: "No one may buy or sell except one who has the mark or the name of the beast" (Rev. 13:17). I have no idea or opinion what precisely that may be, but I can say that it *functions* economically as a barrier to market entry. As a result of the mark, those who refuse to compromise their faith for the sake of economic privilege must endure additional hardship and injustice.

By contrast, when "Babylon" finally falls (as it always does), "the merchants of the earth"—those who accepted the mark—"will weep and mourn over her" (Rev. 18:11). Misunderstanding the nature of true wealth, as did the Laodiceans, they cry out, "Alas, alas, that great city, in which all who had ships on the sea became rich by her wealth!" (Rev. 18:19) The Venerable St. Bede frames their sorrow in terms of uncertainty: "Observe that every single person of those who lament, weeps not only for the loss of riches, but for the sudden and unforeseen ruin of the deceitful world."[8] Like the five foolish virgins, the Bridegroom's sudden coming leaves them in the darkness (Matt. 25:1–13).

---

8    The Venerable Bede, *The Explanation of the Apocalypse*, trans. Edward Marshall (n.p., 1878), 125.

## A Vision of the Bride

AS FOR THOSE WHO REMAIN faithful, an archangel shows St. John their true destiny: "'Come, I will show you the bride, the Lamb's wife.' And he carried me away in the Spirit to a great and high mountain, and showed me the great city, the holy Jerusalem, descending out of heaven from God" (Rev. 21:9–10). On this vision, St. Victorinus of Pettau offers a healthy corrective to overly literal misinterpretations: "The kingdom of Christ is now eternal in the saints, although the glory of the saints shall be manifested after the resurrection."[9] In the descent of the Holy Spirit at Pentecost, we already have in our present world embassies of this new Jerusalem in the Church.

"Now eternal," we possess in part that which in its fullness we anticipate. Thus, we all, as "kings and priests" (Rev. 5:10) of God's Kingdom, act as its ambassadors (the literal meaning of "apostles") to the world, offering a foretaste, a glimpse, a revelation of that "life of the age to come," to quote the Creed. Let us, then, for the sake of this present age, meditate on that heavenly city, never expecting we can establish it through our efforts, yet never wavering in our belief that it can, will, and does come in the grace of God's good time.

> Old men and old women shall again sit
> In the streets of Jerusalem,
> Each one with his staff in his hand
> Because of great age.
> The streets of the city
> Shall be full of boys and girls
> Playing in its streets.
> (Zech. 8:4–5)

> And there shall be no more curse, but the throne of God and of the Lamb shall be in it, and his servants shall serve him. (Rev. 22:3)

> And the Spirit and the bride say, "Come!" And let him who hears say, "Come!" (Rev. 22:17)

---

9   Victorinus of Pettau, *Commentary on the Apocalypse of the Blessed John*, in ANF 7:360.

Let us, too, following two thousand years of Orthodox Christians before us, say, "Come!" Let us witness to this revelation, even with our material resources, of what our world will one day become if today we heed the call to repentance: "Come!" And let us never tire in waiting for our Bridegroom, who answers even still, "Surely I am coming quickly!" (Rev. 22:20)

# Part 2 Summary and Discussion Questions

## Summary

As Orthodox Christians, we do not read the Scriptures alone but with the Church, consulting Fathers and theologians throughout the centuries to help us interpret God's word. In reading the Bible, we should follow the rule of St. Vincent of Lérins: universality, antiquity, and consent. We should hold true to the fundamentals of our Faith consistently passed down to us through the centuries and not overemphasize exceptional opinions we may happen to find in Holy Tradition. At the same time, by developing a biblical theology of wealth, poverty, and care for the poor, we can better avoid prooftexting—taking verses out of context—when we cite the Bible today.

The Law consists of the first five books of the Old Testament: Genesis, Exodus, Leviticus, Numbers, and Deuteronomy. It contains not just commandments but stories, laws, and poetry. According to the Fathers, its moral laws, such as the Ten Commandments, are grounded in natural law. Its civil laws are an application of the moral law to a particular context: the tribes, and later the kingdom of Israel. And its ceremonial laws regulated Israel's relationship to God and foreshadowed the coming of Christ. In every respect, the Lord gave the Law to distinguish His people from the surrounding nations and to witness to them, including through its many economic provisions against theft, fraud, and injustice.

The Prophets include the historical books of the Old Testament, like the books of Kingdoms (Samuel and Kings), along with prophecies named for the prophets through whom they were given, like Jeremiah. In the Prophets, the Lord judges His people according to the Law, calls them to repentance, punishes them when they forsake Him, and promises a coming Messiah or Christ who will sit on the throne of David and establish an eternal Kingdom. Unfortunately, Israel does not remain faithful: Their earthly kingdom is divided into Israel and Judah, and eventually each is exiled through foreign conquest. But the Lord restores the Jews to Jerusalem and even rebuilds His demolished Temple. In the Prophets, the three messianic roles of prophet, priest, and king become divided between the people, the Temple, and the kingdom. Later, educational institutions, such as synagogues and gymnasiums, further broaden the range of social institutions among God's people.

In the Writings—poetic and wisdom literature—we encounter pragmatic wisdom alongside mystical reflection. Job and Ecclesiastes confront us with the problem of evil and existential despair, while both, in their own ways, offer hope in the midst of suffering. Proverbs, Ecclesiasticus, and the Wisdom of Solomon offer prudential advice, including in economic matters, grounded in the image of the divine Wisdom through whom God created the world and impressed His Wisdom upon it. And most important of all, the Psalms teach us to pray while at the same time they prefigure the coming of Christ.

The Gospel depicts Jesus as divine Wisdom Incarnate, the Son of God come to preach good news to the poor—not only the materially impoverished and marginalized but each one of us who depends upon God's grace and mercy. Through His death and Resurrection, Christ delivers us from sin, corruption, death, and the devil, fulfills the Law, and invites us to take up our crosses and follow Him, living lives of mercy and love in all our personal relations. The Law is good, and it's even a necessary and enduring framework for justice, but the Gospel is perfect. We cannot neglect impersonal justice, but we also cannot reduce the Gospel to Law without losing the essentially personal love, grace, and mercy only the Gospel can provide.

The Apostles emphasize the role of Christians as witnesses (literally "martyrs") to the Gospel story and message. Though citizens of worldly kingdoms, our ultimate citizenship is in heaven. Yet we best witness to our heavenly patriotism by ascetically serving the forgotten, destitute, and needy among us. For some this means radical renunciation. For others it means prudent stewardship of the resources God has given them. In all things, by the power of the Holy Spirit, the apostles witnessed, through their sufferings, to the hope of the resurrection the Cross and Pascha won for us. In the midst of hostile cultures, they adapted the motif of exile to frame their relationship as lights to the world shrouded in darkness.

Last, the biblical Apocrypha—mystical texts we do not read liturgically—focus on hope and faithfulness in the midst of uncertainty. The churches in each city are embassies of the Kingdom of heaven. Yes, it also talks about beasts, dragons, and the Antichrist, but these images come from recurring motifs throughout Scripture and history. Anyone who denies the Incarnation and appropriates the honor due to Christ is an antichrist. Any social privilege that acts as a barrier to Christian participation in business and society is a mark of the beast. Any kingdom saturated by blasphemy and greed is Babylon. In the midst of these things in every age, even while warning of their final expression at the end of time, the Church, as Christ's beloved Virgin Bride, waits patiently for her Bridegroom's return. She witnesses not only to what Christ has done but to "the life of the age to come"—the unimaginable joy, peace, and love of God's coming Kingdom that breaks into the world in the present through the Sacraments.

## Discussion Questions

- How does our Orthodox understanding of how to read the Bible differ from an evangelical Protestant point of view?
- What does the Law have to say about our social and economic relations?
- How do the many stories in the Law provide context for its commandments?
- What do the Prophets say about justice, wealth, and poverty?
- What do the Writings teach about wealth and wisdom, poverty and folly?
- How does the Gospel relate to the Law, Prophets, and Writings?

- In what ways does the Gospel go beyond the Law in terms of mercy for the poor and marginalized?
- How do the examples and teachings of the Apostles help us better understand how to witness to the Gospel today?
- How do the books of the biblical Apocrypha help us find peace in the midst of darkness and uncertainty?

PART 3

# Church History

CHAPTER 15

# Why Does History Matter?

I N THE FILM ADAPTATION OF *The Fellowship of the Ring*, Frodo (Elijah Wood) first sees Gandalf (Sir Ian McKellen) riding down the road to the Shire in a carriage loaded with fireworks for his uncle Bilbo's "eleventy-first" birthday, and Frodo calls out to the aged wizard, "You're late!"

"A wizard is never late, Frodo Baggins," Gandalf reprimands, "nor is he early. He arrives precisely when he means to." Unable to keep a straight face, they both crack up laughing.[1]

For Gandalf, the statement may have been a joke, but his larger-than-life stature (literally and figuratively) nevertheless makes the moment memorable for more than its levity. Indeed, Gandalf tirelessly traveled Middle Earth in his quest to defeat Sauron, and Bilbo's birthday served as convenient cover for serious business. Gandalf's arrival in the Shire sets in motion all the events that follow—at exactly the right time.

Having surveyed biblical insights for Orthodox Christian social thought in Part 2, we cannot just jump to the present or even, say, to Adam Smith. We still must cover two thousand years of Church history . . . or we might just say, history.

---

1    *The Lord of the Rings: The Fellowship of the Ring*, directed by Peter Jackson (New Line Cinema, 2001), 178 min.

## Making History

IT HAS BEEN ARGUED THAT the Hebrew account of Creation and the final judgment, combined with the Christian conviction that Jesus Christ came in "the fullness of the time" (Gal. 4:4; see Eph. 1:10) and "in these last days" (Heb. 1:2), actually created and necessitated the idea of history as we understand it today. At the least, "a historian," wrote Fr. Georges Florovsky, "precisely as historian . . . cannot evade the major and crucial challenge of this actual history: 'Who do men say that I am?' (Mark 8:28)."[2]

While historians such as Herodotus existed before the Church began, there are important differences between ancient pagan and Christian conceptions of history. Not only did many pagans presume that history had no ultimate trajectory and instead repeated itself in a series of recurring cycles, but according to Jaroslav Pelikan "the historians of classical antiquity . . . concentrated on contemporary events." By contrast, "according to Eusebius" of Caesarea, known for his *Ecclesiastical History*, "the decisive event . . . had not been in his own lifetime, but had taken place in the life of Jesus Christ."[3] "The sense of history," wrote Fr. Alexander Schmemann, "its irreversibility, the unrepeating nature of time, and within this time the uniqueness and unrepeated quality of each event and each person, were all profoundly alien to Hellenic psychology."[4]

By Pelikan's account, as "the early generations of Christian believers . . . carried out the task of finding a language that would not collapse under the weight of what they believed to be the significance of the coming of Jesus, they found it necessary to invent a grammar of history."[5] Thus, not only did they, in the sense described above, create history as we know it, their theology, too, had to be historically and biblically informed in order to best uphold their convictions amidst the pressures of the world around them.

---

2   Florovsky, "The Predicament of the Christian Historian," in *Christianity and Culture*, The Collected Works of Georges Florovsky, vol. 2 (Belmont, MA: Nordland Publishing Company, 1974), 53.
3   Jaroslav Pelikan, *Jesus Through the Centuries: His Place in the History of Culture* (Yale University Press, 1985), 31.
4   Alexander Schmemann, *The Historical Road of Eastern Orthodoxy*, trans. Lydia W. Kesich (SVS Press, 2003), 39.
5   Pelikan, *Jesus Through the Centuries*, 21.

# *The Plan for Part 3*

FOLLOWING THEIR LEAD, PART 3 of this book surveys the historical theology of care for the poor, together with the economic history in which it arose, in nine chapters each framed by biblical motifs.

The first chapter features the Church, the new Israel, in pagan Rome, where the themes of pilgrimage and exile, already present in the New Testament but taken from the Old, shape the Church's understanding of its position in the sporadically hostile empire.

The second and third chapters examine the idea of a Christian kingdom, in particular Christian Rome from St. Constantine to the fall of Constantinople, drawing from the time of the prophets in the kingdoms of Israel and Judah. What does it mean for a state—or an emperor, for that matter—to be "Christian"? Should bishops be apologists for the crown or prophetic critics, who like Nathan fearlessly rebuke the king for his sins and who like Isaiah advocated for the poor and oppressed? And what sort of society did the laws of this new Christian civilization create?

The fourth chapter journeys into the desert—as did the children of Israel after the Exodus from Egypt—to examine the history of monastic charity, asceticism, and enterprise. Despite their vows of poverty, monks both East and West often found themselves blushing at the "embarrassment of riches," sometimes virtuously accumulated and administered but other times viciously gained and selfishly held.

The fifth and sixth chapters explore Western Orthodox witness from the fall of Rome to the Great Schism. Our biblical motif will be apostolic witness, as we follow the monastic missions of the Celts and the doctrinal sturdiness of Rome. How did Christianity and classical civilization survive the Dark Ages? And in what sense were they really dark? The "Dark Ages" narrative too often obscures much unheralded light regarding Christian views of taxation, true happiness, penance, monastic order and missions, and the perpetual dangers of entangling religion and the state.

The seventh chapter follows the Abrahamic faith (as in the biblical patriarch) of Middle Eastern Orthodox Christians after the Islamic conquests in the seventh century. In the wake of their world's end, they found new life and discovered new insights regarding mercy and justice, reasoned discourse, economic inequality, and ecumenical solidarity.

The eighth chapter examines the apocalyptic character of the unique enculturation of Orthodoxy among the medieval Rus'. From the conversion of St. Vladimir of Kiev through the Tatar conquest to the Stand at the Ugra River, there existed more than three centuries of kenotic spirituality and free, egalitarian social relations that are surprisingly relevant to our modern contexts today.

Last, the ninth chapter examines Orthodox social thought in the Russian Empire. In the Old Testament (and beyond) the non-Davidic, Hasmonean dynasty of the priestly Maccabees afforded the Jews a time of freedom in the midst of a period otherwise marked by exile and occupation. Similarly, imperial Russia, despite its institutional abnormalities, stands out as an oasis for the Orthodox during a time elsewhere marked by foreign conquerors and *dhimmitude*—second class status under Islamic regimes—and it will bring us to the Church's first encounter with the Social Question in the nineteenth century, which marks the beginning of modern Christian social thought.

I would understand if some readers object to this framing—it still omits quite a lot of Orthodox history that deserves greater popular attention. But as I am not writing a new Church history so much as uncovering our historical theology, this survey must suffice.

## Such a Time as This

IN THE MEANTIME, WE MUST set the stage. In our look at biblical theology, we caught a glimpse of what Christ's coming "in the fullness of time" meant—the messianic expectations of the Jewish people, the development of Greek philosophy, and some of the better conventions of Roman law. We must add to these the socioeconomic contexts of Church Tradition and Orthodox Christian teachings on wealth, poverty, labor, and charity. Yet far from uncritically praising these contexts, we must remember that in every case the factors that prepared the way for the Gospel at other times proved violently hostile to the Church. Jesus did not turn out to be the Messiah many Hebrews expected. And the Romans not only carried out His unjust execution at their request, but later, as vividly evidenced by Revelation, Rome joined in persecuting the Church as well.

As for Greek philosophy, though St. Paul the Apostle, St. John the Theologian, and many Church Fathers that came after them considered it useful, it also lent its hand: During persecutions under the reign of Marcus Aurelius, known for his introspective Stoic *Meditations*, the Cynic philosopher Crescens denounced St. Justin, resulting in the saint's martyrdom.[6] Another philosopher, the Epicurean Celsus, wrote the first known comprehensive polemic against Christian teaching.[7] And the Neoplatonist Porphyry wrote a fifteen-book attack on the Christian Scriptures as well.[8] The very intellectual establishment that allowed for the Fathers' careful articulation of Church dogma sought, in envious self-preservation, to discredit and destroy what Clement of Alexandria believed to be the "true philosophy": Christianity.[9]

But what of the Roman economy? It, too, just like Jewish culture, Greek philosophy, and Roman law, contained both positive and negative contexts in terms of preparing for the spread of the Gospel.

Roman society consisted of many degrees of stratification, and a complex web of social relations governed everything.[10] The oldest male of a noble estate acted as *paterfamilias*, exercising control over all household life . . . and even death. While from the beginning Roman law required some duties of piety to one's dependents,[11] *patria potestas* ("the power of the father") also gave a paterfamilias extensive authority. At their worst, they viewed their wives (and concubines) as property, divorced freely, abused and sexually assaulted their slaves, aborted and exposed unwanted infants, controlled to whom and whether their children married, and so on.

---

6  Eusebius of Caesarea, *Ecclesiastical History*, 4.16, in *NPNF*² 1:193–195.

7  For Origen's response to Celsus's polemic, which is otherwise lost to history, see Origen of Alexandria, *Against Celsus*, in *ANF* 4:395–670.

8  Porphyry, *Against the Christians*, trans. and ed. R. Joseph Hoffmann (Prometheus Books, 1994).

9  Clement of Alexandria, *The Stromata*, 6.7, in *ANF* 2:492–494.

10  Peter Brown, "Late Antiquity," in *A History of Private Life*, ed. Paul Veyne (The Belknap Press of Harvard University Press, 1987), 235–312.

11  "The Twelve Tables, 451–449 BC," in *Ancient Roman Statutes*, trans. Allan Chester Johnson, Paul Robinson Coleman-Norton, and Frank Card Bourne (University of Texas Press, 1961), 9–18.

Few means of upward mobility existed for those outside of this upper echelon of Roman life. If one were a slave, one could obtain the status of freedman, but often this emancipation involved a debt, formal or informal, to one's patron for being freed. Thus, many tradesman—at best part of a small middle class[12]—worked simply to sustain the lavish lifestyles of their former masters. Through the patronage of a nobleman, a freedman could obtain increased wealth and social status, but even these were often fragile and vulnerable. Military service could also lead to social advancement, such as emancipation for slaves and honors and titles for freedmen and free-born citizens.

For others, whether slave, freedman, or citizen by birth of lesser status, there remained at least one other way to advance: adoption. Sometimes a rich paterfamilias would adopt a son to share a portion of his estate with him—and his social status in the meantime—as an inheritance. This aspect should be familiar to Christians: "When the fullness of the time had come, God sent forth His Son . . . that we might receive the adoption as sons. . . . Therefore you are no longer a slave but a son, and if a son, then an heir of God through Christ" (Gal. 4:4, 5, 7). We gain the status of sonship now. The Kingdom of heaven, indeed the entire cosmos, is the "estate" of God that His adoptive heirs—each of us, male or female—inherit. Even the metaphor St. Paul used in this passage, writing to Gentile Christians in Roman Asia Minor, depends on "the fullness of the time."

Yet the societal institution of the Roman family, too, became a source of conflict between Church and empire. For one example among many, St. Perpetua, a noblewoman martyred in Carthage on March 7, AD 203, while in prison, repeatedly had to refuse her pagan father's pleas to deny Christ to save her life. In particular, she recorded in her diary that he begged her, "Give up your resolution; do not destroy us all together; for none of us will speak openly against men again if you suffer aught," and, more bluntly, "give me not over to the reproach of men." She recognized that he said these things "fatherly in

---

12  Helen Rhee, "The Social, Economic, and Theological World of Early Christianity," in *Loving the Poor, Saving the Rich: Wealth, Poverty and Early Christian Formation* (Baker Academic, 2012), 1–48.

his love,"[13] but one cannot miss his concern for his own status. In many cases the Gospel broke the very familial bonds and economic structures considered most essential to social life.

We should expect similar consonance and conflict in our own time. By exploring more of these features in the coming chapters, going beyond pagan Rome, we'll be able to learn from what complemented and what clashed with social and economic contexts throughout Church history. We'll see examples of what principles guided Orthodox Christian social action, as well as what worked and what didn't. As for us, not only did Christ come "in the fullness of the time" and "in these last days," but the time remains full, and our days, too, remain "these last days." We must also take on at least one more biblical role: that of Esther, unexpectedly given the opportunity to be queen of Persia and to intervene to save her people from genocide. "Who knows," asked her uncle Mordechai, "whether you have come to the kingdom for such a time as this?" (Esth. 4:14)

Today we face our own challenges, in a wide variety of contexts, for the sake of the poor, suffering, and marginalized, for both the Kingdom of God and the common good. Through Jesus Christ, "the turning point of history,"[14] to quote Pelikan, and through two thousand years of unique and unrepeatable people, events, societies, economies, and empires since, even today we, too, may be best positioned and equipped "for such a time as this."

---

13    *The Passion of Saints Perpetua and Felicity*, in Internet Medieval Sourcebook, ed. Paul Halsall (Fordham University, 1996), https://sourcebooks.fordham.edu/source /perpetua.asp, a revision of W. H. Shewring, trans., *The Passion of Perpetua and Felicity* (Sheed and Ward, 1931).

14    Pelikan, *Jesus Through the Centuries*, 21.

CHAPTER 16

# The Catholic Church in Pagan Rome

I N 1941, THE LIBERAL BIBLICAL scholar Rudolf Bultmann asserted, "We cannot use electric lights and radios and, in the event of illness, avail ourselves of modern medical and clinical means and at the same time believe in the spirit and wonder world of the New Testament."[1] Based on Bultmann's reservations, one might expect ancient pagans, whose religion rested on literal myths, to more readily accept "the spirit and wonder world of the New Testament," rather than dismissing it, as did Pliny the Younger, as "depraved and excessive superstition,"[2] and approving the execution of its adherents. The hinge on which all objections turned, unbeknownst to the objectors, comes down to a single reality: *catholicity.* Many rival, Gnostic "Christianities" claimed apostolic authority, but there was only one Catholic Church. Catholicity bound together the worldview of ancient Orthodox Christians, their faith in Jesus Christ, the hierarchy and Sacraments of the Church, *and* their ascetic service to the needy. Thus, it must shape our social thought today. Of course, being Orthodox, I don't mean *Roman* Catholic. The official name of the Orthodox Church is, in fact, the Orthodox Catholic Church. What, then, does *catholic* mean?

---

1   Rudolf Bultmann, "New Testament and Mythology: The Problem of Demythologizing the New Testament Proclamation (1941)," in *New Testament and Mythology and Other Basic Writings,* trans. and ed. Schubert M. Ogden (Fortress Press, 1984), 4.

2   Pliny the Younger, Letter 10.96: "To the Emperor Trajan," in *Letters,* trans. William Melmoth, rev. by W. M. L. Hutchinson, vol. 2 (G. P. Putnam's Sons, 1926), 403.

## *Orthodox and Catholic*

JUST A FEW YEARS BEFORE Pliny, on the road to martyrdom in Rome, St. Ignatius of Antioch warned the Church in Smyrna against the Gnostics: "They care nothing about love: they have no concern for widows or orphans, for the oppressed, for those in prison or released, for the hungry or the thirsty. They hold aloof from the Eucharist . . . because they refuse to admit that the Eucharist is the flesh of our Saviour Jesus Christ . . . which, in his goodness, the Father raised [from the dead]."[3] Ministries of love for the materially impoverished necessarily follow from our paschal confession that "Christ is risen." Even our bodily needs matter to God, and our care for others witnesses to Christ's Resurrection. "By this all will know that you are My disciples," Jesus taught, "if you have love for one another" (John 13:35).

Saint Ignatius goes on to clarify, "You should regard that Eucharist as valid which is celebrated either by the bishop or by someone he authorizes. Where the bishop is present, there let the congregation gather, just as where Jesus Christ is, there is the Catholic Church."[4] As Christ is to the whole Church, so the bishop is to his congregation. Considering the context, then, this first known use of the phrase "the Catholic Church" inseparably unites the Incarnation and Resurrection, the mystical presence of Christ in the Eucharist, care for the poor and oppressed, and the unity of the Church under episcopal authority.

The Greek for *catholic* here is *katholike*, from *kata*, meaning "through," and *olos*, meaning the "whole." Many today define catholic as "universal," meaning "throughout the whole *world*." That's true, but for St. Ignatius, "holistic" might fit better. Catholicity is the loving communion in Jesus Christ between Creator and creation, heaven and earth, spiritual and material, clergy and laity, universal and local, even rich and poor, for "you are all one in Christ Jesus" (Gal. 3:28).

According to historian Peter Brown, in Jesus' teaching on "treasure in heaven" (Matt. 19:21), "The primal joining of heaven and earth was mirrored

---

3   Ignatius of Antioch, To the Smyrnaeans, 6.2–7.1, in *Early Christian Fathers,* ed. Cyril C. Richardson (Westminster Press, 1953), 114.
4   Ignatius, To the Smyrnaeans, 8.1–2, 115.

113

in society itself. The starkly antithetical poles of rich and poor were brought together, through almsgiving. Through these two primal joinings, the greatest gulf of all—that between God and humankind—was healed."[5] The cosmic catholicity of the Gospel includes our social world. Because the first Christians emphasized this communion between rich and poor, they contrasted with Greek philosophy by universalizing many social norms pagan philosophers commended only to the Roman elite, including things like philanthropy and the taming of one's passions. As Brown elsewhere concluded, "The surprisingly rapid democratization of the philosophers' upper-class counterculture by the leaders of the Christian church is the most profound single revolution of the late classical period."[6]

The ancient philosopher and physician Galen even remarked in amazement, "There are among them [i.e., the Christians] those who possess such a measure of self-control with regard to food and drink and who are so bent on justice, that they do not fall short of those who profess philosophy in truth."[7] Christians of all classes outdid ancient philosophers most of all by their ascetic mastery over the fear of death through their catholic faith in the resurrection. This fortitude, too, Galen noticed: "Fearlessness of death and the hereafter"—one of the highest goals of ancient philosophy—"is something we witness in them every day."[8] Nevertheless, the early apologists wrote to the Roman authorities in order to persuade them to *stop* killing Christians. They didn't fear death, but unless it seemed unavoidable, ancient Christians didn't *want* it either.

## At Home in Exile

BY THE SECOND CENTURY, BAPTISM put one's life in danger. Compounding this risk, terrible rumors spread: "Three charges," wrote St. Athenagoras,

5    Peter Brown, *Treasure in Heaven: The Holy Poor in Early Christianity* (University of Virginia Press, 2016), 6.

6    Peter Brown, "Late Antiquity," in *A History of Private Life,* ed. Paul Veyne (The Belknap Press of Harvard University Press, 1987), 251.

7    Quoted in Ibn Abi Usaibia, *The History of Physicians,* trans. L. Kopf (Institute for African and Asian Studies, The Hebrew University, 1956), 150.

8    Quoted in Usaibia, *History of Physicians,* 150.

"are brought against us: atheism, Thyestean feasts [i.e., cannibalism], and Oedipean intercourse [i.e., incest]."[9] In apologies like that of St. Athenagoras, written to refute these misconceptions, we glimpse how the Catholic Church viewed the hostile pagan world. For example, the *Epistle to Diognetus* claims that Christians "live in their own countries, but only as aliens. They have a share in everything as citizens, and endure everything as foreigners. . . . They obey the established laws, but in their own lives they go far beyond what the laws require."[10] They viewed themselves in the mode of Israel's Babylonian exile, where the prophet Jeremiah instructed the people to "seek the peace of the city" (Jer. 29:7) in which they now lived. Accordingly, St. Justin the Philosopher claimed, "We are in fact of all men your best helpers and allies in securing good order."[11]

In his own answer to pagan rumors, St. Justin described early Christian gatherings, including the administrative structure of their catholicity: "What is collected is deposited with the president [i.e., the bishop], and he takes care of orphans and widows, and those who are in want on account of sickness or any other cause, and those who are in bonds, and the strangers who are sojourners among [us], and, briefly, he is the protector of all those in need."[12] By contrast, according to Brown, "The idea of a steady flow of giving, in the form of alms, to a permanent category of afflicted, the poor, was beyond the horizon of [upper class pagans]."[13]

Father Alexander Schmemann provides further detail. By the third century, "The Church had its own cemeteries and almshouses, conducting an extensive charitable activity."[14] To this detail we may add the observation of Brown: "In 248 the church of Rome had a staff of 155 clergy and supported some fifteen hundred widows and poor. Such a group . . . was as large as the city's largest trade association."[15] This description helps us contextualize St.

---

9   "A Plea Regarding Christians by Athenagoras, the Philosopher," in *Early Christian Fathers*, 303.
10  Epistle to Diognetus, 5.5, 5.10, in *Early Christian Fathers*, 217.
11  "The First Apology of Justin, the Martyr," in *Early Christian Fathers*, 247.
12  Justin Martyr, 67, 287.
13  Brown, "Late Antiquity," 262.
14  Alexander Schmemann, *The Historical Road of Eastern Orthodoxy*, trans. Lydia W. Kesich (SVS Press, 2003), 47.
15  Brown, "Late Antiquity," 270.

Cyprian's rebuke of the schismatic Novatians during this same time. By starting their own sect only for the *cathari* ("the pure"), they *"departed from charity and from the unity of the Catholic Church."*[16]

As for individual Christians, our earliest teachings highlight four fundamental ascetic doctrines: prudent almsgiving, responsible receiving, profitable labor, and a patronage of prayer. While the Fathers commended all almsgiving, the *Didache* ("The Teaching of the Twelve Apostles") relates a saying that recommends discernment: "Let your donation sweat in your hands until you know to whom to give it,"[17] warning especially about supporting itinerant prophets. Both the *Didache* and the *Epistle of Barnabas* furthermore recount another saying for those who receive: "Do not be one who holds his hand out to take, but shuts it when it comes to giving."[18] And where would one get anything to give? "Do good," the *Shepherd of Hermas* records, "and of all your toil which God gives you, give in simplicity to all who need."[19] We see again here, as well as in the *Didache* and *Barnabas*, that principle of St. Paul that "by laboring . . . you must support the weak" (Acts 20:35).

Last, St. Hermas of Rome also describes an image of harmony across social classes: the elm and the vine. The elm (the rich), according to his vision, bears no fruit on its own but provides the shade needed for the vine (the poor) to flourish. Thus, "the poor, interceding with the Lord for the rich, complement their wealth, and again, the rich helping the poor with their necessities complement their prayers."[20] Both benefit each other and together bear fruit to God through a sort of reciprocal patronage, uniting the material patronage of the wealthy with the spiritual patronage of the poor.[21]

---

16    Cyprian of Carthage, Epistle 75: "To Magnus," 1, in *ANF* 5:397, emphasis added.

17    "The Teaching of the Twelve Apostles, Commonly Called the Didache," 1.6, in *Early Christian Fathers*, 172.

18    "Didache," 4.5, 173. Compare to Epistle of Barnabas, 19.9: "Be not one who stretches out the hands to take, and shuts them when it comes to giving," in *The Apostolic Fathers*, trans. Kirsopp Lake, 2 vols. (Harvard University Press; William Heinemann, 1912–1913), 1:405.

19    "Shepherd of Hermas," Mandate 2.4, in *The Apostolic Fathers*, 2:73.

20    "Hermas," Parable 2.8, in *The Apostolic Fathers*, 2:147.

21    On Roman patronage, see Helen Rhee, *Loving the Poor, Saving the Rich: Wealth, Poverty, and Early Christian Formation* (Baker Academic, 2012), 14–19 (Greco-Roman patronage), 65 (the elm and the vine in *Hermas*).

## *The Lion and the Fire*

IN THESE WAYS AND MORE, in their service for the Kingdom of God, the first Christians contributed to the common good of Rome. Tertullian even notes that Christians participated in nearly every trade and social rank.[22] Still, St. Athenagoras objects to the emperors, "While everyone . . . enjoy[s] equal rights under the law . . . you have not cared for us who are called Christians in this way."[23] The nations in which Christians sought "the peace of the city" at times waged war against the Church.

We see a vivid illustration of this animosity in the Martyrdom of St. Polycarp, a letter "to all those of the holy and Catholic Church who sojourn in every place."[24] In Israel's exile, the Babylonians threw the prophet Daniel into the lion's den and his friends into the fiery furnace, despite their service to the king. But God stopped the mouth of the lion and "the Son of God" (Dan. 3:25) preserved the three holy youths in the flames. Similarly, when Polycarp was brought to the arena in Smyrna, the crowd "asked the Asiarch Philip that he let loose a lion on [him]. But he said . . . he had brought the wild-beast sports to a close. Then they decided to shout with one accord that he burn Polycarp alive."[25] Yet "when the flame flashed forth . . . the fire made the shape of a vaulted chamber . . . and made a wall around the body of the martyr."[26] Thus, protected from the mouth of the lion and preserved amidst the flames, "the lawless men . . . commanded an executioner to go to him and stab him with a dagger."[27]

Despite many protests of learned Christians throughout the second and third centuries, martyrdoms like that of St. Polycarp marked this age of exile. However, though the Church's catholicity would endure, the paradigm of exile would soon collapse in Rome when something utterly unthinkable happened in the early fourth century: The emperor became a Christian. A Christian kingdom required new perspectives. But that's a story for the following chapters.

---

22 Tertullian, *Apology*, 92, ANF 3:49.
23 Athenagoras, "A Plea," 1, in *Early Christian Fathers*, 301.
24 "Martyrdom of Polycarp," in *Early Christian Fathers*, 149.
25 "Martyrdom of Polycarp," 12.2–3, 153.
26 "Martyrdom of Polycarp," 15.1–2, 154–155.
27 "Martyrdom of Polycarp," 16.1, 155.

# CHAPTER 17

# Prophets of Christian Civilization

I N THE SEVENTH *HARRY POTTER* book and the first part of its film adaptation, there is a scene where Harry (Daniel Radcliff), the young wizard protagonist, attends a wedding. In the previous book and film (spoiler alert!), his mentor Dumbledore, the most powerful wizard in the world, was betrayed and murdered. Harry, an orphan, feels directionless without Dumbledore's fatherly guidance and unsafe without the reassurance of his presence. Moved by a tribute to Dumbledore in the wizard newspaper *The Daily Prophet*, Harry happens to meet the column's author at the reception. What starts as a cordial and complimentary conversation about the deceased elder quickly degenerates when an eavesdropping socialite (Matyelok Gibbs) interjects her own unsolicited commentary.

In the course of their discussion, Harry learns that Dumbledore has a brother; that his family lived in Harry's birthplace, Godric's Hollow; and that they moved there after Dumbledore's father murdered three muggles (non-magical people). The woman then asks Harry, who is bewildered by these and more disenchanting details, "Honestly, my boy, are you sure you knew him at all?"[1] Many students of history can relate to this sort of demystification of their historical heroes. But just as Harry's encounter with a truer picture of Dumbledore eventually led him back to a place of respect

---

1   *Harry Potter and the Deathly Hallows—Part 1*, directed by David Yates (Warner Bros. Pictures, 2010), 146 min.

and admiration for him, so also, if we look to history unafraid of what evils it may contain, we see that the Church has not erred even in its veneration of certain emperors.

We must not conveniently hide behind a naïve dichotomy between the "good" Church and the "evil" state. History complicates such simplistic analyses, and Christians cannot turn a blind eye to history. We may correctly identify and rightly condemn any number of public or personal sins of the emperors St. Constantine or St. Theodosius, for example, but the Church still bids us venerate them as saints. So also, simply being a bishop or other clergy does not ipso facto guarantee someone's sanctity. If we can muster the courage to countenance the messy details of history, where expectations and reality so often clash, we will see how the Church developed new paradigms for social engagement in a Christian empire.

## *A Bright and Splendid Day*

AFTER THREE CENTURIES OF BRUTAL, intermittent persecutions in pagan Rome, the fortunes of the Church suddenly and dramatically changed when the emperor, whom we know as St. Constantine, confessed himself a Christian after a profound conversion due to his vision and victory at the Milvian Bridge. Eusebius of Caesarea relayed the surprise and relief of Christians across the Roman Empire in vivid terms: "Finally a bright and splendid day, overshadowed by no cloud, illuminated with beams of heavenly light the churches of Christ throughout the entire world." He continued, commenting on the declaration of religious liberty proclaimed in 313 in the so-called Edict of Milan: "And not even those without our communion were prevented from sharing in the same blessings, or at least from coming under their influence and enjoying a part of the benefits bestowed upon us by God."[2]

For a short period of time, this statement held true. Equal religious liberty was all the early apologists asked for the Church—it is a thoroughly Christian ideal—and at first it was all that St. Constantine established. In particular, Milan differed from a previous statement of religious tolerance toward

---

2    Eusebius of Caesarea, *Ecclesiastical History*, 10.1, in *NPNF*[2] 1:369.

Roman Christians in 311 in one specific way: "And we decree still further in regard to the Christians, that their places, in which they were formerly accustomed to assemble, and concerning which in the former letter [in 311] sent to thy devotedness a different command was given . . . shall be restored to the said Christians, without demanding money or any other equivalent, with no delay or hesitation."[3] The Church remembers the Edict of Milan as the moment of her liberation in ancient Rome because it not only acknowledged the right for individuals to be Christian, but it affirmed and restored the property rights, and thus the liberty, of the Church. "You shall not steal" (Ex. 20:15) applied to the state in Christian Rome just as much as it did in ancient Israel in the case of Ahab and Jezebel, who murdered Naboth for his vineyard (see 3 Kingdoms/1 Kin. 21). The Church Fathers in Christian Rome often used the paradigm of the Prophets during the kingdoms of Israel and Judah as a lens for interpreting their relationship to the now-Christian state, prophetically exhorting Christian rulers to respect the natural law and stay out of Church business.

So, too, at their best, Christian rulers sought to apply a Christian understanding of God's Law to Roman law. For example, St. Constantine left a lasting legacy in terms of Byzantine monetary policy through minting a new coin: the *solidus*. The solidus maintained its value until the eleventh century, ensuring the reliability of commercial transactions and acting as a safeguard against inflation. Thus, we see that the principle of "honest scales, honest weights, an honest ephah, and an honest hin" (Lev. 19:36) applied to Christian civilization just as well as to ancient Israel, being grounded in the same prohibition of theft by which the Church's property rights and equal liberty were acknowledged.

## Christian Prophets

UNFORTUNATELY, EQUAL RELIGIOUS LIBERTY SOON turned to unequal privilege that would cast a long shadow over centuries to follow. After the Council of Nicaea in 325, Jaroslav Pelikan notes, St. Constantine "issued an edict against heretics on that basis, forbidding them to gather and

---

3    Edict of Milan, 9, in Eusebius of Caesarea, *Ecclesiastical History*, 10.5, in NPNF[2] 1:379.

confiscating their church buildings and places of assembly. That edict treated Christian dissenters far more harshly than it did pagans."[4] "Persecution," laments Schmemann, "which transformed the schismatics into martyrs, only strengthened them."[5]

In time, like court prophets of the Old Testament, Arian bishops eventually turned the machinery of the state against the Orthodox. When the emperor fell into heresy, Orthodox bishops and others took on the mantle of Elias and other outcast prophets, calling Christian emperors to repent and reform their faith. In his *History of the Arians*, written against the Arian emperor Constantius, St. Athanasius reasserted the ancient independence of the Church: "Where is there a Canon that a Bishop should be appointed from Court?"[6] He continued, "There have been many Councils held heretofore; and many judgments passed by the Church; but the Fathers never sought the consent of the Emperor."[7] Saint Athanasius then evoked images from the Prophets, adopting a new mode of engagement with the powers of this world: "Wherever there is a pious person and a lover of Christ (and there are many such everywhere, as were the prophets and the great Elijah) they hide themselves" from Constantius.[8] Moreover, he chided, "the Emperor . . . is the patron of the heresy, and wishes to pervert the truth, as Ahab wished to change the vineyard [of Naboth] into a garden of herbs."[9] This was not just a matter of supporting bad ideas; it involved expropriating church property from the Orthodox and giving it to Arians.

We see this prophetic role of the Church again in the eighth century, with St. John of Damascus's defense of holy icons. Writing from outside Christian Rome, whose territory by that time had been curtailed by the Arab conquests, he asserted, "Political good order is the concern of emperors, the ecclesiastical

---

4    Jaroslav Pelikan, *Jesus Through the Centuries: His Place in the History of Culture* (Yale University Press, 1985), 53.

5    Alexander Schmemann, *The Historical Road of Eastern Orthodoxy*, trans. Lydia W. Kesich (SVS Press, 2003), 68.

6    Athanasius of Alexandria, *Arian History*, 7.51, in NPNF² 4:288.

7    Athanasius, *Arian History*, 7.52, 4:289.

8    Athanasius, 7.53, 4:289.

9    Athanasius, 7.52, 4:290.

constitution that of pastors and teachers. This is a piratical attack, brothers."[10] Once again, like St. Athanasius, St. John of Damascus evoked imagery from the Prophets to describe the unjust deposition of St. Germanus, Patriarch of Constantinople: "Saul tore the garment of Samuel, and what happened? God tore from him his kingdom and gave it to David the most meek. Jezebel persecuted Elias, and the dogs bathed in her blood. Herod did away with John, and he gave up his life eaten of worms. And now the blessed Germanus, radiant in his life and his words, is flogged and sent into exile, and many other bishops and fathers whose names we do not know. Is not this piracy?"[11] Without a baseline level of due process in society, injustice and tyranny reign.

## The Davidic Model

SAINT JOHN OF DAMASCUS ALSO points us to a positive model of the Christian state and magistrate, with his mention of King David. We rightly regard David as a saint, even a prophet, yet the Scriptures do not shy away from recounting his fall into covetousness, adultery, and murder (see 2 Kingdoms/2 Sam. 11–12). No military victory or worldly accomplishment makes him a saint. Indeed, David had so much blood on his hands that the Lord refused to let him build His Temple (see 1 Chron. 22:7–8). Rather, what makes David a saint, a model of repentance, is his prayer, "Have mercy upon me, O God, / According to Your lovingkindness" (Ps. 50/51:1). David repented when confronted by Nathan, a court prophet who actually acted faithfully before the Lord, proving David still to be, in the last analysis, "a man after [God's] own heart" (1 Kingdoms/1 Sam. 13:14).

So also, the Church remembers St. Theodosius, for example, not only for convening the Council of Constantinople but, when boldly confronted by St. Ambrose in Milan, for famously repenting of the massacre he caused in Thessaloniki: "The ruler of the world stripped of his robe and diadem"[12] and made

---

10  John of Damascus, *Three Treatises on the Divine Images*, 2.12, trans. Andrew Louth (SVS Press, 2003), 69.

11  John of Damascus, *Three Treatises*, 2.12, 69.

12  Peter Brown, "Late Antiquity," in *A History of Private Life*, ed. Paul Veyne (The Belknap Press of Harvard University Press, 1987), 271.

to kneel among the penitents, as historian Peter Brown put it. Saint Constantine had removed sacrifice and *latreia* from the cult of the emperor, effectively reducing it to an extravagant fan club, because he genuinely believed only Jesus Christ to be both God and man. In the humbling of St. Theodosius, we see how, indeed, the Christian emperor was no god but a human being as much in need of salvation, and subject to just laws, as anyone else—a positive legacy that persisted for centuries. Even in the late 1000s, the emperor Alexios I Komnenos and his whole household submitted to public penance.[13]

Thus, while the freedoms of non-Christians faced some unfortunate restrictions in the Christian era of ancient Rome, we nevertheless see positive social and political fruit of the Church's liberty as well. The paradigm of the Prophets proves a vivid mode of social engagement when the ruler claims the name of Christian, and though many of us do not live under officially Christian states today, lessons and opportunities remain. As Fr. Georges Florovsky put it, "The state is never very favorable to the criticism coming from the church unless the state itself is avowedly Christian. The same is true of economic society."[14]

Our societies and parishes include many politicians and businesspeople today, and this prophetic stance can inform both positive and negative interactions with the Church. In the person of St. John Chrysostom, we will see in the next chapter how the response to criticism may not be "very favorable." Yet with a better understanding of the Roman and Byzantine economy and the development of civil and canon law, we will also see how, in historical context, ancient Christian preaching in that same spirit did not amount to a call for revolution. Rather, it meant a fuller, organic realization of the original catholicity of the Christian communion, which, Schmemann tells us, blossomed into "a special sort of Byzantine humanism"[15] that remains applicable to our very different contexts today.

---

13   See *NPNF²* 14:27.

14   Georges Florovsky, "The Social Problem in the Eastern Orthodox Church," in *Christianity and Culture*, vol. 2, The Collected Works of Georges Florovsky (Nordland Publishing Company, 1974), 139.

15   Schmemann, *Historical Road*, 220.

# CHAPTER 18

# Byzantine Humanism

I N THE POWERFUL ENDING OF *Schindler's List*, Oskar Schindler, after sacrificing so much of his own wealth and risking his own life to save the lives of some 1,200 Jews in Nazi Germany, says, weeping, "I could have got more out." He looks around at the possessions he could have sold: "This car . . . why did I keep this car? Ten more people right there." "I didn't do enough," laments the man who did far more than too many others.[1]

In our exploration of Orthodox social thought in Christian Rome, we cannot neglect the shining example of St. John Chrysostom, who urged his hearers to make such loving humility their lifestyle. "John Chrysostom made himself exquisitely unpopular in Constantinople," historian Peter Brown records, "by his habit of following with his eyes individual great landowners and courtiers as they strode in and out of the basilica during his sermons, marking them out by such a penetrating and public glance as the actual perpetrators of the sins and social wrongs he was denouncing."[2] Already by the third century, the Roman elite—not bourgeois entrepreneurs but the inheritors of large estates—had become increasingly socially removed from the plebs of the cities in attempt to curry imperial favor due to increased taxation for national defense. To their chagrin, Patriarch Chrysostom refused to host lavish banquets for high society, instead dedicating himself and the Church's

---

1   *Schindler's List*, directed by Steven Spielberg (Universal Pictures, 1993), 195 min.
2   Peter Brown, "Late Antiquity," in *A History of Private Life*, ed. Paul Veyne (The Belknap Press of Harvard University Press, 1987), 275.

resources to serving the common people. Thus, when his piercing gaze and prophetic criticism turned upon the empress Eudoxia herself, motiving the latter to exile him, the people revolted, causing him to be immediately recalled—the first time, at least. The second time rioters burned the cathedral, and Chrysostom ended up dying in exile, uttering the last words, "Glory to God for all things," a hard and wise saying reminiscent of Old Testament Writings like Job and Ecclesiastes.

## Radical Preaching, Slow Social Change

A RADICAL CONCEPTION OF STEWARDSHIP lies at the heart of Chrysostom's preaching against the "great landowners and courtiers" of his day. To be clear, he never claimed that wealth itself is evil. Indeed, he explicitly rejected that perspective: "Neither is wealth an evil, but the having made a bad use of wealth."[3] Canon 12 of the Council of Sardica (modern-day Sophia, Bulgaria) in 343 even made provision for bishops to visit and manage estates *they* owned, in order that from their fruits they may "help the poor" and so that "their private affairs will suffer no loss from their absence."[4]

Rather, what bothered Chrysostom, and what may be radical even to us today, is the mistaken idea that the more someone gives, the greater good they have done. If that were true, then moral worth could be measured in money, and those with the most to give could be the most righteous. But where then would be the virtue of the poor? Where would be the widow's mite (Mark 12:41–44)? Rather, as St. Symeon the New Theologian put it in the eleventh century, echoing Chrysostom, we should all imagine God saying to us, "By what possessions of yours do you claim that you give alms to your brethren, and through them to Me? I have given you all these things, not to you alone, but to all men in common."[5] This duty of stewardship is referred to, in Roman Catholic social thought, as the "universal destination of goods."[6] Just as in many of

---

3    John Chrysostom, *Against Publishing the Errors of the Brethren*, 2, in *NPNF*[1] 9:236.
4    *The Council of Sardica*, Canon 12, in *NPNF*[2] 14:426.
5    Symeon the New Theologian, "Discourse 9.6," in *Symeon the New Theologian: The Discourse*, trans. C. J. deCatanzaro (Paulist Press, 1980), 155.
6    See Pontifical Council for Justice and Peace, *Compendium of the Social Doctrine of the Church* (Reprint April 2005), §171–184, https://www.vatican.va/roman_curia/pontifical

our Lord's parables, in the Kingdom of heaven we should consider ourselves mere stewards of what ultimately belongs to God, confessing as Jesus bids us, "We are unprofitable servants. We have [only] done what was our duty to do" (Luke 17:10). In so doing, like Schindler we would never believe our service to the needy could be "enough," instead making such service a way of life.

Based on this teaching, one might expect that a Christian empire must have meant a radical restructuring of the entire economic system of the time. The reality is yes and no. Brown records that "many of the regions of the empire of 'New Rome' were characterized by marked agrarian growth and by increased commercial interchange,"[7] to the point that historian Evelyn Patlagean notes the medieval Byzantine economy by the eleventh century depended in part upon expansive trade with Italians, Russians, Jews, Muslims, and others.[8] Indeed, while the Fathers are often critical of unjust business practices, some nevertheless praise the providence of God in spreading resources over the earth so that people would have to sail the seas to trade with one another. As St. Basil the Great put it, "The sea is good in the eyes of God . . . because it brings together the most distant parts of the earth, and facilitates the inter-communication of mariners. By this means it gives us the boon of general information, supplies the merchant with his wealth, and easily provides for the necessities of life, allowing the rich to export their superfluities, and blessing the poor with the supply of what they lack."[9] Thus, international trade, according to St. Basil, brings together far-off people to hear of one another's lives and care for one another's needs.

These are all good things, but none of them are uniquely Christian. And while these commercial aspects of Byzantium are significant, all economies of the time remained largely agrarian, lacking anything comparable to the vast division of labor of our modern industrial and post-industrial eras. Long-term,

---

_councils/justpeace/documents/rc_pc_justpeace_doc_20060526_compendio-dott -soc_en.html.

7    Peter Brown, *Treasure in Heaven: The Holy Poor in Early Christianity* (University of Virginia Press, 2016), xviii.

8    Evelyne Patlagean, "Byzantium in the Tenth and Eleventh Centuries," in *A History of Private Life*, ed. Paul Veyne (The Belknap Press of Harvard University Press, 1987), 558.

9    Basil the Great, *Hexæmeron*, 4.7, in NPNF² 8:75. See also Wilson Whitener and Alexander William Salter, "Wealth and Commerce in Eastern Christian Thought," *Journal of Markets & Morality* 26, no. 1 (2023): 105–125.

year-over-year economic growth and attendant affluence virtually did not happen anywhere in the ancient and medieval worlds. Subsistence living, fragile to the dangers of plague, drought, and war, continued as the prevailing norm.

But that is not the whole story. The best bishops remained "the protector[s] of all those in need,"[10] as St. Justin described them in the second century, first of all through managing a network of alms distribution throughout the empire. For the sake of financial accountability, Canon 26 of the Council of Chalcedon even required all bishops to appoint stewards to "manage the church business . . . so the administration of the church may not be without a witness; and that thus the goods of the church may not be squandered, nor reproach be brought upon the priesthood."[11] Financial accountability is as Orthodox as the Definition of Chalcedon, and we'll see how Orthodox Christology formed the theological basis for more significant social reforms.

## *Discovering Christian Humanism*

Saint Basil the Great, called such not because of his undeniable theological ability but for his deep and active love for the poor, so faithfully and creatively took up the bishop's catholic vocation as to found a complex at the gates of Caesarea, known as the Basileiad, that cared for the poor, hungry, sick, and dying, providing spiritual as well as material support. This served as the world's first hospital, a model for generations to come, offering far more than a passing handout to the needy but fully realizing the teaching of Christ, as Clement of Alexandria put it, to "make a friend. But a friend proves himself such not by one gift, but by long intimacy"[12] (see Luke 16:9). Saint Basil, above all, was such a friend to the needy.

This ministry was not something extra or "tacked on" to St. Basil's theological achievements, however. Within both the theory and practice of the Church, we find the beginnings of a new, personalistic worldview: "Christian humanism," wrote Fr. Alexander Schmemann, "faith in the whole man and

---

10   Justin Martyr, "First Apology," 67, in *Early Christian Fathers,* ed. Cyril C. Richardson (Westminster Press, 1953), 287.
11   *The Fourth Ecumenical Council: The Council of Chalcedon,* Canon 26, in NPNF[2] 14:285.
12   Clement of Alexandria, *Who Is the Rich Man That Shall Be Saved?,* 32, in ANF 2:600.

his absolute value, is the final result of the Christological disputes and a genuine discovery of Orthodoxy."[13] We see this in that most perfect statement of all Orthodox doctrine from St. Gregory the Theologian: "That which [Christ] has not assumed He has not healed; but that which is united to His Godhead is also saved."[14] Once again, we arrive at the ancient catholicity of the Church: The whole human person, body and soul, individually and in community, must be cared for and brought into communion with the Body of Christ.

Thus did the catholicity of the Church persist despite Christians' dramatic shift in social status in Christian Rome. The bishop's role as "the protector of all those in need" expanded, even in terms of the law. Saint Constantine, Schmemann notes, "granted bishops the judiciary right,"[15] meaning that the ecclesiastical courts of canon law acted as legal alternatives to the civil courts. "In the later Byzantine era," writes Fr. John McGuckin, "even in the larger cities, episcopal courts came to be preferred by the people to the civil alternative of a hearing before the magistrate, not only because the penalties were less severe for the offenders, but also for their deeper sense of pastoral care."[16] As St. Paul commanded, "Dare any of you, having a matter against another, go to law before the unrighteous, and not before the saints? Do you not know that the saints will judge the world? . . . How much more, things that pertain to this life?" (1 Cor. 6:1–3) The existence of canon law alongside Roman civil law made for a more just, pastoral, humane, and merciful society. But civil law had its merit, too.

The emperor St. Justinian brought to completion the work of codifying Roman law, attempted first under Diocletian and then again under Theodosius II. Through the Justinian *Code*, says McGuckin, the emperor "was able to ensure that the ancient achievement of the concept of the rule of law"—that all people, including politicians, must be equally subject to just laws—"was able to pass alive into the ferment of the medieval world"[17] and beyond. *Justinian's*

---

13  Alexander Schmemann, *The Historical Road of Eastern Orthodoxy*, trans. Lydia W. Kesich (SVS Press, 2003), 177–178.

14  Gregory Nazianzen, Epistle 101: "To Cledonius the Priest against Apollinaris," in *NPNF²* 7:440.

15  Schmemann, *Historical Road*, 95.

16  John Anthony McGuckin, *The Ascent of Christian Law: Patristic and Byzantine Formulations of a New Civilization* (SVS Press, 2012), 277.

17  McGuckin, *Ascent of Christian Law*, 251.

*Institutes,* moreover, grounded civil law in the natural law and evaluated the superiority of Roman civil law to the *juris gentium,* the common laws of all nations, by its closer proximity to the natural law, for example in the many ways Christian Rome surpassed other nations in offering paths to emancipation for slaves.[18] As John Meyendorff wrote, "The extent to which both the State and the Church practiced social welfare is wider than one usually imagines, even if the clearly objectionable institutions inherited from paganism, such as slavery, were only humanized without being fully suppressed."[19] What makes slavery "clearly objectionable" is the fact that all people are created free by God by virtue of their humanity, i.e., according to the natural law, as the *Institutes* admit.

## A Symphonic Society

IN ST. JUSTINIAN'S SIXTH *NOVELLA,* he first articulated the Byzantine principle of *symphonia* to delimit the relationship between Church and state: "If the priesthood is above reproach from any quarter and stands before God with confidence, and if the imperial authority organizes the commonwealth committed to it rightly and fittingly, there will be a balanced harmony to ensure whatever may be of value to the human race."[20] Given their roles as judges, however, the emperor goes on to stipulate requirements for bishops and clergy—what many would consider an overreach of civil power today. That said, while historians disagree on the extent to which the lines between Church and state may have been blurred in Byzantium, simplistic assessments of the Church as wholly beholden to imperial power prove groundless in the light of the far more complex historical record, which includes the prophetic posturing of many bishops and monks, as we saw in the last chapter.

Symphonia enabled the unique historical harmony between canon and civil law, which McGuckin says demonstrated that "the Church is fundamentally,

---

18 Peter Birks and Grant McLeod, trans., *Justinian's Institutes* (Cornell University Press, 1987).

19 John Meyendorff, *Living Tradition: Orthodox Witness in the Contemporary World* (SVS Press, 1978), 194.

20 Justinian, *Novella, 6,* in *From Irenaeus to Grotius: A Sourcebook in Christian Political Thought,* eds. Oliver O'Donovan and Joan Lockwood O'Donovan (Eerdmans, 1999), 194.

essentially committed to the notion of the rule of law."[21] He continues to elaborate the social implications: "Bound to acknowledge that concept as a fundamental spiritual value, binding together believer and non-believer alike, the Church can never give its assent to random governance, tyranny, or a self-congratulatory governmental system that does not elevate the rights of the needy alongside the privileges of the rich." For example, Canon 75 of the Council of Carthage in 419 even stipulated the emperor's duty to provide civil defenders for the poor, "chosen under the supervision of the bishops,"[22] to act as intermediaries between them—legal and social caseworkers, we might say.

McGuckin goes on to insist on the relevance of the underlying ethos and principles of Eastern Christian Roman law for our societies today: "Men and women, of whatever race, or rank, both rich and poor, educated and illiterate, were given equality under the eye of God. . . . Their lives were raised to infinite value as icons of the divinity, their rights and privileges as the divine icons could never be lost."[23] The rule of law and the image of God are fundamental to any Orthodox social ethic, as they underly the Church's catholicity and the social message of her great preachers and teachers, St. John Chrysostom and St. Basil not least of all. "It is on this basis," McGuckin goes on, "that Christian civilization was founded, one which remains untarnished in Christian theory today, and which one day may be used once more to rebuild a society's value system."[24]

Guided by these principles, hopefully any Orthodox Christians today who aim to "rebuild [our] society's value system" will bring this Byzantine humanism with them. Yet alongside and in dialogue with this civilizational paradigm grew another, complementary Christian mode of civilization, service, and enterprise that cannot be neglected in our survey of Church history: monasticism. In my next chapter, we will venture into the desert to explore what it looks like when the fundamentally ascetic nature of society receives its fullest and most faithful attention.

21  McGuckin, *Ascent of Christian Law*, 269.
22  *Canons of the CCXVII Blessed Fathers Who Assembled at Carthage, Commonly Called the Code of Canons of the African Church*, Canon 75, in NPNF[2] 14:479.
23  McGuckin, *Ascent of Christian Law*, 275.
24  McGuckin, 275.

CHAPTER 19

# Monastic Enterprise

IN THE EARLY TWENTIETH CENTURY, the Protestant church historian Adolf von Harnack observed that "in Western monasticism we have to recognise a factor of the first importance in Church and civilisation."[1] The sociologist Max Weber, Harnack's contemporary, also acknowledged this—for the West—in his major work *The Protestant Ethic and the Spirit of Capitalism*. By contrast, both figures dismissed the Christian East. According to Weber, "Labour is . . . an approved ascetic technique, as it always has been in the Western Church, in sharp contrast . . . to the Orient."[2] Harnack claimed, "The Greek monks . . . to-day as a thousand years ago, live 'in silent contemplation and blissful ignorance.' To work they give only just as much attention as is necessary for a livelihood."[3]

Unfortunately, in English few scholars have investigated the economic significance of Orthodox monasticism as a whole. Thankfully, some scholars have examined specific periods and locales, and together their accounts paint a brighter picture of the monastic contribution to Orthodox social thought and action.

---

1   Adolf von Harnack, "Monasticism," in *Monasticism: Its Ideals and History and The Confessions of St Augustine*, trans. E. E. Kellet and F. H. Marseille (Williams and Nortgate, 1911), 65.
2   Max Weber, *The Protestant Ethic and the Spirit of Capitalism*, trans. Talcott Parsons (Routledge, 1992 [1930]), 158.
3   Harnack, "Monasticism," 56.

## *Seeking First the Kingdom*

BUT WHY MIGHT ONE EXPECT monasticism and asceticism to have economic significance? The answer comes in the Gospel of our Lord Jesus Christ: "Therefore do not worry, saying, 'What shall we eat?' or 'What shall we drink?' or 'What shall we wear?' . . . But seek first the kingdom of God and His righteousness, and all these things shall be added to you" (Matt. 6:31, 33). Though seeking only God's Kingdom in their ascetic way of life, monastics nevertheless provided for their—and many others'—material needs. What is asceticism, then?

Asceticism derives from *askesis*, Greek for "exercise." Ascetic practices are to virtue what physical exercise is to bodily fitness. In Orthodox Tradition, asceticism isn't a Gnostic ethical dualism where the spirit is good and matter evil. Rather, it means daily living the reality of Christ's Resurrection, dying and rising with Him, growing in virtue, and "seek[ing] first the kingdom of God." Thus, we fast, for example, in order to acquire the spirit of the desert, where Moses reminded Israel that the Lord "allowed you to hunger . . . that He might make you know that man shall not live by bread alone; but . . . by every word that proceeds from the mouth of the LORD" (Deut. 8:3).

Communion with God and others cannot exist apart from ascetic self-denial. If we never say, "No," to ourselves, we will never make room for our neighbor, not to mention for God. In this way, according to S. L. Frank, "Every Christian must in a certain sense be a 'monk' in the eternally pagan world."[4] Thus, Christos Yannaras even emphasizes asceticism's ontological significance: "Relation is . . . a constant ascetic effort to let go of the resistance of self-sufficiency. . . . It is the dynamic mode by which existence is realised as loving communion."[5]

Furthermore, society cannot exist without an economy—the production, exchange, distribution, and consumption of the goods necessary for life and flourishing. One key factor of production is labor, an ascetic discipline especially effective at fighting *akedia* or listlessness. Saint John Cassian tells us,

---

4   S. L. Frank, *The Light Shineth in the Darkness*, trans. Boris Jakim (Ohio University Press, 1989), 144.

5   Christos Yannaras, *The Inhumanity of Right*, trans. Norman Russell (James Clarke & Co., 2021), 68.

"By persevering in work the monks dispel listlessness."[6] Monasticism grew as a movement of men and women dedicating their lives to Jesus Christ through the essential "ascetic effort" necessary for "loving communion," including, among other disciplines, one of the essential factors of any productive economy: labor. We should be surprised if it *didn't* have significant civilizational impact.

## *The Desert a City*

AFTER THE CONVERSION OF ST. Constantine, many who had been too timid or who simply imitated the emperor now readily joined the Church. In response, many others, worrying over worldly influence, imitated ascetics like St. Paul of Thebes and St. Antony the Great. As Fr. Georges Florovsky noted, "It was precisely from the Christened Empire that the flight commences, the flight into the desert."[7] One might assume monastics also left "worldly" commerce behind, but history tells a much different tale. Not only through donations but also through enterprise were "all these things . . . added to" the first Christian monks.

Saint Athanasius tells us that even in St. Antony's time "the desert was made a city by monks."[8] According to James E. Goehring, the first Egyptian monks practiced sharecropping, rope and basket weaving, and farming. They sold goods at market. They owned boats and shipped products up and down the Nile. Contrary to common assumptions, "Ownership and transfer of property was relatively common."[9] "Altogether," writes Peter Brown, "in the relation of monks to property, to housing, and to culture, the monastic movement of fourth-century Egypt had a strong element of what the modern

---

6   John Cassian, "On the Eight Vices," in *The Philokalia*, trans. and eds. G. E. H. Palmer, Philip Sherrard, and Kallistos Ware, vol. 1 (Faber and Faber, 1983), 90.

7   Georges Florovsky, "Christianity and Civilization," in *Christianity and Culture*, vol. 2, The Collected Works of Georges Florovsky (Nordland Publishing Company, 1974), 124.

8   Athanasius of Alexandria, *The Life and Affairs of Our Holy Father Antony*, in *Athanasius: The Life of Anthony and the Letter to Marcellinus*, trans. Robert C. Gregg (Paulist Press, 1980), 42–43.

9   James E. Goehring, *Ascetics, Society, and the Desert: Studies in Early Egyptian Monasticism* (Trinity Press International, 1999), 50.

French call *bobo*—the bourgeois bohemian."[10] Indeed, historian Helen Rhee has noted, "Monastic poverty in reality was more patterned after economic self-sufficiency than destitution."[11] This, however, was not egocentric but rather a fulfillment of St. Paul's instruction that "by laboring . . . you must support the weak" (Acts 20:35).

Indeed, Christian monasticism has been inseparable from commerce since the very beginning. We see in the *Sayings of the Desert Fathers* a monk who worries, "The trader is soon coming, and I have no handles to put on my baskets."[12] Another monk overhears this, removes the handles from his own baskets, and claiming he made extra, gives them to the worrying monk, enabling that monk to sell his baskets to provide for his needs. In another story, Abba Pistamon reassures a monk uncomfortable with making a profit, "Abba Sisois and others used to sell what they made. There is no harm in this." He then exhorts him, "However much you have, do not stop making things, do as much as you can provided that the soul is undisturbed."[13]

In a time of rare upward mobility, with only a small "middle class" of merchants, tax collectors, and tradesmen, a new social sphere appeared that wasn't desperately poor, though monks were considered "holy poor"—worthy recipients of alms. Nevertheless, monks also produced and profited, reinvesting in their monasteries, operating ministries, and distributing alms to the needy. While the Greek word for monk, *monachos*, originally meant "solitary," St. Pachomius's coenobitic (communal) model has historically been the Eastern norm, and many monasteries even followed the teaching of St. Basil, bringing the spirit of the desert not only to rural towns but urban metropolises, where there are many more neighbors to love.

Monasticism especially benefited women, who, apart from marriage, as the story of St. Nicholas and the gold coins illustrates, formerly might have faced the grim possibilities of slavery or prostitution if their fathers couldn't support

---

10    Peter Brown, *Treasure in Heaven: The Holy Poor in Early Christianity* (University of Virginia Press, 2016), 87.
11    Helen Rhee, *Loving the Poor, Saving the Rich: Wealth, Poverty, and Early Christian Formation* (Baker, 2012), 184.
12    *Sayings of the Desert Fathers*, 17.16, in *Western Asceticism*, trans. Owen Chadwick (The Westminster Press, 1958), 184.
13    *Sayings of the Desert Fathers*, 6.11, 80.

them. Not only did monasticism offer a better alternative, but the greatest preachers of the Church commended celibacy to both men and women as the highest path of perfection.

## *Monastic Liberty*

MOREOVER, MONASTERIES MARKED A SIGNIFICANT expansion of what we call the "private sector" today. Though monasteries typically include chapels and the monastics who inhabit them dedicate their lives to prayer, in Byzantium private ownership was initially common. Just as the Church did not view herself as free apart from property rights, so also some monasteries insisted on freedom from state *and Church* control, as one Byzantine monastery's founder warned, "It is my desire that this ... monastery remain independent until the end of the world, and free and unenslaved by emperors and patriarchs and monasteries and metropolitans and archbishops and bishops, by archimandrites and superiors, in short, by all men."[14] In contrast to the ideal of symphonia, Fr. John Meyendorff noted, "[The] polarity between the 'already now' and the 'not yet' was ... constantly proclaimed by the large and prosperous Byzantine monastic movement, whose withdrawal from society and non-conformity to the standards imposed by the empire served constantly as a prophetic reminder that there *cannot* be total 'harmony' before the *Parousia*."[15] To give a sense of scale, Fr. Alexander Schmemann records, "At the outset of the struggle with iconoclasm the number of monks in Byzantium had reached a hundred thousand—an almost incredible percentage of the population."[16] Monastic independence, though tolerated, did not avoid conflict—iconoclasm being a prime example.[17]

---

14 "*Areia: Memorandum* and *Typikon* of Leo, Bishop of Nauplia, for the Monastery of the Mother of God in Areia," in *Byzantine Monastic Founding Documents*, eds. John Philip Thomas and Angela Constantinides, vol. 1 (Dumbarton Oaks Research Library and Collection, 2000), 968.

15 John Meyendorff, *Living Tradition: Orthodox Witness in the Contemporary World* (SVS Press, 1978), 196.

16 Alexander Schmemann, *The Historical Road of Eastern Orthodoxy*, trans. Lydia W. Kesich (SVS Press, 2003), 210.

17 For more on the anti-monastic nature of iconoclastic regimes, see Philip Jenkins, *A Storm of Images: Iconoclasm and Religious Reformation in the Byzantine World* (Baylor University Press, 2023).

Later, in the fourteenth century, some called on the state to confiscate monastic property, arguing monks owed the empire for military protection and that they didn't know how best to use their resources. But the state (or Church) also would want to take monastic property because monasteries enjoyed exemption from taxes, generous donations, and in some cases abundant production. In response, St. Nicholas Cabasilas wrote a defense of the monasteries, claiming that "rulers have a right to manage subjects' property, but this does not extend to private, only to common [i.e., public] property. . . . Neither rulers of communities nor judges, nor even emperors with universal rule, may demand an account of what the proprietor does with it, even should he waste it."[18] Confiscation of monastic property would violate not only inheritance law, by which monasteries acquired much of their land, but the basic human dignity of monks. After all, said Cabasilas, "the privilege of speech and the freedom of decision . . . are what make man what he is."[19] He later mused, "How could there ever be a stable form of government which made it impossible to live in freedom?"[20] He further drew more general implications: "Who, then,—what craftsman, farmer, merchant—will take the trouble to make money, knowing that everything he earns will go to other people? How can anyone sustain the pursuit of wisdom when struggling against poverty?"[21]

Despite material prosperity's potential good, however, Orthodox monastic history demonstrates the common teaching of the Scriptures and the Fathers that though wealth isn't inherently evil, we must vigilantly guard against the temptation it brings. Father Sergei Bulgakov identified this phenomenon of wealth-generating monasteries as "an example of the dialectic of history which moves by contradictions: the ascetic denial of wealth leads to its accumulation."[22] As Weber put it, "the whole history of monasticism is in a certain sense the history of a continual struggle with the problem of the

18   "Nicholas Cabasilas," 10, in *From Irenaeus to Grotius: A Sourcebook in Christian Political Thought*, eds. Oliver O'Donovan and Joan Lockwood O'Donovan (Eerdmans, 1999), 478.
19   "Cabasilas," 25, 480.
20   "Cabasilas," 26, 480.
21   "Cabasilas," 26, 481.
22   Sergius Bulgakoff, *Social Teaching in Modern Russian Orthodox Theology* (Seabury-Western Theological Seminary, 1934), 9.

secularizing influence of wealth"[23]—in the Christian East, I would add, just as much as the West.

## *Renewal and Decay*

FIRST, CONSIDER THE POSITIVE EXAMPLE of the Kykkos Monastery on Cyprus. According to Victor Roudometof and Michalis N. Michael, in 1554 "there were 30 monks and a few employees—a shepherd, two vineyard guards and six other employees."[24] Over time, Kykkos acquired land through purchases, rent-to-own arrangements, donations, bequests, and inheritance. The monastery also "bought houses with yards, shops, building plots in the cities, vineyards and gardens."[25] After 1850, "the monastery was one of the most important producers on the island."[26] At the end of the Ottoman era, Kykkos owned seventy-two shops, thirteen annexes, ten churches, 15,148 acres of land, 429 vineyards, eleven water mills, eleven olive mills, and part of a ship. Kykkos employed goldsmiths and commissioners for exportation. It also acted as Cyprus's only bank, borrowing and lending money at interest. In the twentieth century, it resisted British colonialism. From 1983 to 2003, annual income increased tenfold, from approximately €770,000 to €7.7 million, which Kykkos used to fund charity work, renovations, and other cultural ventures, demonstrating, in my assessment, their success against "the secularizing influence of wealth." In 2010, the monastery continued to own extensive land holdings, several factories, and was "one of the main stakeholders in the Hellenic Bank of Cyprus."[27]

By contrast, consider the example of the Solovetskii Monastery in Russia during the Time of Troubles (1599–1615). Metropolitan St. Philip II of Moscow originally founded their saltworks, among other enterprises, during his time as abbot there, before he was called to Moscow and later martyred for defending the people's freedom against Ivan the Terrible. Alas, the monastery

23  Weber, *Protestant Ethic*, 174.
24  Victor Roudometof and Michelis N. Michael, "Economic Functions of Monasticism in Cyprus: The Case of the Kykkos Monastery," *Religions* 1 (2010): 58.
25  Roudometof and Michael, "Economic Functions of Monasticism in Cyprus," 62.
26  Roudometof and Michael, 66.
27  Roudometof and Michael, 72.

did not continue in his saintly spirit. Historian Isaiah Gruber refers to salt as "white gold,"[28] the oil of its day, and Solovetskii had the largest market share in Russia. Gruber writes, "Major institutions such as the 'state within a state' centered at Solovki commanded impressive revenues. . . . These were the mega-corporations of a society continually professing spiritual motives in all realms of life—whether political or social, intellectual or economic, sexual or military. In fact, the vast majority of *ecclesiastic* documents that have survived for the perusal of historians are simply business records of income and expense."[29] Over the sixteen years of the Time of Troubles, the monks recorded "purchases totaling 116,517.095 rubles"[30] (approximately $250 million in 2010 dollars), while their yearly almsgiving in 1605, for example, amounted to only "0.16 rubles."[31]

How might we explain this tragic accounting? The economist Nathan Smith offers an insightful model of monastic decay and renewal.[32] Schmemann points to this phenomenon in Byzantium "from the beginning of the seventh century."[33] In his response to Weber, Bulgakov observes a similar cycle in Russia.[34] Zealous for the perfection of the Gospel, hermits flee to the wilderness. Like St. Antony, their reputations spread and others follow, planting the seeds of civilization in formerly uncultivated "deserts." But as monasteries grow in material prosperity, opportunistic people join, watering down their piety, pushing the zealous either to spiritual reform or flight to the wilderness again. Solovetskii's economic success would have made the monastery attractive to anyone simply desiring to survive the Time of Troubles, rather than only zealots for the Gospel. Thus, its conduct, though inexcusable, was sadly understandable.

---

28  See Isaiah Gruber, "Black Monks and White Gold: The Solovetskii Monastery's Prosperous Salt Trade during the Time of Troubles of the Early Seventeenth Century," *Russian History* 37 (2010): 238–249.

29  Gruber, "Black Monks and White Gold," 238–239.

30  Gruber, 247.

31  Gruber, 247.

32  Nathan Smith, "The Economics of Monasticism," ASREC Working Paper Series (September 6, 2009): 1–47.

33  Schmemann, *Historical Road*, 211.

34  Sergey N. Bulgakov, "The National Economy and the Religious Personality (1909)," *Journal of Markets & Morality* 11, no. 1 (2008): 165.

In later chapters, we'll see some better examples from the Rus', as well as the Church's early confrontation there with the modern "Social Question." As St. Maria Skobtsova observed, "In pre-Petrine Russia . . . behind all the varied manifestations of monastic creativity, it was still perfectly clear that life would present this creativity with very specific demands. The supply met a demand. Monastery schools, monastery colonies, monastery farms, monastery publishing houses, monastery educational and cultural centers, and, often, monastery fortresses—and all that was a sure, strong, and steadfast framework for the holiness hidden within them."[35]

Despite Solovetskii, considering the broader survey of Orthodox monastic enterprise herein, I believe we need more Orthodox monasteries in the hearts of our cities, especially in the West, to model the ascetic self-denial essential to society; to demonstrate the value of virtuous enterprise; and to bear witness that if we "seek first the kingdom of God and His righteousness" (Matt. 6:33), the common good might just be added to us as well.

---

35   Maria Skobtsova, "Toward a New Monasticism I: At the Heart of the World," in *Mother Maria Skobtsova: Essential Writings*, trans. Richard Pevear and Larissa Volokhonsky (Orbis Books, 2003), 92.

CHAPTER 20

# Western Witness

O RTHODOX CULTURAL COMMENTATOR ROD DREHER has made a career of claiming, "There are people alive today who may live to see the effective death of Christianity within our civilization."[1] To justify this worry, Dreher appeals to the philosopher Alasdair MacIntyre. Drawing on MacIntyre's *After Virtue*, Dreher once argued for what he called the "Benedict Option." By Dreher's telling, "The sixth-century Rule of Saint Benedict . . . played a powerful role in preserving Christian culture throughout the so-called Dark Ages."[2] But the idea of the early medieval era in the West as the "Dark Ages" is historically outdated. In Dreher's defense, he is just following MacIntyre, who had anachronistically claimed that St. Benedict and his followers, "Set themselves to achieve . . . the construction of new forms of community . . . so that both morality and civility might survive the coming ages of barbarism and darkness."[3] Were that the case, one might be historically justified in pursuing the "Benedict Option" today.

But this is anachronistic for a number of reasons. The most obvious one is that St. Benedict, as Dreher correctly noted, composed his Rule in the *sixth* century, but the barbarians came in the *fifth*. But Dreher doesn't seem to

---

1    Rod Dreher, *The Benedict Option: A Strategy for Christians in a Post-Christian Nation* (Sentinel, 2017), 8.
2    Dreher, *The Benedict Option*, 4.
3    Alasdair MacIntyre, *After Virtue: A Study in Moral Theory*, 2nd ed. (University of Notre Dame Press, 1984), 263.

notice this inconsistency. The extent of the ensuing "darkness" is also debatable, but even granting the idea of a "Dark Ages," it was hardly passive withdrawal that reignited the Latins' civilizational lights. As much credit is due to the active missionary efforts of St. Columbanus and the Celts as to St. Benedict. Another major factor is the complicated rise of the papacy and, most importantly, the (re)creation of the Western Roman Empire under Charlemagne. The actual history of Orthodox social thought in the West between the fall of Rome (410) and the Great Schism (1054) emits much unheralded light. This chapter will focus on the aftermath of the fall of Rome, examining the common good in terms of what happens when society collapses, episcopal solidarity in the rise of the papacy, how to find true happiness in dark times, and the civilizational significance of monastic rules and penitential manuals for social order and evangelism. Thus, it will paint a clearer picture of early medieval Western Europe too often oversimplified with the label "Dark Ages."

## *Barbarians at the Gates*

THE SACK OF ROME BY the Visigoths in 410 shook Latin Christians to the core. Saint Jerome compared Rome to "another Jerusalem,"[4] describing its ruin in gruesome terms reminiscent of the latter's fall (see Lam. 2:20; 4:10). He had personal contacts in Rome, including one St. Marcella, who had been beaten by barbarians hoping to find valuables in her house. Yet he notes, writing to her younger friend St. Principia, "Christ softened their hard hearts. . . . The barbarians conveyed both you and her to the basilica of the apostle Paul."[5] Nevertheless, St. Marcella died not long after.

By contrast to St. Jerome, as bishop of Hippo in Latin North Africa, St. Augustine had closer contact with Roman refugees, and he found himself having to defend the Faith from pagans who blamed Christianity for the Eternal City's downfall. Saint Augustine wrote his *City of God*, latching onto this practice of ecclesiastical sanctuary noted by St. Jerome, "Contrary to the custom of war, these bloodthirsty barbarians spared" pagans who took

---

4    Jerome, *Letters*, 127, in *NPNF*² 6:256.
5    Jerome, 6:257.

refuge in churches "and spared them for Christ's sake."[6] "All the spoiling," he notes, "was the result of the custom of war. But what was novel, was that savage barbarians showed themselves in so gentle a guise."[7] Had the Arian Visigoths instead been heathens, even Roman pagans couldn't have expected such mercy. When society fell apart, the force of Christianity contributed to the common good by elevating the conduct even of Rome's plunderers.

Another notable account comes from Marseille, where the priest Salvian, a refugee from the Rhineland writing after the Vandals conquered North Africa, blamed the victims. He claimed that "in [Roman] Carthage the servants of God were scarcely allowed to appear in the streets and public squares without mockery and cursing."[8] But when the Vandals came, "How unlike the Romans did these barbarians prove themselves, in cleansing the stains of our disgrace!"[9] He viewed the Vandals as God's judgment and lauded their moral reforms. While he pointed out many "monstrous vices"[10] of the Romans, he especially focused on burdensome taxation: "The poor . . . alone pay the taxes."[11] An unfair tax system had injured the common good.

That said, it is worth noting with Peter Brown that "Salvian's relentless precision on matters of taxation betrays the clear but narrow focus of his own field of vision. . . . When Salvian spoke of the *pauperculi*—the 'poor little guys' . . . he did not mean the lower classes. . . . They were people like himself,"[12] i.e., minor aristocrats. Taxes had become oppressive to them because of the need to pay soldiers and mercenaries for civil war in the Western empire. In fact, Brown insists, "The vagaries of civil war," rather than an "invasion," "accounted for the movements of barbarian groups at this time."[13] When taxes weren't sufficient, "license to pillage . . . [was] extended by rival [Western] emperors . . . in

---

6   Augustine of Hippo, *City of God*, in NPNF[1] 2:2.
7   Augustine of Hippo, 2:5.
8   Salvian, *On the Government of God*, trans. Eva M. Sanford (Columbia University Press, 1930), 8.5, 230.
9   Salvian, *On the Government of God*, 7.22, 219.
10  Salvian, 7.22, 219.
11  Salvian, 7.22, 219.
12  Peter Brown, *Through the Eye of a Needle: Wealth, the Fall of Rome, and the Making of Christianity in the West, 350–550* AD (Princeton University Press, 2012), 448.
13  Brown, *Through the Eye of a Needle*, 388.

lieu of pay."[14] Civil strife led to economic injustice in the form of burdensome
taxation and eventually led to the breakdown of the social order.

Contrary to Salvian's narrow account, the Vandals were actually oppressive to their new Catholic subjects. As Fr. John Meyendorff notes, when the
Vandals took Latin North Africa, "imperial Roman laws which deprived heretics of civil rights were applied to the Orthodox."[15] The same religiously intol-
erant laws used to privilege the Church can just as easily be used to persecute
her should the political winds shift. Moreover, "The capture of Carthage in
439 was accompanied by massacres."[16] The Orthodox in Vandal North Africa
faced continual oppression. Nevertheless, according to Brown, "If the old
world lived on anywhere, in the West . . . it was in the pirate city of Carthage,"[17]
which commercially thrived under the Vandals while the Italian, Gallic, and
Iberian economies contracted, in part due to the loss of African tax revenue.
The "old world" that "lived on" was the best of Roman culture, civilization,
and identity preserved in Christian Rome, otherwise known as *Romanitas*.

## When in Rome

THE FACT THAT THE VANDALS adapted Roman laws wasn't unique.
According to historian Diarmaid MacCulloch, "Everyone wanted to be
Roman: the memory of the empire stood for wealth, wine, central heating and
filing systems, and its two languages, Latin and Greek, could link Armagh to
Alexandria."[18] As Meyendorff noted, "The fifth century marked the collapse
of the imperial system in Italy, Germany, Britain, Gaul, Spain and Northern
Africa, but not of the imperial 'idea,' or the Graeco-Roman civilization."[19] As
for the Church in these lands, "Their relationships with Rome were in a way
similar to those maintained by distant Eastern churches—the Armenian, the

---

14    Brown, 389.
15    John Meyendorff, *Imperial Unity and Christian Divisions: The Church 450–680 A.D.* (SVS
    Press, 1989), 146.
16    Meyendorff, *Imperial Unity*, 146.
17    Brown, *Through the Eye of a Needle*, 402.
18    Diarmaid MacCulloch, *A History of Christianity: The First Three Thousand Years* (Pen-
    guin, 2009), 343.
19    Meyendorff, *Imperial Unity*, 127.

Georgian, the Persian, the Indian—with their mother-church in Antioch."[20] In short: They were autocephalous. He continues to say, "The invasions— especially the sack of Rome by Alaric in 410—terrified contemporaries, but the Germanic barbarians had neither the strength, nor the desire to destroy the age-long [Roman] culture."[21] And how did they maintain continuity with the past? Not only did they adopt many Roman laws and customs, except for the Vandals, they generally tolerated Orthodox Christians.

Given the role of Orthodox bishops in Roman society, these barbarians had good reason to tolerate the Catholic Church. Since St. Constantine, bishops had exercised the judiciary right alongside secular magistrates. As Fr. Andrew Louth put it, "Bishops were figures of local authority, and had come to exercise a role in local government and the administration of justice."[22] It was, at least, a Dark Age for the former aristocracy, devastated by barbarian plunder. But Brown remarks that the Church remained relatively untouched in the late fifth century and that, "The leaders of the churches realized that they—and not the great lay landowners . . . were, at last, truly [materially] wealthy."[23] The Church stewarded that wealth to protect the poor and preserve Roman civilization. As Meyendorff notes, "The Roman popes became, in the West, the symbol of *Romanitas*"[24] and the preservers of what was left of the common good.

In so doing, Pope St. Leo the Great helped develop a new papal self-identity. He twice saved the people of Rome from massacre: "It was quite natural for [Leo] . . . to act and to be seen as a guardian of the *Romanitas*," wrote Meyendorff, in "meeting with Atilla in 452" and "succeed[ing] in preventing the invasion of Italy by the Huns; or when, in 455, he negotiated . . . the sparing of Rome's population and treasures by the invading Vandals."[25] His example paints a picture of Christian witness for how to safeguard the common good when the Church has a position of privilege and authority amidst civil conflict and hostile new political powers.

---

20   Meyendorff, 329.
21   Meyendorff, 127.
22   Andrew Louth, *Greek East and Latin West: The Church* AD *681–1071* (SVS Press, 2007), 71.
23   Brown, *Through the Eye of a Needle*, 530.
24   Meyendorff, *Imperial Unity*, 128.
25   Meyendorff, 149.

In the practical absence of any other Roman authority, St. Leo exclusively appropriated for Rome the idea of bishops as successors to St. Peter.[26] Even so, St. Leo's conception was still far from modern notions of the papacy, though it certainly contributed. Ironically, the Western Church first began to be *Roman* Catholic precisely when the Roman Empire *fell* in Italy. Yes, St. Leo's conception of his role as pope consolidated power in the papacy, but he also sent a clear message of solidarity to all those Western Orthodox who struggled under harsh new regimes, acting as their advocate and representative. For example, the Ostrogoths founded their kingdom with its capital in Ravenna, where previous Western emperors had withdrawn from Rome in the fourth century, but the barbarians relied on the pope for legitimacy and diplomacy with Constantinople, of which they became legal "guests."

## Consolation in Dark Times

NEVERTHELESS, NOT ALL ORTHODOX CHRISTIANS escaped persecution. In the government of the Gothic king Theodoric, we find St. Severinus Boethius: "Noble, wealthy, accomplished, universally esteemed for his virtues . . . to all men a signal example of the union of merit and good fortune," as his translator H. R. James described him. But "within a year he was a solitary prisoner at Pavia, stripped of honours, wealth, and friends, with death hanging over him."[27] Meyendorff tells us he "was accused of plotting with Byzantium against Gothic rule,"[28] an accusation Boethius denied and said was manufactured by his rivals. In the fate of Boethius, we see the closest picture to the idea of Dark Ages: "After the gradual disappearance of the Roman educated class, represented by men like Boethius, executed by Theodoric in 524 . . . there could be little concern for the preservation of the Greco-Latin philosophic

---

26   This idea had previously, as in St. Irenaeus, been applied to all bishops who faithfully passed on the universal, apostolic tradition. See Irenaeus of Lyons, *Against Heresies*, 3.3, in *ANF* 1:415–416, where he applies it to both Rome and Ephesus. So also, at Chalcedon, Gray notes, "The bishops accepted and praised Leo [as mouthpiece of St. Peter] *because* he taught the same thing as Cyril [of Alexandria]." Patrick T. R. Gray, *The Defense of Chalcedon in the East* (Brill, 1979), 9.

27   Anicius Manlius Severinus Boethius, *The Consolation of Philosophy by Boethius*, trans. H. R. James (E. P. Dutton & Co., 1914), x.

28   Meyendorff, *Imperial Unity*, 220.

tradition."[29] The copying of classical sources like Cicero and Virgil all but disappeared afterward until the ninth century.

Boethius translated some works of Aristotle into Latin, and his *Consolation of Philosophy*, written while under house arrest awaiting execution, provides an artful witness to the unique Christian synthesis of Greco-Roman philosophical ethics and metaphysics. The *Consolation* is a dialogue between Lady Philosophy—philosophy personified—and Boethius, despairing of his misfortune.

Losing everything gave Boethius a rare clarity about material riches: "If those things the loss of which thou lamentest had been thine," he imagines Fortune herself saying to him, "thou couldst never have lost them."[30] Lady Philosophy, noting the increased anxiety protecting one's wealth brings, ironically adds, "Oh, wondrous blessedness of perishable wealth, whose acquisition robs thee of security!"[31] Moreover, when Fortune abandoned him, she did him a favor: "In departing she hath taken away *her* friends, and left thee *thine*. . . . Cease, then, to seek the wealth thou hast lost, since in true friends thou hast found the most precious of all riches."[32] When we seek our independence in wealth, it makes us more dependent, insecure, unhappy, and alone. But Philosophy reminds him, "We . . . counted independence in the category of happiness, and . . . God is absolute happiness."[33] The world tells us true happiness, true human flourishing, comes from things like wealth and fame, but only when Boethius lost these things did he clearly see the source of true happiness: communion with God.

Boethius's Christian appropriation of Greco-Roman philosophy also continued in Gaul and far beyond, through the works of St. John Cassian. Cassian's *Conferences* and *Institutes* translated the spirit of the desert fathers into Latin and often served Cassian's own contemporary needs. Western monasticism began with St. Martin of Tours, who had bequeathed a less-rigorous—we might even say "bourgeois"—discipline, allowing for private property.

---

29  Meyendorff, 294.
30  Boethius, *Consolation of Philosophy*, 2.2, 38.
31  Boethius, 2.5, 53.
32  Boethius, 2.8, 65.
33  Boethius, 3.12, 117.

Cassian didn't condemn non-monastic wealth, used virtuously, but he insisted that his monks in Marseille should shun personal possessions, and his influence quickly spread.

## *Monastic Missions*

SAINT PATRICK, FOR EXAMPLE, SPENT time in Lérins before bringing Christianity to the Celts in Ireland, spreading Cassian-inspired monastic spirituality there. The Celtic Church was structured through monastic government, where abbots and even abbesses like St. Brigid sometimes exercised greater authority than bishops. These monasteries established both civic and economic order, which helped missionaries spread Christianity across the rural, clan-based communities. The Celts furthermore developed a new form of missionary martyrdom: *peregrinatio,* or "pilgrimage." Louth writes, "In the course of this *peregrinatio,* these Irish monks established monasteries abroad: St Columba at Iona in Scotland (563), St Aidan at Lindisfarne in the north of England (635) and St Columbanus at Luxeuil in central France (c. 590)."[34] As we say of the apostles, "their voice goes out through all the earth" (Ps. 18/19:4 NRSCE). These Celtic missionaries might even be a resource for our diaspora communities in the West today.

Notably, St. Columbanus spread Celtic monasticism throughout Gaul, Switzerland, and finally to Bobbio in Northern Italy. The Celts also proliferated a new spiritual tool: the penitential manual or tariff book. These guidebooks functioned as the equivalent of hyperlocal, constitutional canons for Christian communities, centered around the authority of abbots. They set guidelines for what penance best remedied particular sins, originally presenting themselves in this medical mode rather than economic or legal. As *The Penitential of Cummean* put it, they provided "medicine for the salvation of souls."[35] But that doesn't mean it wasn't concerned with the economic side of the common good. Due to its use as a guide for the care of all Christians, not just monastics, it does not presume complete nonpossession but rather

---

34   Louth, *Greek East and Latin West,* 102.

35   Oliver Davies, ed. and trans., *The Penitential of Cummean,* in *Celtic Spirituality,* (Paulist Press, 1999), 230.

dictates, "He who steals someone else's property by any means shall restore four times as much to him whom he has injured."[36]

As for monastics, St. Columbanus composed his own influential Rule for monks, widely used and even approved by the Fourth Council of Mâcon in 627. For several centuries, it was in some places observed together with St. Benedict's Rule, both serving as constitutional documents and sharing a lot in common. Both insist on strict obedience to the abbot.[37] Both instruct that "every day we must pray, labor, and read."[38] Both elevate the recitation of the Psalms.[39]

Furthermore, both *The Penitential of Cummean* and St. Benedict's *Rule* make accommodations for personal weaknesses and effort, including for children.[40] Families often offered children to monasteries as "oblates"—gifts to God—imitating Hannah and Samuel (1 Kingdoms/Sam. 1) or St. Anna and the Theotokos, but sometimes probably due to economic hardship, too. Monastic poverty always beats *real* poverty. Before dismissing this odd practice, we ought to remember the desperation of some at the time. Monasteries offered poor families an alternative way of providing for their children when previously no alternative to starvation or neglect may have been available.

Saint Benedict's Rule furthermore dictates a clear, well-organized division of labor,[41] even offering guidelines for monastic artisans, instructing them to sell their wares "a little cheaper than by men in the world,"[42] which, though likely well-intended, would have undercut secular competitors, potentially pushing them out of those markets if monastic supply could meet demand on its own. Combined with being able to subsidize their revenues through donations, strict limitations on consumption, and their tax-exempt status, the growth of Western monastic enterprise comes as no surprise. Moreover,

---

36   *The Penitential of Cummean*, 235.

37   *The Rule for Monks by Columbanus*, in *Celtic Spirituality*, 246–247; D. Oswald Hunter Blair, ed. and trans., *The Rule of St. Benedict*, 2nd ed. (Sands & Co., 1907), §5.

38   *Rule for Monks by Columbanus*, 248. Cf. *Rule of St. Benedict*, §48.

39   *Rule for Monks by Columbanus*, 250–252; *Rule of St. Benedict*, §18.

40   *The Penitential of Cummean*, 245; *Rule of St. Benedict*, §30, §37, and §59.

41   Nevertheless, St. Benedict was not entirely unique in this detail either. Compare, for example, several of the monastic guidelines in Uinseann Ó Maidin OCR, trans., *The Celtic Monk: Rules & Writings of Early Irish Monks* (Liturgical Press, 1996).

42   *Rule of St. Benedict*, §57, 151.

monasteries became a major social, political, and economic force as free contact with Western Catholics did what the force of the Byzantine state could not: convert the Arians to Orthodoxy.

Clovis (Louis), king of the Franks, converted to Orthodoxy in 508 under the influence of his Catholic wife, Queen Clotilde. In Spain, "Nicaean catholicism was adopted as the official religion of the Visigothic, previously Arian, kingdom of Toledo under King Ricared (589),"[43] notes Meyendorff. As for the Ostrogoths and Vandals, in the mid-sixth century, St. Justinian reconquered Italy and North Africa, once again prohibiting Arianism and restoring Rome to communion with Constantinople. By contrast to the peaceful conversions in France and Spain, the devastation of this war added as much to the economic regression of the West as did the barbarian "invasions." It also contributed to the continued rise of the papacy, as "the Church represented the only remaining moral and economic power."[44] Indeed, the Byzantines had long used the bishop of Rome as a go-between with the Gothic kingdoms, so they established an exarch in Ravenna instead of reintroducing a Western emperor.

There would not be another Roman emperor in the West until after the Eastern Romans again retreated. But this chapter ought to have disabused us of thinking that Christianity, or even Romanitas, had been lost to some "Dark Ages" that never were. Orthodox Christianity remained alive and well in the West, creatively adapting to new challenges. Moreover, even before and apart from St. Benedict's Rule, Roman culture lived on, too, as we'll see in the next chapter—for both better and worse.

---

43    Meyendorff, *Imperial Unity*, 321.
44    Meyendorff, 293.

CHAPTER 21

# The Return of Rome

**T**HE POLITICAL ELEVATION OF THE pope in the West coincided with continual state-sponsored heresy in the East, from Monenergism to Monothelitism to Iconoclasm, during which time, for the most part, Rome remained a "rock" of Orthodoxy, which contributed to its spiritual self-importance. Pope St. Leo's contribution of the most controversial phrase in the Definition of Chalcedon ("in two natures") ensured Rome's unwavering defense of the Fourth Ecumenical Council and its pivotal role in the Sixth. Moreover, Iconoclasm could have little force in the distant West, especially after the Lombards captured Ravenna. Yet despite Rome's rise to power, it is during this period that one of the most humble figures took the papal throne: St. Gregory the Great, whom we refer to as "Dialogos" for his *Dialogues*. And contrary to Rod Dreher and Alasdair MacIntyre's assertions, it was through the Carolingian revitalization of the West that St. Benedict's Rule became the monastic standard, rather than the Rule being the direct agent of that revitalization.

It is easy, from our Orthodox perspective, to say that then the *real* Dark Ages began. But the long shadows of this era exist alongside bright lights of mission and social reform. True, the events of these centuries led to the Great Schism in 1054, yet Rome proved the last holdout of Western resistance to altering the Creed. As with the rest of history, the causes are complex. Popular polemics obscure many contributions to Orthodox social thought from Western saints we still venerate today. Those contributions, as we will see, include

150

more on the importance of monastic order and missions, as well as the perpetual dangers to both the Kingdom of God and the common good that come
with entangling religion and the state.

## True Greatness

BY THE MID-SIXTH CENTURY, BYZANTIUM came back, at least in Italy
and Latin North Africa, entailing closer communication and cooperation
between Rome and Constantinople. "In 579," writes Fr. John Meyendorf,
"pope Pelagius II ordained [St. Gregory Dialogos] a deacon and sent him
as his *apocrisiarius* [ambassador] to Constantinople, where he stayed seven
years."[1] In his *Dialogues*, St. Gregory recorded that he met St. Leander of
Seville there, who in 589 "brought the whole nation of the Visigoths to the
true faith of Christ."[2]

The Spanish Church unfortunately would be influential in more than
one way. In addition to intolerance toward other religions, especially Judaism, Meyendorff notes that the independence of Spain meant "no authority,
whether Roman, or Constantinopolitan, was able to do much about a fateful
event: the inclusion of the Filioque in the Creed, as an anti-Arian affirmation,
in connection with King Ricared's conversion."[3] What began as local pecu-
liarities would over centuries find their way into the broader West.

By contrast, St. Gregory became the first monk-turned-pope in 590. The
deep, ascetic legacy of Egypt, Syria, Gaul, Italy, and Ireland was ascendent in
Rome. In St. Gregory we see one of the few popes ever worthy of later papal
claims of leadership and authority—precisely because he denied those very
claims. As Christ had commanded, "He who is greatest among you shall be
your servant" (Matt. 23:11). Saint Gregory adopted for himself the title, "Servant of the Servants of God," and in his reaction to St. John the Faster calling
himself "Ecumenical Patriarch," the pope ironically proved the defender of

---

1   John Meyendorff, *Imperial Unity and Christian Divisions: The Church 450–680 A.D.* (SVS
    Press, 1989), 301.
2   P. W., trans., *The Dialogues of Saint Gregory, Surnamed the Great: Pope of Rome & the First
    of that Name*, ed. Edmund G. Gardner (Philip Lee Warner, 1911), 3.31, 157.
3   Meyendorff, *Imperial Unity*, 323. I am unsure why, theologically, anyone thought our
    anti-Arian Creed needed additional "anti-Arian affirmation."

the traditional, Eastern understanding of the papacy. He wrote to the patriarchs of Alexandria, Jerusalem, and Antioch to dissuade them from so elevating the Patriarch of Constantinople. But when Pope St. Eulogius of Alexandria in turn referred to St. Gregory as "Universal Pope," the latter chastised him: "If your Holiness calls me Universal Pope, you deny that you are yourself that which you say I am universally. God forbid!"[4]

Nevertheless, St. Gregory "also expressed his belief that Peter, even *now*, is present in his (Roman) successors,"[5] and he was still concerned with spreading the influence of Rome and Christian Roman civilization, at least in the West. He sent St. Augustine of Canterbury to the Angles and Saxons. Before Rome could assert its authority over the whole Church in the West, it had to become a proper patriarchate first, which ultimately would be "a phenomenon of the Carolingian Age,"[6] according to Meyendorff. During the Byzantine papacy, the Frankish, Celtic, Spanish, and African Churches remained autocephalous, calling their own councils and managing their own affairs.

The English Church, however, through St. Augustine's mission, would be the first *Roman* Catholic mission, taking up the mantle from the Celts. "The English church," writes Meyendorff, "accepting Roman jurisdiction more directly than the church in France, remained faithful to one major aspect of the old Celtic tradition: its missionary zeal extended not only to the British Isles, but also to continental Europe,"[7] including modern-day Belgium, the Netherlands, and Germany. According to Diarmaid MacCulloch, "Anglo-Saxon and Celtic Christians between them made the Atlantic Isles in the seventh and eighth centuries a prodigious powerhouse of Christian activity. . . . They also followed the sea routes which Columbanus had pioneered into

---

4    Gregory the Great, Epistle VIII: "To Eulogius of Alexandria," quoted in Meyendorff, *Imperial Unity*, 306. The controversy itself seems to have been something of a misunderstanding—hyperbolic titles were common in Byzantium, which may explain St. Eulogius's nonchalance about grand titles and, by contrast, St. Gregory's confusion, given his Latin context.

5    Meyendorff, 330.

6    Meyendorff, 331.

7    Meyendorff, 320.

mainland Europe, conscious that they had received Christianity by mission and determined to do the same for others."[8]

Understanding social dynamics of the time was key to these missionaries' success in new social and economic circumstances. Sensitive to the tendency for most people to follow elites, influencers, and leaders, Anglo-Saxon missionaries typically "went straight to the top when preaching the faith. That way they could harvest a whole kingdom."[9] That said, medieval people in the West did not value individuality as we do today: "Groups mattered more than single people, and within groups there was no such thing as social equality. Most people expected to spend their lives being given orders and showing deference."[10] Yet MacCulloch cautions, "The missionaries of Christianity spoke to them of love and forgiveness shaping the purposes of God, and there is no reason to believe that ordinary folk were too obtuse to perceive that this could be good news."[11] Everyone needs the mercy of the Gospel, from the powerful to the poor. In these missions, Anglo-Saxons also spread Celtic monasticism and ascetic literature, along with Roman liturgy and loyalty, making new converts and renewing Christian communities. Meyendorff notes, "Even the old monastery of St Benedict in Monte-Cassino, South of Rome, was revived in 729 by the English monk Willibald."[12]

However, Rome during this period constantly struggled against, well, more barbarians: "At the end of the sixth century Byzantine power in Italy was shattered by a central European people known as the Lombards,"[13] writes MacCulloch. The Byzantines held the Lombards out of Ravenna and Rome, but the Lombards—some Arian, some pagan—oppressed Catholics in their lands and always threatened Rome. Meanwhile, Meyendorff notes, "The remaining great wealth of the Church, made it into a banker of the imperial administration. . . . St Gregory the Great, in one of his letters, called himself

---

8   Diarmaid MacCulloch, *A History of Christianity: The First Three Thousand Years* (Penguin, 2009), 341.
9   MacCulloch, *A History of Christianity*, 343.
10  MacCulloch, 343.
11  MacCulloch, 344.
12  Meyendorff, *Imperial Unity*, 320.
13  MacCulloch, *A History of Christianity*, 329.

the paymaster of the imperial troops."[14] Importantly for our purposes, however, he continues, "This role of imperial ally did not prevent the Church from using its resources for extensive social work, especially when it was led by holy men like Pope Gregory, and from being viewed as the 'treasury of the poor.' "[15]

## Two Wills, One Empire

MEYENDORFF EMPHASIZES THAT EVEN "WHILE clearly maintaining the moral authority of his see [seat], the pope understood his ministry in terms of service, rather than power. . . . He formally acknow[le]dged the rights, *i.e.* the total judicial independence, of the African church."[16] During the Monothelite controversy, "Byzantine Africa, with its capital in Carthage, appeared as the most secure area of the whole empire. . . . As the East was invaded by Arabs and as the Lombards constantly threatened Italy, Africa was able to host numerous refugees and its exarch . . . tended to believe that he was holding the trump-card in the military and political struggles of the day."[17] He adds, "Among the Eastern refugees, also living in Africa, was Maximus,"[18] i.e., St. Maximus the Confessor.

With Constantinople overrun by Monothelites, the West provided crucial sanctuary for Orthodox from the East. The Byzantine exarch in Carthage, Gregory, was suspected of plotting a coup, and St. Maximus was implicated (a charge he denied). Despite what Meyendorff calls a "subservient attitude of the popes during this period," he notes: "Pope St Martin I, also a former *apocrisiarius* in the imperial capital . . . was elected without imperial confirmation. He welcomed orthodox refugees from the East, including the great St Maximus the Confessor, and held a council of 105 bishops which condemned Monotheletism. Dragged to Constantinople by the exarch [of Ravenna] Theodore Calliopas, the pope was tried, condemned, tortured and exiled to the Crimea (653), where he died in 655."[19] The judgment of Meyendorff rings true

---

14    Meyendorff, *Imperial Unity*, 296–297.
15    Meyendorff, 297.
16    Meyendorff, 304.
17    Meyendorff, 363.
18    Meyendorff, 363.
19    Meyendorff, 308.

here: "The participation of the patriarchate in these shameful events makes this period, morally, the lowest point in the history of the church of Constantinople."[20] Episodes like this highlight the dark side of symphonia, when Church and state are too intertwined and the Church becomes corrupted by political power.

The theological issue here is important for our understanding of catholicity: It is by virtue of the Incarnation that bishops' apostolic authority matters, that the Eucharist is affirmed to be the Body and Blood of Christ, that we hope in the Resurrection, and that Christians must always "remember the poor" (Gal. 2:10). In Christ all former divisions are united, recognized in two natures and two wills, without separation, division, confusion, or change. Vladimir Lossky warned, "In the history of Christian dogma all the Christological heresies come to life anew and reappear with reference to the Church. . . . Monothelitism in ecclesiology is expressed above all in a negation of the economy of the Church in regard to the external world"—i.e., for the common good—"for the salvation of which the Church was founded."[21] The same is true of society. The emperor aimed to make his fundamentally secular will the only will for all the Church, ultimately in contradiction to the principle of symphonia. The former ecclesiological error subsumes the human into the divine, the latter political error subsumes the divine into the human. Another way to put that is that they both confuse the Kingdom of God and the common good.

Against this error, Pope St. Martin wrote to Emperor Constans, "It is always the case that the preservation of the state goes together with the flourishing of the orthodox faith."[22] Saint Martin clearly presumed that the Church better contributes to the common good when it is free of political influence. So, too, Meyendorff observes, "Maximus explicitly denied the emperor any right to define dogma: 'No emperor,' he said, 'was able to convince the inspired Fathers to come to an agreement with heretics. . . . It is for the priests to inquire into and define what concerns the dogmas of the

---

20  Meyendorff, 367.

21  Vladimir Lossky, *The Mystical Theology of the Eastern Church* (SVS Press, 1976), 186.

22  Martin I, Letter of Pope Martin and the Synod to Constans II, in *The Acts of the Lateran Synod of 649*, trans. Richard Price (Liverpool University Press, 2014), 416.

catholic Church.'"[23] Like Pope St. Martin, St. Maximus would also face arrest, sham trial, torture, and exile, where he would die before ever seeing the fruit of his fight for the truth. The entanglement of the state in Church matters led to the violation of the most basic standards of justice. Only years later would the Sixth Ecumenical Council finally vindicate their cause.

## The Carolingian Renaissance

POSSIBLY THE LOWEST MORAL FAILING of that Byzantine theocracy would come over the next century and a half with Iconoclasm. "The radical change in Byzantine imperial policies which would occur under the iconoclastic emperors Leo III (717–741) and Constantine V (741–763)—forceful imposition of iconoclasm, confiscation of the pope's Sicilian revenues, and cutting all military support of the papacy against the Lombards—put an end to the period of 'Byzantine' papacy," notes Meyendorff. "Pope Stephen II looked for support elsewhere and switched his loyalty to the Franks (754)."[24] Given the circumstances, it is easy for me, at least, to sympathize with Pope Stephen. By violating the property rights of the pope and failing in their duty to protect Western Christians as subjects of their empire, the Byzantines gave Rome little choice.

Meanwhile, in Merovingian France, "'Do-nothing kings' (rois-fainéants) delegated power to 'palace mayors' . . . . One of them, Charles Martel, successfully stopped the Arabs at the famous battle of Poitiers (732)." In 751, Martel's son Pippin forced Childeric into a monastery and made himself king. At the same time, according to MacCulloch, "The Lombards had finally ejected the Byzantine emperor's representative from Ravenna, and they overran the remaining Byzantine territories in Italy as far south as Rome. King Pippin recaptured these lands, but he did not return them to imperial government: instead (to the fury of the Byzantines) he gave them to Pope Stephen." In so doing, "he founded one of Europe's most enduring political units, the Papal States."[25]

---

23 Meyendorff, *Imperial Unity*, 367.
24 Meyendorff, 309–310.
25 MacCulloch, *A History of Christianity*, 348.

The Iconoclastic emperors at this time were too busy murdering the Orthodox among them to do anything about this new development. The Frankish kingdom passed from Pippin to his son Charles. "Charles's reign was long, 768 to 814," MacCulloch details, "and history soon christened him Charles the Great—*Carolus Magnus*—Charlemagne."[26] Father Andrew Louth summarizes the most momentous event of his reign, when in the year 800, "on Christmas Day 25 December, at the beginning of the third mass of Christmas, Pope Leo [III] solemnly crowned Charlemagne 'Emperor of the Romans' to the acclamation of those present."[27] The (re)establishment of a Western Roman emperor brought with it a social renaissance: "The Carolingian *renovatio*," which continued after Charlemagne's death in 814, "was an attempt to recover the Latin foundations of Western culture,"[28] largely through the most powerful social institution it had: monasticism. Monasteries by this time were able to boast of centuries of spreading the Kingdom of God and preserving the common good in the West, and along with that came political influence.

According to Louth, "[St.] Benedict of Aniane came to advise the imperial court on monastic reform, and in the early years of the ninth century, the monastic reform became imperial policy. . . . At councils in Aachen in 816 and 817 . . . it was required that all monasteries in the Empire adopt the Rule of St Benedict."[29] Nevertheless, according to Oliver Davies, "Columbanus's text . . . had considerable influence on subsequent monastic Rules, including the *Concordia Regularum* by Benedict of Aniane."[30] A new society, with a new economy, grew out of this monastic foundation.

Even so, much of the Carolingian Renaissance was simply new, and it was around this time that the Nordic Vikings—more barbarians—began raiding the Celtic and Anglo-Saxon monasteries of northern Europe and the British Isles. "The monasteries seem to have been an especial target of the Vikings," notes Louth, "because many monasteries were repositories of wealth," i.e., banks. Christians could expect other Christians to steer clear of monasteries

---

26  MacCulloch, 348.
27  Andrew Louth, *Greek East and Latin West: The Church* AD *681–1071* (SVS Press, 2007), 70.
28  Louth, *Greek East and Latin West*, 140.
29  Louth, 107.
30  Oliver Davies, ed. and trans., *Celtic Spirituality* (Paulist Press, 1999), 40.

as sanctuaries from violence and, thus, often entrusted valuables with the monks, preserving a space for the peaceful growth of people's wealth. However, for the pagan Vikings, "raiding a monastery was an early medieval equivalent of a bank robbery."[31] Thus, the Celtic and English Churches were in no condition to lead a renaissance. Charlemagne's new empire looked elsewhere and in the next centuries developed a new conception of society.

## New Society, New Creed

LOUTH EXAMINES "THE NOTION THAT became popular in the eleventh century of the 'three orders of society': those who fight, those who pray, and those who work."[32] He explains it was partly "a way of usefully conceptualizing a society in which earthly rule, *regnum* ['those who fight'], and spiritual rule, *sacerdotum* ['those who pray'], united to rule society as a whole, for which those 'who worked' provided the necessary economic foundation."[33] Another word for that is feudalism.

Feudalism was thus the product of Christian social thought in the early medieval West, and the lesson in this case is that, in the service of political power, Christian social thought can have its dark side, too. Salvation became a system of market transactions, much later leading to the sale of indulgences and the Protestant Reformation. In the meantime, feudalism worked like this: Nobles owned the land and fought in wars. The Church also owned land, but she fought a spiritual battle, through prayer, for the preservation of the empire. And in both cases, peasants worked the land in exchange for security and intercession. Other than military plunder, the chief economic engine was agrarian.

But plunder should not be passed over too quickly. According to MacCulloch, "Charlemagne's Christianity did not prevent him taking up arms against other Christians. . . . The best that could be done was persuade posterity that the conquered were either all pagans or Christian deviants needing

---

31    Louth, *Greek East and Latin West*, 177.
32    Louth, 294.
33    Louth, 294.

renewal."[34] Though the Celtic penitential manuals that had inspired this new social order condemned all killing and assigned severe penance for it, the new society worked out a troubling division of labor: "Those who fight" would simply pay, through donations, "those who pray" to do their penance for them. In so doing, they separated the illness of sin from its remedies, reducing discipline meant for healing the soul to an economic exchange, one that contributed to a growing "embarrassment of riches" for Western monasteries.

The monastery of Fleury emerged as the most important in this era, MacCulloch tells us, due to "a dramatic act of theft."[35] Put simply: monks of Fleury stole the relics of St. Benedict. We can at least say on that account that they deviated from the tariff books and Rules, which prohibited all theft, though perhaps they did penance later. Regardless, "As early as the eighth century, Fleury drew on its de facto possession of the bones of Benedict to negotiate the right to appeal directly to the pope against any bishop of the Frankish Church, and during the ninth century the abbey continued to enhance this useful weapon through creative manuscript forgeries,"[36] likely including the *Donation of Constantine,* used for centuries to justify papal claims against Orthodox conciliarity. In return, "Popes were not slow to reward Fleury's succession of consecrated crimes with further privileges."[37] Through a strange synthesis of Celtic monastic government and Anglo-Saxon dedication to the pope, the central authority Rome had long claimed for itself became a reality in the West through Fleury.

But the Franks didn't just incorporate insights from the Celts and Anglo-Saxons. "The Carolingians inherited much from the Visigoths of Spain," writes Louth, including "the form of the Niceno-Constantinopolitan Creed used in the liturgy."[38] In the West's defense, both St. Hilary of Poitiers and St. Augustine had included the notion that the Holy Spirit proceeds from the Father "and the Son" (filioque) in their works on the Trinity. If one could only read Latin and didn't understand the precise distinctions of theological

---

34   MacCulloch, *A History of Christianity,* 347.
35   MacCulloch, 354.
36   MacCulloch, 360.
37   MacCulloch, 360.
38   Louth, *Greek East and Latin West,* 142.

Greek, one might not get why, as St. John of Damascus put it, "We do not speak of the Son as Cause or Father, but we speak of Him both as from the Father, and as the Son of the Father. . . . And we do not speak of the Spirit as from the Son: but yet we call Him the Spirit of the Son."[39] But even though Rome agreed with the filioque theologically, the popes to their credit resisted including it in the Creed up to the eleventh century, on the grounds that they could not unilaterally alter the product of an Ecumenical Council. By the time they accepted it, East and West had become so estranged that the technical issue cited for the Great Schism in 1054 was neither the filioque nor the authority of the pope, but the fact that Eastern Christians use leaven in the Eucharist while Latins don't. Neglect and mistreatment from the Byzantines led Rome to strike out on its own. The need to establish a new role for itself in rebuilding the common good of Western society fed into Rome's self-importance. Different social visions, as much as theological disagreement, led to tragic ecclesiastical division.

The next chapter will tell the story of Orthodox social thought in the Middle East, from the Islamic conquests, through the Byzantine reconquest and the Crusades, to the modern era, but the lessons of this chapter should not be ignored. Politics, though necessary for establishing the baseline of justice needed for a stable economy, often becomes the enemy of peace, and lack of communication, coldness, and petty self-aggrandizement have a power to tear asunder even what God has joined together. Yet I still insist, these were not "Dark Ages," due to the shining lights of saints like Gregory the Great, Celtic and Anglo-Saxon missionaries, Pope Martin I, and even Benedict of Aniane. This "Second" Benedict's reforms, despite their political motivations, did indeed revive the fervor of scholarship and education while spreading monastic order and its many blessings, including economic blessings, throughout the West. Like any other period or place in Church history, we must not only disown the darkness of the West but learn from its light.

---

39   John of Damascus, *An Exact Exposition of the Orthodox Faith*, 1.8, in NPNF[2] 9:11b.

CHAPTER 22

# Middle Eastern Melkites

A FTER A CATASTROPHIC CLIMATE DISASTER, in which countless people perish and whole civilizations vanish in little more than a month, one man must find his way in the world that remains. He walks the earth— fighting wars, evading the powerful, encountering foreign faiths—hoping one day to find his true home through the promise of a chosen child. No, this isn't the plot to *The Stand*, *Waterworld*, *The Giver*, or *The Road*. This is the story of the biblical patriarch Abraham.

According to the Law, when the descendants of Abraham brought their tithes at harvest for "the Levite, the stranger, the fatherless, and the widow" (Deut. 26:12), they had to confess, "My father was a Syrian, about to perish" (Deut. 26:5), followed by the story of the Exodus. Thus, through the faith of Abraham (the "Syrian" referred to), the promise of the coming of Christ carried on through the generations. But even though God promised Canaan to Abram as his home, he lived there as a stranger, amidst powerful pagans.

In the aftermath of the Islamic conquests of the Middle East, Orthodox Christians found themselves in an equally precarious situation—second-class citizens in their homelands, tolerated and protected but also oppressed, and now on equal social footing with other Christians. Their story, like any other place and period in Church history, is messy. Yet though often "about to perish," in these new circumstances after their world's end, they found new life, new fruitfulness, and new insight into the importance of justice, mercy, and inequality. Orthodox social thought must be able to address these issues today as well. In our pluralistic contexts, we can learn from their reasoned and ecumenical approach.

## The End of the World

ACCORDING TO DIARMAID MACCULLOCH, "IT was natural that many Christians should assume that the Arab conquests signalled [sic] the end of the world."[1] If ever there were a "Dark Ages," in terms of the emergence of a hostile, post-Christian, post-Roman society, it happened in the Middle East, not the West. Father John Meyendorff provides a succinct summary: "Damascus fell in 635 and Antioch in 638. . . . Symbolically, the most sensational event of these years was the capture of Jerusalem in February 638."[2] He later continues, "The Arab conquest [of Egypt] was a gradual process, which lasted from 639 to 646, and was accompanied by massacres and pillaging."[3] Even Miaphysite Christians, who rejected Chalcedonian Orthodoxy and sometimes suffered state-sponsored harassment in Byzantium, shared a postapocalyptic outlook with the Orthodox.[4]

The Orthodox under the patriarchates of Antioch, Jerusalem, and Alexandria were known as "Melkites," from the Semitic root of "kingdom," called such for their communion with the Patriarch of Constantinople, New Rome and capital of the "kingdom" of the Romans. Melkites did not, however, blindly follow the emperor or the Ecumenical Patriarch; rather, Middle Eastern Orthodox often opposed state-sponsored heresy such as Monenergism, Monothelitism, and Iconoclasm. Saint Sophronius, the Orthodox Patriarch of Jerusalem, not only refuted Monenergism, he negotiated the surrender of the city, saving its by-then defenseless inhabitants. According to Meyendorff,

---

1    Diarmaid MacCulloch, *A History of Christianity: The First Three Thousand Years* (Penguin, 2009), 261.

2    John Meyendorff, *Imperial Unity and Christian Divisions: The Church 450–680 A.D.* (SVS Press, 1989), 357.

3    Meyendorff, *Imperial Unity*, 359, citing Alfred J. Butler, *The Arab Conquest of Egypt* (The Clarendon Press, 1902), 298.

4    See Samuel Noble and Alexander Treiger, ed., *The Orthodox Church in the Arab World 700–1700: An Anthology of Sources* (Northern Illinois University Press, 2014), 14.

"His diplomatic wisdom of 638 set the pattern of Christian survival in the Middle East."[5] That entailed "the preservation of Christian churches and the property rights of Christians, on the condition that they would not manifest their faith in the streets, avoid preaching to Muslims, would not prevent conversions of Christians to Islam, and adopt an attitude of submissiveness and loyalty."[6] This tolerance wasn't true religious liberty, but the Church received greater legal standing than she had in pagan Rome. Samuel Noble and Alexander Treiger summarize, "In exchange for the payment of a head tax (the *jizya*) and submission to a number of other restrictions, they were granted permission to organize their religious communities on autonomous lines and were exempted (indeed, forbidden) from military service."[7]

While this arrangement did mean periods of stability and tolerance, MacCulloch notes, "Whether Christians found themselves oppressed in the new situation depended on the personality and outlook of the new Muslim authorities."[8] Some churches were confiscated and converted into mosques. Building restrictions made the maintenance of churches difficult, such as the Holy Sepulchre. And the jizya could be painful and likely provoked many conversions to Islam. Nevertheless, the persistence of Christians despite all these disincentives illustrates an important point: Human behavior cannot be reduced to economic motivations. Economism—the name for that idea—cannot explain the endurance of the Church in the Middle East after the end of the world.

Rather, faith, "accounted to Abraham for righteousness" (Rom. 4:9), grounded Orthodox Christians in these new circumstances. One of the first Christian works of this period comes to us from the monastery of Mt. Sinai: *The Ladder of Divine Ascent* by St. John Climacus. While written for monks, the first step includes these wonderful instructions for those "living carelessly in the world": "Do whatever good you may. Speak evil of no one. Rob no one. Tell no lie. Despise no one and carry no hate. Do not separate yourself from the church assemblies. Show compassion to the needy. Do not be

---

5    Meyendorff, *Imperial Unity*, 358.
6    Meyendorff, 358.
7    Noble and Treiger, *The Orthodox Church in the Arab World*, 15.
8    MacCulloch, *A History of Christianity*, 262.

a cause of scandal to anyone. Stay away from the bed of another. . . . If you do this, you will not be far from the kingdom of heaven."[9] In substance, this advice is just Ten Commandments morality, i.e., natural law. Climacus was no extremist. He knew monasticism wasn't for everyone, so he commended basic moral standards for non-monastics, including prohibiting theft and promoting almsgiving.

We can even catch a glimpse of the lives of some such common, non-monastic Christians through the seventh-century travelogue of one bishop Arculf, a Celt from Gaul, recorded by St. Adamnan of Iona: "On the 15th of September, annually, an immense multitude of people of different nations . . . meet in Jerusalem for the purpose of commerce, and the streets are so clogged with the dung of camels, horses, mules, and oxen, that they become almost impassable, and the smell would be a nuisance to the whole town. But, by a miraculous providence, which exhibits God's peculiar attachment to this place, no sooner has the multitude left Jerusalem than a heavy fall of rain begins . . . and ceases only when the city has been perfectly cleansed."[10] We probably shouldn't hastily assume the rain meant God blessed the commerce, but maybe. The people did at least wait until the day *after* the Exaltation of the Cross (first observed earlier that century), and perhaps that liturgical motivation brought them to Jerusalem in the first place.

## *Ecumenical Insights*

THE END OF THE EIGHTH century brings us to another shining light of Middle Eastern monasticism: St. Isaac the Syrian, who made a point in his *Mystic Treatises* to remind Christians that Christian social thought can never simply be satisfied with justice, at which the natural law aims. Rather, only through "surpassing justice by mercy" do we receive "the crown . . . of the perfect under the new covenant."[11] As evidence of ecumenical solidarity, it is worth noting,

---

9    John Climacus, *The Ladder of Divine Ascent*, trans. Colm Luibheid and Norman Russell (Paulist Press, 1982), 78.

10   Adamnan of Iona, "The Travels of Bishop Arculf in the Holy Land," in *Early Travels in Palestine*, ed. Thomas Wright (Henry G. Bohn, 1848).

11   Isaac the Syrian, "Treatise IV," in *Mystic Treatises by Isaac of Nineveh*, trans. A. J. Wensinck (Koninklijke Akademie Van Wetenschappen, 1923), 30.

as does Fr. Andrew Louth (and others), "These extraordinary works of ascetic theology" were written "by a 'Nestorian' bishop" yet "destined . . . to become among the most valued collections of ascetic wisdom in the world of Byzantine orthodoxy and beyond."[12] Though all his life a member of the officially Nestorian Church of the East that rejected the Third Ecumenical Council, we Orthodox still venerate St. Isaac as one of our own, as do Roman Catholics and Miaphysites.

Only briefly bishop of Nineveh, St. Isaac was a monk, and he composed several ascetic works full of wisdom for Orthodox social thought today. Saint Isaac often opposes justice and mercy in rhetorically provocative ways. While one could read this juxtaposition as incompatibility, his ideal of "surpassing justice" should probably be contextualized with his condemnations of injustice: "Be treated unjustly rather than treat unjustly," he writes elsewhere.[13] Mercy *transcends* justice; injustice violates it. Furthermore, sometimes justice can be a distraction from mercy: "If thou settest up as thy aim to practice mercy," he writes, "train thyself not to pursue justice in other fields, lest thou appear to work with one hand and to spill with the other."[14] Justice is the purview of law, and thus state power. But Christ's Kingdom is "not of this world" (John 18:36), and the schisms between Christians of this time, exacerbated by state power in Christian Rome, once again show the peril of confusing the Gospel with politics.

Saint Isaac's universal appeal likely comes from this emphasis on mercy, but he also models irenic engagement with other Christian traditions, admonishing "against reading books which accentuate the differences between the confessions, with the aim of causing schisms."[15] Middle Eastern Christians did dispute with one another over theology, but for persuasion rather than triumphalism. Indeed, as Samuel Noble points out, "The two most significant themes in Christian Arabic literature—defense of Christianity vis-à-vis Islam and intra-Christian Christological debates—were by necessity often

---

12 Andrew Louth, *Greek East and Latin West: The Church AD 681–1071* (SVS Press, 2007), 165–166.
13 Isaac the Syrian, "Treatise L," 234.
14 Isaac the Syrian, "Treatise IV," 30.
15 Isaac the Syrian, "Treatise IV," 34.

discussed in terms of 'reason' rather than purely in terms of 'revelation.'"[16] In this regard St. John of Damascus stands out as, in a sense, the father of Scholasticism in the eighth century for his *Fount of Knowledge*.[17]

## Natural Theology

WE CAN EVEN SEE THIS approach expanding to a sort of "natural theology"—reasoned argument for the essentials of religion—in the work of Theodore Abu Qurra in the early ninth century. Theodore uses reasoned natural theology, clearly influenced by Aristotle, to argue for the truth of Christianity, acknowledging some common ground between all religions. In the process, he acknowledges the existence of "worldly goods"—food, clothing, shelter, and so on—desires for which God gave us "that we might obtain them and enjoy happiness."[18] Yet he also puts these in their proper place. Each of us has higher, spiritual desires, and like St. Severinus Boethius, Abu Qurra affirms, "The object of such desires is God, in and of Himself."[19] Moreover, "He generously grants Himself to us, and we dwell with Him and touch Him, partaking of His sweetness and happiness through these desires. . . . Through Him, we become gods and enjoy Him forever."[20] Of course, for Theodore, "we dwell with [God] and touch Him" through a life of virtue in Jesus Christ.

---

16   Samuel Noble, *The Kitāb al-Manfaʿa of Abdallāh ibn al-Faḍl al-Anṭākī, Critical Edition, Translation and Commentary*, PhD Dissertation (KU Leuven, 2022), 51.

17   See John of Damascus, *The Fount of Knowledge*, in *Saint John of Damascus: Writings, The Fathers of the Church: A New Translation*, trans. Frederic H. Chase, vol. 37 (Fathers of the Church, Inc., 1958). While the structure of this work's chapters does not quite follow the familiar Scholastic order of objections, contrary claims, responses, and replies, the Damascene nevertheless heavily interacts with previous authorities, whether philosophers or Church Fathers before him, weighing and sifting through their opinions and systematizing them all into a coherent whole in a way that never before had been done, though we can see unsystematic antecedents, for example, in the *Ambigua* of St. Maximus the Confessor and the works of others. Latin translation of *The Fount of Knowledge* (or at least the third part, *An Exact Exposition of the Orthodox Faith*) also influenced Peter Lombard and Thomas Aquinas, among others.

18   "Theodore Abu Qurra," trans. John C. Lamoreaux, in *The Orthodox Church in the Arab World*, 81.

19   "Theodore Abu Qurra," 80.

20   "Theodore Abu Qurra," 81.

As regimes changed throughout the Middle East, Christians often suffered. The rule of law, that bright contribution to Orthodox social thought of Byzantine humanism, deteriorated in Muslim society as the number of Christians diminished. "Muslims went from being a minority to being a majority in Iran in 800 and in the majority in Syria and Egypt in 900," notes Panchenko.[21] In the ninth century, another Western pilgrim, Bernard, recorded rampant corruption during his journey to the Holy Land via Alexandria.[22] Everywhere he and his companions went, local officials ignored letters ensuring their safety, instead extorting bribes.

Bernard did, however, note that Christians still lived in relative freedom and admirably used it to practice Christian social action. He stayed at a hostel established by Charlemagne, and he noted that Christians sought to rescue their imprisoned brethren who couldn't pay the jizya. Christians still flourished in trade, finance, education, medicine, and public administration. However, even though they were now in the minority, Christians' relative prosperity, says Panchenko, "caused an ever-growing resentment from ordinary Muslims. At the end of the ninth century and especially in the first third of the tenth century, numerous cases of religious strife and unrest, looting, and the destruction of churches are mentioned."[23]

In the early tenth century, the Byzantines reconquered northern Syria, reestablishing community with the Melkites. Yet according to Panchenko, "Each triumph by [Emperor] Nicephoras Phocas provoked anti-Christian pogroms in Egypt, Palestine, and Syria."[24] No doubt, those Christians liberated by the Byzantines couldn't help but feel the plight of their brethren. In Antioch at this time, the theologian Abdallah ibn al-Fadl al-Antaki stands out for wrestling in multiple works with the problem of inequality—a perennial question but especially pronounced in his time and context. Why do some suffer while others enjoy abundance?

21   Constantin A. Panchenko, *Arab Orthodox Christians Under the Ottomans 1516–1831*, trans. Brittany Pheiffer Noble and Samuel Noble (Holy Trinity Seminary Press, 2016), 20.
22   Bernard the Pilgrim, "The Voyage of Bernard the Wise," in *Early Travels in Palestine*, 24–30.
23   Panchenko, *Arab Orthodox Christians*, 25.
24   Panchenko, 25.

Noble notes again that "the most consistently present theme in [Ibn al-Fadl's] works is the importance of reason in articulating and understanding Christian belief."[25] Ibn al-Fadl reasons that our individuality is given by God as a matter of Providence: "Were it not for these features, one might marry his mother or a family member without knowing it and also one would not be prevented from committing injustice, theft, and murder since he would know that he could not be distinguished from others."[26] We should be wary of individualism as a form of one-sided social thought, but individuality definitely matters. God made each person unique and irreplaceable. But why do these individual differences include inequalities? For example, he asks, why do some live longer than others? He answers, "As for the reason for disparity among people in terms of shortness and length of life, this is in order to establish proof of the Resurrection,"[27] as well as Providence and Judgment Day.

Ibn al-Fadl even extends this argument to economic inequality. Without it, "Society would cease functioning, and no one would be motivated to be a physician, a weaver, a tailor, a farmer or to pursue any other craft, as this is difficult, and thus their evils would multiply."[28] The implication here is that higher-skilled jobs rightly command higher incomes. Nevertheless, he is no apologist for the status quo: "The benefits of disparity are not hidden. They include ... the possibility for virtue to be performed both in wealth and in poverty; in wealth, by doing good to the weak, and in poverty through patience and thankfulness."[29] Inequality enjoins upon us duties toward one another. Moreover, wealth remains susceptible to temptation, and poverty can be used for our good.[30]

## The Crusades and Beyond

UNFORTUNATELY FOR MIDDLE EASTERN CHRISTIANS, further inequality would be imposed upon them. MacCulloch details the "exceptional

---

25   "Abdallah ibn al-Fadl al-Antak," in *The Orthodox Church in the Arab World*, 172.
26   "Abdallah ibn al-Fadl al-Antak," 179.
27   Ibn Al-Fadl, 180.
28   Ibn Al-Fadl, 181.
29   Ibn Al-Fadl, 181.
30   Ibn Al-Fadl, 181.

. . . episode of persecution under [Egyptian] Caliph al-Hākim from 1004 to 1013, which included the destruction of the Church of the Holy Sepulchre in Jerusalem—one of the sparks of . . . Latin Christians to reconquer the Holy Land."[31] The fall of Syria to the Seljuk Turks led Emperor Alexios I Komnenos to seek help from the West. Hoping to heal the Great Schism, Pope Urban II accepted and sent armies on the first Crusade, which successfully (miraculously, they thought) established the County of Edessa, Principality of Antioch, County of Tripoli, and Kingdom of Jerusalem.

One might expect that the return of Christian rule would mean improved circumstances for Middle Eastern Christians, but according to Panchenko, "The situation of Syrian Christians did not improve. The Latins prevented their Eastern coreligionists from having full social standing. . . . The local population soon felt the brunt of the Western feudal system and the level of exploitation became higher than it had been previously."[32] The Crusaders established rival Latin patriarchs in Antioch and Jerusalem, while the Orthodox Patriarch of Antioch "fled to Constantinople."[33] Yet Noble and Treiger add, "Though this state of affairs . . . sometimes caused resentment on the part of the local Christians, in many places there is also evidence of ecclesiastical symbiosis and liturgical communion between the Latin and the Greek and Arab Orthodox clergy."[34] Indeed, Middle Eastern Christians with secular vocations were now subject to the rigid inequalities of Western feudalism, but monastics, who in the feudal system served the essential and privileged role of "those who pray," were generally respected and even patronized.

When the Crusader states fell at the end of the thirteenth century, Melkites became dependent upon outside benefactors. A significant Serbian and Georgian presence could be found at Mar Saba, the Holy Sepulchre, and at other sacred sites, for example. Panchenko further notes how "Middle Eastern

---

31  MacCulloch, *A History of Christianity*, 277–278. He adds, "Hākim's atypical actions should not be attributed to Islam as much as to insanity, which eventually led him to proclaim himself Allah, whereupon he was murdered by outraged fellow Muslims." Indeed, other than during his reign, fortunes of Christians in Egypt greatly improved before and after his time.

32  Panchenko, *Arab Orthodox Christians*, 36.

33  Noble and Treiger, *The Orthodox Church in the Arab World*, 30.

34  Noble and Treiger, *The Orthodox Church in the Arab World*, 30.

churches . . . remained willing to accept alms from any benefactor. The monks of the Monastery of Sinai . . . had chapels for the Syrian Jacobites, the Armenians, and the Copts [all Miaphysites]. . . . In the fifteenth century, the monastery designed a special cell and, later, a chapel dedicated to St Catherine . . . for Latin-rite services."[35] The hardship of the times motivated an admirable solidarity between Christians of different traditions.

Given their destitution by the fifteenth century, the Melkites' restoration once again to community with Greek and other Orthodox under the comparatively stable Ottomans marked a social improvement, in contrast with the apocalyptic accounts of Constantinople's fall among the Byzantines. In the seventeenth century, Antiochian Patriarch Macarius III even traveled extensively through the Ottoman Empire, Wallachia, Moldova, Ukraine, and Muscovy, collecting alms to right Antioch's finances, which had fallen victim to usurious creditors, taking many merchants and paupers under his protection along the way.[36] His son, Paul of Aleppo, noted in particular how Muscovy at this time flourished through relatively free markets within Moscow and relatively free trade between Moscow and Greeks, Persians, and "Franks" (Germans and English).[37]

Melkite merchants also prospered under the Ottomans, in part through trade with the Franks. This emergent middle class sometimes used their influence for good, for example by thwarting interference from Constantinople in the selection of the Patriarch of Antioch. However, their dealings with Roman Catholics, combined with the Antiochian Patriarchate's need for help from Latin missionaries in educating their people, contributed to the schism of 1724 in which the Latins established a rival patriarchate (permanently, this time) in communion with Rome (whose members are sometimes referred to as "Melkite Catholics" today).

---

35  Panchenko, *Arab Orthodox Christians*, 66.
36  Paul of Aleppo, *The Travels of Macarius, Patriarch of Antioch*, trans. F. C. Belfour, 2 vols. (The Oriental Translation Fund, 1836).
37  Paul of Aleppo, *Travels of Macarius*, 2:114: "The trade of the Muscovites is rudely free; and their sales are abundant, as they are not asked for tribute or taxes, nor are oppressed by any tyrannical collectors." This relates to the internal economic freedom of the Moscow markets. For free trade with foreign merchants, see 1:267, where Paul observes that "Greek merchants" were not charged any "toll" for trade, and that merchants from other lands more than made up for the tolls they paid in gifts they received from the tsar.

Nevertheless, despite the Melkites' struggles since their world's end in the seventh century, their history teaches many lessons relevant for Orthodox social thought today. When times got tough, the Orthodox worked together with Christians of other traditions to protect their people from persecution and material hardship. Average Orthodox Christians, neither monastic nor clergy, lived out their faith by helping those in need from the resources they earned in various trades. Saint Isaac the Syrian contributed to a better understanding of the difference between justice and mercy, the Law and the Gospel. Other Arab Orthodox Christians modeled respectful disagreement through reasoned dialogue. That same reflection led to Ibn-al-Fadl's insights regarding the necessity of economic inequality and the responsibilities such inequality imposes on those with greater material resources. Last, international commerce brought with it cultural encounter, as well as opportunities to aid those in need far removed from our own contexts, as Serbians, Georgians, and Moscow did for the Melkites. Following their example, hopefully this overview has been sufficient that we all might confess with new meaning, "My father was a Syrian, about to perish" (Deut. 26:5). In the meantime, we, too, like Macarius III, must journey to the Rus' to see the origins, trajectory, trials, and social contributions of the last independent Orthodox civilization from the fall of Constantinople to Greek independence after 1821.

# CHAPTER 23

# A New Christian People: The Rus'

O N FEBRUARY 24, 2022, RUSSIA invaded Ukraine. I have opinions about this tragic bloodshed between predominantly Orthodox Christian peoples, but it would be an error to politicize our history. As the British lord and Roman Catholic historian John Acton put it, "Each age is worthy of study—to be understood for its own sake . . . not as a stepping stone to the present."[1] The history of the Church among the Rus' is firstly Orthodox Christian history, and we deprive ourselves of a great resource for Christian social thought today if we let our views of the present overshadow our reception of the past. Yet as Acton said elsewhere, "History is not a master but a teacher. It is full of evil."[2] If I faithfully give the past its due, "full of evil" though it be, I hope to disappoint any who would so abuse it in order to celebrate and justify, rather than mourn, our own evils today. As St. Maria Skobtsova put it, "We have no right to wax tenderhearted over all our past indiscriminately. . . . We should aspire to the lofty and combat the sinful."[3]

In that light, let us agree to make the prophecy of Isaiah our prayer: "They shall beat their swords into plowshares, / And their spears into pruning hooks; / Nation shall not lift up sword against nation, / Neither shall they learn war

---

1  John Emerich Edward Dalberg-Acton, *Essays in Religion, Politics, and Morality*, ed. J. Rufus Fears, Selected Writings of Lord Acton, vol. 3 (Liberty Fund, 1988), 621.
2  Acton, *Essays*, 620.
3  Maria Skobtsova, "Under the Sign of Our Time," in *Mother Maria Skobtsova: Essential Writings*, trans. Richard Pevear and Larissa Volokhonsky (Orbis Books, 2003), 114.

anymore" (Is. 2:4). This prophecy of the Day of the Lord actually fits well the biblical motif of this chapter: the apocalyptic character of the Russian reception of the Gospel and the principle of kenotic love derived from it. This principle constitutes a unique contribution to Orthodox Christian social thought, and it runs like a golden thread through the history of the Rus', from the generosity of St. Vladimir, to his grandson's legal reforms, to the new society of Novgorod, even to saints after the rise of Moscow.

## An Apocalyptic People

VLADIMIR, PRINCE OF KIEV, AFTER uniting the warring Slavs and other clans and towns of ancient Rus' became convinced that they needed a new religion, so he sent envoys to representatives of major religions. Reporting the glory of Hagia Sophia to Vladimir, his envoys to Constantinople famously declared, "We knew not whether we were in heaven or on earth."[4] Less well remembered, however, the *Primary Chronicle* also records that the Byzantine envoys *to* Kiev made the best impression upon Vladimir through their teaching on salvation history, using an icon of the Last Judgment as their visual aid: "Happy are they upon the right," sighed Vladimir, "but woe to those upon the left!" To which the Byzantine emissary replied, "If you desire to take your place upon the right with the just, then accept baptism!"[5]

In 988, the Rus' did accept baptism, becoming at the eleventh hour "a new Christian people,"[6] and they recorded this legend because these details mattered to them. Jesus Himself taught that those "on the right" will be "happy," because whatever "you did . . . to one of the least of these My brethren, you did it to Me" (Matt. 25:40). By all accounts, St. Vladimir, as we know him, took that condition seriously. "Vladimir died in the orthodox faith," records the *Primary Chronicle*. "He effaced his sins by repentance and by almsgiving, which is better than all things else."[7] Such is the chroniclers' common assessment

---

4  Samuel Hazzard Cross and Olgerd P. Sherbowitz-Wetzor, trans. and ed., *The Russian Primary Chronicle: Laurentine Text* (The Medieval Academy of America, 1953), 111.

5  Cross and Sherbowitz-Wetzor, *Russian Primary Chronicle*, 110.

6  Cross and Sherbowitz-Wetzor, 119.

7  Cross and Sherbowitz-Wetzor, 125.

of good princes, who "constantly accepted advice, guidance, and instruction from the Church, and recognized it as the authority of conscience,"[8] as Fr. Alexander Schmemann noted. The *Primary Chronicle* also calls St. Vladimir "the new Constantine of mighty Rome"[9]—an image the Rus' would revisit at a later time.

The writing of such chronicles evinces an early concern for scholarship and history. Saints Cyril and Methodius created the Cyrillic alphabet for Old Slavonic in their mission to Bulgaria, and the Bulgarians passed it, along with their books, to the Rus', who took to them eagerly. Illiteracy and lack of education are significant contributors to poverty, and conversely, literacy and education are themselves forms of wealth, as well as contributing factors to increased material well-being. Thus, the spread of literacy due to Orthodox missions among the Rus' also contributed to their common good. Indeed, literacy was so central to Russian culture that as a result, in the eleventh century, Metropolitan St. Ilarion of Kiev enthusiastically voiced his appreciation, saying, "We do not write for the ignorant, but for them that have feasted to fulfillment on the sweetness of books!"[10] While the pope in the West and the patriarchs of the East said to one another, "I have no need of you," the Rus' fell in love with books. But which books?

The answer is not philosophy or science books. Instead, "The poverty of intellectual culture in ancient Russia is amazing," wrote G. P. Fedotov. "For seven centuries . . . we know of no scientific work in Russian literature, not even a dogmatic treatise."[11] Rather, "Most of the translations pursued merely practical and edifying aims."[12] That included, however, "Most of the genuine treatises and sermons of the ancient fathers concerning the end of the world, the coming of the Antichrist and Christ."[13] All books were unquestionably viewed as sacred because nearly all were Christian religious works, and they

---

8    Alexander Schmemann, *The Historical Road of Eastern Orthodoxy*, trans. Lydia W. Kesich (SVS Press, 2003), 298.
9    Cross and Sherbowitz-Wetzor, *Russian Primary Chronicle*, 124.
10   Ilarion of Kiev, "Sermon on Law and Grace," in *Sermons and Rhetoric of Kievan Rus'*, trans. Simon Franklin (Harvard University Press, 1991), 4.
11   G. P. Fedotov, *The Russian Religious Mind*, ed. John Meyendorff (Nordland Publishing Company, 1975), 1:38.
12   Fedotov, *Russian Religious Mind*, 1:45.
13   Fedotov, 1:49.

lacked the common distinction today between Scripture and other works of Holy Tradition. By Fedotov's account, the Rus' did not even seem to have had a complete translation of the Bible until the fifteenth century, instead using an apocryphal summary in place of the historical books of the Old Testament.[14] Nevertheless, at a time when biblical Latin and Greek had become incomprehensible to many hearers, "only the Slavic nations of Europe listened to the Gospel and could understand something of it."[15] Though humble compared to the great empires of their day, the Rus' uniquely enjoyed a treasure greater than any material wealth.

## *The Prince and the Moneylenders*

BIBLICAL YET APOCRYPHAL, PRACTICAL YET apocalyptic, scholarly yet unscientific, historical yet eschatological—What result did this strange mixture yield? Russian piety and sainthood in this period already had a character of its own—what Fedotov and others refer to as "kenoticism": "In the kenotic religion, which takes its pattern in the humility of Christ, man humiliates himself not only before God but before the lowest members of society."[16] The term refers to Philippians 2:7, in which St. Paul tells us that Christ "made Himself of no reputation [*eauton ekenosen*], taking the form of a bondservant." Visitors to St. Sergei of Radonezh's Holy Trinity Monastery, for example, were alarmed to discover the filthy gardener was also the abbot.[17]

We can see this kenotic ideal on a social level as well. Compared to Byzantium, which had inherited and baptized a highly stratified social order from

---

14   Fedotov, 1:42.
15   Fedotov, 1:57. We should note that, outside of Europe, Christians in the Middle East also had recent Arabic translations of their biblical books, thanks to Abdallah ibn al-Fadl al-Antaki. See Constantin A. Panchenko, *Arab Orthodox Christians Under the Ottomans 1516–1831*, trans. Brittany Pheiffer Noble and Samuel Noble (Holy Trinity Seminary Press, 2016), 32–33.
16   Fedotov, 1:391.
17   Epiphanius the Wise, "The Life, Acts, and Miracles of Our Blessed and Holy Father Sergius of Radonezh," in *Medieval Russia's Epics, Chronicles, and Tales*, ed. and trans. Sergei A. Zenkovsky, rev. ed. (Penguin, 1974), 262–289. Notably reflecting the Russian love for books, St. Sergei's life begins with him praying to God as a boy to be cured of illiteracy (262–263).

Rome, the Rus' were barely literate before their baptism. True, their cities had princes and boyars (landed aristocrats), but in the Kievan and Mongol periods the seed of the Gospel found far more egalitarian soil. Russian chronicles, infused with a strong sense of the eschatological, did not hesitate to characterize even peasant revolts as divine judgment for the sin of a prince. Moreover, several cities had a citizens' council, called a *veche*, where even free peasants participated in government through voting.

I'll explore that in more detail momentarily, but we should also acknowledge some continuity with Byzantium. For example, in early twelfth-century Kiev, the city faced a crisis over usurious lending. Lenders, compounding interest three times a year, imposed oppressive rates on borrowers. In 1113, upon the death of the prince Sviatopolk II, the city descended into unrest and the people called for St. Vladimir II Monomakh, grandson of St. Vladimir the Great, to be their prince. Monomakh reformed the laws, establishing limits on interest-bearing loans, though not abolishing them altogether.[18] Similarly, while Church canons forbade *clergy* to lend at interest,[19] Byzantine law, for the most part, simply capped the maximum rate of interest.[20] Historian George Vernadsky calls this allowance a "failure of the Eastern Church," claiming that "the Greek Orthodox Church forbade the practice of 'usury' in exactly the same words as did the Roman Catholic Church."[21]

Vernadsky does not substantiate this claim, however, and I personally haven't found an Orthodox writer who prohibits usury, taking that to

---

18   See George Vernadsky, trans., *Medieval Russian Laws* (W. W. Norton & Company, 1947), 43–45, including the extensive note on Article 53.

19   See Nicaea 17; Carthage 5; Carthage 16; Laodicea 4; Trullo 10; Apostles 44; Arabic Nicene 15; and Nyssa 6, all of which can be found in *NPNF*² 14. Of these, only Nyssa 6 is clearly directed at the laity at all, and to my knowledge it is not an ecumenically accepted canon like the rest.

20   The rate varied over time and circumstance, but I know of only one instance in which a ban on all interest was attempted, and it proved unworkable. See *Novella* 83 of the iconoclastic emperor Leo, available at https://droitromain.univ-grenoble-alpes.fr/Anglica /NL83_Scott.htm.

21   Vernadsky, *Medieval Russian Laws*, 8. Vernadsky's account is also contradicted by historian of economics Marjorie Grice-Hutchinson's *Early Economic Thought in Spain, 1177–1740* (Liberty Fund, 2015), 21.

entail *all* interest, in "exactly the same words" as Roman Catholics before St. Tikhon of Zadonsk in the eighteenth century.[22] To be sure, the Scriptures and Church Fathers harshly condemn as usurers those moneylenders who exploited the poor and desperate, lending to those unable to repay as justification for dispossessing them. But the Fathers' concerns are always interpersonal and grounded in a more Stoic understanding of natural law, i.e., that which accords with or violates our nature as human beings. Saint Gennadios Scholarios, for example, while speaking of *justice*, simply prohibits merchants from lending with "*heavy* interest"[23] and only later, when addressing *mercy*, exhorts his hearers to lend to anyone who asks without "demand[ing] interest."[24] In the West, by contrast, Aristotle's understanding of usury as all interest, based on his understanding of the nature of money, became the standard.[25]

The upshot of this philosophical distinction is that while the Orthodox Church is not without its historical failings, I do not think the morality of lending is one of them, and St. Vladimir Monomakh is a shining example. By contrast with the agrarian West, Vernadsky does note that a "'money economy' was one of the essential features of Byzantium. As to Kievan Russia, its economic growth and blossoming was chiefly the result of an extensive commerce with both Byzantium and the Orient. . . . Not only was there then in

---

22  Tikhon of Zadonsk, *Journey to Heaven*, trans. George D. Lardas (Holy Trinity Monastery, 1991), 132–135. Notably, St. Tikhon also preserves patristic reasons for denouncing usury such as "not to take from those who do not have" (133), grounding the condemnation in exploitation of the poor, alongside identifying all interest with usury: "To take more than what is lent is usury," (132) as was common in the West.

23  Gennadios Scholarios, "Concerning the Foremost Worship of God: Or the Evangelical Law in Summary," 8, in *From Ashes to Ruin: Selections from the Writings of St. Gennadios Scholarios,* trans. John Palmer (New Rome Press, 2022), 53, emphasis added.

24  Scholarios, "Concerning the Foremost Worship," 67.

25  This cannot be explained through a lack of knowledge of Aristotle in the East, as it was the West, not the East, that went for centuries without much access to his works. See David Bradshaw, *Aristotle East and West: Metaphysics and the Division of Christendom* (Cambridge University Press, 2004). We ought, rather, to conclude that those many Eastern Church Fathers who knew of Aristotle's view of usury instead deliberately chose biblical and Stoic language in their own teachings. One way of distinguishing these views would be to call Aristotle's view "objective" or "impersonal" while the Fathers' view tends to be more "subjective" or "personal."

Russia a strong merchant class, but the princes themselves invested heavily in both overland and oversea commercial transactions. Loans at interest constituted an important corollary of such transactions."[26] By keeping interest in check but not prohibiting it, St. Vladimir Monomakh served both justice and commerce, which in turn facilitated the "economic growth and blossoming" of the Rus'.

The Law of Moses, in fact, did not prohibit all lending at interest either, stating, "To a foreigner you may charge interest, but to your brother you shall not charge interest" (Deut. 23:20). The difference between a foreigner and "your brother," of course, is a matter of familiarity. The first, fundamentally commercial relation is impersonal, while the second familial relation is personal, as is the relation of clergy to their people. We may additionally add that the Law prescribes special care of those foreigners living among God's people, i.e., those who had become part of the community (see Deut. 24:17). Thus we shouldn't assume the basis of this command is racial preference or tribalism. Rather, the foreigner asking for a loan would not be a desperate member of one's community but likely a traveling merchant, who might reasonably be expected to pay back a loan with interest. In Orthodox Church history, we see this impersonal/personal distinction in the difference between civil law and canon law, reflecting the impersonal nature of justice in the former and the personal nature of mercy in the latter. We should not expect civil laws to fully accord with the Gospel, and in the case of lending, we see in both Byzantium and the Kievan Rus' that the state maintained justice while the Church preached mercy.

Monomakh, moreover, was no stranger to the kenotic love of the Gospel, as his *Instruction* to his children demonstrates. "First of all," he wrote, "for the sake of God and for the salvation of your own souls, retain the fear of God in your hearts and give alms openhandedly, for generosity is the source of all virtue."[27] He furthermore exhorted them, "Above all things: Forget not the poor, but support them to the extent of your means. Give to the orphan, protect the widow, and permit the mighty to destroy no man. Take not the life of the just

---

26 Vernadsky, *Medieval Russian Laws*, 9.
27 Vladimir Monomakh, "Instruction to His Children," in Zenkovsky, *Medieval Russia's Epics, Chronicles, and Tales*, 94.

or the unjust, nor permit him to be killed. Destroy no Christian soul, even though he be guilty of murder."[28]

Monomakh fought many battles, so unfortunately he did not live up to his ideal ethic of life described here, but it is still admirable. According to Christ, "peacemakers"—not warriors—"shall be called sons of God" (Matt. 5:9). But sometimes warriors are necessary. Sometimes in our sinful world there is a "time to kill" (Eccl. 3:3), and in that sense even a time to "sin boldly,"[29] as Martin Luther put it. But the Gospel teaches us that the Cross is a standard of peace, and the early Rus' would even seal their treaties by kissing the Cross, with their bishops acting as peacemakers.[30] They regarded the breaking of such an oath to be a dire sin. We ought to have faith that if God can reconcile us sinners to Himself, then He can reconcile us to one another as well. We can see that peacemaking faith, even if not fully realized, in St. Vladimir Monomakh.

## A Kenotic Civilization

THE CLANS IN THE ERA of the Kievan Rus' continued to war with one another intermittently until (and after) the Tatar conquest, which chroniclers apocalyptically attributed to divine judgment. Though the Mongols mostly cut short the unique civilizational trajectory of the medieval Rus', we do not need to speculate as to what it might have become. Novgorod and the cities and territories subject to it escaped the devastation of the Golden Horde by preemptively surrendering. While the rest of the Rus' faced humiliating abuse as vassals of the pagan Mongols, Novgorod remained free at the price of a tax. As a result, "Novgorod was not an outlandish growth in Russian life," claimed Fedotov, "but the most Russian element in it, the element which was most free of Tatar admixture, and in addition contained, as it were, the possibility for a free culture to develop in the future."[31]

---

28  Monomakh, "Instruction to His Children," 97, the original is italicized and in verse.
29  Martin Luther, Letter to Melanchthon, August 1, 1521, in *Luther's Works: Letters I*, ed. and trans. Gottfried G. Krodel, vol. 48 (Fortress Press, 1963), 282.
30  Fedotov, *The Russian Religious Mind*, 1:299–314.
31  Fedotov, 2:188.

"Was Novgorod a republic?" asked Fedotov. "Yes, at least for three and a half centuries of its history, from the twelfth to the fifteenth centuries."[32] The Republic of St. Sophia, as Novgorod referred to itself, included one other republic as well: Pskov, which later enjoyed its own independence from 1348 to 1510. "The territory of Novgorod was immense," notes Fedotov. "All Northern Russia as far as the Urals and even a section of Siberia lay under her authority and her law,"[33] surpassing the territory even of Moscow.

We can surmise some of Novgorod's theological underpinnings from what we know of how it functioned. "The Archbishop-elect of Novgorod the Great and Pskov, Hieromonk Theophilus," begins the Novgorod Charter of 1471, "in his court—the ecclesiastical court—shall conduct trials in accordance with the rules of the holy fathers—the Nomocanon; and he shall give equal justice to every litigant, be he boyar, or a middle-class burgher, or a lower-class burgher."[34] Rule of law—"equal justice" before the law—comes first. And lest anyone think this impartiality is only an ecclesial matter, "The president of the council of masters was the archbishop," says Fedotov. "In effect, he was the one who was 'president' of the republic, to draw a modern analogy. . . . His name was drawn by lot from those of the candidates elected by the veche. The three lots on the altar in the Cathedral of St. Sophia symbolized the divine will for the fate of the city-state."[35] Thus, while "supreme authority in the Novgorod republic belonged . . . to the veche," which "elected the entire administration,"[36] in the case of the archbishop, God cast the deciding vote.

Yet Novgorod had its darker side as well. The first Russian heretics, the Strigolniki, arose in Pskov, spread to Novgorod, and bore a strikingly egalitarian and democratic character. Protesting the charging of fees for sacramental services, the Strigolniki rejected the sacramental and hierarchical aspects of the Church, both essential aspects of catholicity. These fees were common

---

32   Fedotov, 2:188.
33   Fedotov, 2:187–188.
34   The Charter of the City of Novgorod, Article 1, in Vernadsky, *Medieval Russian Laws*, 83. Though the charter only applied to Novgorod at this time, since Pskov was already independent, the archbishop of Novgorod remained "Archbishop of Novgorod . . . and Pskov."
35   Fedotov, *The Russian Religious Mind*, 2:190–191.
36   Fedotov, 2:189.

because Novgorod was a commercial republic, relying on international trade for its economy. Despite hostilities between Orthodox and Roman Catholics, including prince St. Alexander Nevsky having to repel the Second Swedish Crusade, the German Catholic Hanseatic League remained a major trading partner for Novgorod.[37] Commerce was the basis of peaceful relations with Moscow, too, including Novgorod eventually accepting the authority of its grand prince.[38] Of necessity, it no doubt had a larger merchant class—and thus a larger middle class—than many societies of the time, making these fees more understandable. But as is often the case, a taste for freedom and equality only grows the desire for more of it, and sometimes this hunger manifests itself in the sin of envy, as in the case of the Strigolniki. Thus, they harshly condemned both the rich and the Church.

Pskov and Novgorod did not respond to the Strigolniki with tolerance. Fleeing persecution in Pskov, the Strigolniki settled for some time in Novgorod, yet that did not bring an end to their troubles. In a 1375 peasant riot—one of several in Novgorod's history—three Strigolniki were thrown from the Volkhov Bridge and drowned in the river. Perhaps these riots evince a dark instability underlying democratic Novgorod, but to be fair, it is worth noting Fedotov's observation that violent unrest was actually rare, and "for the most part the 'masters' [*sovet gospod*] were able to reconcile the hostile parties before bloodshed occurred."[39] He notes, moreover, that "less innocent blood was shed in Novgorod in all the centuries of its existence than in the few days that Ivan the Terrible visited it in 1570."[40] What led to that?

## *The Rise of Moscow*

MOSCOW OCCUPIED A PRECARIOUS PLACE during the Mongol period. The Metropolitan of the Rus' transferred to Moscow from Kiev, which by the

---

37   Pavel V. Lukin, "German Merchants in Novgorod: Hospitality and Hostility, Twelfth-Fifteenth Centuries," in *Baltic Hospitality from the Middle Ages to the Twentieth Century: Receiving Strangers in Northern Europe*, ed. Wojtek Jezierski, Sari Nauman, Christina Reimann, and Leif Runefelt (Palgrave Macmillan, 2022), 117–142.
38   Fedotov, *The Russian Religious Mind*, 2:189.
39   Fedotov, 2:190.
40   Fedotov, 2:190.

fourteenth century had been absorbed into the Grand Duchy of Lithuania. Moscow's grand prince negotiated a sort of haven for the Rus' by becoming the Golden Horde's chief deputy. The Rus', for their part, not only faced Mongol oppression but continued internecine conflicts with each other. The political unity established under St. Vladimir had dissolved, despite a unity of faith. Under these circumstances, Moscow grew in influence and attracted many Rus' who wished simply to better their material conditions.

By the fifteenth century, several major events molded the self-identity of Russian Orthodox Christians. Many felt betrayed by the Council of Ferrara-Florence (1431–1449). In 1453, Constantinople fell. There was no longer an Orthodox "tsar" (as the Rus' called the emperor), despite many liturgical references to such a personage. But Moscow, meanwhile, had to deal with another "tsar"—the Mongol khan. Moscow, having slowly built its power for centuries, made a stand in 1480 at the Ugra River and in effect declared to the Mongols independence for all the Rus'—and their subjugation to Moscow.

Centuries of Mongol dominance could not but leave a deep psychological impression. "'Tatarism'—lack of principle and a repulsive combination of prostration before the strong with oppression of everything weak—unfortunately marked the growth of Moscow and the Muscovite culture from the very beginning,"[41] noted Schmemann. Tatarism, by Schmemann's account, would be the polar opposite of kenoticism, and thus a bipolar social character developed in Russian lands—both principles remaining present. It was under these circumstances that the mythology of Moscow as "Third Rome" arose in Orthodox social thought. Contrary to popular appropriation, its intention was to remind the grand prince that the Christian sovereign had a duty to both the Church and the people. Such protest was embodied in the enterprising abbot-turned-metropolitan St. Philip II, who spoke out against Ivan IV ("the Terrible") and his brutal *oprichnina* (suppression of the aristocracy, confiscation of lands and property, and rule by political police), which ultimately resulted in the saint's martyrdom.

Thus, by the end of the sixteenth century, the Orthodox world within and without looked terribly dark. All other Orthodox lands fell to the Ottoman

---

41    Schmemann, *Historical Road*, 305.

Turks and the Time of Troubles followed Ivan IV. Yet Orthodoxy proved adaptable to several political forms, resilient in the face of tyranny, and uniquely concerned with kenotic, self-giving love for the poor, including in its purest and most lofty polities, economies, and laws, however imperfect and sinful they, to their credit, admitted themselves at times to be. Moreover, here already we see the seeds of both good and evil in the Russian Empire, to which we'll turn in the next chapter.

CHAPTER 24

# The Russian Empire

I N AN EPISODE OF *THE Simpsons* titled, "The Seemingly Never-Ending Story,"[1] Moe, owner of the local pub, tries to lose his friends and sometime bar denizens to win a woman's love. He proceeds to throw them out of his tavern one by one, until he stops before evicting Barney, the town drunk, realizing that he had already thrown him out twice before. "Barney, how do you keep getting back in?" he asks before tossing him out a third time. The scene ends with Barney emerging behind Moe in the doorway for a fourth time.

In the Hellenization of the Maccabees, we see a similar story. Despite trying to isolate themselves from the outside world, it kept coming back, whether they were ready for it or not. The story of the Russian Empire follows this same trajectory. After the fall of Constantinople and other Orthodox lands to the Ottoman Turks, Russia alone remained free. But despite anti-Western attitudes, Western ideas kept popping back up in new forms, including in ways that would transform the Church's senior leadership from a Patriarch to a Holy Synod. Moreover, generation after generation sought to expel Western ideas while simultaneously embracing *other* Western ideas. Like Moe trying to evict Barney from his tavern, the task proved a fool's errand (and in my view continues to be one today). If we can take a step back from polemical impulses, we can see a way of engaging with the West—and

---

1  *The Simpsons*, season 17, episode 13, "The Seemingly Never-Ending Story," directed by Raymond S. Persi, written by Ian Maxtone-Graham, featuring Maurice LaMarche, aired March 12, 2006, on Fox.

the modern world it bequeathed to us—in non-reactionary terms. The question is not what is Western and what is Eastern, but what is Orthodox? In the principle of sobornost', Orthodox thinkers of this era gave us an answer that has implications not only for ideological debates but for service to the poor in the modern world.

## *Prelude to the Empire*

TEMPORARILY IN 1667, THEN LONG-TERM in the Treaty of Perpetual Peace of 1686, the Polish-Lithuanian Commonwealth ceded Kiev to Russia, bequeathing to the Orthodox in Kievan lands a history of religious tolerance and theological education. Despite all the violence and turmoil in Western Europe, the Commonwealth excelled in religious liberty, including for the Orthodox. In that context of freedom, Kiev became a center of Orthodox theology.[2]

Metropolitan Peter Mohyla of Kiev founded the academy there that bears his name, which raised the theological standard among the Rus' as it carried on the Scholasticism that medieval Byzantium had embraced long before.[3] Mohyla's 1645 catechism gained pan-Orthodox acceptance and use over the following decades, establishing a basis for generalization about the common person's exposure to Orthodox teaching.[4] Largely based on the Roman Catholic Tridentine Catechism, but still preserving distinctive Orthodox theological commitments, here we see an attempt to think deeply about Christian duties in our social and economic life, especially in Mohyla's treatment of familial, civil, and Church authority in the Fifth Commandment ("Honor your father and mother"—Ex. 20:12) and of property and charity in the Eighth Commandment ("You shall not steal"—Ex. 20:15), among others.

Regarding the Fifth, Mohyla highlights the debt all people owe to their parents for their very existence, as well as their upbringing, only then extending the command to include any other legitimate authorities. Nevertheless,

---

2   *Konfederacja Warszawska* (1573), http://www.literatura.hg.pl/varsconf.htm.
3   Marcus Plested, *Orthodox Readings of Aquinas* (Oxford University Press, 2012).
4   Peter Mogila, *The Orthodox Confession of the Catholic and Apostolic Eastern Church*, trans. Philip Ludwell III, ed. J. J. Overbeck (Thomas Baker, 1898).

he cautions, "We must be careful that nothing be contrary to the *Glory of God* or his most holy *Commandments,* always remembering that we must obey God rather than our *Parents*: According to the *Doctrine of Christ* (Matth. x. 37), *He that loveth Father or Mother more than me is not worthy of me.*"[5] So, too, any other authorities. Regarding the Eighth, he notes that the prohibition against theft extends to in any way "*violently withholding the Right of another.* Hereby is also forbidden the taking away another's good Name and Reputation, the exacting too much of one's Hireling or Tenants, and the imposing too hard Conditions of Service on them. This likewise respects *Usury.*"[6] He adds, "This Commandment regardeth, also, all just Contracts and Bargains, in which we are required to be strictly true and upright, that we defraud not one another."[7]

Unfortunately, the Rus' did not always live out Mohyla's wise interpretation of these commandments. When the Tsar Feodor III died, political operatives exploited resentment of soldiers for harsh treatment by their superiors to incite the Moscow Uprising of 1682. Rioters murdered boyars, military personnel, and several members of the royal family in front of the ten-year-old heir Peter, known to history as Peter the Great, the first Russian emperor. When he came of age, he was determined to modernize Russia, inclusive of the Orthodox Church, into a kingdom of law and order. To reform the Church, he promoted the most-educated bishops—most of which at that time were Kievan—ultimately favoring Feofan Prokopovich, who became Metropolitan of Novgorod and Pskov.

Though educated in Rome, unlike others who followed the same path, Prokopovich had a profound spiritual crisis upon seeing the ecclesiastical corruption of the Eternal City and reading Martin Luther's *On the Babylonian Captivity of the Church.* He eventually fled Rome, scandalizing East-West relations there, and he spent time in German lands, presumably absorbing more Lutheran theology, including political theology. Because of his Lutheran leanings, most Orthodox historians do not remember Prokopovich fondly, but we still ought to consider his context.

---

5   Mogila, *Orthodox Confession,* 158, italics original.
6   Mogila, 160, italics original.
7   Mogila, 160.

As Andrey V. Ivanov points out in his book *A Spiritual Revolution*,[8] Russia did need reform and modernization. Tatar despotism continued on in Moscow's tsars, reaching its height in Ivan the Terrible and the Time of Troubles. The absence of higher education during this period meant that despite a genuine flowering of monasticism at this time, the rest of society remained feudal, which was often a hard and cruel life with few other pathways for upward mobility.

Indeed, feudal serfdom became widespread only during the Muscovite period, and medieval and modern monasteries contributed to this societal transformation, as evidenced by the controversy between the Possessors and Non-Possessors.[9] The former, such as St. Joseph of Volokolamsk, defended monastic property for the sake of providing social services. The latter, such as St. Nilus of Sora, criticized monasteries for being corrupted by opulence and owning serfs. The Stoglav Synod of 1551 ruled in favor of the Possessors, but given that both Joseph and Nilus are venerated as saints, we can deduce a certain ecclesiastical unease with that outcome. In my own judgment, the Possessors were correct in principle—monasteries, too, have property rights—but in practice they had abused their rights by violating the rights of others in contributing to the spread of serfdom. The Non-Possessors raised serious concerns that remained unresolved up to the eighteenth century.

## A Russian Reformation

THE ERA OF ST. PETERSBURG'S ascendancy, including Prokopovich's Church reform, sought to solve such real and serious problems. The merits of the means chosen, however, certainly deserve debate. In 1721, following Lutheran examples, Feofan's *Spiritual Regulation* replaced the Patriarch of Moscow with the Holy Synod.[10] While many view this new arrangement as one-sided dominance of the state over the Church, Prokopovich successfully

---

8   Andrey V. Ivanov, *A Spiritual Revolution: The Impact of Reformation and Enlightenment in Orthodox Russia* (University of Wisconsin Press, 2020).
9   Schmemann, *The Historical Road of Eastern Orthodoxy*, trans. Lydia W. Kesich (SVS Press, 2003), 317–318.
10  Alexander V. Muller, ed. and trans., *The Spiritual Regulation of Peter the Great* (University of Washington Press, 1972). Prokopovich is the author.

campaigned to make the Holy Synod equal, rather than subject to, the Senate, arguably giving the Church greater influence in the empire, at least for its first century. As Fr. Alexander Schmemann put it, "state and Church interpreted the imperial authority in different ways."[11] Like anything in history, we should expect to find some good, some bad, and some ugliness in the Synodal period of Russian Orthodoxy.

On the positive side, while the Protestant Reformation led to the permanent fracturing of the Western Church, many Protestant ideas, as well as some Roman Catholic counterpoints to them, passed into Orthodoxy comparatively peacefully. Furthermore, nothing came uncritically. By the eighteenth century, many Western Christian traditions had already distinguished themselves from one another and solidified their perspectives. Within and across these traditions, various movements also developed, often specifically in response to developments in modern philosophy, science, and society. Not only Prokopovich, but others after him incorporated what doctrines they believed were compatible with Orthodoxy while keeping the Liturgy unchanged. While Fr. Georges Florovsky criticized this,[12] Schmemann points to the positive side: "Mental discipline returned for the first time to the Church, and education and the inspiration of creative work returned as well."[13]

Prokopovich incorporated Lutheran ideas into his catechism, using Luther's *Smaller Catechism* as its basis. One of the sharpest contrasts to Mohyla's catechism comes in Prokopovich's treatment of the Fifth Commandment, where he lists duties to the emperor and civil authorities "in the first place,"[14] i.e., *before* the honor due to fathers and mothers (which gets third place after ecclesiastical authority). After him, Metropolitan Platon Levshin of Moscow took the Westminster *Larger Catechism* as inspiration for his own 1763 catechism.[15] And Metropolitan St. Filaret of Moscow followed a more Pietist line

---

11 Schmemann, *Historical Road*, 333–334.

12 Georges Florovsky, *Ways of Russian Theology, Part One*, vol. 5, The Collected Works of Georges Florovsky (Nordland Publishing Company, 1979).

13 Schmemann, *Historical Road*, 336.

14 *The Russian Catechism*, trans. Jenkin Philipps (W. Meadows, 1725), 10.

15 See *The Orthodox Doctrine of the Apostolic Eastern Church; Or, a Compendium of Christian Theology*, ed. G. Potessaro (Whittaker & Co.; Oliver & Boyd; Dunnill & Palmer, 1857).

in his 1830 catechism,[16] adding, albeit begrudgingly, some aspects more in line with Roman Catholicism due to shifting pressures in the empire in his day. Collectively, rather than merely parroting Western ideas, these catechisms, along with Mohyla's work before them, should be viewed as Orthodoxy's first entrance into the broader theological conversation of modern Christian civilization. In addition to theology proper, all of them give us insight into Orthodox social thought at the time and remain useful references. Common themes include proper stewardship—rather than condemnation—of material wealth, the protection of private property, the prohibition of usury, the need for almsgiving, and social duties between parents and children, citizens and rulers, and Church members and Church authorities.

Prokopovich's monastic and ascetic reforms, however, involved both bad and ugly circumstances, too. He often minimized or dismissed ascetic practices as superstitious, failing to see them as the essence of the Gospel in action, dying and rising with Christ daily. Moreover, the number of monasteries and monks dropped to less than a quarter of what they had been. Further, the state misappropriated monasteries for supposedly "practical" uses—for example, as military retirement homes, hospitals, and even prisons—assuming wrongly that monks pursuing the Kingdom of God had no benefit for the common good.

Nevertheless, far more disgracefully, the Church, principally in its monastic estates, by this time owned over a million male serfs and their families and treated them shamefully. By the mid-eighteenth century, peasant revolts against the monasteries led to state intervention. The empress Catherine the Great freed all ecclesiastical serfs with her February Manifesto of 1764. After that time and up to the twentieth century (not coincidentally, in my view), Russia saw a monastic revival, and the bishops became defenders of the remaining serfs against abuse by landowners. Russian serfs would not be fully freed until Emperor Alexander II's 1861 Emancipation Manifesto, authored by St. Filaret, which the nobles were compelled to accept due to their extensive debts to the state. Peasants became full citizens, with the right to marry

---

16   See *The Longer Catechism of the Orthodox, Catholic, Eastern Church*, trans. R. W. Blackmore, in *The Creeds of Christendom with a History and Critical Notes*, ed. Philip Schaff, vol. 2 (Harper & Brothers, 1889), 445–542.

without landlords' approval, own land, and start businesses. The land, however, came at a heavy price to buy or rent. Thus, the newly freed serfs quickly fell into debt of their own.

Circumstances could have been different. Under the influence of Enlightenment ideas, many boyars and bishops hoped through the eighteenth century that Russia would adopt a constitution. Any outside observer at the time would guess that Russia would be the first traditionally Orthodox polity to adopt liberal rights, freedoms, and institutions. Metropolitan Platon openly called for a constitution. And Alexander Pushkin earned himself a brief exile with his "Ode to Liberty." When the Decemberists sought to take advantage of the brief interregnum in 1825, some of them had copies of Pushkin's poem with them. But after the Decemberists murdered Emperor Nicholas I's negotiator, he ordered his soldiers to turn their cannons on the crowd. The empire's short-lived constitution remained nearly a century away.

## (Re)discovering Sobornost'

WHILE REFORM CONTINUED AFTER THIS time, for many the winds of progress had left their sails. The dashed hopes of the intelligentsia contributed to the creation of a classic Russian literary type: the "superfluous man." Again, think of Pushkin—his Eugene Onegin would have joined the civil service in a previous age. Instead, he lives a profligate life, just waiting for his uncle to die so he can inherit his estate. He represents a generation who saw their vocation robbed from them by a monarch whose rule they resented. Pushkin's characters become stuck going through the motions of social custom out of sync with whatever ideals they may have left. "Habit was given us in distress," wrote Pushkin, "By Heaven in lieu of happiness."[17] The Jews got the Pharisees during the Hasmonean dynasty and the Zealots under Roman rule; the Russians got Fyodor Dostoevsky's Ivan Karamazov[18] and,

---

17  Alexander Pushkin, *Eugene Onéguine: A Romance of Russian Life*, trans. Henry Spalding (Macmillan and Co., 1881), 55.

18  Fyodor Dostoyevsky, *The Brothers Karamazov*, trans. Constance Garnett (The Modern Library/Random House, 1950).

ultimately, the Bolsheviks. Yet Dostoevsky, at least, had further influences that deserve our attention today as much as his novels.

First, Nicholas I's suppression of Enlightenment ideas, including the Russian Bible Society, didn't come from nowhere. The intellectual tide had been turning for more than a decade. Yet this new antagonism toward Western influence was not the end of creative Orthodox intellectual endeavor. Slavophiles such as Alexei Khomiakov, in response to Western polemics, reached back into Holy Tradition to find the core essence of the Church. What did they find? Sobornost'—the spiritual unity of all, even the world itself, with God in love through the Church.[19] The term derives from the Slavonic translation of "catholic" in the Creed, and rightly so. As we saw in pagan Rome, so too the Slavophiles' understanding of sobornost' resonates strongly with the early Church's understanding of its catholicity—not merely a term for doctrinal purity or universal authority, but the cosmic weight of the Incarnation as "ministry of reconciliation" (2 Cor. 5:18) through the ecclesiastical hierarchy, Sacraments, and everyday ascetic charity. Those familiar with *The Brothers Karamazov* will rightly think of sobornost' in terms of Fr. Zosima's sermon: "Love all of God's creation, the whole and every grain of sand in it. Love every leaf, every ray of God's light. Love the animals, love the plants, love everything. If you love everything, you will perceive the divine mystery in things."[20] Dostoevsky furthermore cited St. Tikhon of Zadonsk as inspiration for Fr. Zosima. Saint Tikhon, embodying the eighteenth-century spirit of constructive dialogue with the West and social reform at home, authored a spiritual manual that, among other topics, contains chapters on rich and poor, lenders and borrowers, sellers and buyers, and employers and employees. He affirmed that "riches are a gift of God bestowed upon men, for *the earth is the Lord's, and the fulness thereof* (Ps. 24/23:1)." Yet he continued, "They are given you, O Christian, not for your sake alone, but also for the sake of the poor."[21] Despite the romantic rhetoric of Fr. Zosima's sermon, the practically minded

---

19   Boris Jakim and Robert Bird, trans. and ed., *On Spiritual Unity: A Slovophile Reader* (Lindisfarne Books, 1998).
20   Dostoyevsky, *The Brothers Karamazov*, 382–383.
21   Tikhon of Zadonsk, *Journey to Heaven: Counsels on the Particular Duties of Every Christian*, trans. George D. Lardas (Holy Trinity Monastery, 1991), 130.

St. Tikhon served as Dostoevsky's model of sanctity. Indeed, the philosopher Nikolai Berdyaev even summed up the Russian contribution to philosophy as *"concrete idealism,"*[22] a combination of deep philosophy with practical concern and embodiment. And one philosopher in particular served as inspiration not only for Dostoevsky but all Orthodox social thought that would follow.

## Vladimir Soloviev

MANY BELIEVE THAT DOSTOEVSKY BASED the character of Alyosha on his young friend Vladimir Soloviev. In Soloviev, we find the first example, and a shining one, of distinctly *modern* Orthodox social thought, comparable to figures like Pope Leo XIII or Abraham Kuyper in the West. Soloviev's moral philosophy builds on Immanuel Kant and echoes St. Athenagoras of Athens in its person-centered, or "personalist," core: "Pity which we feel towards a fellow-being acquires another significance when we see in that being the image and likeness of God. We then recognise the unconditional worth of that person; we recognise that he is an end in himself for God, and still more must be so for us. We realise that God Himself does not treat him merely as a means."[23]

Soloviev's *Lectures on Godmanhood*, despite their metaphysical and theological focus, begin with a refutation of materialistic socialism and scientific positivism.[24] Moreover, the third part of his magnum opus on moral philosophy, *The Justification of the Good*, focuses on "The Good through Human History," i.e., through the development of human society.[25] It contains chapters on law, economics, and criminal justice, all within a broad vision of society where Church, state, and economy—perhaps more accurately what we might

---

22  Nikolai Berdiaev, "Philosophical Verity and Intelligentsia Truth," in *Vekhi: Landmarks—A Collection of Articles about the Russian Intelligentsia,* trans. and ed. Marshall S. Shatz and Judith E. Zimmerman (M. E. Sharpe, 1994), 13, italics original.

23  Vladimir Solovyov, *The Justification of the Good,* rev. ed., ed. Boris Jakim, trans. Natalie A. Duddington (Eerdmans, 2005), 154, emphasis original.

24  Vladimir Solovyov, *Lectures on Godmanhood,* trans. Peter Zouboff (Dennis Dobson Ltd Publishers, 1948). Zouboff's introduction, it should be noted, is heavily influenced by his Roman Catholic perspective. In Zouboff's defense, Soloviev did express sympathies with papal claims and wrote in favor of reunion with Rome, but his thought is thoroughly influenced by Orthodoxy, and he never left the Orthodox Church.

25  Solovyov, *Justification of the Good,* 173–403.

call "culture"—each grew from the soil of the family and the moral impera-
tives of piety, altruism, and asceticism, respectively. These developed into distinct realms of life meant to work together in Chalcedonian terms—without
separation, division, confusion, or change—for the good of all. Furthermore,
Soloviev rightly refused to reduce all economic questions to ethics: "The
important domain of human material relations is studied on its technical side
by political economy [and] financial and commercial law, and falls within the
scope of moral philosophy only in so far as *exchange* becomes *fraud*."[26] One
may, and should, quibble with various aspects of Soloviev's vision of a "free
theocracy," but those who wish to contribute to Orthodox social thought in
the present ought at least to start with Soloviev.

Unfortunately, Soloviev died in 1900 at the age of fifty. All the promise of
the twentieth century—the adoption of a constitution that included democratic government and protections for freedom of conscience and other
basic rights, as well as, in 1917, the restoration of the Moscow Patriarchate—
disappeared under the shadow of the Bolshevik Revolution. As Fr. Alexander
Schmemann wrote, "Simultaneously with the growth of light in Russia there
was a growth of darkness as well, and it is a terrible warning, judgment, and
reminder that the darkness proved the stronger."[27]

How did it come to that? And where did we go from there? To answer those
questions, we must backtrack to the era in which this chapter began, but in
the West rather than the East. We must come to some understanding of the
origins and basic teachings of modern economics before we can examine and
evaluate more contemporary Orthodox attempts to contribute to the broader
conversation of Christian social thought today. I will attempt to do exactly
that in the final two parts of this book.

---

26   Solovyov, 309.
27   Schmemann, *Historical Road*, 340.

# Part 3 Summary and Discussion Questions

## *Summary*

OUR MODERN UNDERSTANDING OF HISTORY as a progression from a beginning to an end owes a debt to our Christian Faith. Eusebius of Caesarea may be the first historian to presume that the central event of history happened in the past: the Incarnation, death, and Resurrection of Jesus Christ. Our confession that Jesus is the Christ, the Son of God, commits us to valuing the importance of history. Thus, we should learn from the story of the Church throughout history and the world, West, East, Middle East, and beyond. And we should consider that just as Roman infrastructure and Greek philosophy prepared the world to receive the Gospel, so also did Roman law and society. At the same time, the Gospel also sharply clashed with these social forces when Christian charity challenged Greco-Roman piety, idolatry, and social elitism.

In pagan Rome, Christians witnessed to Christ's Resurrection through their fearlessness in the face of torture and death, being prepared for the contest of martyrdom through asceticism. They understood the Church to be catholic—not just universal but holistic—binding together all things in Christ through the Sacraments, under the bishops, and manifest by their love for orphans, widows, the poor, and oppressed. They participated in all levels of Roman society, but they rejected cultural practices corrupted by sin, advocating for universal religious liberty.

With the conversion of St. Constantine, the Church received back her confiscated property, obtained freedom from persecution, and became an essential part of the constitution of Christian Rome. Bishops received the judiciary right to judge cases in their own courts according to canon law, which offered an organized system of mercy alongside the civil law, grounded in natural law, that aimed at justice through the rule of law. Saint Justinian articulated the relationship of Church and state as symphonia, acknowledging a separate sphere of authority in the empire in which the emperor did not exercise supreme sovereignty. But proximity to power sometimes corrupted bishops. Dissenting promoters of Orthodoxy like St. Athanasius, St. Ambrose, and St. John Chrysostom prophetically spoke out against heresy, tyranny, and neglect of the poor. At the same time, the Church expanded her charitable ministries, including through St. Basil's Basileiad, offering both physical and spiritual care to those suffering and dying. This work flowed from their humanist understanding that Christ assumed the whole of our human nature in order to heal it entirely, and thus every aspect of our lives—material, spiritual, social, and so on—matters to God.

In order to preserve the austere discipline of the early Church, beginning in the late third century, some Christians dedicated themselves to asceticism in the institution of monasticism. From its start, in both the East and West, monasticism had an important economic component: Monks consumed little, worked hard, and produced goods to sell, providing for their needs and giving alms to the poor. Monastic enterprise was extensive. The first monks owned boats and shipped goods up and down the Nile. They offered spiritual and material support to rural villages. Even many cities first began with a hermit's cell. In Byzantium, many monasteries were founded on private estates and viewed themselves as distinct from Church and state, despite their spiritual core. They connected their freedom in society with the ownership of their property, as most clearly articulated by St. Nicholas Cabasilas. While many monasteries lived up to their ideals—viewing wealth and poverty as good or evil only to the extent that they were used for righteousness or sin—some struggled to resist secularization and corruption, which served as a warning for others.

Next, the story of Orthodoxy in the West from the fall of Rome to the Great Schism reveals a richer account of the rise and fall of civilization than is often told. Barbarians such as the Goths and Visigoths had been invited into Roman lands to fight as mercenaries in civil wars, but when aristocrats and emperors couldn't pay them—even by means of oppressive taxation—then the barbarians set their sights on Rome. While many consider the following centuries the "Dark Ages," this period contained rich cultural and intellectual production, from philosophers like St. Boethius to monastic writers inspired by St. John Cassian. Celtic penitential manuals spread monastic discipline to rural villages, and Celtic missionary exile ultimately converted the Arian barbarians to Orthodoxy. Meanwhile, the popes of Rome fought for Orthodoxy and the Roman cultural heritage of the West, eventually sending out missionaries of their own, such as St. Augustine of Canterbury. Monasticism continued to flourish in the West, with St. Benedict's Rule as the crowning achievement. Like Celtic rules, it contains detailed advice about the finances, order, and almsgiving of Benedictine monasteries. Ultimately, to the chagrin of the Byzantines, Rome would restore the Western Empire in the controversial figure of Charlemagne, whose reforms used the social power of monasteries to enforce the "three orders" of feudalism: those who fight (nobles), those who pray (priests and monks), and those who work (everyone else). Further estrangement from the East would lead to the Great Schism in the eleventh century.

Meanwhile, in the Middle East, the Holy Land fell to Islamic invaders in the seventh century. Christian independence was preserved, but only in the humiliating second-class status of dhimmitude. Nevertheless, Melkites (as Orthodox of Syria, Palestine, and Egypt were called) continued their long tradition of theological reflection and social action. Figures like St. John of Damascus, Theodore Abu Qurra, and Abdallah ibn al-Fadl al-Antaki built upon reason and natural law to contribute to the Scholastic method. Melkites also found points of ecumenical solidarity and appreciation with Miaphysite and Nestorian Christians, such as St. Isaac the Syrian, and later, after the Great Schism, even with Latins. The Ottoman Empire, while marking the tragic end of Byzantium, brought centuries of stability to Melkites that allowed them to flourish again, including through international trade and travel in the modern era.

Last, the story of Orthodoxy among the Rus'—from the Kievan period, through the Tatar conquests, the Republic of Novgorod, the Polish-Lithuanian

Commonwealth, and eventually the rise of Moscow—contains many timeless treasures for Orthodox social thought. The Rus' developed their own ascetic ideal in the concept of *kenoticism*, lowering oneself below the lowest member of society. Their more egalitarian outlook on society originally emphasized the rule of law and took on a more democratic character, though not without problematic inequalities like slavery, and later serfdom. And the Russian Empire, rather than becoming completely Westernized, marks the return of the Orthodox to the broader conversation of Christian civilization. Saints and scholars from this period established universities, wrote catechisms, and reimagined what society might become, for better as well as worse. This period, too, saw the rediscovery of catholicity in the concept of sobornost' and the rise of Russian literature and philosophy, including the shining lights of Fyodor Dostoevsky and Vladimir Soloviev. It also saw the Orthodox East's first encounter with the "Social Question" of the industrial era—though it was cut short by the tragic events of the Russian Revolution—which serves as a warning for us today and raises the question of how such a thing could come about.

## Discussion Questions

- God used Greek philosophy and Roman law, infrastructure, and society to prepare the way of the Gospel. In what ways might God be preparing the way in our own time and contexts? How might these same things also become hostile to the love of Christ?
- What does it mean to call the Church "catholic"? How does this relate to wealth and poverty today?
- What lessons can we learn about mercy and justice for the poor from Christian Rome and Byzantium? How could we translate the positive features of Christian civilization to our largely secular contexts?
- How can the history of monastic enterprise serve as a model—and a warning—for Orthodox Christians in the business world today? What role could the everyday asceticism of even non-monastics play in business ethics and corporate culture?
- How might the witness of the Western Orthodox after the fall of Rome serve as a model for civilizational revitalization today?

- In what ways could the Scholastic method of Melkite Christians contribute to more faithful ecumenical cooperation in thinking through issues of our modern economies and caring for the poor?
- How can we, in all our vocations, better follow the example of the Medieval Rus' in kenotic, self-emptying love for the lowest, most marginalized and forgotten people in our world today?
- What lessons and dangers for Orthodox Christian social thought can be gleaned from the rise and fall of the Russian Empire?

# Modern Economics

CHAPTER 25

# What Is Economics?

Why do politicians—of every party—so often fail to deliver on their promises to voters? A cynic would answer "dishonesty," and no doubt many politicians simply do not respect the truth. But I think at least as often they lack the requisite knowledge and know-how to keep their promises—or, for that matter, to make realistic promises in the first place. Often they blame their rivals just to cover for the fact that they promised something they could not practically deliver. Either they lack the necessary resources, the means to acquire them, or the means to use them. Perhaps all three. Good intentions are not enough. For that matter, a person with bad intentions cannot achieve what they want without a proper understanding of how our economies work either—a small silver lining to the inconvenient reality that prudent management of scarce resources is necessary to achieve any goals we have in this life, political or otherwise.

That's what economics is about—prudent management of scarce resources—and if we want to figure out how to effectively live out our Orthodox Tradition of love for our neighbors today, especially the poor, we need to know some basics of what economics is, where it came from, and how modern economies work. The common textbook definition of economics comes from the English economist Lionel Robbins: "Economics is the science which studies human behaviour as a relationship between ends and scarce means which have alternative uses."[1] What did he mean by that?

## Defining Economics

"SCARCE" DOES NOT MEAN "HARD to find" or even "static." We do have renewable resources, for example. And others result from productive processes, and thus, the supply of them can be increased. Rather, scarcity means that the current supply of a resource, if used for one purpose, would restrict our ability to use it for another. "The Manna which fell from heaven may have been scarce," wrote Robbins, "but, if it was impossible to exchange it for something else or to postpone its use, it was not the subject of any activity with an economic aspect."[2]

In this sense, we could say economics studies "opportunity cost." That is, the costs of doing something includes the "cost" of not being able to do other things with those same resources. Robbins gives the example of a student who wants to study both math and philosophy but only has the time and ability to focus on one and must choose between them. The student must economize on her time and talent, and thus, even though there is no money involved in the choice (presuming they have the same financial cost) the decision is still economic. Economics is not only, or even primarily, about money. Nor is the "market" economists talk about the same as the stock market. Economists care about how and why people use their resources for some things and not others and what incentives might persuade them to change their behavior. A market is any relationship of exchange, where people trade the products of their labor and capital for others', redistributing the wealth of the economy to meet the needs of consumers and increase overall welfare.

## Defining Political Economy

THE BEGINNING OF MODERN ECONOMICS is often attributed to Adam Smith. Smith, however, taught moral philosophy at the University of Glasgow

---

1    Lionell Robbins, *An Essay on the Nature & Significance of Economic Science* (Macmillan & Co., 1932), 15.
2    Robbins, *Nature & Significance*, 13.

in the eighteenth century. While his work *An Inquiry into the Nature and Causes of the Wealth of Nations* (1776) established political economy as a distinct academic discipline in its own right, the work does have moral concerns, and his other major work, originally published in 1759, *The Theory of Moral Sentiments*, focused on moral psychology as much as ethics. He revised both several times before his death in 1790, indicating that the publication of his *Wealth of Nations* did not diminish his interest in moral behavior.

I note this historical context because political economy, what Adam Smith did, had not yet become modern economics. Political economy requires big-picture thinking, including morality and other noneconomic values. We shouldn't think of modern economics as inherently immoral, but economists today do not often claim to make moral judgments. They care about telling people how economies work and how certain policies will likely motivate people to behave differently. They also point out the estimated or actual costs of policies—you know, those things politicians too often ignore when making promises to voters. Some people today argue that economists still presume some inherent moral values, and some of those claims may have merit. Nevertheless, I see this "value-free" nature of economics as an opportunity for us to cultivate a fruitful dialogue between the moral commitments and social principles of Orthodox social thought, on the one hand, and modern economic science, on the other.

We should still make political economy our goal: Economics alone cannot be sufficient, in the same way that well-intended politicians (and citizens, for that matter) can't just rest on their good intentions. Our world has limits that constrain what we can accomplish, whether or not we want to acknowledge them. "I, wisdom, dwell with prudence" (Prov. 8:12), says the Scripture. Prudence is one of the four cardinal virtues—along with justice, temperance, and courage—listed in Wisdom 8:7 and has been a hallmark of Greek philosophy and Christian ethics through the centuries. Moreover, through virtue, obtained through ascetic effort, we actualize within us the grace of God given to us through the Sacraments and we grow in communion with Jesus Christ. So if learning a little about economics can help us be more virtuous, we ought to take the opportunity to do so, even if it may require some ascetic effort.

Indeed, to dig a little into the root of the word "economics," Jesus even told a parable (Luke 16:1–13) about a steward (*oikonomos*) that gets at the spiritual importance of political economy: "There was a certain rich man who had a steward, and an accusation was brought to him that this man was wasting his goods. So he called him and said to him, 'What is this I hear about you? Give an account of your stewardship, for you can no longer be steward'" (Luke 16:1–2). Economics studies efficiency. That shouldn't be valued above all else, but it should be valued. The opposite of efficiency is waste, and God does not want us to waste the resources of His creation. Doing so jeopardizes our position before God as caretakers of the world He made.

That said, Jesus continues the parable, telling us that the steward then used the master's resources to make friends, and in so doing, though the steward is described as "unjust," the master commended him for recognizing that there are more valuable things in life than money. Those friends would help the steward if he lost his income. Efficiency is good, but it must also be directed at good goals. Economics is good, but it must be used for the love of our neighbors.

## The Plan for Part 4

IN ORDER TO ASSIST US in our stewardship of God's creation today for the love of our neighbors, the next seven chapters tell the story of modern economics, considered historically and assessed in the light of Orthodox social thought. I must apologize from the start that readers wholly unacquainted with economics may feel inundated with unfamiliar names. Keeping everything straight may require some ascetic effort. I hope, however, that by situating some of the key insights of economics within the historical development of the science by specific people, it will feel less abstract and more personal. Modern economics results from the work of generations of real people who often had explicitly moral concerns and goals. Thus, like reading biblical genealogies, we should at least hear some of their names and stories because they can help us better understand wealth and poverty, specifically how to get more of the former in order to have less of the latter for our neighbors today.

In the first chapter, I will explore precursors to modern economics in late Scholastic theology in the West. Many of the principles of modern economics can be found in early modern penitential manuals and legal treatises, which also include some relevant Christian moral analyses of property, money, and lending that we ought to be familiar with and consider.

Next, Adam Smith deserves a whole chapter of his own. People still read him today, and for good reason, even if they often do so one-sidedly and then skip almost everyone who came after him. We won't be doing that, however, as we will examine insights from both his *Wealth of Nations* and his *Theory of Moral Sentiments*, then proceed in the following chapter to discuss the next generation of economists.

The era following Smith, known as classical political economy, made real advancements not just in the understanding of economic life but in actual policies that aided the poor. Many of these classical political economists were Western Christians; several were even ministers. They advocated for the abolition of slavery in Britain. They also fought for free trade and for reform to Elizabethan "poor laws," with mixed results in the latter case. And they raised—and addressed—new theoretical problems that remain relevant today.

After these classical economists, we will need to consider some socialists and other social reformers. While most socialist figures from this time are marginal to economic science today, we need to know something about the ideas of Karl Marx, as they were so consequential and disastrous in the Christian East and sadly still remain prevalent worldwide today. But we should also take time to consider the Christian socialists, especially the Anglican minister F. D. Maurice, who complicate any simplistic identification of socialism with revolutionary Marxism. And we need to acknowledge the important work of evangelical social reformers, like Lord Shaftesbury, who rejected socialism.

Having given these social reformers their due, next we can examine how the academic discipline of economics responded to the challenge of Marxism through what is known as the "Marginal Revolution." Economists did adapt their science to the challenges of Marxist analysis, just not how Marxists hoped they would. This era led to a refinement of the science and the beginnings of what we know as economics today, in contrast to political economy.

Mathematics began to play a larger role, and economists began to view their discipline as more akin to the hard sciences, i.e., as "value-free." Nevertheless, this distinction does not mean they had no moral concerns, nor that they believed economics did not need morality.

Closing this series of chapters, the last two will briefly look at the contribution of John Maynard Keynes, the origins of modern macroeconomics in the social and civilizational crises of the early twentieth century, and some reactions to it within the discipline. Keynes offered a new perspective on unemployment, inflation, deficits, debt, and saving. Modern economics today owes a significant debt (no pun intended) to Keynes and post-Keynesian theorists, but dissenting voices from other important schools of economic thought— such as Austrian, Ordoliberal, and Chicago—deserve our familiarity as well. Together, they represent the range of likely views of contemporary economists, who nevertheless still agree on many of the fundamentals of their science.[3] In the course of surveying their contributions, we will also see that the "Great Divergence" between economics and morality came only recently, which raises the opportunity for Orthodox social thought to enhance economic analysis today.

If these chapters only teach greater familiarity with those fundamental economic principles for my readers and why they matter for Orthodox social thought, I will be satisfied. We need to have a better understanding, however imperfect, of basic economics than the rhetoric of the average politician, blogger, or social media meme. On the one hand, as a by-product it may make us a little more jaded about politics today. But who knows? Maybe, on the other hand, some of you readers intend to run for office. In that case, I hope these chapters will help you be the change you—and others—want to see. Most of all, I hope these chapters will empower readers to contribute to a wider conversation with other Christians about how to carefully live out our Faith together today for both the Kingdom of God and the common good.

---

3    For a brief survey, see Jay W. Richards, "What Economists Know, Believe, and Debate," *Journal of Markets & Morality* 23, no. 1 (2020): 117–130.

# CHAPTER 26

# Scholastic Economics

W HY IS WATER, A SUBSTANCE every living being needs for its survival, so cheap, whereas yachts, a luxury no one needs and few people get to enjoy, are so expensive? Think about it: Measured in the cost of a bottle of water, a yacht costs hundreds of thousands of bottles of water—enough water to float a yacht in! Why? Why doesn't the price of something reflect how much people need it? Isn't that what *valuable* should mean?

Consider another paradox: In the fifteenth and sixteenth centuries, everyone knew the value of gold and silver. The Spanish, fresh off the Reconquista of the Iberian Peninsula from the Muslim Moors, in the same year (1492) discovered the "New World" and set out to extract as much gold and silver as they could from the Americas. "What were the effects on Spain of such extraordinary and unexpected good fortune?" asks economic historian Marjorie Grice-Hutchinson. She answers, "A trade boom set in. Prices rose . . . doubling themselves in the first half of the sixteenth century and again in the second."[1]

So Spanish commerce experienced a "trade boom," but the overall result of all the new gold and silver was inflation: Prices doubled twice. Grice-Hutchinson puts this inflation in perspective: "From contemporary observers it evoked prophecies of doom. . . . Spain found herself increasingly unable to sell her products abroad, and increasingly threatened by foreign

---

1    Marjorie Grice-Hutchinson, *Early Economic Thought in Spain, 117–1740* (Liberty Fund, 2015), 96.

competition."[2] If "prophecies of doom" sounds like hyperbole, consider that Revelation 6:6 warns of hyperinflation that causes basic staples—"a quart of wheat" and "three quarts of barley"—to rise to a whole day's wages ("a denarius"). Grice-Hutchinson goes on to summarize the long-term results: After 1650, "Spain, to whom the conquest of the Indies might have brought lasting progress, entered a long period of economic stagnation."[3] In the meantime, however, during the "trade boom," "Spanish universities had come to occupy a foremost place among those of Europe. In particular, the University of Salamanca was famed for the brilliant teachers who were attracted to its chairs."[4]

## The School of Salamanca

FOUNDED BY FRANCISCO DE VITORIA, a notable defender of the rights and dignity of Native Americans against their mistreatment by Spanish colonists, the School of Salamanca has since been acknowledged as an important forerunner to the modern disciplines of economics and international law, among others. It is better to think of the School of Salamanca as a school of thought, however, as many figures associated with it taught elsewhere. What did these writers—all of whom were theologians, philosophers, and moralists—contribute to a more scientific understanding of economic life? This chapter will focus on their contributions to a better understanding of the nature of property, money, and lending, and how those contributions relate to Orthodox Christian social thought.

To begin with, these thinkers were Scholastics who wrote, in part, in the tradition of late ancient Celtic penitential manuals, advising confessors how best to care for merchants with troubled consciences. We should not think of Scholasticism as a philosophy but as a method of reasoned inquiry in which "Questions, Articles, Objections, Distinctions, Solutions, and Conclusions follow one another in dutiful procession, and the most trivial statements are supported by a heavy apparatus of citations,"[5] as Grice-Hutchinson notes. It

---

2    Grice-Hutchinson, *Early Economic Thought*, 96.
3    Grice-Hutchinson, 97.
4    Grice-Hutchinson, 97.
5    Grice-Hutchinson, 98.

still forms the basis for good academic writing today, in fact. The Scholastic method came to the West through its encounter with Muslim philosophers, such as Averroes and Avicenna, who also transmitted their knowledge of Aristotle, whose works had been largely lost in the West. Arabic translations of Aristotle's works—and for that matter the origins of the Scholastic method itself—came to the Muslims through Arab Christians. These Christians dominated the education professions in the Middle East and highly valued reasoned inquiry for the sake of their apologetics, scientific endeavors, and ecumenical relations. So how does it work?

Let's begin with the philosophical foundation: natural law. Natural law is rooted in the Scriptures and Greek philosophy, and virtually every Church Father, East and West, speaks of sin as "against nature" and virtue as living "according to nature."[6] By the sixteenth century in the West, in combination with their own peculiar intellectual development via Thomas Aquinas, natural law had come to take on some more specific meanings.[7] Relevant to our discussion here, John T. Noonan notes a distinction between primary and secondary natural law: "The natural law is unchangeable in its primary principles, though in its secondary principles it may be changed by being ignored or, on the other hand, by being developed."[8] Thus, for example, "Before the Fall, says William of Auxerre, nature indicated that property should be held commonly. After the Fall, in the present state of sin, nature permits private ownership."[9] This latter principle that "nature permits private ownership" is something nearly all legal systems, in various ways, have always acknowledged. "Private property is thus commanded by the *ius gentium* [the law of all peoples] or the secondary principles of natural law."[10] In this way, late

---

6    Stanley S. Harakas, *Toward Transfigured Life: The* Theoria *of Eastern Orthodox Ethics* (Light and Life Publishing, 1983); *Living the Faith: The* Praxis *of Eastern Orthodox Ethics* (Light and Life Publishing, 1992).

7    For historic, Orthodox Christian perspectives on Thomas Aquinas, see Marcus Plested, *Orthodox Readings of Aquinas* (Oxford University Press, 2012).

8    John T. Noonan, *The Scholastic Analysis of Usury* (Harvard University Press, 1957), 25.

9    Noonan, *Scholastic Analysis of Usury*, 29. It should be noted that for some, private property may even have a place in Paradise. See Francisco Suarez, "What Kind of Corporeal or Political Life Men Would Have Professed in a State of Innocence," *Journal of Markets & Morality* 15, no. 2 (2012): 543–563.

10   Noonan, 29.

Scholastic thinkers theologically and philosophically grounded their under-standing of private property.

## Inflation

WE VIVIDLY SEE THIS GROUNDING of natural law in the work of Juan de Mariana. Though one might expect some leniency for Mariana, given his advanced age, he faced the Inquisition for his 1609 *Treatise on the Alteration of Money*. The Vatican placed his book on the Index Expurgatorius, its list of banned books, because it criticized the rulers of his day. His work can teach us about the nature of inflation, both in terms of economics (how inflation works) and morality (why it is wrong deliberately to cause it).

In his treatise, Mariana grounds his discussion of inflation upon the moral duties rulers owe their citizens with respect to their property: "The private goods of citizens are not at the disposal of the king. Thus, he must not take all or part of them without the approval of those who have the right to them."[11] With this principle, he anticipates the rallying cry of the American Revolution—"No taxation without representation!"—by nearly two centuries: "New taxes should not be imposed on subjects without their free consent—not by force, curses, or threats."[12] Why? Because to do so is theft, which violates the natural law and, for that matter, the Law of God in the Ten Commandments.[13]

Mariana's treatise reveals that inflation didn't just come from the influx of new gold and silver to Spain. The king also had been debasing coins, minting new coins of less pure metal, in violation of the biblical injunction to "have a perfect and just weight, a perfect and just measure" (Deut. 25:15). To Mariana, this inflationary policy amounted to a tax imposed apart from the consent of the governed: "1,000 gold pieces of new money . . . will not be more useful for living than 800 previous ones. Therefore, people scarcely coping with previous

---

11   Juan de Mariana, *A Treatise on the Alteration of Money*, trans. Patrick T. Brannan (CLP Academic, 2011), 18.

12   Mariana, *Treatise on the Alteration of Money*, 17.

13   On the relation between these two for the Late Scholastics, see Noonan, *The Scholastic Analysis of Usury*, 26–27.

taxes will be oppressed by a new and very heavy one. Among those affected will be churches, monasteries, hospitals, gentlemen, and orphans—no one to be spared."[14]

Why does it work that way? Another Scholastic, Martín de Azpilcueta, gives further insight: "Money increases or decreases its value . . . when there is great lack or need. . . . It is worth more where and when there is a great lack of it than where there is a great abundance."[15] That is, as Alejandro Chafuen explains, "Nearly all the Late Scholastics shared the idea that the quantity of money is one of the main factors influencing its value."[16] Supply and demand determines the value of money. Where it is in "great abundance," people value it less. Where it is too scarce, they value it more. In the former case, people need more money to purchase something that would cost less in the latter. So, too, by this same principle we can explain why bottles of water cost less than yachts—water is abundant, but yachts are scarce.

This variability of money's value holds with regards to regional scarcity, as Azpilcueta notes, but also universally, as Chafuen notes: "Mariana formulated a principle that bears remarkable resemblance to what economists today call 'Gresham's Law'—bad money tends to drive out good money."[17] If the king mints more copper money without changing the coins' denomination and exchange rate, everyone will want the devalued copper currency for the brief period that it can buy them more than an equal amount of silver. But the effect will quickly be that merchants raise prices to adjust, thus devaluing money as a whole. This currency manipulation can be disastrous: "Commerce, when interfered with, is like milk that is so delicate that it is spoiled by the most gentle breeze. As a matter of fact, money," observed Mariana, "is the ultimate foundation of commerce. When it is altered, everything else resting upon it will necessarily collapse."[18]

---

14  Mariana, *Treatise on the Alteration of Money*, 85.
15  Martín de Azpilcueta, *On Exchange*, trans. Jeannine Emery (CLP Academic, 2014), 94.
16  Alejandro A. Chafuen, *Faith and Liberty: The Economic Thought of the Late Scholastics* (Lexington Books, 2003), 62.
17  Chafuen, *Faith and Liberty*, 67. Gresham's Law is named for Thomas Gresham, an English financier in the sixteenth century who criticized the debasing of English coins at the time.
18  Mariana, *Treatise on the Alteration of Money*, 85.

## Usury

THE LATE SCHOLASTICS INHERITED THEIR definition of money from Aristotle, as Grice-Hutchinson notes, "The idea of money as a medium of exchange, measure of value, and store of value . . . reappears constantly throughout their work."[19] This definition served them well, but another aspect of Aristotle's monetary theory did not: "Aristotle's dictum [that] Money does not beget money"[20] caused them to reject all interest on loans as sinful usury, notes Chafuen. Confusing the impersonal nature of the Law with the personal nature of the Gospel, they asked, did not Christ himself command, "lend, hoping for nothing in return" (Luke 6:35)?

Noonan notes, "The Third Lateran Council had excommunicated . . . men who had been convicted in a court of taking usury, or who were 'notorious by fact' by publicly setting themselves up to lend money at a profit."[21] On the one hand, Noonan continues to say that "the canon had the practical effect of excommunicating only the professional lenders who made usury their business," i.e., "pawnbrokers who made loans for consumption purposes to the poor at high rates: their usual charge was 43½ per cent per annum."[22] That certainly could have been sinful, exploitative usury, making it a serious concern for Christian social thought. Yet on the other hand, the economist Joseph Schumpeter notes that for the Scholastics usury "does not necessarily involve the exploitation of the needy: this element . . . was not a constituent of the scholastic concept of usury."[23] Why not?

The Scholastics' intellectual struggle came down to Aristotle's definition of money as fundamentally unfruitful in itself. And, indeed, the word *usury* does simply originate as a term for interest. But it was not the only term in Hebrew, Greek, or Latin,[24] and in our time we helpfully tend to differentiate between interest as a neutral term and usury as a sinful kind of interest. That said, the

19   Grice-Hutchinson, *Early Economic Thought in Spain*, 108.
20   Chafuen, *Faith and Liberty*, 122.
21   Noonan, *Scholastic Analysis of Usury*, 34.
22   Noonan, 34.
23   Joseph A. Schumpeter, *A History of Economic Analysis*, ed. Elizabeth Boody Schumpeter (George Allen & Unwin Ltd; Oxford University Press, 1954), 103.
24   On some of these terms, especially the Hebrew, see the Lutheran Scholastic Johann Gerhard, "On Interest and Usury," *Journal of Markets & Morality* 22, no. 2 (2019): 557–596.

Scholastics' natural law concern in this case was not primarily the violation of *human* nature through vice but the violation of the nature of *money*, which would be irrational and only in that sense vicious.

## Giving Credit Its Due

SO HOW DID THESE GREAT minds in the West escape what would seem to be an intractable problem? Commerce needs credit to function, and commerce had exploded upon the discovery of the Americas, but credit would be too scarce apart from interest. Pious merchants, worried over the salvation of their souls, came to confessors for guidance. Surely they could not leave their families starving and homeless. But in order to work their trade they needed credit. Some of them even made lending itself their trade. Were they literally damned if they did and damned if they didn't?

First, the Scholastics had help from the East, inasmuch as the rediscovery of the Justinian *Code* in the Middle Ages in the West birthed an abundant legal commentary tradition they could draw from. Chafuen explains, "Scholastic authors agreed with Roman lawyers that [certain] extrinsic titles . . . could justify an interest payment to a lender. *Damnum emergens* ['resulting harm'] provides that the lender is entitled to ask the borrower for compensation whenever he incurs losses due to the loan. According to *lucrum cessans* ['loss of benefit'], the lender may ask the borrower to compensate him for the gain he forgoes by not investing his money elsewhere."[25] They also agreed that tardy repayment could justify interest.

These categories helped Western Scholastics distinguish between legitimate payment beyond the principal of a loan and usury. Again, for some this was a matter of their livelihoods, as Luis de Molina even noted a relation between lending at interest and inflation that results in losses to lenders: "The one who when lending foresees that later he will have to buy at a higher price whatever he needs for his family, may agree to an increment equivalent to that loss."[26] That is, if money tomorrow won't buy as much as money today, in order to be repaid in full lenders may ask for compensation for the value that will be

---

25    Chafuen, *Faith and Liberty*, 120.
26    Luis de Molina, *A Treatise on Money*, trans. Jeannine Emery (CLP Academic, 2015), 132.

lost to inflation. Thus, we should also regard interest that does not exceed the rate of inflation to be okay.

Cardinal Thomas Cajetan even noted that while one could not charge for the use of money or time (which, it was thought, is the common property of all), one could hope for a gift of gratitude—and in fact God demanded gratitude. Thus, the difference between usury and licit interest came down to the intentions of the lender: "Either such a lender hopes for something beyond the capital from his end [and] is thus committing usury, or he hopes for something from the friendly affection of the person to whom he makes the loan and thus does not sin."[27] While perhaps such "friendly affection" couldn't be written into a contract and enforced by law, it could be expected based upon custom and enforced through social pressures.

Many Protestant authors, representing a similar spectrum of opinions, also wrote commentaries on usury. One of them, in particular, usually and rightly receives some notable credit for advancing the discussion: John Calvin. According to Bernard W. Dempsey (again, using usury to mean all interest), "The idea of John Calvin, Charles du Moulin, and Claude de Saumaise that usury was not evil in itself but only in its excess, was not new, having been a standard textbook objection since the days when the Albigensian heretics had been answered by Antoninus; and the same view had been held by the Greek schismatics,"[28] i.e., we Orthodox.

What did Calvin say? First of all, he rejected Aristotle's definition of usury: "Who doubts that idle money is wholly useless? Who asks a loan of me does not intend to keep what he receives idle by him. Therefore the profit does not arise from that money, but from the produce that results from its use, or employment."[29] Indeed, Calvin, commenting on Luke 6:36, rightly notes that "while [Christ] would command loans to the poor without expectation of repayment or the receipt of interest, he did not mean at the same

---

27 Thomas Cajetan, *On Exchange and Usury*, trans. Patrick J. Brannan (CLP Academic, 2014), 74.

28 Bernard W. Dempsey, *Interest and Usury* (Dennis Dobson, Ltd., 1948), 114–115.

29 John Calvin, *De Usuris Responsum*, in *Usury Laws: Their Nature, Expediency, and Influence—Opinions of Jeremy Bentham and John Calvin, with Review of the Existing Situation and Recent Experience of the United States by Richard H. Dana, David A. Wells, and Others* (The Society for Political Education, 1881), 35–36.

time to forbid loans being made to the rich with interest; any more than in the injunction to invite the poor to our feasts, he did not imply that the mutual invitation of friends to feasts is in consequence to be prohibited"[30] (see Luke 14:15–24).

We might think, for example, of the parable of the talents, where the rich master scolds his steward for failing to lend his talent at interest to the banker (see Matt. 25:14–30)—neither party to the loan would be poor in that case. However, Calvin does not, for this, therefore think that all lending at interest should be allowed: "If all usury is condemned, tighter fetters are imposed on the conscience than the Lord himself would wish. Or if you yield in the least, with that pretext very many will at once seize upon unlicensed freedom."[31] He even goes so far as to confirm the common prejudice of his time in saying, "It is very rare for the same man to be honest and yet be a usurer."[32] It would take another two centuries for harmful taboos around merchants and moneylenders—often simply a product of aristocratic scorn more than dispassionate observation—to dissipate.

## An Orthodox Assessment

REFLECTING ON THE ECONOMIC CONTRIBUTION of the Late Scholastics in the West, Schumpeter lamented, "The Eastern [Roman] Empire survived the Western for another thousand years, kept going by the most interesting and most successful bureaucracy the world has ever seen. Many of the men who shaped policies in the offices of the Byzantine emperors were of the intellectual cream of their times. They dealt with a host of legal, monetary, commercial, agrarian, and fiscal problems. We cannot help feeling that they must have philosophized about them. If they did, however, the results have been lost."[33] I'm not so sure that such Eastern reflection doesn't exist, though, simply untranslated and overlooked. But even if he's right, I don't think it is fair to say the Orthodox didn't make any important contributions.

---

30  Calvin, *De Usuris Responsum*, 33–34.
31  Calvin, 33.
32  Calvin, 34.
33  Schumpeter, *History of Economic Analysis*, 73.

To the extent Schumpeter is right, Grice-Hutchinson's account of Spain gives us an explanation for this apparent silence. The Spanish economy experienced such a sudden transformation that theologians there could not ignore it. Their literature then spread throughout the Latin academy more broadly, across Western Europe. Meanwhile, the Turks conquered Constantinople in 1453, and Peter Mohyla and his monastic brotherhood wouldn't found his Academy in Kiev until 1615. Furthermore, the Christian East did not experience these same economic problems in any comparable way, so naturally we shouldn't expect Orthodox Christians to have spent as much time reflecting on them.

That said, as already noted, the Scholastic method itself owes a debt to Middle Eastern Christians, including Orthodox Melkites like St. John of Damascus, Theodore Abu Qurra, and Abdallah ibn al-Fadl al-Antaki, among others. The very intellectual method and tools used in the West to adapt their Christian social thought to changing times owe a debt to the Christian East, even if only indirectly. And many medieval Orthodox theologians in Byzantium were themselves Scholastics and did, in fact, think through similar topics. Juan de Mariana's defense of citizens' property rights, for example, resonates with St. Nicholas Cabasilas's defense of monastic property in the fourteenth century.[34] Mariana may not have read Cabasilas—although he was very well-read—but his insights are broadly Christian, not limited to early modern Spain. Being Western doesn't make his contributions un-Orthodox.

As for the Late Scholastic treatment of usury, Grice-Hutchinson notes (unhelpfully using the term *usury* to mean any interest), "The canon law of the eastern Church did not forbid usury. A widely-used Syrian code of the late fifth or early sixth century allows usury on loans of corn up to a maximum rate of 25 percent a year, and on loans of money up to 1 percent monthly."[35] She concludes, "The Emperor Justinian, therefore ... was acting in harmony with the rules of the eastern Church in drawing up a series of enactments that regulated but did not forbid usury."[36] And, of course, we've already seen in

---

34 "Nicholas Cabasilas," in *From Irenaeus to Grotius: A Sourcebook in Christian Political Thought*, ed. Oliver O'Donovan and Joan Lockwood O'Donovan (Eerdmans, 1999).

35 Grice-Hutchinson, *Early Economic Thought in Spain*, 21.

36 Grice-Hutchinson, 21.

chapter 23 that this was also the case among the Orthodox of the medieval Rus', who were building upon the legal heritage of Byzantium. Without Aristotle's understanding of money, no comparable intellectual controversy over lending happened in the East.

Indeed, while the Fathers have harsh words for moneylenders in their homilies, in the context of canon and civil law in Byzantium, Grice-Hutchinson is correct to say that "as a general rule, the fathers wrote with the indignation of moralists, not the objectivity of legislators."[37] Again and again, the Fathers primarily concern themselves not with the nature of money as such, like Aristotle, but specifically with "the exploitation of the needy,"[38] in contrast to Western Scholastics.

To be fair, however, in response to dramatic economic changes, Western theologians carefully and faithfully engaged the new problems of their day, overcoming such obstacles within their own tradition. "The economics of the [Scholastic] doctors," wrote Schumpeter, with only a dash of hyperbole, "absorbed all the phenomena of nascent capitalism and, in consequence . . . served so well as a basis of the analytic work of their successors, not excluding A[dam] Smith."[39] In 1600, the world had just begun to get richer. By 1800, the growth rate of global wealth, beginning in Western Europe, would reach an inflection point from which humanity has never returned. What insights coincided with and contributed to that? And how should we Orthodox Christians understand them? The answer begins in the next chapter with Adam Smith.

---

37  Grice-Hutchinson, 21.
38  Schumpeter, *History of Economic Analysis*, 103.
39  Schumpeter, 94.

CHAPTER 27

# Adam Smith

I N THE 2000 CULT CLASSIC film *High Fidelity*, Rob (John Cusack) describes what makes a good date: "What really matters is *what* you like, not what you *are* like."[1] Of course, as Christians, we should care what people *are* like more than *what* they like, but the point stands that the convergence of our sentiments plays an important role in our relationships. As C. S. Lewis put it, "The typical expression of opening Friendship would be something like, 'What? You too? I thought I was the only one.'"[2]

At the dawn of our contemporary world, one moral philosopher spent an inordinate amount of time dissecting precisely how "what you like" relates to "what you are like": Adam Smith. "According to Smith," writes Eric Schliesser, "our senses have some structure of the external world built into their normal functioning from the start."[3] In Smith's work, we find a method for discovering God's inner architecture of social life. And without a basic understanding of his work, we cannot ever hope to apply the timeless insights of Orthodox Christian social thought to our economic life today. Smith will help us understand the origins of both moral culture and material wealth, as well as the role of the state in ensuring justice and what

---

1    *High Fidelity*, directed by Stephen Frears (Buena Vista Pictures Distribution, 2000), 113 min.
2    C. S. Lewis, *The Four Loves* (Geoffrey Bles, 1960), 77.
3    Eric Schliesser, *Adam Smith: Systematic Philosopher and Public Thinker* (Oxford University Press, 2017), 57.

social distortions happen when the state goes too far beyond that limited vocation.

## Smith vs. the Mercantilists

NEARLY TWO HUNDRED YEARS PASSED between the Late Scholastics and Smith. In the meantime, social taboos against merchants greatly diminished due in part to the rise of mercantilism.[4] With the discovery of the Americas, European commerce exploded. Concurrently, warring European powers after the Protestant Reformation reached an uneasy settlement in the Peace of Westphalia in 1648, roughly marking the birth of the modern nation state. Thus, merchants, desiring to benefit from international trade, balanced that desire against national interests. They urged statesmen to guard the "balance of trade," which according to Douglas A. Irwin consisted of minimal tariffs on natural resources and high tariffs on things manufactured in other countries.[5]

As the Scots mercantilist James Steuart put it in 1767, their reasoning went like this: "The balance of [domestic] work and [foreign] demand promotes the foreign and domestic interests of a nation, equally. The *first*, by advancing her power and superiority abroad; the *last*, by keeping every one employed and subsisted at home."[6] Thus, he promoted subsidies on domestic production alongside tariffs and prohibitions on foreign imports for the purpose, as he saw it, of protecting domestic manufacturing jobs.[7] Steuart wrote for shrewd statesmen, who would assign populations to different employments, encourage good habits, and pull the levers of commercial policy in order to "play against one another as if they were playing at chess."[8]

By contrast, in the sixth and final edition of Adam Smith's *Theory of Moral Sentiments* (which we'll call "TMS" for short), published in 1790,[9] he adds the

---

4  Douglas A. Irwin, *Against the Tide: An Intellectual History of Free Trade* (Princeton University Press, 1996), 28–29.
5  Irwin, *Against the Tide*, 39.
6  James Steuart, *An Inquiry into the Principles of Political Œconomy: Being an Essay on the Science of Domestic Policy in Free Nations*, 2 vols. (A. Miller and T. Cadell, 1767), 1:493.
7  Steuart, *Principles*, 505.
8  Steuart, 494.
9  The first edition was published in 1759.

following warning about the statesman he calls a "man of system," who "seems to imagine that he can arrange the different members of a great society with as much ease as the hand arranges the different pieces upon a chess-board." However, "in the great chess-board of human society, every single piece has a principle of motion of its own, altogether different from that which the legislature might choose to impress upon it."[10] The attempt to play chess by social and economic engineering is *foolish*, because each person is naturally free and unpredictable, and *immoral*, because to ignore that freedom violates the rules of justice.

As noted, this passage comes from Smith's TMS, not his *Wealth of Nations* (which we'll call "WN"). Why might he have added it to his work on morality instead of his work on economics? What did Smith think he was doing in his overall intellectual project that might connect the two?

## *Smith's Social Science*

WHILE THE LATE SCHOLASTICS BUILT on natural law in their economic investigations, James Otteson notes, "Adam Smith did not advocate or rely on a theory of natural law or natural rights."[11] However, Smith does care about what is "natural," and as we'll see, he does think that matters for morality. But instead of deduction from natural law principles, Smith sought to discover laws of nature through inductive investigation, inspired by Isaac Newton's approach to the physical sciences.[12] What did he discover? The logic and components of spontaneous order.[13]

---

10  Adam Smith, *The Theory of Moral Sentiments*, 6th ed., 6.2.2, in *The Theory of Moral Sentiments; or, An Essay towards an Analysis of the Principles by Which Men Naturally Judge Concerning the Conduct and Character, First of Their Neighbours, and Afterwards of Themselves. To Which Is Added, A Dissertation on the Origin of Languages*, new ed. (Henry G. Bohn, 1853), 342–343. Henceforth, TMS. On the sixth edition, see Erik Matson, "A Brief History of the Editions of TMS, Part 2," *Adam Smith Works*, December 4, 2020, https://www.adamsmithworks.org/documents/erik-matson-brief-history-of-the-editions-of-tms-part-2.
11  James Otteson, *The Essential Adam Smith* (Fraser Institute, 2018), 58.
12  Otteson, *The Essential Adam Smith*, 13.
13  For the Scottish Enlightenment background to Smith's understanding of spontaneous or emergent order, as well as self-love and interest, see Orlando Samões, "On Seeing

In his book expounding the Orthodox social principle of sobornost', S. L. Frank observed, "All that is generally accepted in society, e.g., mores, habits, fashions, even law . . . and the prices of goods . . . exists without any special contract or agreement, appears 'spontaneously' in some manner and not as the consciously set goal of the general will."[14] Smith used his Newtonian method to write about all of these phenomena. Building upon the work of Otteson,[15] we can summarize Smith's contribution in TMS and WN in Table 27.1:

### Table 27.1: Adam Smith's Social Science

|  | TMS | WN |
|---|---|---|
| **Motivating Desire** | Mutual Sympathy to Be Loved and Lovely | Truck, Barter, and Exchange to Better One's Condition |
| **Rules Developed** | Justice, Propriety, and Merit (Exchange of Sentiments) | Justice, Bargaining (Economic Exchange) |
| **Local Knowledge** | Beneficence, Discovered Through Sympathy | Self-Love or Interest, Discovered Through Sympathy |
| **Currency** | Sentiments and Judgments | Money, Goods, and Services (Product of Labor) |
| **Unintended Order** | Common Moral Culture | Economy (Division of Labor) |
| **Feedback Mechanism** | Interaction with Others Produces Impartial Spectator/Conscience | Interaction with Others Produces Market Price |

---

Invisible Hands: Adam Smith's Benevolence and Self-Love," *Journal of Markets & Morality* 25, no. 2 (2022): 217–236.

14   S. L. Frank, *The Spiritual Foundations of Society* (Ohio University Press, 1987), 36.

15   See Otteson, *The Essential Adam Smith*, 31–32; James R. Otteson, *Adam Smith's Marketplace of Life* (Cambridge University Press, 2002), 286–287.

In the rest of this chapter, I will explain these terms so that this table can serve as a handy reference. While I encourage everyone to read Smith, he admits regarding his own writing style, "I am always willing to run some hazard of being tedious" for the sake of clarity.[16] This table effectively cuts through the tedium.

## Motivating Desire

IN TMS, SMITH BEGINS, "HOW selfish soever man may be supposed, there are evidently some principles in his nature, which interest him in the fortune of others, and render their happiness necessary to him, though he derives nothing from it, except the pleasure of seeing it."[17] He next focuses on the "pleasure of mutual sympathy." "Sympathy, for Smith," says one Smith scholar, "was ... a mechanism for moral judgment that allowed the agent to judge the appropriateness of all behavior."[18] According to another, for Smith "sympathy is put to work by an even more fundamental principle in human nature, the desire to agree."[19] Smith spends pages on propriety, i.e., polite behavior. In learning to be polite, we learn to adjust our behavior to others'. We do this because "man naturally desires, not only to be loved, but to be lovely; or to be that thing which is the natural and proper object of love."[20] Or as Theodore Abu Qurra put it, "Each of us desires ... to love all and be loved by all."[21]

Smith sees a similar phenomenon in economics. In WN, Smith begins, "The greatest improvement in the productive powers of labour ... seem to have been the effects of the division of labour."[22] He illustrates this with the

---

16  Adam Smith, *An Inquiry into the Nature and Causes of the Wealth of Nations*, 5th ed., 2 vols. (Methuen & Co., 1904), 1.1.4, 31. Henceforth, WN.

17  Smith, TMS, 1.1.1, 3.

18  Pratap Bhanu Mehta, "Self-Interest and Other Interests," in *The Cambridge Companion to Adam Smith*, ed. Knud Haakonssen (Cambridge University Press, 2006), 246.

19  Knud Haakonssen, *The Science of a Legislator: The Natural Jurisprudence of David Hume and Adam Smith* (Cambridge University Press, 1981), 49.

20  Smith, TMS, 3.2, 166.

21  "Theodore Abu Qurra," trans. John C. Lamoreaux, in *The Orthodox Church in the Arab World, 700–1700: An Anthology of Sources*, ed. Samuel Noble and Alexander Treiger (Northern Illinois University Press, 2014) 80.

22  Smith, WN, 1.1.1, 5.

example of the pin factory, in which, by dividing the steps of pin-making into different tasks, "ten persons . . . could make among them upwards of forty-eight thousand pins in a day. . . . But if they had all wrought separately and independently . . . they certainly could not each of them have made twenty, perhaps not one pin in a day."[23] He next surmises, "As it is by treaty, by barter, and by purchase, that we obtain from one another the greater part of those mutual good offices which we stand in need of, so it is this same trucking disposition which originally gives occasion to the division of labour."[24] Thus, the division of labor comes from our desire to better our condition, just as moral culture comes from the desire to love and be loved.

## *Rules Developed*

IN TMS, SMITH OUTLINES GENERAL rules of justice, as well as propriety and merit, whereby society takes its moral shape. He defines justice as protection of what Otteson calls the "3 Ps"[25]: persons, property, and promises (e.g., contracts). In the 3 Ps, justice dictates that we don't harm one another, and that doing so merits the censure of law and state punishment. As such, it constitutes a largely "negative virtue,"[26] embodying what some call the "Silver Rule" that can be found across religions: "What you hate, do not do to anyone" (Tobit 4:15, NRSVCE). Smith calls justice "sacred"[27] and insists, "Justice . . . is the main pillar that upholds the whole edifice"[28] of society. Beyond justice, Smith also notes that through seeking mutual sympathy, we quickly discover rules of appropriate conduct: "A man is mortified when . . . he looks round and sees that nobody laughs at his jests but himself."[29] Similarly, we learn certain acts are virtuous and thus praiseworthy, while others are vicious and blameworthy.

---

23   Smith, WN, 1.1.1, 7.
24   Smith, WN, 1.1.2, 17.
25   Otteson, *The Essential Adam Smith*, 21.
26   Smith, TMS, 2.2.1, 117.
27   Smith, TMS, 2.2.2, 119.
28   Smith, TMS, 2.2.2, 125.
29   Smith, TMS, 1.1.2, 10.

In WN, we see the fundamental place of the rules of justice in Smith's rejection of mercantilism: "All systems either of preference or of restraint . . . being thus completely taken away, the obvious and simple system of natural liberty establishes itself of its own accord." What is this system? "Every man, *as long as he does not violate the laws of justice,* is left perfectly free to pursue his own interest his own way, and to bring both his industry and capital into competition with those of any other man, or order of men."[30] Rather than playing chess with people's livelihoods, the state ought to protect them from foreign invasion (military), harm to one another (police and courts), and provide basic public works that would be unprofitable for private enterprises,[31] such as subsidizing primary education.[32] Moreover, in the "system of natural liberty," exchanges have their own natural rule of bargaining: "Give me that which I want, and you shall have this which you want."[33]

## Local Knowledge

In TMS, BENEFICENCE ("DOING GOOD") largely cannot be legislated because its specific demands can only be known through local knowledge. As Otteson put it, "Without detailed knowledge of the specific situations of both the recipient and the giver, we cannot know what beneficence requires. . . . Smith argues that beneficence should properly be left not to government but rather to individuals on the basis of their localized knowledge and individual judgment."[34] Thus, Smith claims, "Beneficence is always free, it cannot be extorted by force."[35] Unlike justice, beneficence is a positive virtue, "meaning that to fulfill it we must engage in positive action to improve others' situations."[36] Basically, it's the Golden Rule: "As you want men to do to you, you also do to them" (Luke 6:31). Nevertheless, Smith does admit that states should enforce some general duties of beneficence: "The laws of all civilized

---

30 Smith, WN, 2.4.9, 184, emphasis added.
31 Smith, WN, 2.4.8, 185.
32 For a discussion of this, see Otteson, *The Essential Adam Smith,* 64.
33 Smith, WN, 1.1.2, 16.
34 Otteson, *The Essential Adam Smith,* 22.
35 Smith, TMS, 2.2.1, 112.
36 Otteson, *The Essential Adam Smith,* 21.

nations oblige parents to maintain their children, and children to maintain their parents, and . . . many other duties of beneficence." Yet he cautions, "Of all the duties of a lawgiver, however, this . . . requires the greatest delicacy and reserve."[37] Parenting and elder care constitute a gray area for Smith since while neglect doesn't actively harm a child or elder, it does passively harm them. Children and infirm elders cannot provide for their own needs. Unlike the butcher, brewer, and baker, they actually do require what they "stand in need of . . . from the benevolence"[38] of others.

In WN, Smith similarly notes the local nature of knowledge of others' "self-love" or "interest." However, self-love doesn't mean selfishness (think of Lev. 19:18: "You shall love your neighbor *as yourself*"). Rather, Smith shows how we must concern ourselves with others—again as a matter of sympathy. As Erik Matson put it, "Habitual sympathy . . . engenders knowledge of circumstance."[39] Smith observed, "Man has almost constant occasion for the help of his brethren, and it is in vain for him to expect it from their benevolence only. He will be more likely to prevail if he can interest their self-love in his favour, and shew them that it is for their own advantage to do for him what he requires of them."[40] Smith argues against the mercantilists' economic policies not just because they are unjust, but because they are ultimately *impossible*. "Too often, legislators or others presume to know best how interests are to be served," one Smith scholar summarizes. "In attacking that presumption, Smith . . . is arguing that relevant agents be allowed to judge their own interests rather than having them judged by the powerful who . . . are likely to be guided by *their* interests."[41] Indeed, throughout WN, as Schliesser notes, Smith "is concerned with institutions that improve the lot of the working poor."[42] As Otteson reminds us, "Pharaohs, emperors, kings, and aristocrats

---

37 Smith, TMS, 2.2.1, 116.
38 Smith, WN, 1.1.2, 16.
39 Erik W. Matson, "The Edifying Discourses of Adam Smith: Focalism, Commerce, and Serving the Common Good," *Journal of the History of Economic Thought* 45, no. 2 (June 2023): 312.
40 Smith, WN, 1.1.2, 16.
41 Mehta, "Self-Interest and Other Interests," 251. See also Otteson, *The Essential Adam Smith*, 41.
42 Schliesser, *Adam Smith*, 193.

have long been able to take care of themselves," but "Smith is worried instead about the everyday common man,"[43] who, Smith presumes, understands his own needs better than anyone else.

## Currency

IN TMS, OUR SENTIMENTS AND judgments play the role of currency, or we might say, they are the "means of communication." Smith observes, "How are the unfortunate relieved when they have found out a person to whom they can communicate the cause of their sorrow! Upon his sympathy they seem to disburden themselves of a part of their distress: *he is not improperly said to share it with them.*"[44] For Smith, "this continuous exchange . . . underlies all human culture."[45]

In WN, the currency is, of course, money, as well as goods and services: "The butcher seldom carries his beef or his mutton to the baker, or the brewer, in order to exchange them for bread or for beer; but he carries them to the market, where he exchanges them for money, and afterwards exchanges that money for bread and for beer."[46] However, all of these, to Smith, ultimately represent something else: labor. Specifically, what we get from our labor is then exchanged for the products of the labor of others in order to meet our needs while thereby meeting theirs.

## Unintended Order

IN TMS, THE RESULT OF people's striving to love and be loved, and conversely to judge and avoid judgment, is their moral culture. Many have differed in their opinion of Smith's theology,[47] but we can at least say he attributes the resulting unintended system of order to the wise intentions of our Creator: "When by natural principles we are led to advance those ends which

43  Otteson, *The Essential Adam Smith*, 38.
44  Smith, TMS, 1.1.2, 12, emphasis added.
45  Haakonssen, *The Science of the Legislator*, 49.
46  Smith, WN, 1.1.5, 34.
47  For a variety of perspectives, see Paul Oslington, ed., *Adam Smith as Theologian* (Routledge, 2011).

a refined and enlightened reason would recommend to us, we are very apt . . . to imagine that to be, the wisdom of man, which in reality is the wisdom of God."[48] Schliesser even supplies a Christological passage from earlier versions of TMS: "The doctrines of revelation coincide, in every respect, with those original anticipations of nature; and, as they teach us how little we can depend upon the imperfection of our own virtue, so they show us . . . that the most powerful intercession has been made, and that the most dreadful atonement has been paid for our manifold transgressions and iniquities."[49] Whatever Smith's doctrine, we can say he believed nature demonstrates God's wisdom and draws us to live out His designs for our flourishing, including how to live morally upright lives.

We see this again in WN, where Smith highlights the emergence of the division of labor: "This division of labour . . . is not originally the effect of any human wisdom, which foresees and intends that general opulence to which it gives occasion. It is the necessary, though very slow and gradual, consequence of a certain propensity in human nature which has in view no such extensive utility; the propensity to truck, barter, and exchange."[50] As greater and greater specialization within a business leads to greater production and, thus, greater "opulence" for all, so also through exchange, we extend the division of labor—and its resulting "opulence"—throughout society between enterprises, even between nations. Thus, with the exception of national security concerns, Smith supported free trade. By contrast, "In the lone houses and very small villages which are scattered about in so desert a country as the Highlands of Scotland, every farmer must be butcher, baker and brewer for his own family."[51] Everything the solitary highlander's family needs must be the product of his own labor, and thus his life will be hard and poor. Far from

---

48    Smith, TMS, 2.2.3, 126–127.
49    Quoted in Schliesser, *Adam Smith*, 341. On theological differences between the editions of TMS, see Erik W. Matson, "God, Commerce, and Adam Smith through the Editions of *The Theory of Moral Sentiments*," *Journal of Markets & Morality* 24, no. 2 (2021): 269–288. Otteson notably claims, "Smith was apparently a Christian and hence seemed to believe both that God created us and that He intends for us to be happy." Otteson, *The Essential Adam Smith*, 29. Others, like Schliesser, think Smith was a deist rather than a Christian.
50    Smith, WN, 1.1.2, 15.
51    Smith, WN, 1.1.3, 19.

individualism,[52] Smith thinks we are radically dependent upon one another, both morally and economically.

## Feedback Mechanism

IN TMS, SMITH NOTES THAT through others' reactions to our own conduct, we eventually abstract the image of a wholly "impartial spectator," a "man within the breast," i.e., our conscience, that checks our behavior, even when no one else is around. "These natural pangs of an affrighted conscience are the demons, the avenging furies, which, in this life, haunt the guilty, which allow them neither quiet nor repose,"[53] says Smith. Of course, we might rightly object that the conscience is *more than* the echo of society, and that demons are *more than* a guilty conscience. Smith may, at times, confuse how we come to know something with *what* something actually is. Nevertheless, we do agree that people have consciences and are tormented by demons. Moreover, we can also agree with Smith that "The All-Wise Author of Nature . . . has made man . . . the immediate judge of mankind; and has in this respect, as in many others, created him after his own image . . . to superintend the behaviour of his brethren."[54] Thus, the "man within the breast" reflects not just the echo of society but the image of God within every human being. In this way, whenever we act, our consciences give us moral feedback.

In WN, the market price, discovered from the bargaining of buyers and sellers, serves as a feedback mechanism. Smith contrasts this with the "natural price," which is essentially the total *cost* of labor, land, and capital ("stock") of any given product. The market price is what others are willing to pay for it: "If at any time [supply] exceeds the effectual demand, some of the component parts of its price must be paid below their natural rate."[55] As a result, just as the judgments of the impartial spectator correct our moral behavior, prices correct

---

52  This charge is often brought against Smith by people who, I must assume, rely too heavily on secondary sources rather than on Smith's actual words. See, e.g., Christos Yannaras, *The Inhumanity of Right*, trans. Norman Russell (James Clarke & Co., 2021), 40.

53  Smith, TMS, 3.2, 173.

54  Smith, TMS, 3.2, 185.

55  Smith, WN, 1.1.7, 59.

economic behavior. If a product's price is too high, no one will buy it. Either the price must be lowered, or if it can't without loss, people will divert their resources—land, labor, and capital—to a product that will profit them. No mercantilist chess master needed! "The All-Wise Author of Nature" has providentially designed us to respond to market prices and economize on our resources, creating new wealth and providing for one another through exchange.

## *An Orthodox Assessment*

FROM OUR ORTHODOX PERSPECTIVE, I find it significant that Smith distinguishes in his two major works between three social spaces and standards: law, which ensures justice; markets, through which we better our conditions; and private beneficence, through which we care for those unable to care for themselves. Law works through fear of punishment. Markets work through hope of reward. And beneficence works through mercy and love. Earlier in this book, in discussing the perfection of the Gospel in chapter 12, I noted what the Fathers call three "different stages of perfection"[56]—the slave, the steward, and the son—who each obey God from these same motivations, respectively. But each, being grounded in worldly imagery, also tells us something about our social life that augments Smith's analysis.

We need law and government, but if the state swallows up the whole of society, that totalitarian society becomes despotism—the rule of "masters" (despots) over slaves. We need economic exchange to provide for our needs and the needs of others. But some of the most meaningful relationships in our lives—family, friendships, Church—would be degraded if reduced to contracts and calculations. Nor do we want a government that runs on bribes. Last, we need beneficence and love in our communities, families, and friendships, but we don't want nepotism (rule by family connection) in government or cronyism (government privilege for friends of politicians) in our economies.

Knowing love to be the highest motivation, we should prioritize what can be done through beneficence. What can't be accomplished through beneficence, we should do through the next highest stage: exchange. What remaining social

---

56   John Cassian, *Conferences*, 11.12, in *NPNF*² 11:420.

good can't be accomplished through beneficence or exchange must be done by the state. Otherwise, as Smith notes, society would have no foundation of justice on which to build. Thus, this biblical and ascetic tradition in Orthodox social thought could further enlighten Smith's "system of natural liberty."

But why should we want to do that? In the years since Adam Smith, many of his insights have been put into practice. What has been the result? According to development economist Amartya Sen, "The big divergence in prosperity between the rich and the poor countries of the world gathered momentum in the nineteenth century. This largely happened *after* Smith—and the development strategies that were pursued followed principles and policies on which Smith had thrown pioneering light."[57] But that's not all. Not only has wealth increased, but poverty has decreased. According to Otteson (writing in 2018), "We have gone from 75 percent of the world living in extreme poverty, to just 9 percent. . . . Since just 1970, the proportion of the world's population living at humanity's historical norm of between $1 and $3 per person per day has dwindled from 27 per cent of the population to today, for the first time in history, below 5 percent. . . . And those countries that have most closely approximated Smithian political economy have done best."[58] I cannot overstress this point: For most of human history, global wealth remained nearly flat until 1600, and only really took off around 1800. The vast majority of people suffered in poverty, if not also from oppression as slaves, serfs, or indentured servants. When communities, societies, cities, states, and nations even partially give Smith's "obvious and simple system of natural liberty" a chance, more hungry are fed, more naked are clothed, more homeless are housed, and according to Adam Smith, that is a testament to the reflection of divine Wisdom in human nature. If we hope to do these things anywhere today (as we should), we ought to incorporate Smith's insights into our understanding of Orthodox Christian social thought.

But if all this happened *after* Smith, who first put his ideas into practice? The answer is classical political economists. The next chapter tells their story.

---

57  Amartya Sen, "Adam Smith and Economic Development," in *Adam Smith: His Life, Thought, and Legacy,* ed. Ryan Patrick Hanley (Princeton University Press, 2016), 282.

58  Otteson, *The Essential Adam Smith,* 69.

CHAPTER 28

# Classical Political Economy

IN AN EPISODE OF STAR *Trek: Deep Space Nine*,[1] Jake Sisko (Cirroc Lofton) and Nog (Aron Eisenberg) overhear a conversation between Nog's enterprising uncle Quark (Armin Shimerman) and his employee who forgot to cancel an order for "yamok sauce." "Now what am I supposed to do with five thousand wrappages of Cardassian yamok sauce?" asks Quark. Quark and Nog are Ferengi, aliens whose culture comedically caricatures modern capitalism: They value profit above all else, especially "gold-pressed latinum." Nog's entrepreneurial, Ferengi instincts alert him to opportunity: "Five thousand wrappages. That's a lot of yamok sauce. . . . It'd be a shame to let it to go to waste." Soon the two boys go off on an adventure, trading yamok sauce for "self-sealing stem bolts," and the stem-bolts for a plot of land on the nearby planet Bajor. Finally, when Quark hears the Bajoran government needs the land to build a reclamation facility, Nog confesses to trading Quark's merchandise for the land, and they finally earn the profit Nog wanted.

The episode illustrates one contribution of the classical political economists: Say's Law. Named for Jean-Baptiste Say, the short version is that supply creates its own demand, that a truly useful product, in the hands of enterprising people, will empower them to demand products from others. Say observed that "the mere circumstance of the creation of one product immediately

---

1   *Star Trek: Deep Space Nine*, season 1, episode 15, "Progress," directed by Les Landau, written by Peter Allan Fields, aired May 10, 1993, in syndication.

opens a vent for other products"[2] and acknowledged that people also create economic value through exchange: The profit of one party does not require a loss by another. Adam Smith distinguished between productive and unproductive labor, implying that only manual laborers producing products created economic value. Say improved on Smith by rejecting that distinction: "The labour of the philosopher, whether experimental or literary, is productive; the labour of the adventurer [*entrepreneur*] or master-manufacturer is productive, although he perform no actual manual work."[3]

Say even coined a new term: *entrepreneur*, which his translator gives as "adventurer," above. The entrepreneur identifies overlooked opportunities to connect supply and demand, either creating a new product or, like Jake and Nog, creating value through exchange, because a quality product really will find a market. Say describes entrepreneurship in terms resembling the Protestant work ethic: "This kind of labour requires a combination of moral qualities, that are not often found together. Judgment, perseverance, and a knowledge of the world, as well as of business."[4] Entrepreneurs employ these virtues in taking risks to create previously unimagined value for the world. Sometimes they fail—and Say thought they should not be protected from failing—but when they succeed, the benefits far exceed their own material or individual profit.

Thus, Say and the other classical economists implemented Smith's vision for the sake of alleviating poverty, while also contributing their own insights. Though they achieved some positive results, such as the repeal of the 1815 Corn Law, their revision of the Elizabethan Poor Laws shows how good reasoning can be misguided. Harsh conditions of the working poor led to very different attempts at reform in the following generation. But I start with Say because his insights, like Smith's, turned out in hindsight to be the most predictive, and thus most relevant today. When other economists at the time worried about predictions of overpopulation that did not pan out, Say saw the limitless

---

2    Jean-Baptiste Say, *A Treatise on Political Economy; On the Production, Distribution, and Consumption of Wealth*, trans. C. R. Prinsep, new American ed. (J. B. Lippincott & Co., 1857 [1803]), 134–135.

3    Say, *Treatise on Political Economy*, 85.

4    Say, 330.

potential of human creativity, or as St. Augustine put it, "an inexhaustible wealth in [human] nature."[5]

This chapter will explore how classical and Christian political economists appropriated Adam Smith's insights into Christian social thought, emphasizing the need for religious and moral instruction to go hand in hand with sound economic analysis, including an appreciation for the benefits of entrepreneurship and international trade.

## The Principle of Population

MANY CHRISTIAN MINISTERS ALSO LABORED as economists, starting with the first to follow Smith: Thomas Robert Malthus. An Anglican parson in Wotton, Surrey, Malthus saw rural poverty firsthand among his parishioners, who were saved from starvation only by the Poor Laws, which required landlords to provide emergency subsistence for their peasants. In his *Essay on the Principle of Population*, Malthus adopted Smith's method to try to explain—and alleviate—the pauperism he encountered.

Like Smith, Malthus noticed a motivating desire at the root of a social phenomenon. But in Malthus's case, the phenomenon he sought to explain was poverty instead of wealth. He identified the motivating desire as the drive to procreate. He also observed "the constant tendency in all animated life to increase beyond the nourishment prepared for it,"[6] because though people multiply, limited soil restricts the expansion of agriculture. Put simply, people and animals multiply, but crops can only add. As a result, left unchecked, we reproduce faster than we can grow food to feed everyone. The commands to "be fruitful" and to "multiply" (Gen. 1:28) conflict in this emergent disorder of poverty. As Malthus put it, "Taking the whole earth . . . and, supposing the present population equal to a thousand millions, the human species would increase as the numbers, 1, 2, 4, 8, 16, 32, 64, 128, 256; and subsistence

---

5    Augustine of Hippo, *City of God*, 22.24, in NPNF¹ 2:503.
6    Thomas Robert Malthus, *An Essay on the Principle of Population: A View of Its Past and Present Effects on Human Happiness with An Inquiry into Our Prospects Respecting the Future Removal or Mitigation of the Evils Which It Occasions*, 6th ed. (Reaves and Turner, 1888 [1798]), 2. Henceforth, *Principle of Population*.

[i.e., crops] as, 1, 2, 3, 4, 5, 6, 7, 8, 9. In two centuries the population would be to the means of subsistence as 256 to 9."[7]

So why don't things actually work that way? Other than starvation, Malthus identified positive checks and preventative checks to population. Positive checks were not positive in the sense of being "good." They include all sorts of misery, including "severe labour,"[8] poverty, war, and disease. Preventative checks, on the other hand, Malthus did consider good. They most notably include chastity and delayed marriage (and thus delayed childbearing), brought on by education and civilization. Worried about poverty and starvation, Malthus urged his readers to employ preventative checks against overpopulation in order to minimize people's suffering. After Malthus, notes Ross B. Emmett, "The Smithian optimism is turned, not into pessimism, but into an economic world that always faces limits imposed by scarcity."[9]

While contemporary economists believe we have good reason not to worry about overpopulation today, Malthus's *Essay* does accurately describe most of history . . . until about the time he wrote it. For example, 1,600 years prior to Malthus, Tertullian observed, "The whole world . . . is becoming daily better cultivated and more fully peopled. . . . [But] our numbers are burdensome to the world, which can hardly supply us from its natural elements." He continues, "pestilence, and famine, and wars, and earthquakes have to be regarded . . . as the means of pruning the luxuriance of the human race."[10] Before the Industrial Revolution and Adam Smith, virtually all societies existed in this "Malthusian Trap," as economists call it.

Malthus saw vast and influential implications of his principle. For example, supply and demand apply to labor as well, and for Malthus this led to a practical conclusion about poverty policy: The Elizabethan Poor Laws needed to be reformed, because the more people compete for the same jobs, the lower

---

7   Malthus, *Principle of Population*, 6.
8   Malthus, 8.
9   Ross B. Emmett, "Nineteenth-Century British Christian Socialism: Association rather than Competition," *Journal of Markets & Morality* 26, no. 1 (2023): 13.
10  Tertullian, *A Treatise on the Soul*, 30, in *ANF* 3:210. In context, he does first celebrate the cultivation of the earth and the spread of civilization, arguing against the Pythagoreans who believed in reincarnation. Basically, he argues if population can increase so significantly, there must not be a finite number of human souls being reincarnated every one thousand years.

wages they command. Yet the Poor Laws fed people who didn't work, meaning that landowners received less profit from their crops—both because they
had less to sell and greater costs—and thus, even with fewer workers, they had
less to pay those who *did* work. The Poor Laws also meant that young people had no incentive to delay marriage, since if they couldn't find work, the
Poor Laws would support them. Taken together, Malthus concluded, the Poor
Laws "may be said therefore to create the poor which they maintain."[11] Borrowing from Roman Catholic social thought, we might say Malthus saw the
Poor Laws as "structures of sin"[12] that unjustly perpetuated poverty. Other
classical economists concurred. As David Ricardo put it, "every friend to the
poor must ardently wish for their abolition."[13] As for other *Christian* economists, according to A. M. C. Waterman, "At their hands, over the next thirty-
five years, Malthusian political economy was . . . received into the body of
Christian social thought."[14]

## Christian Classical Economists

THOMAS CHALMERS, AN EVANGELICAL, PRESBYTERIAN minister,
latched onto Malthus's emphasis on chastity and Christian education: "It is
to a moral restraint on the numbers of mankind, and not to a physical enlarge-
ment of the means for their subsistence, that we shall be henceforth beholden
for sufficiency or peace in our commonwealth."[15] Chalmers saw Malthus's
principle as linking together Christian morality and the market economy:
"There is an indissoluble connexion between the moral character and the

---

11   Malthus, *Principle of Population*, 303.
12   See Pontifical Council for Justice and Peace, *Compendium of the Social Doctrine of the
     Church*, (Reprint April 2005), §332, https://www.vatican.va/roman_curia/pontifical
     _councils/justpeace/documents/rc_pc_justpeace_doc_20060526_compendio-dott
     -soc_en.html.
13   David Ricardo, *Principles of Political Economy and Taxation* (George Bell and Sons, 1908
     [1817]), 84.
14   A. M. C. Waterman, *Revolution, Economics and Religion: Christian Political Economy
     1798–1833* (Cambridge University Press, 1991), 57.
15   Thomas Chalmers, *On Political Economy, in Connexion with the Moral State and Moral
     Prospects of Society*, vol. 1, in *The Works of Thomas Chalmers*, vol. 19 (William Collins,
     1836 [1832]), 83.

economic comfort of the peasantry; and the doctrine of Malthus is the *vinculum*"—i.e., the connecting tie—"by which to explain it."[16] He furthermore criticized the Poor Laws in Smithian terms for, in his view, attempting to accomplish by justice what should be a matter of private beneficence.[17]

Richard Whately, who advanced from professor of political economy at Oxford to Church of Ireland archbishop of Dublin, more often, and more optimistically, emphasized civilizational, preventative checks on population, acknowledging "causes which tend to the gradual increase of wealth, in a ratio even greater than the increase of population, and to the growth of all that we call by the collective name 'Civilization.' "[18] While Chalmers urged economists to pay more attention to Christian morality, Whately, more confident in the progress of civilization, urged Christians to pay more attention to political economy: "It is not a sign of Faith . . . to decline meeting any theorist on his own ground, and to cut short the controversy by an appeal to the authority of Scripture."[19] He nevertheless appeals to Scripture to support this: "It is for us to 'behave ourselves valiantly for our country and for the cities of our God,' instead of bringing the Ark of God into the field of battle to fight for us."[20]

One of the most able-minded opponents of the Poor Laws stands as a link back to the Late Scholastic analysis of inflation. Edward Copleston, an English churchman, wrote to the prime minister Robert Peel, showing how, according to Waterman, "The increase of poverty in the early sixteenth century" did not result from the Poor Laws, as Malthus maintained, but "arose instead from 'the depreciation of money' " due to the gold and silver from Spanish colonialism. Rather, "The Elizabethan Poor Law was enacted as a remedy."[21] In the early nineteenth century, the Bank of England issued paper money in difficult times, with no gold or silver standard to anchor its value. Later, it kept printing money for *any* reason it wanted. Copleston lists both war *and* peace

16   Chalmers, *On Political Economy*, 40.
17   Chalmers, 417.
18   Richard Whately, *Introductory Lectures on Political Economy*, 2nd ed. (B. Fellowes, 1832), 130.
19   Whately, *Introductory Lectures*, 31.
20   Whately, 32. In particular, he contrasts the faithful words of David in 2 Kingdoms/2 Samuel 10:12 with the rashness of the sons of Eli in 1 Kingdoms/1 Samuel 4:1–11.
21   Waterman, *Revolution, Economics and Religion*, 189.

as reasons cited, for example. Faced with the resulting monetary instability, "every expedient is resorted to by [the poor laborer's] employer before that of a permanent rise of wages."[22] In short, while the worker's wages technically stayed the same, they really took a pay cut because that same amount couldn't buy as much as it used to. This situation impoverished them.

The state then implemented Poor Laws as a remedy, but this only exacerbated the problem by encouraging early marriages and further lowering wages. As for alternative solutions to the Poor Laws, with the exception of Malthus,[23] who supported the 1815 Corn Law tariffs on grain, Copleston and nearly all other classical economists, including the Christian ones, supported free trade, which expanded the market for grains and lowered their prices. The issue may be politically complicated today, but the economics remains clear: By extending the division of labor through international trade, prices fall and life becomes more affordable. That's good news for the poor. Orthodox Christian social thought today would need very good, noneconomic reasons for opposing international trade.

## Say's Missing Insight

UNLIKE SMITH, WHOSE WORK HAS largely been vindicated by subsequent history, contemporary readers likely suspect something must have been missing in Malthus's analysis. After all, today we have eight times as many people and, to our shame, throw away uneaten food every day. Sure, we've had more than our fair share of "positive checks"—wars, plagues, natural disasters, murderous tyrannies, and the like. Even so, *how* did we get all this *food*? Why didn't Malthus's predictions pan out?

The answer is Say's entrepreneurial insight: Wealth ultimately comes from the creativity of people. People aren't the problem. They are the solution, when left to God's design. Made in His image (Gen. 1:28), we create good

---

22   Edward Copleston, *A Letter to the Right Hon. Robert Peel, M. P. for the University of Oxford, on the Pernicious Effects of a Variable Standard of Value, Especially as It Regards the Condition of the Lower Orders and the Poor Laws* (John Murray, 1819), 36.

23   See Boyd Hilton, *The Age of Atonement: The Influence of Evangelicals on Social and Economic Thought, 1795–1865* (Clarendon Press, 1988), 66.

things from God's good creation to do good in the world. Say, for example, gave more credit than Malthus to the role of technology in improving food production,[24] and this indeed has been a major factor historically. Back then, no one could have imagined all the technologies we have today, from selective breeding of crops, pesticides, and improved fertilization to canning, packaging, preservatives, and refrigeration. But Say at least understood the value of creativity. And others did see a glimpse. For instance, the secular economist John Stewart Mill commented that if American corn "should ever substitute itself for wheat as the staple food of the poor," then "it would require perhaps some generations for population" to outpace food production.[25]

As for America, political economy made its debut there through a group of Christian natural theologians known as the "clerical economists" (though not all of them were ordained). Bradley W. Bateman notes that, as the United States had abundant land at its disposal, "Malthus's ratios made little or no sense."[26] Thus, these economists were more influenced by Smith and Say. "When the freedom of commerce is not restricted," wrote Episcopalian minister John McVickar, "each country necessarily devotes itself to such employments as are most beneficial to each. This pursuit of individual advantage is admirably connected with the good of the whole."[27] Why? "Providence, by giving different soils, climates, and natural productions to different countries, has evidently provided for their mutual intercourse and civilization."[28] "Before the discovery of the agents now in use," wrote the Baptist pastor Francis Wayland, "the most vivid imagination could never have conceived of the benefits which they have already conferred upon society. There is no reason to suppose, that we are now more capable of fathoming the goodness of God, than our ancestors were three or four hundred years ago."[29] Confident of God's beneficent Wisdom, by which we are "fearfully and wonderfully made" (Ps.

---

24  Say, *A Treatise on Political Economy*, 90.
25  John Stuart Mill, *Principles of Political Economy with Some of Their Applications to Social Philosophy* (Longmans, Green and Co., 1923 [1848]), 195–196.
26  Bradley W. Bateman, "Christian Theology and American Economics: From the Free Market to Socialism," *Journal of Markets & Morality* 26, no. 1 (2023): 70.
27  John McVickar, *Outlines of Political Economy* (Augustus M. Kelley, 1966 [1825]), 69.
28  McVickar, *Outlines of Political Economy*, 69.
29  Francis Wayland, *The Elements of Political Economy* (Bould and Lincoln, 1856 [1837]), 59.

138/139:14), Wayland did not fear a future of want and starvation but imagined a more peaceful and harmonious future.

## *Two Wins and a Loss*

WHILE, ALAS, CLASSICAL POLITICAL ECONOMY cannot claim to have achieved world peace, it did have its victories. The new science scored one of its first big "wins" in the abolition of the slave trade in Britain in 1807, and then slavery altogether, across the rest of the British Empire, in 1833. Though evangelical activists like William Wilberforce played the most important role, virtually all classical economists, including the Americans, rejected slavery, and abolitionists of the time credited Adam Smith as a forerunner.[30] And to his great credit, when Malthus heard that pro-slavery members of Parliament used his principle to defend the slave trade, he rushed to the printers just in time to add a long note to the very end of the second edition of his *Essay* in 1807, calling such an appeal "most unwise in the friends of the slave-trade."[31]

Malthus's *Essay* recommended replacing positive checks on population that cause misery with the preventative checks of morality and civilization. Rather than benefiting Africa by depopulating it, he said, the slave trade kept it from developing: "The state of Africa . . . is exactly such as we should expect in a country where the capture of men was considered as a more advantageous employment than agriculture or manufactures."[32] Europeans wrongly regarded Africans as inherently barbaric. Rather, "As long as the nations of Europe continue barbarous enough to purchase slaves in Africa we may be quite sure that Africa will continue barbarous enough to supply them."[33] In this case, at least, the demand created the supply, and only by changing the

---

30  Thomas Clarkson, *The History of the Rise, Progress, and Accomplishment of the Abolition of the African Slave-Trade by the British Parliament*, vol. 1 (Longman, Hurst, Rees, and Orme, 1808), 258–259.

31  Malthus, *Principle of Population*, 508. My thanks to Ross Emmett for drawing my attention to this. See Ross B. Emmett, "Malthus, the Slave Trade, and the Civilizing Effect of the Preventive Checks" (June 11, 2014), available at SSRN: https://ssrn.com/abstract =2449035 or http://dx.doi.org/10.2139/ssrn.2449035.

32  Malthus, 509.

33  Malthus, 509.

moral culture and legal structures fueling that demand could the supply ever be stopped.

Another win came in the repeal of the Corn Law in 1846. Free trade really did reduce the price of grains, which benefitted all British subjects—especially the poor—with the exception of farm-owning aristocrats. The Cobden-Chevalier Treaty in 1860, drastically reducing tariffs between France and the United Kingdom, would further lead to free trade agreements across most Western nations. In Smith's day, he lamented the "variety of goods of which the importation into Great Britain is prohibited."[34] The classical economists changed all that. Public support has waxed and waned, but free trade has continued to spread that "universal opulence" Smith observed to more and more people ever since.

Not every victory for classical political economy amounted to a win, however. In 1834, the British Parliament passed the Poor Law Amendment Act. On the one hand, it allowed for greater freedom of movement for peasants and entailed the building of "workhouses" for the poor who had no work. On the other hand, influenced by both Malthus's principle and Jeremy Bentham's utilitarianism[35] (to minimize pain and maximize pleasure for the greatest number of people), cities made the conditions of these workhouses purposefully harsh to motivate the jobless to find work. Yet as the Industrial Revolution marched on, men and women labored under even harsher conditions. The utilitarian "moral calculus" did not compute: Many people still preferred the workhouses to factories and mines. The new science of political economy had clear blind spots.

## An Orthodox Assessment

FROM OUR ORTHODOX POINT OF view, I find Say's entrepreneurial insight that all kinds of labor produce economic value to be the most helpful, as it

---

34  Adam Smith, *An Inquiry into the Nature and Causes of the Wealth of Nations*, 5th ed., 2 vols. (Methuen & Co., 1904), 1.4.2, 418.

35  Jeremy Bentham, *Writings on the Poor Laws*, vol. 1 (Clarendon Press, 2001). Secular political economists like Mill tended to adopt utilitarianism as their moral philosophy. See John Stewart Mill, *Utilitarianism*, in *The Utilitarians* (Dolphin Books, 1961), 399–472.

reflects our creation in God's image. He created us to create! And in so doing, to serve one another. Along these lines, just like Say, Fr. Sergei Bulgakov similarly complained about how Adam Smith distinguished between productive and unproductive labor: "Although . . . a purely methodological differentiation . . . [Smith] established a profound and completely illegitimate middle ground that divides economic and spiritual activity."[36] Thus, Bulgakov pointed to this theological side of Say's thought: Economic activity has profound spiritual significance, and spiritual activity has economic significance, as we saw in the case of monastic enterprise in chapter 19. In this way, Say's insight can enhance our conception of Orthodox Christian social thought.

As for Malthus's principle of population and the value of a moral culture of chastity, Vladimir Soloviev, though more critical of laissez-faire (i.e., non-interventionist) economics in his day,[37] nevertheless concurs with Malthus that "the unlimited increase of population . . . is not ordained by any physical, and, still less by any moral law. . . . Normal economics are possible only in connection with the normal family, which is based upon rational asceticism and not upon unchecked carnal instincts."[38] Curiously, neither Malthus nor any other classical economist comments on what, according to the principle of population, historically must have been the necessary and significant alleviation of human misery through the institutionalization of sexual restraint, beyond marriage, in monasticism. Recall Fr. Alexander Schmemann's observation that "at the outset of the struggle with iconoclasm the number of monks in Byzantium had reached a hundred thousand—an almost incredible percentage of the population."[39] In addition to charity and enterprise, we

---

36    Sergey N. Bulgakov, "The National Economy and the Religious Personality (1909)," *Journal of Markets & Morality* 11, no. 1 (2008): 160.

37    Vladimir Solovyov, *The Justification of the Good*, rev. ed., ed. Boris Jakim, trans. Natalie A. Duddington (Eerdmans, 2005), 284. That said, as we've seen, his attempt to distinguish between "psychological and moral, and not economic, causes" cannot apply to Adam Smith or to most of the classical economists, who understood their whole discipline to be moral and the roots of human behavior to be motivated by psychological desires, reactions, and reasoned reflection. Soloviev's moral analysis of economic life, though insightful, sometimes suffers from sweeping and unsubstantiated generalizations.

38    Solovyov, *Justification of the Good*, 309.

39    Alexander Schmemann, *The Historical Road of Eastern Orthodoxy*, trans. Lydia W. Kesich (SVS Press, 2003), 210.

could call this an unseen contribution to civilization by monasticism. We may not need to worry about overpopulation today, but for most of history before 1800, Malthus's analysis holds up, and monasticism must have been a powerful "preventative check."

As for why we don't need to worry about overpopulation, in addition to creative, entrepreneurial solutions, trade has made a huge impact. Christians, even saints, have disagreed on the merits of international trade throughout history. Nevertheless, we must admit that even in our Orthodox Tradition there have been some who equally admired the working of divine Wisdom through international commerce as did the classical economists. Saint Gregory the Theologian, for example, wondered in amazement, "And how doth [God] bring upon [the sea] the Nautilus that inhabits the dry land (i.e., man) in a little vessel, and with a little breeze . . . that earth and sea may be bound together by needs and commerce?"[40] The Christian classical economists shared his wonder. We should, too.

But we should also keep in mind the shortcomings of industrialization and classical political economy. In addition to the failed reform of the Poor Laws, even the supply of potential labor created its own demand: Young children went to work down in the mines, in factories, and up chimneys, which led to their mistreatment, injury, disease, and tragically early deaths. The division of labor continued to expand, but despite genuine gains from trade, opulence did not, in the short term, prove as "general" as Smith predicted, due to such social injustice. At first, the new industrial economy better resembled Malthus's "positive checks" of misery.[41] The "Social Question" had arrived in Britain. Social activists and reformers, including many Christians, could not and did not look on indifferently. The next chapter will tell some of their stories as we explore socialism and social reform.

---

40    Gregory of Nazianzus, "Oration 28: The Second Theological Oration," 27, in *NPNF*² 7:298. See also Wilson Whitener and Alexander William Salter, "Wealth and Commerce in Eastern Christian Thought," *Journal of Markets & Morality* 26, no. 1 (2023): 105–125.

41    Malthus, in fact, criticized both of these problems—harsh working conditions and child labor—in his day. See Malthus, *Principle of Population*, 308, 475–476.

CHAPTER 29

# Socialists and Social Reformers

ON FEBRUARY 21, 1848, KARL Marx and Friedrich Engels wrote, "A spectre is haunting Europe—the spectre of Communism."[1] The very next day, revolution came to Paris. Crowds of protestors clashed with soldiers, but on February 24, King Louis Philipe abdicated, clearing the way for the Second Republic. Revolutionaries once again took up the principles of 1789— liberty, equality, and fraternity—but now they were intermixed with socialism. Discontent with working conditions and the potato famine, and inspired not by Marxism but French socialists, the French overthrew and remade the reigning social order. Similar democratic revolutions spread across Europe, some resulting in short-term success, some violently suppressed, others motivating more peaceful, constitutional reforms.

The revolutions spread as far as Ireland, but not to Britain, the birthplace of the Industrial Revolution and classical political economy. Why not? How did the British address the shortcomings of their new economy? Did Marxism make a difference, since it originated there? If not, who helped their society to overcome the unjust treatment of workers and child labor? After addressing Marxism, this chapter will answer these questions by examining first the Christian socialists, led by F. D. Maurice, then more importantly the work of evangelical social reformers, especially Lord Shaftesbury. These Christians,

---

1    Karl Marx and Friedrich Engels, *Manifesto of the Communist Party*, in *The Marx-Engels Reader*, ed. Robert C. Tucker, 2nd ed. (W. W. Norton & Company, 1978), 473.

acting upon theological convictions, demonstrate that a more humane society does not require violent revolution.

## The Marxist Worldview

AS A STUDENT OF HISTORY, I must admit I don't see the appeal of Marx and Engel's claim that "the history of all hitherto existing society is the history of class struggles."[2] Indeed, shouldn't any Orthodox reader, at least, find it absurd that "Pope and Czar" together "entered into a holy alliance"? Pope Pius IX condemned Emperor Nicholas I over forced conversions of Eastern-rite Catholics to Orthodoxy. Yet Marx and Engels ask their readers to believe that, behind the scenes, these rulers *really* formed two pillars of a vast international conspiracy to oppress the proletariat and prop up the bourgeoisie. The appeal, no doubt, comes from Marxism's powerful ability to interpret genuinely harsh social conditions through a comprehensive worldview. In the next chapter, we'll see how the economics profession responded to Marxism's analytical claims, but first we need to understand these philosophical underpinnings.

Marxism depends on deterministic "historical materialism," i.e., it denies the reality of spiritual things while claiming that all history results from fate. To be fair, though reductionistic, Marxism does acknowledge many social forces, but it regards material relations as basic and ultimate: "Because . . . every succeeding generation finds itself in possession of the productive forces acquired by the previous generation," wrote Marx, "a coherence arises in human history . . . as the productive forces of man and therefore his social relations have been more developed." He continues, "Hence . . . material relations are the basis of all [our] relations."[3] Joseph Schumpeter clarified, "Marx did not hold that religions, metaphysics, schools of art, ethical ideas and political volitions were either reducible to economic *motives* or of no importance. He only tried to unveil the economic *conditions* which shape them and which account for their rise and fall."[4]

---

2    Marx and Engels, *Manifesto of the Communist Party*, 473.

3    Karl Marx, "Society and Economy in History," in *The Marx-Engels Reader*, 137.

4    Joseph Schumpeter, *Capitalism, Socialism, Democracy*, 3rd ed. (Harper & Row, 1950), 11.

Of course, each generation does inherit material conditions. Matter matters, as we Orthodox sometimes say. But people also inherit spiritual conditions. For Engels, however, these merely represent "ideologies," vestiges of primitive superstition: "Religion, philosophy, etc. . . . have a prehistoric stock . . . of what we should today call bunk."[5] "Ideology," for Marxists, refers to a "false consciousness,"[6] a "bourgeois illusion"[7] ultimately arising from one's material circumstances. What that means is you might *think* you like your job or believe the Creed, but *really* everyone—even "Pope and Czar"—has been conditioned merely to think so by oppressive material conditions and the social forces that arise from them. In this way, Marxists reduce all history to the unfolding, Manichean dialectic of class struggle: "Oppressor and oppressed . . . carried on . . . a fight that each time ended, either in a revolutionary re-constitution of society at large, or in the common ruin of the contending classes."[8]

Against this conception, Fr. Sergei Bulgakov, formerly a Marxist economist before his return to Orthodoxy, emphasized that "the determining power in the spiritual life of man is his religion—not only in the narrow sense of the word, but in a wider sense as well, i.e., the highest and ultimate values which one admits as being *beyond* him and *higher* than himself and also his practical relation to these values."[9] In fact, we can see this in Marxism. Engels has such faith in Marx's historical dialectic as a force "*beyond* him and *higher* than himself" that he regards even Marx as incidental to its discovery: "The time was ripe for it and . . . it simply *had* to be discovered."[10] No credit goes to the free creativity of his friend. Rather, Engels pays homage to the all-powerful, blind, and impersonal dialectic of history. Put simply, Marxism ultimately has no place for *persons*, only strictly material *things*.

Marx, furthermore, adds a messianic dimension: We suffer because of "the great historical movement arising from the conflict between the productive

---

5    Friedrich Engels, "Letters on Historical Materialism," in *The Marx-Engels Reader*, 763.
6    Friedrich Engels, 766.
7    Friedrich Engels, 767.
8    Marx and Engels, *Manifesto of the Communist Party*, 473–474.
9    Sergei Bulgakov, *Karl Marx as a Religious Type: His Relation to the Religion of Anthropotheism of L. Feuerbach*, trans. Luba Barna (Nordland, 1979), 41.
10   Engels, "Letters on Historical Materialism," in *The Marx-Engels Reader*, 768.

forces already acquired by men and their social relations" and "the terrible wars which are being prepared between the different classes." What will
save us?—"the practical *and violent* action of the masses by which alone these
conflicts can be resolved."[11] Rather than Christ, Marx makes the masses the
savior of his system. Marxism promises a classless society, free of private property, oppression, scarcity, and religion. But with the benefit of hindsight, we
know that such "violent action" has only *spread* inequality, theft, oppression,
starvation, and hopelessness, whether across Eastern Europe in traditionally
Orthodox lands, or throughout Asia, Africa, and the Americas, even today.
Revolutionaries sacrificed millions of unique and irreplaceable lives for a
future that never came, and never can come, because every human person,
created "in the image of God" (Gen. 9:6), contains God-given freedom, creativity, and inviolable dignity no deterministic dialectic can ever explain.

Outside of German and Russian socialist and economic literature, Marxism had little influence until the Russian Revolution, after which the Soviet
propaganda machine began promoting it and printing Marx's works.[12] Social
reform across Europe in the nineteenth century came from others, some
socialist and some not, and in Britain, Christians played a major role.

## Christian Socialism

CHRISTIAN SOCIALISM BEGAN WHEN F. D. Maurice, an Anglican minister, heard of a planned Chartist rally in London in April 1848. While socialism
at the time lacked a political component, focusing instead on organized labor,
the Chartists demanded legal reform. Authorities suppressed the rally before
it could start, but it motivated Maurice to send his fellow churchman Charles
Kingsley to fetch the young lawyer J. M. Ludlow. Together, they wrote a series
of tracts called *Politics for the People*,[13] attempting to reach out to disaffected
workers on behalf of the Church of England.

---

11  Marx, "Society and Economy in History," in *The Marx-Engels Reader*, 141, emphasis
    added.
12  See Phillip W. Magness and Michael Makovi, "The Mainstreaming of Marx: Measuring
    the Effect of the Russian Revolution on Karl Marx's Influence," *Journal of Political Econ-
    omy* 131, no. 6 (June 2023): 1507–1545.
13  See *Politics for the People* (John W. Parker, West Strand, 1848).

In France, the anarchist Pierre-Joseph Proudhon had declared, *"Property is robbery!"*[14] But while the Paris Revolution unfolded, across the English Channel Maurice preached a series of sermons on the Lord's Prayer in which he claimed, "Property is holy."[15] What did he mean? "Beneath all distinctions of property and of rank lie the obligations of a common Creation, Redemption, Humanity."[16] In particular, God created all people to be one universal, divine family, with God himself for their Father. But the selfishness of sin has alienated us from one another. However, redeemed through Jesus Christ, all humanity once again can call upon God as "Our Father" (Matt. 6:9) in the Church. As such, "The name Father loses its significance for us individually, when we will not use it as the members of a family."[17] To Maurice, property defines the nature of our relationships—and thus responsibilities—to our neighbors, our brothers and sisters. That makes it holy.

Thus, when Maurice heard that the Chartists had planned a demonstration days after he finished his sermons, he believed his place in society as an Anglican minister, aristocrat, and historical theologian[18] entailed responsibilities to disaffected workers in the neighborhood around Lincoln's Inn, where he served as chaplain. Maurice, Kingsley, and Ludlow wrote *Politics for the People* to persuade others of the upper classes to join them. It did not make much of an impact. Kingsley's 1850 novel *Alton Locke*, which imaginatively tells the story of the hardships of a poor laborer, probably did better at spreading awareness about industrial working conditions.[19]

Yet under Maurice's leadership, the trio pressed on, most importantly through a weekly Bible study and biweekly conferences with local labor leaders, both led by Maurice. The Christian socialists promoted entrepreneurial

---

14    Pierre-Joseph Proudhon, *What is Property?* in *The Works of P. J. Proudhon*, vol. 1 (Benj. R. Tucker, 1876), 12, emphasis original.

15    F. D. Maurice, *The Lord's Prayer: Nine Sermons Preached in the Chapel of Lincoln's Inn* (Macmillan, 1861), 65. This quote is from his fifth sermon, given on March 12, 1848.

16    Maurice, *The Lord's Prayer*, 65.

17    Maurice, 6.

18    On the relation between Maurice's appreciation for the Church Fathers and his Christian socialism, see Dylan Pahman, "The Origins and Aims of F. D. Maurice's Christian Socialism," *Journal of Markets & Morality* 26, no. 1 (2023): 27–49.

19    Charles Kingsley, *Alton Locke: Tailor and Poet, an Autobiography*, new ed. (MacMillan and Co., 1893 [1850]).

worker cooperatives as a way to give people a greater share in factory profits and self-determination over their careers. These didn't succeed either, due to mismanagement and legal obstacles. According to Ross B. Emmett, "Until 2000, Ludlow's cooperatives continued to operate with the risk of personal liability." They would continue to bear this risk until "Tony Blair, who often acknowledged his intellectual debt to earlier Christian socialists ... expanded provisions made before the World Wars to provide limited liability to cooperatives."[20] Limited liability is an important legal protection for business owners. It means that if a business goes bankrupt, creditors must be content with what can be paid from the company's assets. They cannot go after owners' personal property. Without it, business ventures are often too risky to get off the ground.

While Ludlow and every other Christian socialist would be glad to hear the good news about limited liability for worker cooperatives, for Maurice it's beside the point. He conceived of Christian socialism as an educational and evangelistic project, engaging opposing views with the utmost charity and eschewing "party spirit." Contrasting himself with secular socialists, Maurice claimed, "I assume that to *be* the only possible condition of society which they wish to *make* the condition of it."[21] How so? He believed that "if they begin to look earnestly at the Bible history, at the creeds of the Christian Church, at the records of it from the Day of Pentecost to this time, I believe they will find more and more, that they have the ground there, the only one upon which they can stand or work."[22] Indeed, he even recommended to Ludlow that if people wanted communism, in the sense of collective ownership of property, "every monastic institution properly so called was a Communist institution to all intents and purposes."[23]

---

20  Ross B. Emmett, "Nineteenth-Century British Christian Socialism: Association rather than Competition," *Journal of Markets & Morality* 26, no. 1 (2023): 19.
21  F. D. Maurice, *Tracts on Christian Socialism*, no. 1: "Dialogue between Somebody (a Person of Respectability) and Nobody (the Writer)," in *Democratic Socialism in Britain*, ed. David Reisman, vol. 2: *The Christian Socialists* (Routledge, 1996), 8.
22  Maurice, *Tracts on Christian Socialism*, no. 1, vol. 2, 7.
23  F. D. Maurice, To Mr. Ludlow, Bradley, Newton Abbot, August 13, 1849, in *The Life of Frederick Denison Maurice: Chiefly Told in His Own Letters*, ed. F. Maurice, 2 vols. (Charles Scribner's Sons, 1884), 2:7. Unfortunately, Maurice did accept the common

As for this "ground" that the Church had and socialists needed but couldn't see, Maurice continues, "They will not read in the Divine book of a great strife of individual competitors, but of a Divine family, expanding itself into a Divine nation, of a universal society growing out of that nation."[24] Ultimately, Maurice had his own worldview, rooted in the Scriptures and Church history.[25] Redemption begins with a family in the calling of Abram, then a nation in ancient Israel, and finally all humanity in the Church, where we receive "the Spirit of adoption by whom we cry out, 'Abba, Father'" (Rom. 8:15). Each new phase does not abolish but rather includes what came before.

Thus, according to historian Jeremy Morris, "Maurice claimed that the Catholicity of the Church was served, not by absolute uniformity, but by local diversity. Locality and persistence in time were complementary elements of the function of liturgy as a 'sign' of Catholicity."[26] In this way, Maurice's worldview combined catholicity, subsidiarity, and the three Lutheran "creational estates" of family, state, and church. Thus, the locus of Christian activism, for Maurice, should be the local parish of the national church.

Most importantly, though, Maurice wanted to educate working class people about their place in this divine order, as members of God's divine family. Like the Christian political economists, he wanted to impart moral instruction. Rather than the class war of revolutionary socialists like Marx, Maurice promoted class cooperation. The workers so loved Maurice as a pastor that when the publication of his *Theological Essays* led to his dismissal from King's College in 1854,[27] they recruited him as president of the Working Men's College, the first institution of humane, adult education for workers in Europe. "If the distinction between a freeman and a slave . . . is identical with the

---

caricature of Eastern monasticism as quietist. See F. D. Maurice, *Social Morality*, 2nd ed. (Macmillan & Co., 1872), 275.

24  Maurice, *Tracts on Christian Socialism*, vol. 2, 7.

25  For more on this, see Dylan Pahman, "The English Kuyper and the Dutch Maurice," *Journal of Economics, Theology and Religion* 4 (2024), https://j-etr.org/2024/02/19/the
-english-kuyper-and-the-dutch-maurice/.

26  Jeremy Morris, "A Social Doctrine of the Trinity? A Reappraisal of F. D. Maurice on Eternal Life," *Anglican and Episcopal History* 69, no. 1 (2000): 85.

27  F. D. Maurice, *Theological Essays*, 2nd ed. (Redfield, 1854). The issue in question was Maurice's "soft" universalism.

distinction between a Person and a Thing," said Maurice in a series of lectures to promote the new school, "you will seek above all things to make our working people understand that they are Persons, and not Things."[28]

As for economics, like other socialists Maurice contrasted cooperation with competition, likely misunderstanding the latter. As John Stewart Mill noted, "I do not pretend that there are no inconveniences in competition, or that the moral objections urged against it by Socialist writers, as a source of jealousy and hostility among those engaged in the same occupation, are altogether groundless. But if competition has its evils, it prevents greater evil,"[29] namely monopoly and poverty. So on that account, Maurice shared other socialists' confusion. Conversely, he actually knew Mill,[30] and though he rejected Jeremy Bentham's utilitarianism,[31] he expressed measured appreciation for Adam Smith, including his opposition to slavery[32] and his support for free trade.[33] As for the worker cooperatives and the Working Men's College, nothing about them conflicted with classical political economy.

But if the Christian socialist worker cooperatives couldn't turn a profit, and the first wave of the movement fizzled out—or culminated, in Maurice's view—in the Working Men's College, how did working conditions improve in Britain? Evangelicalism deserves the greatest credit.

## Evangelical Paternalism

"IF IN THE FIRST DECADES of the nineteenth century 'Britain's increasing prosperity' was 'a focus for Protestant pride,'" writes Richard Turnbull, "by

---

28  F. D. Maurice, "Learning and Working," in *Learning and Working: Six Lectures Delivered in Willis's Rooms, London, in June and July, 1854; The Religion of Rome, and Its Influence on Modern Civilization: Four Lectures Delivered in the Philosophical Institution of Edinburgh, in December* (Macmillan, 1854), 113.

29  John Stuart Mill, *Principles of Political Economy with Some of Their Applications to Social Philosophy* (Longmans, Green and Co., 1923 [1848]), 793.

30  F. Maurice, ed., *The Life of Frederick Denison Maurice*, 1:75–76

31  Maurice, *Social Morality*, 341.

32  F. D. Maurice, *Moral and Metaphysical Philosophy, Vol. 2: Fourteenth Century to the French Revolution, with a Glimpse into the Nineteenth Century* (Macmillan, 1882 [1847]), 579

33  Maurice, *Social Morality*, 339–340.

the middle decades a greater emphasis on sin and judgment was a reminder of the perils of wealth and moral danger that faced the evangelical entering business."[34] Evangelicalism began as a movement, not a denomination: "The term evangelical has encompassed Anglicans, Quakers, and Pentacostals [sic] alongside independents, Baptists, and Presbyterians."[35] In Britain, we've already seen how evangelicalism interacted with economics on a theoretical level in Thomas Chalmers.

On the practical side, many evangelicals owned businesses, and their pastors exhorted them to work honestly, treat their employees well, and avoid speculation.[36] Their leaders also opposed limited liability because they viewed market consequences as moral training, but "many evangelical businesses did incorporate and often viewed limited liability as beneficial by enabling smaller investors to enter into commercial investments." Nevertheless, "What was needed, all agreed, was prudence and responsibility."[37] According to Turnbull, "Evangelicalism . . . affirmed the market mechanism, demanded discipleship and moral behavior, and reserved a role, albeit limited, for government in preventing abuse."[38] Activists such as Lord Anthony Ashley Cooper, Seventh Earl of Shaftesbury, would take up the cause of that "limited" role, as well as lead the way in charitable missions to address many hardships and injustices of the working poor.

Turnbull describes the paternalist, aristocratic, and agrarian background to Shaftesbury's activism: "The links which bonded people together were not class relationships, but ties that ran vertically through the social system. It preserved England from revolution."[39] Yet that world faded before Shaftesbury's eyes: "Industrialization and commerce threatened the traditional means and methods of encouraging good relationships within the social hierarchy."[40]

---

34  Richard Turnbull, "Evangelicals and Business in Nineteenth-Century Britain," *Journal of Markets & Morality* 26, no. 1 (2023): 52, citing Jane Garnett, " 'Gold and the Gospel': Systematic Beneficence in Mid-Nineteenth-Century England," in *Studies in Church History* 24 (1987): 347–358.
35  Turnbull, "Evangelicals and Business," 52.
36  Turnbull, 57–58.
37  Turnbull, 59.
38  Turnbull, 58.
39  Richard Turnbull, *Shaftesbury: The Great Reformer* (Lion, 2010), 13–14.
40  Turnbull, *Shaftesbury*, 15.

Instead, "Family relationships were . . . replaced by employer relationships. The employment of children was both cheap and effective as their fingers were nimble and wages low. Overwork and ill-treatment were the order of the day. . . . The ill-health, poor conditions, and mistreatment of children working in these factories gave rise to much concern."[41] As Shaftesbury charged Parliament in an 1840 speech, "The future hopes of a country must, under God, be laid in the character and condition of its children."[42]

Unlike Maurice, Shaftesbury "had no truck with the fledgling trade union movement and considered both socialism and Chartism as enemies of the state."[43] Yet he often executed their goals—if not their means—better than they did. He shepherded legislation through Parliament, reforming treatment of the mentally ill, public sanitation, child labor, and work hours. He also supported free trade and Catholic emancipation in Ireland.[44] At the same time, he promoted privately run "ragged schools" to get poor children off the streets and provide basic instruction, religious and remedial, teaching them the Bible alongside reading, writing, and arithmetic. His editor summarized a story Shaftesbury told in an 1849 speech that illustrated their plight: "He recollected a very graphic remark made by one of those children in perfect simplicity, but which yet showed the horrors of their position. The [school]master had been pointing out to him the terrors of punishment in after-life. The remark of the boy was—'That may be so, but I don't think it can be any worse than this world has been to me.' "[45]

People called Shaftesbury the "Poor Man's Earl." His and others' efforts, motivated by their evangelical faith, corrected, however imperfectly, many injustices of the new industrial economy, ensuring humane treatment of "the least of these" (Matt. 25:40). "That Tory paternalism was mixed up in his deeply Christian motivations," says Turnbull about Shaftesbury's involvement with the Ragged School Union, "that an excessive romanticism clouded

---

41  Turnbull, 74–75.
42  "Children Not Protected by the Factory Acts," August 4, 1840, in *Speeches of the Earl of Shaftesbury, K. G. upon Subjects Having Relation Chiefly to the Claims and Interests of the Labouring Class* (Chapman and Hall, 1868), 17.
43  Turnbull, *Shaftesbury*, 83.
44  Turnbull, 117–118.
45  "Emigration and Ragged Schools," July 24, 1849, in *Speeches of the Earl of Shaftesbury*, 255.

his vision—neither of these is denied. However that also should not serve to eclipse the main objectives and motives behind Lord Shaftesbury and his work."[46] Nor, for that matter, should it eclipse his accomplishments. We can and should learn from his tireless efforts to serve the common good of workers and children in his time and context when we think about how best to do so in our own.

## An Orthodox Assessment

THE POWER OF MARXISM DEMONSTRATES the importance of having a worldview that can explain the various problems of modern life and offer solutions. Unfortunately, the Marxist worldview is incompatible with Orthodoxy by being atheist, materialist, and determinist. Orthodox Christian social thought must offer a compelling alternative. Thankfully, F. D. Maurice and Lord Shaftesbury show us how to do that.

F. D. Maurice grounds his Christian socialist worldview in the Lord's Prayer. But he wasn't the first to notice the social nature of this prayer. Saint John Chrysostom taught that each Christian "saith not, 'my Father, which art in Heaven,' but, 'our Father,' offering up his supplications for the body in common, and nowhere looking to his own, but everywhere to his neighbor's good."[47] This leads Maurice to a relational understanding of property, entailing duties that transcend social classes, including extending humane higher education to the working classes. His idea of a "divine order" even touches on catholicity, seeing the Church as the only possible universal society, yet instantiated within national and local contexts. As most historically Orthodox nations have constitutionally established the Orthodox Church, Maurice's "divine order" might especially be a resource for those contexts.

As for Shaftesbury's evangelicalism, it constituted one strain of a broader wave of religious awakenings in the late-eighteenth and early-nineteenth centuries, even, according to Andrey V. Ivanov, spreading to the Orthodox Church,

---

46  Turnbull, *Shaftesbury*, 151.
47  John Chrysostom, *Homilies on Matthew*, 19, in *NPNF*[1] 10:131.

most notably to Metropolitan St. Filaret of Moscow.[48] Common emphases included the Bible, conversion to Christ, the Cross, personal morality, and social activism. Saint Filaret supported Christian education for all, writing an excellent catechism and promoting the Russian Bible society's vernacular translation of the Bible—until it was suppressed by the emperor. His preaching also emphasized the importance of personal encounter with Christ. There is nothing uniquely Protestant about such an idea, and it can be as socially transformative in our world today as it was in nineteenth-century England.

That said, I can't imagine any readers being predisposed to *both* Christian socialism and evangelical paternalism (if either), but both demonstrate genuine and effective efforts—on their own terms, at least—by the first Christians to tackle the modern "Social Question." If readers only take from this chapter that we have more options to fight social injustice and uplift the poor than Marxism, I'll be happy. But we aren't yet finished with Marxism. Marx also made analytical claims. His challenges to economic science were met by the Marginal Revolution, which I address in the next chapter.

---

48  Andrey V. Ivanov, *A Spiritual Revolution: The Impact of Reformation and Enlightenment in Orthodox Russia* (University of Wisconsin Press, 2020), 212.

# CHAPTER 30

# The Marginal Revolution

I N A BRILLIANT MOVE UNITING both geeks and nerds, in 2023 Wizards of the Coast, maker of the collectible card game Magic (The Gathering), announced a sensational crossover product: *Lord of the Rings*-themed Magic cards (just as J. R. R. Tolkien intended!). Wizards even included a one-of-a-kind printing of the coveted "One Ring" card. When Magic player Brook Trafton found it in a pack in June 2023, she was "keen to sell the card directly to another Magic player and collector," according to *Polygon*.[1] She found her buyer in the Grammy-nominated musical artist Post Malone, who bought it for $2 million.

What could possibly explain spending $2 million for a rectangle of cardboard? Marginal utility. This concept forms the centerpiece of the late-nineteenth century Marginal Revolution in economics. It also explains why mainstream economics ultimately rejected Marxist analysis. Discovered simultaneously and independently by William Stanley Jevons in England, Léon Walras in Switzerland, Carl Menger in Austria, and John Bates Clark in the United States, marginal utility led to the mathematization of economics without losing sight of moral concerns. It solved many unanswered puzzles leftover from classical political economy and remains foundational for modern economics today. So how does it work? And how did it serve as a convincing

---

1    Oli Welsh, "Post Malone Has Bought Magic's $2M One Ring Card," *Polygon*, August 2, 2023, https://www.polygon.com/23817181/mtg-one-ring-card-post-malone.

response to Karl Marx? In order to apply Orthodox Christian social thought to the common good of our economies today, we need to understand how prices reflect marginal utility rather than the objective amount of labor it takes to make something. If we can do that, we can understand how profits and businesses do not need to be exploitative but can serve both the Kingdom of God and the common good.

## Marxist Analysis

MARX BEGINS HIS MAGNUM OPUS *Capital* with the premise that "the exchange values of commodities must be capable of being expressed in terms of something common to them all."[2] He distinguishes between "use-value" and "exchange value," because evidently prices do not correspond to the usefulness of things. Marx uses Adam Smith's example: water and diamonds.[3] People need water to live. No one *needs* diamonds. "Diamonds are of very rare occurrence on the earth's surface," reasons Marx, "and hence their discovery costs, on an average, a great deal of labour-time."[4] He believes this means that products "have only one common property left, that of being products of labour."[5] Labor, to Marx, is where prices come from. This is known as the "labor theory of value."

Additionally, Marx claims Aristotle "discovered, in the expression of the value of commodities, a relation of equality,"[6] which Marx also affirms. This idea of "equality in exchange" assumes that two items will only be traded if they are of equal value. Taken together, "as values, commodities are mere congelations of human labour,"[7] and the exchange of two commodities indicates that they represent equal amounts of labor. In order to make a product, a "capitalist" must purchase all the means of production, from materials and

---

2  Karl Marx, *Capital: A Critical Analysis of Capitalist Production*, trans. Samuel Moore and Edward Aveling, ed. Friedrich Engels, vol. 1 (Swan Sonnenschein, 1904), 4.
3  Adam Smith, *An Inquiry into the Nature and Causes of the Wealth of Nations*, 5th ed., 2 vols. (Methuen & Co., 1904).
4  Marx, *Capital*, vol. 1, 7.
5  Marx, vol. 1, 4.
6  Marx, vol. 1, 29.
7  Marx, vol. 1, 18.

machinery (themselves products of labor) to the labor of workers. But if he took his product to market, he would only ever break even, right? How does he get his revenue to exceed his expenses? How does he make a profit?

"The creation of surplus-value," says Marx, can "be explained neither on the assumption that commodities are sold above their value, nor that they are bought below their value."[8] He rules out these explanations because of the principle of equality in exchange, explicitly rejecting Jean-Baptiste Say's insight that exchanges themselves create value.[9] Thus, to Marx the "surplus-value" must come not from the market but from the production process. He presumes the costs to the capitalist of every resource used in making a commodity cannot be changed—*except labor*. In the market, to Marx, employers and employees negotiate as equals, but in the shop, warehouse, mine, or factory, the boss calls the shots. So the capitalist pays the laborer for six hours' worth of product, for example, then requires him to work all day. As a result, "The rate of surplus-value is . . . an exact expression for the degree of exploitation of labour-power by capital, or of the labourer by the capitalist."[10]

Profit, to Marx, amounts to unpaid labor. Thus, he reasons, "The essential difference between . . . a society based on slave labour, and one based on wage labour, lies only in the mode in which this surplus-labour is in each case extracted from the actual producer."[11] The Marxist phrase "wage slavery" refers to this concept. To Marx, a slave and a wage-laborer differ only by the extent of their exploitation. Combined with his "historical materialism," this relationship *really* represents "oppressor and oppressed."[12] Charitably, we could say that to Marx "the practical and violent action of the masses"[13] simply follows the rule of "eye for eye" (Ex. 21:24)—justice in the form of violence for violence, but only if his analysis works.

---

8    Marx, vol. 1, 139.
9    Marx, vol. 1, 141.
10   Marx, vol. 1, 200–201.
11   Marx, vol. 1, 200.
12   Karl Marx and Friedrich Engels, *Manifesto of the Communist Party*, in *The Marx-Engels Reader*, ed. Robert C. Tucker, 2nd ed. (W. W. Norton & Company, 1978), 473–474.
13   Karl Marx, "Society and Economy in History," in *The Marx-Engels Reader*, 141.

## *Marginal Analysis*

So what makes marginal analysis better? While economists did directly respond to Marx, we should remember how marginal (no pun intended) Marx was in his lifetime. While the first-generation marginalists don't seem to have Marx in mind, the Austrian Eugen von Böhm-Bawerk and the Englishman Alfred Marshall certainly did, so I will also draw on their work, as well as Philip Wicksteed, to help us understand marginal utility.

Böhm-Bawerk notes that while Marx's reasoning may be valid, he fails to prove the claims upon which he reasons: "Marx . . . should have given a purely empirical proof in support of a proposition adapted to a purely empirical proof. This, however, Marx does not do."[14] Every summer I teach a research methods seminar, and one thing I emphasize is that empirical claims require empirical evidence. Marx supplies no empirical evidence for the labor theory of value. Rather, he appeals to the authority of Smith and Ricardo, though they did not come to the same conclusions as him. But Böhm-Bawerk notes, "There is yet another and perfectly natural way of testing and proving such propositions: the psychological."[15] He claims Marx doesn't use this method either. We can give Marx more credit. The water/diamond paradox at least starts with a psychological consideration of use-value. However, Marx still didn't give this method its due.

Marginalists noticed that utility, which is just another word for "usefulness," comes in more than one kind. They distinguished between "absolute" or "total" utility and "effective" or "marginal" utility.[16] John Bates Clark gives the example of air: "The cubic mile of air about your dwelling sustains your life; of course it has infinite utility. But has it? Annihilate it and see. Other air at once takes its place."[17] Everyone needs air to breathe, but that is *absolute* or *total*

---

14    Eugen von Böhm-Bawerk, "Karl Marx and the Close of His System," in *Karl Marx and the Close of His System & Böhm-Bawerk's Criticism of Marx*, ed. Paul M. Sweezy (Augustus M. Kelley Publishers, 1975), 66.

15    Böhm-Bawerk, "Marx and the Close of His System," 67.

16    See John B. Clark, *The Philosophy of Wealth: Economic Principles Newly Formulated* (Ginn and Company, 1886), 78; Alfred Marshall, *Principles of Economics: An Introductory Volume*, 8th ed. (Macmillan and Co., 1930), 129.

17    Clark, *Philosophy of Wealth*, 77.

utility, not *effective* or *marginal* utility. Even a cubic mile of air has no effective utility, because as a matter of physics it would be immediately replaced if it disappeared. Thus, says Alfred Marshall, "We cannot trust the marginal utility of a commodity to indicate its total utility."[18] Why does this distinction matter? "The real worth of things to a man is not gauged by the price he pays for them."[19] Rather, says Clark, "it is effective, and not absolute utility that is the basis of wealth and value,"[20] and thus prices.

By only considering total or absolute utility as "use-value," Marx missed marginal utility, too-hastily affirming the labor theory of value. Consider this alarmingly inaccurate statement from Marx: "Whether a man buys his house ready built, or gets it built for him, in neither case will the mode of acquisition increase the amount of money laid out on the house."[21] At least today, the cost of buying a home on the market contrasts sharply with building one.[22] This data, of course, would be an example of the empirical evidence Marx failed to consider. Instead, he simply presumed the price must be the same because the "congealed labour-time"[23] contained in a house doesn't differ whether bought or built.

So also, the amount of labor to produce a Magic (The Gathering) card doesn't change between Brook Trafton finding it in a pack for $13 and Post Malone purchasing it from her for $2 million. The act of opening *that* pack of cards didn't require $2 million-worth more labor than any other. For most readers, the effective value of that "One Ring" Magic card would probably be zero. But for Post Malone this card had $2 million worth of effective utility, which is why it sold for that price. Because of Marxism's inability to explain economic phenomena like this, Marxist analysis based on the labor theory of value is considered pseudoscience by economists today, whether "left-wing," "right-wing," or anywhere in between. How, then, does this effective or marginal utility "work"?

---

18   Marshall, *Principles of Economics*, 129.
19   Marshall, 129.
20   Clark, *The Philosophy of Wealth*, 78–79.
21   Marx, *Capital*, 172.
22   Holly Johnson, "Building a House vs Buying," *Consumer Affairs*, February 10, 2023, https://www.consumeraffairs.com/finance/building-a-house-vs-buying.html.
23   Marx, *Capital*, 6.

First of all, it is *personal*: "The *measure* of value is entirely subjective in nature," wrote Carl Menger, "and for this reason a good can have great value to one economizing individual, little value to another, and no value at all to a third."[24] What makes this "marginal" is the increase or decrease of value a person attributes to an additional unit—or degree of quality—of an economic good: "The satisfaction of any one specific need has, up to a certain degree of completeness, relatively the highest importance, and [then] . . . has a progressively smaller importance, until eventually a stage is reached at which . . . [it] is a matter of indifference." Beyond that, adding more becomes "a burden and a pain."[25] Thus, William Stanley Jevons notes, "The will is our pendulum, and its oscillations are minutely registered in all the price lists of the markets."[26] Following from this, Marshall adds, "The *elasticity* (or *responsiveness*) *of demand* in a market is great or small according as the amount demanded increases much or little for a given fall in price, and diminishes much or little for a given rise in price."[27] Thus, demand for yachts, for example, is highly flexible or *elastic*. No one needs them, so if the price is too high, no one buys them. Demand for insulin, by contrast, is *inelastic*, since many diabetics need it to live, no matter the price.

By contrast, the Marxist Rudolf Hilfering admitted, "Marx is entirely unconcerned with the individual motivation of the estimate of value."[28] He mistakenly accuses marginalists of individualism on this account. Rather, Philip Wicksteed insisted, "We must regard industrial and commercial life, not as a separate and detached region of activity, but as an organic part of our whole personal and social life."[29] And Clark argued, "It is society, not the individual, that makes the estimate of utility which constitutes a social or market valuation."[30] That is, prices in general reflect the average of marginal utility across

24    Carl Menger, *Principles of Economics*, trans. James Dingwall and Bert F. Hoselitz (Ludwig von Mises Institute, 1976), 146.
25    Menger, *Principles of Economics*, 125.
26    William Stanley Jevons, *The Theory of Political Economy* (Macmillan and Co., 1871), 14.
27    Marshall, *Principles of Economics*, 102.
28    Rudolf Hilfering, "Böhm-Bawerk's Criticism of Marx," in *Karl Marx and the Close of His System*, 185.
29    Philip H. Wicksteed, *The Common Sense of Political Economy* (Macmillan and Co., 1910), 3. See also Clark, *The Philosophy of Wealth*, 82.
30    Clark, 83.

all potential buyers. Marshall even shows how utility varies by social class.[31] In the case of the "One Ring" Magic card, most people would not be buyers at any price, but of those interested, Post Malone was not the only person who bid around $2 million. Marginalists simply presume the individual persons who make up society *matter*, whereas Marx does not. Because they account for personal motivations, their analysis more accurately explains real life.

Second, marginal utility is *comparative*: "The price which a person pays for a thing can never exceed . . . that which he would be willing to pay rather than go without it,"[32] says Marshall. We even have a hierarchy of needs and wants: "The feelings of which a man is capable are of various grades," says Jevons. "He is always subject to mere physical pleasure or pain. . . . He is capable also of mental and moral feelings of several degrees of elevation."[33]

That said, this comparative aspect of marginal utility supports Say's insight about the creation of value through exchange. As Léon Walras put it, "His remarkable insight stood him in good stead; the only thing he lacked was a more powerful method of investigation."[34] Marginal analysis—and advanced mathematics, to Walras—constitutes that "more powerful method." "Surplus value" or profit does not come from exploitation of workers—at least not necessarily or directly. Instead of equality of value in exchange, people *stop* exchanging at exactly the point they estimate the value of what they have equals what they are offered. Everyone wants to "get a deal" on their purchase, and in most cases they do. They only exchange when *both* parties think they gain.

In this light we can precisely define profit as when the marginal utility of a product to society (the price people will pay for it) exceeds the marginal utility of the resources used to make it (its cost). Menger notes that, of course, "Men can be in error about the value of goods."[35] We should always ask ourselves why we value what we do, lest we end up with buyer's remorse, like Esau after selling his birthright to Jacob for a bowl of stew (see Gen. 25:29–34). But in general—apart from deception, fraud, or misjudgment—most people

---

31   Marshall, *Principles of Economics*, 103.
32   Marshall, 124.
33   Jevons, *The Theory of Political Economy*, 29.
34   Léon Walras, *Elements of Pure Economics, or the Theory of Social Wealth*, trans. William Jaffé (George Allen and Unwin, 1954 [1874]), 389.
35   Menger, *Principles of Economics*, 120.

consider themselves better off, and thus exchanges are positive-sum in terms of wealth.

## Marginal Morality

SO FAR, WE'VE SEEN HOW marginal utility answers and surpasses Marx's analytical claims, but what then did these economists think about morality and economic progress?

Jevons stated, "I have no hesitation in accepting the Utilitarian theory of morals,"[36] though he rejected Jeremy Bentham's version,[37] instead claiming, "I have never felt that there is anything in that theory to prevent our putting the widest and highest interpretation upon the terms used."[38] As a champion of mathematical methods, Jevons's "utilitarian calculus" was, well, just ordinary calculus applied to marginal utility. Unlike Bentham and Marx, he knew value doesn't inhere within products on the market but rather comes from how potential buyers value those products, which is reflected in prices.

At its worst, utilitarianism tends toward majority rule or an ends-justify-the-means mentality. It also tends toward relativism: Utilitarianism is a theory of what is good, without actually defining *the* good. Instead, utilitarians emphasize that people all have their own, different ideas of the good. They usually claim neutrality regarding those ideas as long as people don't harm one another while pursuing their goals. But how do they determine what constitutes "harm" while remaining neutral about the good? Orthodox social thought can do better than that.

Next, and differently, Walras distinguished between economics as art, science, and ethic. Production takes technical experimentation and knowhow—it is an art. Exchange centers around marginal price analysis—it is a science. Distribution revolves around institutions like property, therefore justice—that's ethics.[39] Rather than utilitarianism, Walras's ethics are personalist, defining injustice in terms of using other people for one's own purposes rather

---

36 Jevons, *The Theory of Political Economy*, 27.
37 Jevons, 12.
38 Jevons, 27.
39 Walras, *Elements of Pure Economics*, 64.

than treating them as ends in themselves. In this light, he notes that distribution involves human freedom and responsibility. If people's choices are "good, there will be a mutual coordination of human destinies; justice will rule. If bad, the destiny of some will be subordinated to the destiny of others; injustice will prevail."[40]

John Bates Clark offers another moral perspective. Clark had a Puritan upbringing and identified as a Christian socialist, which he called "economic republicanism,"[41] at least in 1886 when he wrote his *Philosophy of Wealth*. That work includes chapters on "The Ethics of Trade"[42] and "The Economic Function of the Church."[43]

Regarding ethics, using marginal analysis he noted that in circumstances where the labor market is monopolized by only one company, workers will be at the mercy of their employer due to fear of being unable to meet their most basic needs (a matter of what Marshall called "inelastic demand"). So companies could lay off some workers to reduce wages through competition. Clark supported trades-unions to check such abuses, but he ultimately admitted this practice "has never, in our actual experience, been realized." Even if wages dip for a time, they always rebound higher. The explanation he offers is "our vacant lands. Competition cannot starve men while free farms are waiting for them."[44]

On the Church, Clark notes, "If men were purely material, physical nourishment would suffice for them; but spiritual natures require spiritual nutriment."[45] Furthermore, "The place of worship with its furnishings, the Bibles and book of song, much of the music, and most of the spoken words, are property, bought and paid for,"[46] as any parish council treasurer can remind us. Clark speaks harshly of those churches in his time that sold seats in pews and brought the socioeconomic distinctions of the world into their naves. Rather, like F. D. Maurice he notes that the Church at her most faithful already

---

40  Walras, 77.
41  Clark, *The Philosophy of Wealth*, 199.
42  Clark, 149–173.
43  Clark, 221–235.
44  Clark, 170.
45  Clark, 221.
46  Clark, 226.

realizes the principle of economic cooperation: "That which costs millions of dollars is, in this way, offered without reserve to whoever will take it."[47]

Soon after 1886, Clark would abandon his skepticism of competitive markets. Perhaps the evidence did not bear out his pessimism, or maybe he thought the work of trade unions or other cooperative societies had worked— the reason isn't clear. Nevertheless, one can still find biblical allusions in his last major work, *Social Justice without Socialism*,[48] so his new perspective was not likely due to a loss of faith.

Last, Marshall, whose 1890 *Principles of Economics* was the standard English-language textbook for decades, sees economics as fulfilling a Christian moral vocation: "The dignity of man was proclaimed by the Christian religion: it has been asserted with increasing vehemence during the last hundred years. . . . Now at last we are setting ourselves seriously to inquire . . . whether there need be large numbers of people doomed from their birth to hard work in order to provide for others the requisites of a refined and cultured life; while they themselves are prevented by their poverty and toil from having any share or part in that life."[49]

Nevertheless, Marshall points out big advances in the quality of life since even 1800 in England, while also observing some of the tradeoffs required by the rough transition to what he calls *"Economic Freedom"*[50]: "In a modern society the obligations of family kindness become more intense, though they are concentrated on a narrower area; and neighbours are put more nearly on the same footing with strangers."[51] Yet, "modern methods of trade imply habits of trustfulness on the one side and a power of resisting temptation to dishonesty on the other, which do not exist among a backward people."[52] Reminiscent of Lord Shaftesbury, Marshall supports increased education and play for children, as well as increased upward economic mobility for the poor. He also admits that, in Britain at least, trade unions have contributed to better working conditions.

---

47  Clark, 228.
48  John Bates Clark, *Social Justice without Socialism* (Houghton Mifflin Company, 1914).
49  Marshall, *Principles of Economics*, 3–4.
50  Marshall, 10, italics original.
51  Marshall, 6.
52  Marshall, 7.

Unfortunately, Marshall's worldview has a major drawback: Passing references to "backward races" of people plague his work. One could say he was "a man of his time"—perhaps he simply used terms to refer to less developed economies that only grate against our contemporary standards of propriety. But the early twentieth century featured a worldview called "eugenics" that twisted Malthus's principle of population, combined with Darwinian evolution, to claim some races and classes of people were more advanced than others and that future good could come about by discouraging less advanced people from reproducing. While now debunked, many once considered eugenics serious science. Unfortunately, as a lifetime member of the Cambridge University branch of the Eugenics Education Society, we know Marshall was one of them.

## An Orthodox Assessment

FATHER SERGEI BULGAKOV WROTE IN 1912, "The labor theory of value, at least in pure form, has long been indefensible even within political economy."[53] This chapter has shown, from the words of Marx, why that is the case. While Marxist analysis can be found in almost every other academic discipline (including biblical studies!), it is considered pseudoscience by mainstream economists today, and for good reason: It doesn't accurately describe prices, production, or profits. Orthodox social thought shouldn't be using Marxist analysis to understand our economic life in the same way that people shouldn't use phrenology to understand neuroscience. It is an intellectual dead end.

By contrast, marginal analysis is still used today, and it carries potential to help us better understand the needs of those around us. As Vladimir Soloviev put it, "It is written that man does not live by bread *alone*, but it is not written that he lives without bread."[54] Marginal analysis explains how a per-

---

53 Sergei Bulgakov, *Philosophy of Economy: The World as Household*, trans. Catherine Evtuhov (Yale University Press, 2000), 120. He nevertheless found it philosophically interesting.

54 Vladimir Solovyov, *The Justification of the Good*, rev. ed., ed. Boris Jakim, trans. Natalie A. Duddington (Eerdmans, 2005), 394–395, emphasis original.

son whose basic needs go unmet will put a higher value on food, clothing, shelter, and so on, than on less essential goods. Indeed, we should care for the common good so that others might catch a glimpse of God's Kingdom through us. But that doesn't make those material needs more important than spiritual matters.

Our Orthodox history illustrates this point well. Economists usually rank food, clothing, and shelter as the most basic values. But Christian ascetics and martyrs forgo even these for a more basic need: communion with God—"to live is Christ, and to die is gain" (Phil. 1:21). To be fair, Marshall does at least acknowledge, "Religious motives are more intense than economic." But since "economics is a study of mankind in the ordinary business of life," and "the business by which a person earns his livelihood generally fills his thoughts," he focuses on those things.[55] Clark does a better job attending to basic spiritual needs, and no doubt we could learn from his integration of faith and economics. Similarly, marginal analysis and Orthodox social thought could enlighten one another.

Marshall, on the other hand, is less morally consistent than Clark. When he speaks about Christian principles, he's quite good. And he integrates these well with his economic analysis. But all his moral statements are tainted by his eugenics. Eugenics emphasizes the superiority of the strong, healthy, racially dominant, and noble-born over the weak, disabled, and working class, especially but not limited to racial minorities. It is an inversion of the kenoticism of the medieval Rus' that, by contrast, imitates Christ in serving the lowest and elevating the last. We can learn from Marshall's economics, but we should reject his eugenics.

We could better learn from Walras's personalist approach to political economy. As we've seen in previous chapters, the idea that people should always be treated as ends in themselves and never reduced to mere means is thoroughly Orthodox.[56] Walras's emphasis on justice furthermore resonates with natural law, though he unfortunately opposed "nature" and "freedom" in a way the

---

55   Marshall, *Principles of Economics*, 1.
56   See Athenagoras of Athens, *Treatise on the Resurrection*, 12–13, in *ANF* 2:154–156, discussed in chapter 7; Solovyov, *Justification of the Good*, 152, discussed in chapter 24.

Church Fathers never would.[57] Even so, his political economy might make for an interesting conversation partner with Orthodox social thought as well.

While these moral views differ widely, they demonstrate Schumpeter's observation about the genuinely scientific value of marginal analysis: "The marginal principle per se is a tool of analysis, the use of which imposes itself as soon as analysis comes of age,"[58] regardless of one's creed. He even notes how a few Marxists, such as Emil Lederer,[59] ended up adopting marginal analysis and abandoning the labor theory of value.

Indeed, until the Russian Revolution, Marxists were more willing to modify their worldviews. Schumpeter notes how they "watered down Marx's [prediction of a] spectacular breakdown [of capitalism] . . . to a mere inability of capitalist society to keep up its traditional rate of accumulation."[60] In hindsight, even that prediction didn't pan out—though some today still use the meme "late capitalism" to signify this idea. But to be fair, the time between now and then didn't *lack* crises either. In addition to the Russian Revolution, the next chapter of this section explores economic perspectives on a range of civilizational crises from World War I through the Great Depression and World War II.

---

57   Walras, *Elements of Pure Economics*, 55.
58   Joseph A. Schumpeter, *A History of Economic Analysis*, ed. Elizabeth Boody Schumpeter (George Allen & Unwin Ltd; Oxford University Press, 1954), 836.
59   Emil Lederer, *Technical Progress and Unemployment*, International Labour Office Studies and Reports, Series C (Employment and Unemployment), no. 22 (P. S. King & Son, 1938).
60   Schumpeter, *History of Economic Analysis*, 849.

CHAPTER 31

# The Economics of Crisis

O N JUNE 28, 1914, GAVRILO Princip, a Bosnian Serb, assassinated Austrian Archduke Franz Ferdinand and his wife, Sophie, spurring the July Crisis, in which the nations of Europe activated a series of alliances. Austria-Hungary declared war on Serbia, and World War I began, tearing apart the fabric of European Christendom and finally ending on Armistice Day, November 11, 1918. Exactly five years after the assassination of Franz Ferdinand, the Paris Peace Conference concluded in 1919 with the Treaty of Versailles, in which Germany, the strongest ally of Austria-Hungary, officially surrendered to the Allied powers and accepted their terms, including heavy reparations, disarmament, territorial concessions, and declaration of responsibility for the damages of war.

World War I marked the first of many civilizational crises in the twentieth century, followed by the Russian Revolution, the Great Depression, and World War II, among others. Economists interpreted these crises and offered guidance, for better and worse, to avoid repeating them. The emergence of modern macroeconomics—the study of whole economies and the forces that influence them—marks the last development of economic science and political economy we'll examine in Part 4, beginning in this chapter with its originator: John Maynard Keynes. Keynes's work, and responses from F. A. Hayek and Wilhelm Röpke, clarifies contemporary questions of crisis and monetary policy with a surprising, if unintentional, embrace of the ascetic discipline of memento mori: meditation on death. These economists together can help us see the ascetic foundation of modern monetary policy and its importance for Orthodox social thought today.

## Keynes's Political Economy

KEYNES WORKED AS "OFFICIAL REPRESENTATIVE" of the British Treasury "at the Paris Peace Conference" and "sat as deputy for the Chancellor of the Exchequer on the Supreme Economic Council"[1] before resigning in frustration, as he writes in his 1919 work *The Economic Consequences of the Peace*. This work "launched him to global fame,"[2] according to Phillip W. Magness and Sean J. Hernandez. Keynes "argued cogently that the huge weight of the reparations demanded of Germany and others would impoverish Europe and risk civil war,"[3] notes one editor of his work. In hindsight, Keynes appears prescient. Moreover, in the midst of the Great Depression in 1935, he published his *General Theory of Employment, Interest, and Money*, which offered a blueprint for how policymakers could fight massive unemployment. As early as 1923 he complained, "Economists set themselves too easy, too useless a task if in tempestuous seasons they can only tell us that when the storm is long past the ocean is flat again."[4] The *"long run,"* he argued, "is a misleading guide to current affairs. *In the long run* we are all dead."[5]

Critics often point to this as short-term thinking, but as Samuel Gregg notes, "Strictly speaking, he was not prioritizing the pursuit of short-term advantage over medium- and long-term economic performance."[6] Rather,

---

1    John Maynard Keynes, *The Economic Consequences of the Peace*, in *The End of Laissez-Faire; The Economic Consequences of the Peace* (Prometheus Books, 2004), 49, henceforth *End of Laissez-Faire; Economic Consequences*.

2    Phillip W. Magness and Sean J. Hernandez, "The Economic Eugenicism of John Maynard Keynes," *Journal of Markets & Morality* 20, no. 1 (2017): 83, henceforth "Economic Eugenicism."

3    Robert H. Parks, "Foreword," in *End of Laissez-Faire; Economic Consequences*, 11.

4    John Maynard Keynes, *A Tract on Monetary Reform* (Macmillan and Co., 1929 [1923]), 80.

5    Keynes, *Tract on Monetary Reform*, 80, italics original.

6    Samuel Gregg, "Wilhelm Röpke, John Maynard Keynes, and the Problem of Inflation," *Journal of Markets & Morality* 20, no. 1 (2017): 144.

he argued that inflation doesn't just regulate itself. Inflation, the increase of prices due to the devaluation of money, points to a factor of prices in addition to marginal utility: Prices are *measured in money*. Thus, fluctuations in the value of money affect prices across an economy just as much as the supply of, and demand for, products.

Indeed, as we already saw with the Late Scholastics, the value of money itself depends on supply and demand. Economists call this the "quantity theory of money." But the supply isn't simply the total money but the total money *in circulation*—the total money in use. To Keynes saving money instead of using it creates deflation—the decrease in prices due to the increased value of money—whereas investment keeps money moving. As Lawrence H. White put it, "In Keynes's theory interest is . . . a reward" for using money instead of saving it.[7] Indeed, in the way modern banking works, banks lend out people's money, making profit through interest. They are only required to hold a "fractional reserve"—a small portion—of deposits. Thus, the supply of money actually *increases* through loans.

Keynes noted that if central banks set the interest rate of federal funds low, people will borrow more, investing in capital assets (like houses) and businesses. Low rates encourage borrowing because the total amount people have to pay back will be less than with high rates. Low rates also make borrowing a good hedge against inflation. If a loan only has 2 percent interest, but inflation is 3 percent, the total amount paid back will be *less* than what was borrowed in terms of *real* (the actual buying power) rather than *nominal* (the number of dollars) value. Even in that example, banks are better off lending since the real value of their funds would diminish *even more* if they didn't. So mild inflation incentivizes everyone to lend and borrow, moving more money through an economy, which Keynes thought was a good thing.

As a result of increased investment, current businesses expand and entrepreneurs create new ones, which increases the demand for workers. As a result of inflation, the real value of wages will be cheaper, so businesses will be able to hire more unskilled people in particular, reducing unemployment. Thus, in his *General Theory*, Keynes defined "*full* employment" not as zero

---

7 Lawrence H. White, *The Clash of Economic Ideas: Great Policy Debates and Experiments of the Last Hundred Years* (Cambridge University Press, 2012), 136–137.

unemployment but as "the *maximum* quantity" at "a given real wage."[8] He thought central banks should adjust interest rates and the money supply to maintain full employment, noting that fiscal policy (government spending) contributes to this, too. When governments spend at a deficit (i.e., on credit), it creates inflation but also employment on public works projects. According to Keynes, "If our central controls succeed" in creating full employment, "the classical theory comes into its own again."[9]

All this relates to the Great Depression because, as the US Federal Reserve notes, "From the fall of 1930 through the winter of 1933, the money supply fell by nearly 30 percent."[10] Basically, $10,000 cash in 1930 would buy $13,000 worth of goods in 1933. Why was that bad? Deflation has the opposite effect of everything above: Borrowers end up having to pay back *even more* than they borrowed, and people save more, since the real value of money increases all on its own. But, of course, saving cash and not using it decreases the supply of money in use, causing more deflation. "Together, hoarding and accumulating reduced the supply of money. . . . As the stock of money declined, the prices of goods necessarily followed."[11] As a result, people made a run on banks to withdraw their money, in some cases exceeding banks' fractional reserves. "Deflation forced banks, firms, and debtors into bankruptcy; distorted economic decision-making; reduced consumption; and increased unemployment."[12] In May 1933, unemployment in the US surpassed 25 percent. With this experience as the background, Keynes's *General Theory* seemed heaven-sent.

"While Keynes was writing *The General Theory*," writes Hadley T. Mitchell, "he had come to view economics as a moral science."[13] As we've seen, most economists still expressed ethical views. But Keynes's morality has problems. Under the influence of philosopher G. E. Moore, Keynes rejected not only

---

8    John Maynard Keynes, *The General Theory of Employment, Interest, and Money* (Harcourt, Brace and Company, 1935), 12, emphasis original.

9    Keynes, *General Theory of Employment*, 378.

10   Gary Richardson, "The Great Depression," *Federal Reserve History*, November 22, 2013, https://www.federalreservehistory.org/essays/great-depression.

11   Gary Richardson, "Banking Panics of 1930–31," *Federal Reserve History*, November 22, 2013, https://www.federalreservehistory.org/essays/banking-panics-1930-31.

12   Richardson, "Banking Panics of 1930–31."

13   Hadley T. Mitchell, "The Ethics of Keynes," *Journal of Markets & Morality* 20, no. 1 (2017): 33.

utilitarianism but Christianity and natural law, too. Instead, his core "ethical" commitment was eugenics.

According to Magness and Hernandez, "One repeated theme is his attribution of population problems to the laissez-faire of nature, essentially positioning eugenic-infused policies as a correction to what he saw as a form of market failure."[14] For example, "In 1925 . . . Keynes traveled to Moscow" and gave a lecture with "an astounding thesis to explain the economic woes of the Soviet Union. All but turning a tin ear to the Soviets' destructive foray into centralized industrialization, Keynes suggested an entirely different cause: overpopulation."[15] Given the Soviets' mass murder of millions of their own people, including many Orthodox martyrs, Keynes's statement sounds alarmingly tone-deaf today.

Worse, in June 1926, Keynes gave a lecture at the University of Berlin that "formed the basis for his influential essay 'The End of Laissez-Faire.' "[16] In that essay, Keynes mused, "The time may arrive a little later when the community as a whole must pay attention *to the innate quality* as well as to the mere numbers of its future members."[17] According to Magness and Hernandez, the German press heard the message loud and clear.[18] Despite the terror of Nazism, Keynes never disavowed eugenics, calling it "the most important, significant and . . . genuine branch of sociology which exists"[19] just two months before his death in 1946.

## An Austrian Political Economy

THE WOES OF INTERWAR GERMANY and the rise of Nazism form the background for another economic bestseller: *The Road to Serfdom* by F. A. Hayek, an economist of the Austrian school that traced its roots to Carl Menger, Eugen von Böhm-Bawerk, and others. According to White, "Nobody

---

14  Magness and Hernandez, "Economic Eugenicism," 84.
15  Magness and Hernandez, 85.
16  Magness and Hernandez, 86.
17  John Maynard Keynes, *The End of Laissez-Faire*, in *End of Laissez-Faire; Economic Consequences*, 42, italics added.
18  Magness and Hernandez, "Economic Eugenicism," 86.
19  Quoted in Magness and Hernandez, 79.

was more surprised than Hayek when *The Road to Serfdom* quickly became a popular success."[20] With several abridgments, including by *Reader's Digest*, orders for the book, first published in 1944, rapidly exceeded one million copies, launching Hayek on a speaking tour of the US in 1945. In the book, Hayek used his tools as an economist to analyze the rise of totalitarianism and warn the Allied nations of WWII to avoid the same fate.

According to Hayek, public unrest over competitive markets leads to calls for government regulation. Government regulation then leads to an economy "in which competition is more or less suppressed but planning is left in the hands of the independent monopolies of the separate industries,"[21] which only reduces the dynamism of the economy and creates greater public unrest. Finally, when the results don't satisfy the public, the state takes control, which leads to the nationalization of industries and the direction of production by government instead of by consumer demand through uncontrolled prices.

The resulting inefficiencies create a dilemma for public leaders: "Just as the democratic statesman who sets out to plan economic life will soon be confronted with the alternative of either assuming dictatorial powers or abandoning his plans," writes Hayek, "so the totalitarian dictator would soon have to choose between disregard of ordinary morals and failure." He continues, "It is for this reason that the unscrupulous and uninhibited are likely to be more successful in a society tending towards totalitarianism."[22] Thus, totalitarianism creates a Gresham's Law of leadership: Bad leaders drive out good. Economic intervention leads to the expansion of state power over private life and ultimately to grave moral corruption.

Keynes sought to distance his theories from classical economics, mischaracterizing it as based on greed and laissez-faire (noninterventionism), but Hayek, a classical liberal, saw himself in greater continuity with it. Yet even Hayek stipulated, "It is important not to confuse opposition against this kind of planning with a dogmatic laissez-faire attitude. The liberal argument is in favour of making the best possible use of the forces of competition as a means

---

20  White, *Clash of Economic Ideas*, 168.
21  F. A. Hayek, *The Road to Serfdom* (George Routledge & Sons, 1944), 30.
22  Hayek, *Road to Serfdom*, 101.

of co-ordinating human efforts, not an argument for leaving things just as they are."[23] Moreover, "competition not only requires adequate organisation of certain institutions like money, markets, and channels of information—some of which can never be adequately provided by private enterprise—but . . . an appropriate legal system."[24] He even stresses that "the preservation of competition" is not "incompatible with an extensive system of social services."[25] And he acknowledges the need for environmental regulation when competitive markets fall short.[26]

Echoing Adam Smith's *Wealth of Nations*, Hayek valued competition as a "discovery procedure"[27] in which uncontrolled prices coordinate the plans of buyers and sellers to bring about the best use of resources. In this way, even with today's data, computers, and artificial intelligence, no one could ever assume effective control over a whole economy. Doing so would require restricting economic freedom, rendering prices useless and making economic planning impossible. Breadlines and other massive shortages of basic goods in totalitarian societies illustrate this point.

So Hayek held the variety and spontaneity of nature in higher esteem than Keynes. He was more comfortable with the uncertain and unknowable aspects of social life. Despite common caricatures, Hayek rejected "dogmatic laissez-faire." He valued liberty, private property, and the rule of law. Though a religious agnostic, he even valued tradition and cultural institutions to the extent that they contained tacit social knowledge accumulated over the centuries. Last, he had humility about the limits of economics, claiming that "the economist who is only an economist is likely to become a nuisance if not a positive danger."[28] Indeed, this admirable intellectual asceticism pervades Hayek's work, even if he wouldn't call it that.

---

23     Hayek, 27.
24     Hayek, 28.
25     Hayek, 28.
26     Hayek, 29.
27     F. A. Hayek, "Competition as a Discovery Procedure," *The Quarterly Journal of Austrian Economics* 5, no. 3 (Fall 2002): 9–23, translated by Marcellus S. Snow. Originally given as a lecture in 1968.
28     F. A. Hayek, "The Dilemma of Specialization," in *Studies in Philosophy, Politics and Economics* (Touchstone, 1969), 123.

But Hayek's moral views still have shortcomings. In particular, he has little tolerance for social justice, which he calls a "mirage."[29] He reasons that the phrase tends to be a "black box" that people fill with whatever meaning they want, making it impossible to ever satisfy everyone. There may be some truth to that, but I think most people today, at least, use the term *social justice* to talk about things like "an appropriate legal system" and "an extensive system of social services" for those otherwise unable to support themselves, both of which, we've seen, Hayek thought possible and compatible with competitive markets in some form. In addition, he did admit that while he regretted the use of the phrase "social justice," he regarded philosopher John Rawls's theory of justice—that justice consists in what social rules would be most fair for a person chosen at random—to be "more or less what I have been trying to argue."[30]

## *An Ordoliberal Political Economy*

NEVERTHELESS, WE CAN SEE A more theologically informed moral perspective in the work of Wilhelm Röpke, an economist of the German Ordoliberal school. "A strong anti-Communist and a devout Lutheran Christian with a deep interest in Catholic social teaching," writes Gregg, "Röpke was fascinated by theological and philosophical questions."[31] This becomes clear right from the start of his 1958 work *A Humane Economy*: "I see in man the likeness of God; I am profoundly convinced that it is an appalling sin to reduce man to a means ... and that each man's soul is something unique, irreplaceable, priceless, in comparison with which all other things are as naught."[32] We see again here the personalist moral principle that people are ends in themselves. Röpke then combines this principle with the Christian theological perspective that all people are made after "the likeness of God." From this conviction, Röpke

---

29  F. A. Hayek, *Law, Legislation, and Liberty*, vol. 2, *The Mirage of Social Justice* (The University of Chicago Press, 1976).

30  Hayek, *Law, Legislation, and Liberty*, vol. 2, 100. See also John Rawls, *A Theory of Justice* (The Belknap Press, 1971), which Hayek cites.

31  Gregg, "Problem of Inflation," 142.

32  Wilhelm Röpke, *A Humane Economy: The Social Framework of the Free Market*, trans. Elizabeth Henderson (Henry Regnary Company, 1960), 5.

cared deeply about the moral culture of a free and humane society, without neglecting the insights of modern economics.

"One week after Hitler was appointed Chancellor in early 1933," writes White, "Röpke gave a speech calling the National Socialist [i.e., Nazi] movement a 'revolt against reason, freedom and humanity.' When Hitler's government began expelling Jews from German universities two months later, he denounced the policy."[33] Indeed, all the Ordoliberals opposed Nazism, at great risk to their lives. White notes that Röpke's colleague Walter Eucken "courageously opposed the efforts of Martin Heidegger, the Rector of the University of Freiburg, to expel Jews from the University. During the Second World War, Eucken was active in an anti-Nazi discussion group. He was questioned several times by the Gestapo while some of the other participants were arrested."[34] Röpke, for his part, eventually fled to the Netherlands, then Turkey, later settling down in his homeland of Switzerland.

Writing in 1942, Röpke lamented, "We are experiencing the despair of one who has gone astray, and to be told the way is almost more important to us than to be given bread."[35] Once again, "man shall not live by bread alone" (Deut. 8:3). Echoing Smith's *Theory of Moral Sentiments*, Röpke thinks whole cultures need ascetic self-discipline: Society (not the state) "must have at its command prompt and infallible reflexes. . . . of approval or disapproval, which show us that society is guided by inviolable concepts of value. These reflexes should always begin to function easily and promptly as soon . . . as we enter the border zone where a joke ceases to be a joke."[36] Cultures that blunt these reflexes of basic propriety go "astray."

Unfortunately, Röpke grounded some of his worries in unease about overpopulation, which as we've already noted should not concern us in the midst of our abundance today. Unlike Keynes, though, Röpke thankfully wasn't a eugenicist. Rather, he worried that the mass culture of all classes in population-dense cities leaves them susceptible to populism and atomistic

---

33  White, *Clash of Economic Ideas*, 242.
34  White, 241.
35  Wilhelm Röpke, *The Social Crisis of Our Time*, trans. Annette and Peter Schiffer Jacobsohn (University of Chicago Press, 1950), 1–2.
36  Röpke, *Social Crisis of Our Time*, 12.

individualism: "The place of genuine integration created by genuine communities, which requires the ties of proximity, natural roots and the warmth of direct human relationships, has been taken by a pseudo-integration, created by the market, competition, central organization, by 'tenementing,' by ballot papers, police, laws, mass production, mass amusements, mass emotions and mass education, a pseudo-integration which reaches its climax in the collectivist state."[37]

I call this "unfortunate" because I do not see any reason that densely populated cities are more liable to mob mentalities than communities in the countryside. The Middle Ages had pitchfork-toting villagers, despite "ties of proximity" and "natural roots." That is not to say, of course, that modern, urban society doesn't present genuine challenges in terms of maintaining close community ties, but I find Alfred Marshall's more balanced assessment fits better with the facts.[38] Indeed, Röpke at times echoes sociologist Max Weber's thesis that capitalism depends on a Christian moral foundation it ultimately and necessarily undermines.[39] Similarly, Röpke seems to imply an *inevitable* trajectory of nineteenth-century capitalism culminating in the social breakdown of WWI and the subsequent rise of totalitarianism, despite significant exceptions—not only Switzerland but the Netherlands, Norway, Sweden, Denmark, and Spain maintained their neutrality during the Great War.

Yet to his credit, Röpke didn't just complain about the death of Western civilization, he and the Ordoliberals facilitated its resurrection in West Germany after WWII. In June 1948, Ludwig Erhard, "director of the Economic Administration in the UK-U.S. occupied zone of Germany," issued a massive currency reform and "a sweeping order abolishing many of the price controls and rationing directives then in effect."[40] According to White, "Röpke advised Erhard on the abolition of price controls,"[41] despite American and British

---

37  Röpke, 10.
38  Alfred Marshall, *Principles of Economics: An Introductory Volume*, 8th ed. (Macmillan and Co., 1930), 6–7, quoted in the previous chapter.
39  Max Weber, *The Protestant Ethic and the Spirit of Capitalism*, trans. Talcott Parsons (Routledge, 1992 [1930]).
40  White, *Clash of Economic Ideas*, 231.
41  White, 243.

officials' cautions. "With Erhard's sweeping decontrol measures, the shortages ended, and black markets disappeared. Shops once again had goods to sell."[42] Not only that, "By 1958, West Germany's per capita output had risen three-fold. The country outgrew France and the United Kingdom despite receiving much less Marshall Plan aid. It left East Germany in the dust. This was the era of the *Wirtschaftswunder* or 'wonder economy.'"[43] But it wasn't magic, just sound economics. Put simply, they restored the freedom of prices and money to function properly again, and the potential of human nature to "be fruitful and multiply; fill the earth and subdue it" (Gen. 1:28) went to work.

On economics, the Ordoliberal position can be summed up by Eucken: "State planning of [market] forms—Yes; state planning and control of the economic process—No!"[44] Their position sits somewhat between Keynes and the Austrians. They supported economic liberty, but they also thought that without structural regulation, freedom of contract would crowd out freedom of competition. Since they valued the benefits of competition, they recommended the reduction of barriers to market entry and the use of anti-trust action to break up monopolies. Though Röpke strongly preferred private charity, in general the Ordoliberals also supported public social services. Their political economy still forms the foundation of the German social market economy today.

That said, in sharp contrast to Keynes, the Ordoliberals opposed inflationary monetary policy. While Americans can look back fondly on the economic boom of the Roaring '20s, Gregg notes, "In the early years of the Weimar Republic, hyperinflation developed to the point whereby the German mark, worth 4.2 to the US dollar in 1914, was trading at a rate of four trillion to one by late 1923. The savings of much of the middle class in one of the most populous and industrialized countries in Europe were thus wiped out."[45] As Hayek warned, "It should never be forgotten that the one decisive factor in the rise of totalitarianism on the Continent . . . is the existence of a large recently

---

42   White, 232.
43   White, 233.
44   Walter Eucken, *This Unsuccessful Age: Or the Pains of Economic Progress* (Oxford University Press, 1952), 96.
45   Gregg, "Problem of Inflation," 143.

dispossessed middle class."[46] What they needed—and what, after WWII the Ordoliberal currency reform accomplished—was sharp *deflation* followed by long-term monetary stability. Having lived through such harrowing hyperinflation, Röpke faulted Keynes for basing "his economic revolution on his diagnosis of extraordinary circumstances: the Great Depression."[47] And the restraint Keynes did call for went unheeded. As Röpke pointed out, "One cannot talk Parliament and public opinion into saving and economical management, by exceptionally praising them as virtues, if all the rest of the time they are reviled as folly and sin."[48]

## An Orthodox Assessment

To me, the connecting thread for these economists from an Orthodox perspective is asceticism. Keynes's emphasis on relieving mass unemployment, grounded in the reality of our mortality "*in the long run,*" could be regarded as a sort of economic memento mori, the discipline of "remembrance of death." People do not live forever, and those who are hurting today will not be comforted by assurances that *eventually* everything will work itself out. We must always remember our limitations, including in our economies. Only God is eternal. Businesses, markets, industries, and even whole economies change every day, and people need help getting by. And if economic policy can help, economists may have a unique vocation to do so. That said, just as with Alfred Marshall, we must reject Keynes's eugenics, which unfortunately was central to his political economy. Whatever we may think of Keynesian policies, this "moral" aspect of Keynes's political economy cannot be reconciled with our Orthodox Tradition's emphasis on the inherent dignity of every person created in the image of God.

As for Hayek, his comfort with uncertainty and the limits of knowledge fits well with what we saw in the biblical Apocrypha: learning to wait on God in

---

46  Hayek, *Road to Serfdom*, 155.
47  Gregg, "Problem of Inflation," 144.
48  Wilhelm Röpke, "Keynes and the Revolution in Economics: Economics Old, New, and True," in *The Humane Economist: A Wilhelm Röpke Reader,* ed. Daniel J. Hugger (Acton Institute, 2019), 237–238.

all things. Moreover, our ascetic approach to theology, which emphasizes the limits of what we can know and the transcendent mystery of God's works, fits well with both Hayek's method and his emphasis, like Adam Smith, on spontaneous order. Being religiously agnostic, Hayek probably wouldn't agree with that, but those who build on his insights today might be more open to this connection. Furthermore, his warnings from the *Road to Serfdom* about how one bad policy leads to another, and how the most morally corrupt leaders thrive in totalitarian societies, should help us guard against the temptation to follow anyone who makes big, unrealistic promises, whether in government, the Church, business, or any other sphere of life.

Röpke does a better job directly tying his economics to the Christian principles we Orthodox share. We, too, believe that all people, created in God's image, have inherent dignity that must be respected. Furthermore, his warnings about how he saw the West going astray once again have an ascetic core to them. Just as we need self-discipline for our souls, so also our cultures need to freely exercise self-discipline—rather than having it imposed upon them by law—to sustain themselves. We could see this as a social application of St. Moses the Ethiopian's caution that, in seeking the Kingdom of God, "Travellers who miss their way are still tiring themselves though they are walking no nearer to their destination."[49] The way, Abba Moses tells us, is purity of heart. For Röpke, the common good of modern economies and even Western civilization needs this, too. If he's right that the West had already lost its way in his time, it has been tiring itself out ever since.

Nevertheless, the positive insights of economists like Keynes, Hayek, and Röpke can give us clarity about the crises of the past, including the Russian Revolution, for the sake of Orthodox social thought in the present. In his *Economic Consequences of the Peace*, Keynes rightly pointed out, "The Governments of Europe . . . seek to direct on to a class known as 'profiteers' the popular indignation against the more obvious consequences of their vicious methods. These 'profiteers' are, broadly speaking, the entrepreneur class of capitalists . . . who in a period of rapidly rising prices cannot but get rich

---

49   John Cassian, *Conferences*, 1.4, in *Western Asceticism*, ed. Owen Chadwick, vol. 12, The Library of Christian Classics (The Westminster Press, 1958), 197.

quick whether they wish it or desire it or not."[50] They didn't really "get rich" due to inflation, but by comparison to everyone else, due to rising prices, it looked that way. "By directing hatred against this class," Keynes warned, "the European Governments are carrying a step further the fatal process which the subtle mind of Lenin had consciously conceived. The profiteers are a consequence and not a cause of rising prices."[51] Hayek and Röpke would agree with him on that.

And so, combining Keynes's observations with Röpke's emphasis on Christian moral culture and Hayek's *Road to Serfdom*, we have our answer to one of the questions with which we ended Part 3: Where did the Russian Revolution come from? What wrought this "black miracle," as Fr. Sergei Bulgakov called it, in which "it has been granted to Satan to smite the Russian Job with all his flails"?[52] A mismanaged economy during an unpopular and bungled military conflict, within a culture in crisis, led to resentment against "capitalists" for high prices in an empire that had only just begun to industrialize. Then, dark forces and radical revolutionaries, like Vladimir Lenin, seized the opportunity for "practical and violent action,"[53] to quote Karl Marx once again. A similar "black miracle" played out in Germany two decades later, and across nearly a third of the world in the twentieth century.

But where did the world go from there? And what part can Orthodox social thought play in sanctifying our social and economic orders? The final chapter of this section will review more recent developments in monetary policy, the role of entrepreneurship, and the contemporary divergence between ethics and economics today.

---

50   Keynes, *Economic Consequences of the Peace*, in *End of Laissez-Faire; Economic Consequences*, 247–248.
51   Keynes, 248.
52   Sergius Bulgakov, "The Old and the New: A Study in Russian Religion," *The Slavonic Review* 2, no. 6 (March 1924): 487.
53   Karl Marx, "Society and Economy in History," in *The Marx-Engels Reader*, ed. Robert C. Tucker, 2nd ed. (W. W. Norton & Company, 1978), 141.

# CHAPTER 32

# The Great Divergence

E CONOMIST RUSS ROBERTS, KNOWN FOR his *EconTalk* podcast and his fondness for Adam Smith, made an observation a few years ago that encapsulates the state of modern economics: "Not everything that is important can be quantified. I worry that as economists, we too often are like the drunk at 1 AM looking for his keys under the glare of a streetlight. You go over to help, and when you fail to find the keys, you ask the drunk if he's sure if he lost them here. 'Oh no,' he responds. 'I'm not sure where I lost them. But the light's better here.'"[1] Mathematical modeling and statistical analysis can illuminate our social problems today. But for many modern economists, everything else lies shrouded in darkness. Examining mass shootings, the minimum wage, and the opioid crisis, Roberts uses Smith's observation in *The Theory of Moral Sentiments* that "man naturally desires, not only to be loved, but to be lovely"[2] to invite other economists to pay more attention to what can't be measured: "There isn't a variable for dignity in the data set,"[3] says Roberts.

1   Russ Roberts, "Adam Smith, Loneliness, and the Limits of Mainstream Economics," *Medium*, March 11, 2019, https://russroberts.medium.com/adam-smith-loneliness-and -the-limits-of-mainstream-economics-fobe78940e17.

2   Adam Smith, *The Theory of Moral Sentiments*, 6th ed., 3.2, in *The Theory of Moral Sentiments; Or, An Essay towards an Analysis of the Principles by Which Men Naturally Judge Concerning the Conduct and Character, First of Their Neighbours, and Afterwards of Themselves. To Which Is Added, A Dissertation on the Origin of Languages*, new ed. (Henry G. Bohn, 1853), 166.

3   Roberts, "Adam Smith, Loneliness."

From the Late Scholastics to Adam Smith, the classical economists, the marginalists, and John Maynard Keynes, to F. A. Hayek and Wilhelm Röpke, economists often had moral and sometimes even theological commitments that shaped their political economy. But trends in the twentieth century would push morally informed political economy to the margins of economics today. Economists have only lately become Roberts's man searching for his keys under the streetlight: The Great Divergence, as I call it, between economics and ethics is recent. This chapter charts out some of those trends toward positivism—the idea that economics should be free of moral content—as well as noting a few exceptions. In the process, I'll also discuss the important role of entrepreneurship and, once again, monetary policy. By the end, I hope to show the opportunity for Orthodox Christian social thought to contribute to our own understanding of pressing economic issues for the life of the world today.

## *From Knight to Schumpeter*

NOW, JUST TO BE CLEAR and avoid confusion, when I say that there has been a Great Divergence between ethics and economics, I do not mean to condemn *distinguishing* between morality and economics. After all, we *distinguish* between our Lord's divinity and humanity, while at the same time affirming them to be without separation, division, confusion, or change. Distinguishing is necessary to avoid confusion. The Great Divergence, rather, is a problem of the separation of two things that, while distinguishable in theory, in practice work and exist as one.

We could regard University of Chicago economist Frank Knight as something of the canary in the coal mine. Knight is a complicated figure, about whom it was said, in mock imitation of the Islamic *shahada*, "There is no God, but Frank Knight is his prophet."[4] The meaning of this phrase has been disputed, but at least in his published work, the sense is that Knight acknowledged and insisted upon—while also lamenting—the social importance of religion. Though relatively irreligious and even hostile toward Christianity, he

---

4    Robert H. Nelson, "Frank Knight and Original Sin," *The Independent Review* 6, no. 1 (Summer 2001): 5–25.

thought economics needed a moral, if not religious, foundation. To that end, he dedicated a significant portion of his work to critiquing the compatibility of various ethical systems with the insights of modern economics. "Without an adequate ethics and sociology in the broad sense," wrote Knight in 1939, "economics has little to say about policy."[5]

This statement comes at the end of an article Knight wrote on the ethics of Christianity, which he understood as a naive application of the Golden Rule to all spheres of life, even beyond communities of friendship and familiarity. As Ross B. Emmett summarizes, "Knight argued that the problems of social action in the impersonal context of rules for liberal democratic society cannot be resolved by appeals to Christian personal morality."[6] Actually, in contrast to Adam Smith, Knight didn't even recommend the Golden Rule for personal relations either. Perhaps some Christians in his day wanted the sort of "gospel of love" he critiqued, but his representation of Christian ethics is a straw man, making his critique unpersuasive.

Instead, the important thing about Knight is that even though he rejected Christianity, he still saw that economics needed moral and social thought ("ethics and sociology"). Despite being considered a founder of the influential Chicago school of economics, for a number of reasons Knight's warning went unheeded. One possibility may be that the insights of his major work in 1921, *Risk, Uncertainty and Profit*,[7] which focused on the nature of entrepreneurship, came to be eclipsed by Joseph Schumpeter's 1942 *Capitalism, Socialism, and Democracy*.[8] Similar to Jean-Baptiste Say, Knight focused on issues of character. Entrepreneurship requires that a person be an excellent judge of genuine, incalculable risk, as well as of the reliability and trustworthiness of business partners, in order to profit. Entrepreneurs must be the sort of people who are not crippled by uncertainty but ably plan ahead to account for it. A decade later, Knight gives us more to work with than Keynes's claim

---

5    Frank H. Knight, "Ethics and Economic Reform: III. Christianity," *Economica*, new series 6, no. 24 (November 1939): 422.

6    Ross B. Emmett, "Economics is Not All of Life," *Econ Journal Watch* 11, no. 2 (May 2014): 147.

7    Frank H. Knight, *Risk, Uncertainty and Profit* (Augustus M. Kelley, 1964).

8    Joseph A. Schumpeter, *Capitalism, Socialism, and Democracy*, 2nd ed. (Harper & Brothers, 1942).

that enterprise depends on "animal spirits," i.e., "a spontaneous urge to action rather than inaction."[9] Of course, enterprise requires willingness to take risks, but that doesn't make entrepreneurs' actions impulsive, unplanned, or unreasonable.

Schumpeter, by contrast to Knight, focused more on the broader impact of a dynamic, entrepreneurial economy. He coined the term "creative destruction" to describe how new products and industries transform and displace others, which leads to overall heightened economic well-being. The invention of the automobile, for example, revolutionized transportation and transformed the quality of life for everyone, but it also put many blacksmiths and carriage manufacturers out of business. He even noted that just the possibility of competition is enough to spark innovation—monopolies will still innovate as long as markets are open to even just the possibility of new competition. According to Schumpeter, "Industrial mutation . . . incessantly revolutionizes the economic structure from within, incessantly destroying the old one, incessantly creating a new one. This process of Creative Destruction is the essential fact about capitalism."[10]

For Schumpeter, this "essential fact" was purely a matter of observation, not faith or morality: "A theoretical construction which neglects this essential element of the case neglects all that is most typically capitalist about it . . . it is like *Hamlet* without the Danish prince."[11] Thus, like many twentieth-century economists, Schumpeter emphasized the importance of understanding dynamic economic changes: "In dealing with capitalism, we are dealing with an evolutionary process" as "long ago emphasized by Karl Marx."[12] Indeed, though the term "creative destruction" is often used to defend the benefits of competitive market economies—rightly so, in my opinion—Schumpeter thought the phenomenon pointed to the opposite conclusion.

Without contradiction, we could describe Schumpeter as a positivist, Austrian school, big-business socialist. Despite being raised Roman Catholic

---

9    John Maynard Keynes, *The General Theory of Employment, Interest, and Money* (Harcourt, Brace and Company, 1935), 162.
10    Schumpeter, *Capitalism, Socialism, and Democracy*, 83.
11    Schumpeter, 86.
12    Schumpeter, 82.

and later converting to Lutheranism, Schumpeter's desire to separate moral exhortation from economics comes through again and again in his *History of Economic Analysis*.[13] He was Austrian in terms of his methods and intellectual heritage, but in contrast to Hayek, for example, Schumpeter thought business consolidation and eventually state control were both good and inevitable. He claimed, but did not substantiate, that "big business may have had more to do with creating [a higher] standard of life than with keeping it down."[14] Empirical data since Schumpeter's time contradicts this claim, however. As Matthew Mitchell noted in 2012, "Compared with larger firms, smaller firms are about twice as likely to file 'high-impact' patents."[15] We can also, in hindsight, say that Schumpeter chose a bad example by citing US Steel in this connection.[16] If ever there were a "poster child" for how government intervention and favors lead to corporate decline and stunted dynamism, it would be US Steel.

## *The Rise of Chicago*

PERHAPS BUZZ ABOUT SCHUMPETER'S CONTROVERSIAL and positivist claims simply overshadowed Knight, but we can trace other contributions to the Great Divergence as well. We know Keynes had a moral grounding to his economics, but his followers (thankfully) often overlooked that aspect of his thought. MIT economist Paul Samuelson probably did more than anyone to popularize Keynes's insights through his 1948 *Economics*,[17] one of the standard textbooks for the following two decades. Clearly referencing Keynes, he identified the goal of economics as understanding the causes "of prosperity, full employment, and high standards of living."[18] While Samuelson did note that healthy democracies depend on these things for their survival, he nevertheless argued that economic analysis is worthwhile for its own sake: "A doctor

13  Joseph A. Schumpeter, *A History of Economic Analysis*, ed. Elizabeth Boody Schumpeter (George Allen & Unwin Ltd; Oxford University Press, 1954).

14  Schumpeter, *Capitalism, Socialism, and Democracy*, 82.

15  Matthew Mitchell, *The Pathology of Privilege: The Economic Consequences of Government Favoritism* (Mercatus Center, 2012), 27.

16  Schumpeter, *Capitalism, Socialism, and Democracy*, 83.

17  Paul A. Samuelson, *Economics: An Introductory Analysis*, 1st ed. (McGraw-Hill Book Company, Inc., 1948).

18  Samuelson, *Economics*, 3.

passionately interested in stamping out disease must train himself to observe things as they are. His bacteriology cannot be a different one from that of a mad scientist out to destroy the human race by plague."[19] Samuelson's point is that just as bacteriology is morally neutral, so is economics. What matters is what someone does with it, but such ethical concerns fall outside the competence of economics, which he largely believed to be a social application of mathematics.[20]

However, Samuelson somewhat fell out of popularity after the 1970s. As Lawrence H. White noted, "Keynesian writers . . . had an anomaly on their hands after 1969, when inflation and unemployment were high at the same time."[21] Under Keynesian analysis, inflation should have reduced unemployment. Having both at the same time meant that Keynes had missed something. Mainstream economists found a better alternative in Milton Friedman. With Anna Jacobson Swartz, Friedman cowrote the massive 1963 *Monetary History of the United States*,[22] which among other topics, offered a better account of the Great Depression than Keynes. Thankfully, Friedman wrote extensively and summarized their findings in other works.

" 'Full employment' and 'economic growth' have in the past few decades become primary excuses for widening the extent of government intervention in economic affairs," wrote Friedman. "A private free-enterprise economy, it is said, is inherently unstable. Left to itself, it will produce recurrent cycles of boom and bust. The government must therefore step in to keep things on an even keel."[23] On the contrary, "The Great Depression . . . was produced by government mismanagement rather than by any inherent instability of the private economy," Friedman argued. "A governmentally established agency—the Federal Reserve System—had been assigned responsibility for monetary policy. In 1930 and 1931, it exercised this responsibility so ineptly as to convert what

19    Samuelson, 5.
20    See especially Paul Anthony Samuelson, *Foundations of Economic Analysis* (Oxford University Press, 1947).
21    Lawrence H. White, *The Clash of Economic Ideas: Great Policy Debates and Experiments of the Last Hundred Years* (Cambridge University Press, 2012), 322.
22    Milton Friedman and Anna Jacobson Schwartz, *A Monetary History of the United States, 1867–1960* (Princeton University Press, 1963).
23    Milton Friedman, *Capitalism and Freedom*, 40th anniversary ed. (University of Chicago Press, 2002), 37.

THE KINGDOM OF GOD AND THE COMMON GOOD

otherwise would have been a moderate contraction into a major catastrophe."[24] As for this "mismanagement," Friedman details in another work, "Throughout that period the Federal Reserve System was never concerned with the quantity of money. It did not in fact publish monthly figures of the quantity of money until the 1940s. Indeed, the first mention in Federal Reserve literature of the quantity of money as a criterion of policy was in the 1950s."[25] The massive deflation that caused bank runs, bankruptcy, and unemployment took place because no one at the US Federal Reserve kept track of the monetary supply at all.

For Friedman, then, the goal of monetary policy should be to faithfully manage the money supply by keeping inflation stable and preferably low. Against Keynes's preference for expert discretion, Friedman recommended, "Short of the adoption of . . . a publicly stated policy of a steady rate of monetary growth, it would constitute a major improvement if the monetary authority followed the self-denying ordinance of avoiding wide swings."[26] To Friedman's credit, the Fed's official account of the Great Depression begins by quoting former Reserve chairman Ben Bernanke telling Friedman he was right.[27] And today, the Federal Reserve has a "dual mandate" to ensure both full employment and stable prices, essentially—some would argue, incompatibly—combining Keynes and Friedman. Nevertheless, the US dollar remains the world's reserve currency due to its relative stability, and Friedman deserves his due for his part in that.

## Practical Economists and Defunct Ethics

HOWEVER, FRIEDMAN'S INFLUENCE CANNOT BE limited to monetary policy. Despite studying under Knight at Chicago, Friedman argued, "Positive economics is in principle independent of any particular ethical position or normative judgments."[28] Indeed, according to Emmett, "Chicago rejected

---

24  Friedman, *Capitalism and Freedom*, 38.
25  Milton Friedman, *The Optimum Quantity of Money and Other Essays* (Macmillan and Co., 1969), 76.
26  Friedman, *Optimum Quantity of Money*, 109.
27  Gary Richardson, "The Great Depression," *Federal Reserve History*, November 22, 2013, https://www.federalreservehistory.org/essays/great-depression.
28  Milton Friedman, "The Methodology of Positive Economics," in *Essays in Positive Economics* (University of Chicago Press, 1966), 4.

Knight."[29] Thus, as distinct from Hayek, for example, Friedman regarded economics as "an 'objective' science, in precisely the same sense as any of the physical sciences."[30] Friedman, like Samuelson, spread the conception of economics as not just distinct but separate from ethics, despite also clearly caring about ethical issues in his popular writing and policy work.[31] Like Hayek, Friedman affirmed classical liberal values of individual liberty, private property, self-government, and so on. But non-market, non-state social spheres do not play a major role in his political economy. To him, either a problem can be solved by private enterprise, *or* the state must take action.[32] Friedman's theoretical achievement, high public profile, and positivist conception of economics further reinforced the Great Divergence, bringing us to the present state of things: Russ Roberts's man under the streetlight.

Today, economists largely disagree with Knight and follow Friedman in presuming that economics, apart from ethics and social thought, has a lot to say about policy. They comment on the news, online, and in books about how states, companies, and individuals should run their lives. While we should value the specialized analysis of modern economics and use it to make more prudent decisions, the moment a person says "should" or "ought," their statement has moved into the sphere of morality. Keynes once warned, "Practical men, who believe themselves to be quite exempt from any intellectual influences, are usually the slaves of some defunct economist."[33] The same applies to defunct ethicists, philosophers, and theologians. Indeed, many economists' policy recommendations today reflect a naïve utilitarianism, for example.

## *An Orthodox Assessment*

THE GREAT DIVERGENCE HAS LED to an estrangement between moral perspectives, like Christian social thought, and modern economics. But this

---

29  Emmett, "Economics is Not All of Life," 148.
30  Friedman, "Methodology of Positive Economics," 4.
31  White, *Clash of Economic Ideas*, 310.
32  Friedman, *Capitalism and Freedom*, 39.
33  Keynes, *The General Theory*, 384.

development was recent, and we can even learn from the economic insights of those who contributed to it.

For instance, we can learn from Knight and Schumpeter about the nature and importance of entrepreneurship. We might think of policies that allow for creative destruction as another sort of economic memento mori. Once again, businesses, markets, industries, and economies are as mortal as the people who work in them. Moreover, we believe life does not end in death, but we "look for the resurrection of the dead," as we confess in the Creed. As Christ taught, and as we recall in our memorials for the dead, "Unless a grain of wheat falls into the ground and dies, it remains alone; but if it dies, it produces much grain" (John 12:24). So long as we don't restrict economic dynamism through interference in the market process, creative destruction reflects a similar image of death and resurrection. Combining Schumpeter with Knight, we might even argue that Orthodox asceticism and apocalyptic hope in the face of uncertainty would rightly prepare and orient entrepreneurs for the risk-taking that drives the whole process. I certainly hope asceticism has been, and believe it can be, a spiritual anchor for the many Orthodox business owners in our parishes today.

As for Friedman, once again, there is an unintentional analogy to asceticism in his work when he claims that healthy monetary policy requires self-denial from the experts in charge and adoption of a rule of discipline that cultivates an inner calm. Policy can exacerbate problems just as well as solve them. Just as we need good habits that are not pushed around by our passions, central banks need monetary discipline. While the US Federal Reserve hasn't adopted an official inflation rule, it stands out compared to other nations in terms of its patience and caution when it comes to adjusting interest rates, and that has contributed to the stability of the US dollar as the world's reserve currency. Federal interest rates might seem overly nerdy or trivial or worldly, but the first people to feel the effects of runaway inflation in any economy are the poor, who often have bad credit and who only barely get by living paycheck to paycheck every month. Orthodox social thought cannot do without a decent understanding of what makes for a stable currency.

At the same time, economics still needs a moral foundation, and Orthodox social thought can provide it. The only way not to fall into the presumption that economics is self-sufficient is to practice ascetic self-criticism and study what moral and spiritual perspectives are still alive and well today, rather than defunct. Others may not fully embrace our Orthodox Christian perspective, but anyone bothered by the Great Divergence should be interested in a world-view that thrives in distinguishing and uniting seeming opposites in harmonious symphonia. Divinity and humanity, virginity and motherhood, Jew and Gentile, male and female, rich and poor "are all one in Christ Jesus" (Gal. 3:28), and as St. Ignatius of Antioch put it, "Where Jesus Christ is, there is the Catholic Church."[34] Shouldn't the Orthodox Church also be a place where ethics and economics find full affirmation of both their unique dignity and their need for each other as essential aspects of the life of the world? For those willing to listen—and there are many economists like Roberts who sense this deficiency of their discipline—the last part of this book will survey recent sources and trends in Orthodox Christian social thought.

---

34  Ignatius of Antioch, To the Smyrnaeans, 8.2, in *Early Christian Fathers*, ed. Cyril C. Richardson (Westminster Press, 1953), 115.

# Part 4 Summary and Discussion Questions

## *Summary*

ECONOMICS IS THE STUDY OF the use of scarce resources for limited goals—resources that could have been used for other purposes. Political economy is the broader discipline that seeks to combine economic insights with ethics, history, social theory, even theology, for the sake of just and humane economic development. Orthodox Christian social thought, then, is an Orthodox perspective on political economy. As such, it requires not only knowledge of Holy Tradition but also of economic science.

The Late Scholastics in the early modern West are important forerunners of modern economics. In the wake of the Spanish discovery of the Americas, their penitential manuals and ethical treatises wrestled with economic issues, including inflation and interest, discussing them in terms of supply and demand. At the same time, they morally grounded their political economy in natural law, generally advocating for stable currency and eventually even some forms of interest-bearing loans. The Orthodox East did not have the same crisis of inflation or perspective on usury, but we can still learn from the Late Scholastics' careful treatment of these complicated economic topics.

Adam Smith is rightly considered the founder of modern economics, but his *Wealth of Nations* was part of a broader project to introduce Newton's scientific method into social science. His first work, *The Theory of Moral Sentiments*, follows the same method. Smith analyzed the phenomenon of spontaneously emerging social orders, which he understood to be the work of Providence, focusing on beneficence in his *Theory of Moral Sentiments* and the division of labor and economic markets in *The Wealth of Nations*. People's desires lead them to develop rules of conduct for spontaneous orders. These orders coordinate local knowledge through social feedback mechanisms. In morality, that comes from one's conscience. In markets, it comes through prices. To Smith, the state should handle issues of justice and public works, leaving mercy and mutual care to private charity and markets. Three primary social spheres underly this idea: the state, the market, and what people today call "civil society." Interestingly, these correspond quite well to the Orthodox ascetic stages of the slave, the steward, and the son, who obey God from the same motivations that govern these different social systems. Moreover, Smith's clear distinction between matters of justice and mercy complements our Orthodox understanding of the relation of the Law to the Gospel.

The classical political economists built upon Smith's insights to advocate for the abolition of slavery in Britain, the reform of the Elizabethan Poor Laws, and the end of the Corn Law restrictions on foreign trade. They also added their own contributions to the new social science. Christian political economists built upon the Rev. Thomas Robert Malthus's worries about overpopulation to argue that healthy economies depended on Christian moral education and the virtue of chastity. At the same time, Jean-Baptiste Say noticed that economic value is also created through exchange as well as entrepreneurial production. Among more secular economists, utilitarianism held the strongest moral sway. Along with evangelical activists, they succeeded in their efforts to abolish slavery. They succeeded in reforming the Poor Laws. And they succeeded in lowering barriers to trade, which reduced the cost of living for nearly everyone and only hurt wealthy landowners. However, their reform of the Poor Laws, alongside the harsh conditions of the new industrial economy, produced moral challenges that their analysis proved insufficient to solve: The modern "Social Question" had come to Britain. Orthodox social thought can build upon the Christian political economists' wonder at the workings of Providence, the importance of moral education, and the good of international trade, which at least some Church Fathers acknowledged.

By 1848, the new problems of industrial labor led to social unrest and social-ism. Karl Marx and Friedrich Engels published the *Communist Manifesto*, and democratic revolution spread from Paris across Europe, emphasizing lib-erty, fraternity, and equality. But revolutionary Marxism, with its fatalistic and materialist historical dialectic, did not make much difference in Britain. Instead, more moderate advocates for cooperative labor, such as Christian socialists like F. D. Maurice, established an enduring institution in the Work-ing Men's College, the first institution in Europe to bring liberal higher edu-cation to the working classes. Meanwhile, the evangelical paternalism of men like Lord Shaftesbury made the most difference in terms of reforming laws about child labor, working conditions, and work hours. His efforts to bring remedial education to the poorest children in Britain through "ragged schools" gave them the possibility of a better future. And evangelical preach-ers urged business owners to succeed in the marketplace without neglecting proper care of their workers and the poor. While we should reject the Marx-ist worldview, we can learn from Maurice and Shaftesbury. Maurice's concept of a divine order might especially resonate with Orthodox nations that have established the Orthodox Church. And while today we think of evangelicals as a certain kind of Protestant, the movement transcended Christian tradi-tions at the time, even reaching as far as Metropolitan St. Filaret of Moscow. Personal encounter with Christ, love for Scripture, and an emphasis on the Holy Cross motived Shaftesbury to make a difference in his time, and they can do the same for us today.

The next generation of economists would provide an answer to Marxist analysis through the Marginal Revolution. The Marxist labor theory of value (the idea that the economic worth of goods can be reduced to the labor that produced them) and the principle of equality in exchange (the idea that trade only happens when the items have equal value) do not hold up to the reality that prices represent marginal, rather than total, utility. Prices signify the economic value of a single unit of a product to any potential buyer. They do not signify moral, artistic, or any other value. They are a matter of how people rank their own preferences and needs and to what extent that product fulfills them. Thus, they are not based on labor, and two parties exchange only when each party thinks they will benefit from the trade. Value, and thus profit, can be created through exchange without requiring the exploitation of workers. While Orthodox Christian social thought should prophetically call out real instances of fraud or exploitation, it must also incorporate marginal analysis so as not to be misled by the common idea that all profit is evil. These marginalist economists still had their own moral commitments, from utilitarianism to personalism to Christian socialism to a Christian grounding of economic liberty to, unfortunately, eugenics. We should be wary of utilitarianism and reject eugenics, but Orthodox social thought might build on the others and provide its own insights.

The twentieth century began with a series of crises. John Maynard Keynes rose to popularity during the Great Depression through his analysis of unemployment, investment, and inflation. Unfortunately, his moral foundation was eugenics, the belief that some people are genetically superior to others and that lesser people should be discouraged from reproducing. By contrast, economists such as F. A. Hayek and Wilhelm Röpke analyzed the rise of fascism and warned people about it. Hayek noted that calls for regulation of economic competition led to consolidation and then state control, distorting the price signal and leading to shortages and surpluses. When leaders can't fulfill their economic promises, they are faced with the temptation to assume dictatorial control. When dictators still can't produce their desired economic results, they must either compromise basic morality or liberalize. Röpke focused on the breakdown of Christian moral culture that was needed to sustain liberal economies, worrying especially that mass culture creates the opportunity for demagogues to consolidate power. Orthodox social thought should incorporate their insights through an ascetic lens, helping those who need relief now while embracing intellectual humility about what government action can safely do. So, too, if we agree with Röpke that Western culture has lost its way, we should work to build more reverent cultural institutions rather than trying to impose moral purity through law.

The Great Divergence between morality and economics has come only recently. Joseph Schumpeter contributed the term "creative destruction" to describe how capitalism depends on entrepreneurial change, with businesses, markets, and industries constantly displacing one another, like how the automobile industry replaced the blacksmith. Paul Samuelson popularized

Keynes's theories and contributed to the mathematization of economics. Milton Friedman's analysis of the Great Depression proved more accurate than that of Keynes and his followers. Schumpeter, Samuelson, Friedman, and others' "value-free" understanding of their science led to the divorce of economics from its moral foundations in political economy. But in order to say how individuals, businesses, and governments should behave in our economies today, economics needs a foundation of moral and social thought. Thus, all the insights of modern economics have not advanced beyond the need for moral principles, and Orthodox Christian social thought should be an active voice in that conversation today.

## Discussion Questions

- Why does economics matter for Orthodox social thought?
- Could the Late Scholastics' natural law approach to economic problems be a model for Orthodox social thought? Why or why not?
- How does Adam Smith relate markets, the state, and civil society? How might Orthodox social thought build upon or modify his social theory?
- What did the classical economists add to Adam Smith? How might Orthodox social thought learn from their insights while avoiding their mistakes?
- How might Christian socialists like F. D. Maurice and evangelical paternalists like Lord Shaftesbury help us address social injustice better than Marxism?
- Why doesn't Marxist analysis work? How can Orthodox social thought use marginal analysis to better understand prices, profits, and business today?
- How might the economic understanding of civilizational crisis by John Maynard Keynes, F. A. Hayek, and Wilhelm Röpke help us apply insights from Orthodox asceticism to modern economic struggles today?
- How might Orthodox Christian social thought overcome the "Great Divergence" between moral principles and economic science?

PART 5

# Contemporary Sources
# and Challenges

# CHAPTER 33

# How Should We Think Socially?

I N ORDER TO ENGAGE OUR world and serve the poor with Orthodox Christian social thought today, we must learn to be Christian social thinkers. Up to this point, we've surveyed other Christian traditions, the Bible, Orthodox Church history, and the history of economics. Before we examine more recent Orthodox contributions, we should sketch out a few principles and frameworks that integrate some insights we've covered so far. As Christ said, we must bring from our treasures "things new and old" (Matt. 13:52). In order to better identify what new things really are treasures, we should take stock of the "old" treasures we've already collected. For example, every Christian tradition should at least agree on the common ground of natural law as a basis of public morality and rule of law, the inviolable dignity of each person created in the image of God, and the centrality of Jesus Christ for our salvation. Inspired by our Melkite and Scholastic forebears—using reasonable reflection and surveying common ground as well as differences, deficiencies, and questions—I hope to set the stage for the "new" treasures in this book's final chapters with this integration of our "old" treasures here.

To be sure, however, our task is perilous. Our analysis will not fit easily into some people's intellectual boxes. We cannot be concerned with being "right wing" or "left wing," conservative or progressive, capitalist or socialist, and so on, if what we value most is finding and knowing the truth, rather than simply scoring points for "our side." People consumed by such either/or worldviews may distort our perspective through those filters, but we should press on. If we really value finding the best means to fulfill Christ's command to feed the hungry, clothe the naked, shelter the homeless, visit the imprisoned, welcome the stranger, and comfort those who sorrow, a little discomfort and marginalization should be a small price to pay. After all, Christ himself taught, "Blessed are those who are persecuted for righteousness' sake, / For theirs is the kingdom of heaven" (Matt. 5:10).

Thankfully, the Church has an abundance of wisdom about wealth and poverty that is still relevant for us today. The Scriptures consistently warn of the temptations of riches while commending the struggles of the poor. Nevertheless, they do not call material wealth inherently evil. That sort of dualism fits Gnosticism better than Orthodoxy. Indeed, the Law protects property rights (Ex. 20:15) while also requiring care for the poor among God's people (Lev. 19:9–10). The biblical Writings commend prudent use and management of wealth as well. So, too, Church Fathers like Clement of Alexandria, St. Basil the Great, St. Gregory the Theologian, St. John Chrysostom, and St. John Cassian consistently teach that the only true evil is sin and the only good, virtue. All other things, including material riches, are only evil or good to the extent that they are used for sin or righteousness. Theologians like St. Hermas of Rome and Abdallah ibn al-Fadl al-Antaki additionally note that economic inequalities enjoin responsibilities on both rich and poor toward one another. And while the Edict of Milan, Celtic penitential manuals, the Justinian *Code*, Byzantine monastic constitutions, St. Nicholas Cabasilas, and many more all affirm the right to private property, others like St. John Chrysostom and St. Symeon the New Theologian emphasize that we should view everything we have as ultimately belonging to God. How can what we've learned so far help us faithfully hold all these concepts and commandments together in our world today? We need a map of society.

## The Old Christian Map

BASICALLY EVERY CHRISTIAN TRADITION, INCLUDING our Orthodox Tradition,[1] historically distinguishes between family, state, and church. In an

---

1    This can be seen in Orthodox catechetical literature, in particular their commentary on the Fifth Commandment: "Honor your father and your mother, that your days may be long upon the land which the LORD your God is giving you" (Ex. 20:12).

attempt to adapt this to our modern world, Vladimir Soloviev accounted for the emergence of state, church, and economy historically, as arising from early tribal society where freedom, power, and authority remained undifferentiated in the tribe and only dispersed over time into economies, modern states (in which the tribe becomes the family), and the church. He even connected these to the biblical messianic roles of prophet (economy), king (state), and priest (church). Similarly, the Anglican Christian socialist F. D. Maurice understood family, state, and church in terms of the biblical narrative of their historical emergence and scope—local, national, and universal—with the higher levels of society saturating those lower. Thus, there are local governments within national governments. There are national churches within the universal Church, and local parishes within national churches. Roman Catholics would add that the principle of subsidiarity dictates that the most local level of society should be the first to address any given problem, only seeking help from the next higher level if it proves insufficient to the task. We Orthodox would add that subsidiarity thus requires ascetic self-denial for higher social levels to hold back when they are not needed as well as for lower social levels humbly to admit when they need help. Indeed, no community—church, state, family, or otherwise—can function properly without the ascetic self-limitation of its members. We can chart these social levels as follows in Table 33.1:

### Table 33.1: Levels of Society

| Level | Institution |
|---|---|
| Universal | Church |
| National | State |
| Local | Family |

Presumably all other social spheres and institutions, such as the Working Men's College in London or the Knights of Columbus, would fall within these more general levels of society to varying degrees. Lutherans and Neo-Calvinists would further stipulate that only the church can save the world. All other orders, mandates, or spheres serve primarily just to preserve society from the corruption of sin. We can see something of this in our Orthodox Tradition as well: Soloviev claimed, "The purpose of legal justice is not to transform the world which lies in evil into the kingdom of God, but only to prevent it from changing *too soon* into hell."[2] The Church—not any other sphere—is the world becoming the Kingdom of God. Every non-ecclesial society only becomes a bearer of salvation to the extent that we bring the sacramental grace of Christ into them through our various vocations as members of His Church.

However, these categories seem insufficient for our "new" contemporary world. As general social levels, they work, but Abraham Kuyper would emphasize that new spheres emerge according to a historical dialectic—a gradual, logical process—of sphere sovereignty. The economist Joseph Schumpeter would similarly point to the role of creative destruction. Indeed, many modern Christian social thinkers, including Soloviev and Dietrich Bonhoeffer, have at least added the categories of work, culture, or economy to the three basic institutions of church, state, and family. Economies, furthermore, are not limited to the local or even national levels, even if their ultimate good lies in the material provision of families' needs. We might also wonder about the difference of context between urban, suburban, and rural localities.

So, too, the biblical narrative at least includes a role for religious education in the synagogue distinct from the Temple. Christ Himself even came as a rabbi, a teacher of the Law, not a Temple priest! Of course, in the Divine Liturgy the Church historically combines both of these functions through the Liturgy of the Catechumens (synagogue) and the Liturgy of the Faithful (Temple), but where does education in general fit into our social thought? Is the gymnasium anathema to us, as it was to the Maccabees? More than a few Church Fathers would disagree. So would the early Christian political economists, Maurice, Kuyper, and many others.

To all this, we could add the further complication of religious liberty and pluralism. Has religion displaced church in our societies, even while religion in general has been marginalized by secularization?

And what about transnational governments, like the European Union? National states are not the only game in town anymore. If the

---

2    Vladimir Solovyov, *The Justification of the Good*, rev. ed., ed. Boris Jakim, trans. Natalie A. Duddington (Eerdmans, 2005), 324.

family-state-church map has become inadequate, what other option do we have? Imitating the creativity of Social Gospel thinkers like Walter Rauschenbusch—without his unorthodox theology—we need to draw up a new map more sensitive to the social circumstances we face today.

## Adam Smith's Map

ANOTHER WAY OF MAPPING SOCIAL spaces comes from Adam Smith, who distinguished between the state, which is responsible for maintaining justice; markets, which spontaneously coordinate the local knowledge of others' self-interest through prices for the sake of mutual aid; and beneficent communities and individuals—we might say "civil society"—in which people are spontaneously directed by the local knowledge of their consciences, relationships, culture, social pressures, and circumstances to put aside selfishness and have mercy on their needy neighbors for the sake of love. The expansion of the division of labor through local, national, and international markets accounts for the massive and ongoing reduction of poverty since the nineteenth century, but "man shall not live by bread alone" (Deut. 8:3). As a matter of human dignity and flourishing—the common good—people need not only material provision but justice and mercy as well. Yet even today, we still have relative poverty in the developed world and extreme poverty in some developing nations.

These three social spaces—states, markets, and beneficent relationships—mirror the common Orthodox ascetic motifs of the slave, steward, and son or child of God. The slave obeys God out of fear of punishment, the steward from desire for future reward, and the son purely out of love. While for the Fathers these motifs model degrees of personal spiritual growth, the motivations at their cores map perfectly onto Smith's social spaces: States punish injustice, markets reward labor, and beneficence works good for its own sake. A society that consists solely of the state is totalitarian and despotic, ruled by Smith's "man of system" at best and tyrants at worst, as F. A. Hayek described in his *Road to Serfdom*.[3] Furthermore, a society that only consists of market and state may meet material needs and basic justice, but it lacks the moral culture of love

---

3   See F. A. Hayek, *The Road to Serfdom* (George Routledge & Sons, 1944), discussed in chapter 31 of this book.

needed to sustain itself and make life truly meaningful, as Smith and Wilhelm Röpke argued.

The economist Kenneth Boulding developed a general theory of social systems and dynamics that echoes Smith and our Orthodox ascetic tradition as well.[4] Though not well-known today, Boulding was second winner of the John Bates Clark medal (awarded to economists under forty for exceptional contributions), a devout Quaker, a peace theorist and activist, and a student of the economists Lionel Robbins, Frank Knight, and Joseph Schumpeter, among others.

Boulding distinguished between exchange economies and grants economies. Exchange systems, such as markets, are egalitarian and materially positive-sum. What that means is market actors both give and receive, considering themselves better off for having done so. The logic of exchange systems is, "If you give me good thing A, I'll give you good thing B." The grants economy consists of two distinct, often hierarchical systems: integrative systems and threat systems. The state is a threat system—just laws have clear punishments for those who violate them. The logic of threat systems is, "Give me good thing A, or I will give you bad thing B." Families, on the other hand, are integrative systems that follow the logic, "I will give you good thing A and expect nothing in return." Since these both involve one-way grants, Boulding called them the grants economy.

Knowing to what social systems any institutions belong helps us understand their nature and what happens when they are twisted and abused—what Abraham Kuyper would call "the antithesis." Babies do not earn their mother's milk. States that give out favors are corrupt. Exchanges made under duress are unjust and thus theft. We could also think of this in terms of natural law: Threat systems are meant to keep basic social harm in check along the lines of the Ten Commandments. Exchange systems exist for the provision of human needs. Integrative systems provide loving distribution of spiritual and material goods. When an institution that is proper to one of these systems

---

4    Kenneth E. Boulding, *Three Faces of Power* (Sage Publications, 1989). Boulding also stands out as a relatively recent economist (he died in 1993) who still believed economics to be a moral science. See Boulding, "Economics as a Moral Science," *The American Economic Review* 59, no. 1 (1969): 1–12.

fails to conform to its nature or seeks to absorb others into its purposes, it becomes unnatural and thus sinful.

That said, Boulding emphasized that each of these systems are also "fuzzy sets"[5]—they all contain *dynamics* of the others. Markets need both law (threat) to enforce contracts and trust (integration) between business partners. States require both legitimacy (integration) and social contracts (exchange), in which people receive certain social services and protections in return for their taxes and other contributions. Parents provide for their children out of love, and they want their children to obey out of love, but in order to properly discipline them, they sometimes use both rewards (exchange) and punishments (threat).

This social-scientific approach helpfully complements Christian social thought, but it has inadequacies as well. Analytically, it seems to me there should be four, not just three, general social systems. Integrative systems like the family are personal, materially zero-sum (they don't involve the production or exchange of goods), and hierarchical (in terms of parents' authority over children). States are impersonal, materially zero-sum, and hierarchical (even democratically elected rulers' have authority over private citizens). Markets are impersonal, materially positive-sum (they do involve the production and exchange of goods), and egalitarian (if exchanges are not free relationships between equals, they are corrupt and coercive—not exchanges but theft). But what is both personal *and* materially positive-sum and egalitarian? Boulding admits that friendship seems to satisfy this description, but he doesn't think it scales beyond two-person relations.

## A New Map

HERE, WE MUST GET CREATIVE. Philosophical and theological reflection could fill out this analysis. Wisdom teaches that "there is a friend who sticks closer than a brother" (Prov. 18:24). And though Jesus calls His disciples to be servants, stewards of His Gospel, and children of God, He nevertheless told His apostles, "No longer do I call you servants . . . but I have called you friends" (John 15:15). Indeed, He even puts this friendship

---

5    Boulding, *Three Faces of Power*, 24.

dynamic at the center of the Gospel: "Greater love has no one than this, than to lay down one's life for his friends" (John 15:13), which, of course, is what Christ did for us. We call Him *philanthropos*—the friend (*philos*) of humanity (*anthropos*).

Clement of Alexandria, referencing Luke 16:9, reminds us, "The Lord did not say, Give, or bring, or do good, or help, but make a friend. But a friend proves himself such not by one gift, but by long intimacy."[6] Everyone needs friendship, of course, but policymakers and even some private charities undervalue its immeasurable importance for the poor. No one with family and friends to fall back on becomes homeless, for example. True, reducing homelessness requires increasing the housing supply. But we also need to *decrease loneliness*, which impersonal social systems like markets and the state can never do. Economics is necessary but not enough.

Fathers like St. John Climacus emphasize the spiritual state of friendship with God as one of the highest goals of the ascetic life: "A friend of God is the one who lives in communion with all that is natural and free from sin," while nevertheless withdrawing from the world "for the sake of that which is above nature."[7] Rather than a contradiction, this image of divine friendship fulfills our nature as microcosms, uniting heaven and earth, supernatural and natural, even rich and poor—a likeness of the Incarnation through the catholicity or sobornost' of the Church.

C. S. Lewis even noted that friendship spreads beyond two-person relations and naturally challenges tyrannical authority: "Headmasters and Headmistresses and Heads of religious communities, colonels and ships' captains, can feel uneasy when close and strong friendships arise between little knots of their subjects."[8] Only insecure leaders, however, can be truly threatened by such "little knots" of friendship. Smith or Röpke might further note the importance of friendships for cultivating a healthy moral culture. And in various associations and clubs, we can see the combination of both personal intimacy

---

6    Clement of Alexandria, *Who Is the Rich Man That Shall Be Saved?*, 32, in *ANF* 2:600.
7    John Climacus, *The Ladder of Divine Ascent*, trans. Colm Luibheid and Norman Russell (Paulist Press, 1982), 74.
8    C. S. Lewis, *The Four Loves* (Harcourt Brace, 1962), 88.

and materially positive-sum dynamics, where new wealth is produced outside of strict contracts.

Friendship also helps us better understand close-knit communities, where even markets have stronger personal connections. A small-town restaurant proprietor, for example, might let his customer eat today but pay tomorrow, because he knows her personally and trusts that she is "good for it." They have the personal proximity needed for what Pope Benedict XVI referred to as "reciprocal gifts."[9] Nevertheless, friendship, too, is a "fuzzy set." A local business with familiar, regular customers might also make sales online, simultaneously participating in both personal and impersonal market systems.

We can map these social systems, with examples in brackets, as follows in Table 33.2:

## Table 33.2: Social Systems

| | Personal Economy (Mercy) | Impersonal Economy (Justice) |
|---|---|---|
| **Grants Economy** (Zero-Sum, Hierarchical) | *Integrative Systems* [Families, Charities] | *Threat Systems* [States, Law] |
| **Exchange Economy** (Positive-Sum, Egalitarian) | *Friendship Systems* [Clubs, Local Businesses] | *Market Systems* [Chain Stores, Online Shopping] |

Thus, in addition to Boulding's distinction between the exchange economy and grants economy, we can add the "personal economy" and "impersonal economy," expecting their moral norms to bear some resemblance to the distinction between the mercy of the Gospel and the justice of the Law as outlined earlier in this book. As "fuzzy sets," some institutions will contain more

---

9    Pope Benedict XVI, *Caritas in Veritate*, encyclical letter, June 29, 2009, 39, https://
     www.vatican.va/content/benedict-xvi/en/encyclicals/documents/hf_ben-xvi_enc
     _20090629_caritas-in-veritate.html.

dynamics of one or two of these than others. Families, for example, contain integrative dynamics in terms of parents' care for minor children, but St. Paul describes spouses as "submitting to one another in the fear of God" (Eph. 5:21)—combining reciprocal giving (friendship) with awareness of divine judgment and law (threat).

These systems also help address the problem of contexts mentioned above: Rural, suburban, and urban societies contain differing degrees and instances of these systems, rural being the most personal and urban being the most impersonal, while, of course, remaining "fuzzy sets," too. One-size-fits-all policy or moral exhortation cannot take into account this variety of our social life, again requiring subsidiarity. These contexts matter, because persons and relationships have inviolable human dignity that cannot be ignored without error and sin.

Indeed, this social map additionally helps us see shortcomings of various worldviews. Much of modern, secular life, for example, emphasizes the impersonal economy at the expense of the personal. We often argue about whether a problem is best solved by the market or the state, as if no other options exist. Conversely, nostalgia for traditional societies tends to overemphasize the personal and local, missing the importance of impersonal social spaces. Sometimes Röpke, for example, writes as if everyone should have their own family farm and live in a small, intimate Swiss town. But there are eight billion people in the world, and not everyone could provide for their needs that way. Indeed, taken to an extreme, this kind of romanticism misses the great benefits of the division of labor, as Adam Smith pointed out.

Similarly, Boulding criticized his fellow economists who tended, after the Great Divergence between economics and ethics, to study only the exchange economy. This is referred to as "economism," the mistaken belief that every interaction in life is an exchange. Alternatively, the opposite error would be a zero-sum mentality that views problems of poverty as solely a matter of redistribution of a fixed pool of resources. This sort of person thinks that all the poor need are charity or government assistance. But often what the poor really want and need are friendships, jobs, savings, and credit. People don't just shift wealth around in the grants economy. They *create it* in the exchange economy, as Jean-Baptiste Say and the marginalists pointed out. Unsurprisingly, developing nations have not been lifted out of extreme poverty by international aid but by entrepreneurial creative destruction and their integration as equals into the global exchange economy. Times of crisis and disaster call for aid. It is very important in those circumstances. But development requires a dynamic and flourishing economy.

But where, in all of this, is the Church? Must we restrict her into one system, sphere, or level of society? Or shouldn't we expect that, as a matter of her catholicity, she both includes and transcends all of these, offering each to God through prayer? Accordingly, like the early apologists, I believe religious liberty to be all the Church should want or need, given the imperfection of our fallen world. "Render . . . to Caesar the things that are Caesar's," Jesus taught, "and to God the things that are God's" (Matt. 22:21). Caesar can have his kingdom. Christ's Kingdom is "not of this world" (John 18:36). Caesar's image may be on the money, but God has impressed His image on our human nature, calling each of us to grow in His likeness.

True, Holy Tradition neither requires nor condemns legal privilege for the Church within, or even over, the state, but the martyric Catholic Church in pagan Rome preferred liberty. The Edict of Milan also only acknowledged equal religious liberty and property rights, and we've seen countless warnings about too closely entangling Church and state throughout Orthodox history. Nevertheless, the primitive Church still acknowledged that as Christians lived across all social strata, so too the Church touched all of society through them as citizens, neighbors, craftsmen, merchants, doctors, teachers, servants, parents, children, and so on. As Bonhoeffer put it in his own time and context, "The Christian is at the same time worker, spouse, and citizen."[10]

Legally, at least in the United States, churches are nonprofit organizations and in that sense integrative systems. We call our priests "Father," and everyone receives godparents at their baptism (or chrismation, in the case of converts like me). But our wonderful ethnic festivals, for example, couldn't raise funds if they didn't make a profit over the costs of organizing them. So, too, parishes sell candles, books, and icons without compromising the nature of

---

10   Dietrich Bonhoeffer, *Ethics*, in *Dietrich Bonhoeffer Works*, trans. Reinhard Krauss, Charles C. West, and Douglas W. Stott, vol. 6 (Fortress Press, 2005), 73.

the Church as the "the house[hold] of God . . . the pillar and ground of the truth" (1 Tim. 3:15). Rather, such ecclesial commerce could set an example for a more righteous economy, full of grace, fairness, reciprocation, and mercy. We, as members of the Body of Christ, can then spread that grace of the Holy Spirit into our families, businesses, governments, friendships, and so on, hoping that in so doing we, like the apostles, cast out nets as "fishers of men" (Matt. 4:19). With this new social map as our guide, the final chapters of this book will survey recent theological resources for doing that today.

## The Plan for Part 5

FIRST, WE'LL LOOK AT THEOLOGICAL and philosophical resources from our Orthodox Tradition in the twentieth century. After encountering the "Social Question" in the late nineteenth century, Orthodox thinkers continued to offer guidance for how to serve the poor in our contemporary economies, as well as reflecting more generally on the spiritual nature of our social and economic life. To that end, we'll examine Sophia, sobornost', and liturgical theology, including both sacramentalism and asceticism.

Next, we need to learn from and assess recent Church statements about economic issues. These documents represent a first attempt at bringing the Orthodox Church into the broader conversation of Christian social thought today at the level of official—if only provisional and pastoral—Church teaching. However, we'll also see some ways in which future statements, should there be any, could improve upon the shortcomings of these documents by better listening to Holy Tradition, modern economics, and even other Christian traditions.

After Part 5, I'll conclude with an epilogue, hoping that with all these resources at our disposal, readers might find creative ways to develop and apply Orthodox Christian social thought to the common good for our contexts today, tomorrow, and until Christ returns and establishes His Kingdom in full.

CHAPTER 34

# Sophia

A T THE BEGINNING OF EVERY Orthodox vespers, we read a psalm which marvels at the work of God in all creation: "Man goes out to his work," says the psalmist, "And to his labor until the evening. / O Lord, how manifold are Your works! / In wisdom You have made them all" (Ps. 103/104:23–24). Sophia—Greek for "Wisdom"—is a modern Orthodox concept that emphasizes the connection between God's work of creation and our creative work in the world, whether in terms of our relation to our material resources or to each other. The study of divine Wisdom is called sophiology. Though theologically controversial for reasons I won't get into, the reflection on divine Wisdom from modern Orthodox theologians such as Fr. Sergei Bulgakov and Fr. Pavel Florensky remains insightful for Orthodox Christian social thought today. Here, with the help of other theologians throughout Holy Tradition, I will present a controversy-free account of divine Sophia with the aim of better understanding the spiritual significance of human labor and friendship. Bulgakov highlights the first, while Florensky highlights the second. So I'll start with Bulgakov.

## Bulgakov and Economics

As A YOUNG MAN, BULGAKOV attended seminary, only to lose his faith and become a Marxist economist instead of a priest. But after his dissertation criticizing Karl Marx's analysis of agriculture was rejected, he found his way back to Orthodoxy through German philosophy, according to Fr. Daniel

P. Payne and Christopher Marsh.[1] Bulgakov later served as a representative in the Second Duma of the Russian Empire. He also wrote several essays as a critic of the radical intelligentsia in Russia, most significantly as a contributor to the volume *Vekhi*,[2] which drew condemnation from Vladimir Lenin himself.[3] Bulgakov contrasted the heroic ideal of privileged Russian activists with the Orthodox ideal of the holy ascetic. While revolutionaries didn't care about personal growth, they sought forcibly to make Russian society into a utopia. The Christian ascetic, by contrast, seeks "first the kingdom of God and His righteousness" (Matt. 6:33), unworried as the lilies of the field. The ascetic has tempered, minimal expectations of society but maximal aspirations for their salvation. A few years afterward, in 1912, Bulgakov published a philosophical reflection on political economy, *Philosophy of Economy*,[4] only later finally becoming a priest and focusing on theology. Along with S. L. Frank, Nikolai Berdyaev, and other religious intellectuals, the Soviets exiled Bulgakov from Russia in 1922. In 1924 he settled in Paris, where he helped found the St. Sergius Orthodox Theological Institute, dying there in 1944.

Summarizing Bulgakov's *Philosophy of Economy*, Payne and Marsh note, "Bulgakov was not against economics *per se*; rather, he was against the worldviews that supported the economic systems."[5] In particular, as Marcus Plested notes, "Bulgakov decries any economic system based only on material concerns as inherently deathly, iniquitous, and destructive of the human spirit."[6] But what does this have to do with Sophia?

---

1  Daniel P. Payne and Christopher Marsh, "Sergei Bulgakov's 'Sophic' Economy: An Eastern Orthodox Perspective on Christian Economics," *Faith & Economics* 53 (Spring 2009): 39.

2  Marshall S. Shatz and Judith E. Zimmerman, ed. and trans., *Vehki: Landmarks* (M.E. Sharpe, 1994).

3  V. I. Lenin, "Concerning *Vekhi*," in *Lenin Collected Works*, vol. 16 (Progress Publishers, 1974), 123–131. Lenin especially—and unfairly—criticizes Bulgakov, indicating that the latter's essay touched a nerve in the aspiring revolutionary.

4  Sergei Bulgakov, *Philosophy of Economy: The World as Household*, trans. Catherine Evtuhov (Yale University Press, 2000).

5  Payne and Marsh, "Sergei Bulgakov's 'Sophic' Economy," 44.

6  Marcus Plested, *Wisdom in Christian Tradition: The Patristic Roots of Modern Russian Sophiology* (Oxford, 2022), 39.

We might say that to Bulgakov economy is the fulfillment of the command to "fill the earth and subdue it" and "have dominion" (Gen. 1:28). According to his translator, "In this imperfect world Bulgakov turned to a biblical notion— Sophia—as a way out of the mere labor 'in the sweat of our face' [Gen. 3:19] that characterizes our existence in the fallen world."[7] We saw this biblical notion of divine Wisdom in the biblical Writings in chapter 9. As Dionysius the Areopagite notes, "Even our sense-perceptions themselves may be rightly described as an echo of that Wisdom"[8] by which God made the world. If creation is, in this sense, an "echo" of divinity, then our creative labor can reveal the original goodness of creation: "In rare moments of revelation, we catch a glimpse of what life was once like in the Garden of Eden."[9] As Bulgakov put it, "The empirical world is . . . never wholly separated . . . from the divine Sophia that ever soars above the world, illuminating it through reason, through beauty, through . . . economy and culture."[10]

Nevertheless, Bulgakov's translator notes that rather than utopia, "a 'sophic economy' was not a paradise to be achieved on earth but a constantly present vision inspiring us to work for the restoration of the harmony of nature and culture that humanity had lost in the Fall."[11] With this "sophic" understanding, we can start to see an Orthodox theology of work and culture: Every act of combining our labor with creation, if offered to God and undertaken joyfully, reveals divine goodness and beauty. Our work has become toilsome, but it is still "in the sweat of your face" that "you shall eat" (Gen. 3:19). Our toil reflects the Fall, but the fruit of that labor still fulfills the command to "be fruitful" (Gen. 1:28), exercising dominion over creation and imaging God's rule, His Kingdom, even for the common good of our economies today.

---

7 Catherine Evtuhov, "Introduction," in *Philosophy of Economy*, 10.

8 Dionysius the Areopagite, *On the Divine Names*, 7.2, in *Dionysius the Areopagite: On the Divine Names and the Mystical Theology*, trans. C. E. Rolt (Kessinger Publishing Company, 1991), 149.

9 Evtuhov, "Introduction," in *Philosophy of Economy*, 11.

10 Bulgakov, *Philosophy of Economy*, 145.

11 Evtuhov, "Introduction," in *Philosophy of Economy*, 13.

## Florensky and Friendship

NEXT, WE MUST CONSIDER AN additional insight from Fr. Pavel Florensky: friendship. Florensky was a friend of Bulgakov that the Soviets let stay in Russia because they valued his ability as a natural scientist and mathematician. Yet they could not tolerate his faith for long. In 1933, they rewarded his contributions by falsely accusing him of conspiring with the Nazis.[12] He fought these charges until he realized the sham nature of the trial and that if he pled guilty he might free others who had similarly been falsely accused. The Soviets sentenced him to ten years of forced (scientific) labor, but after moving him from labor camp to labor camp for four years, they executed him by firing squad in December 1937.

"Sophia," writes Florensky, "is a preliminary hint at the transfigured, spiritualized world . . . of the heavenly in the earthly." However, rather than focusing on labor like Bulgakov, he continues, "This revelation occurs in the personal, sincere love of two, in friendship. . . . Friendship, as the mysterious birth of *Thou*, is the environment in which the revelation of the Truth begins."[13] That said, Florensky sees Sophia most especially in monastic elders known for austere, ascetic labor, so his view is not that far from Bulgakov's. If we combine labor and friendship—as we did in the category of the "exchange economy" on our new social map in the last chapter—we can note how much more joyful even the most toilsome work becomes when we labor alongside a friend. Friendship more easily unlocks the revelatory, "sophic" potential of work, and the creativity of both work and friendship also enliven the "grants economy" of families, charities, government, and law. Indeed, friendship's significance cannot be limited to even an enlightened economic perspective.

---

12 While Florensky was no Nazi, he did unfortunately express some troubling anti-Semitic views. See Robert F. Slesinski, "On the 'Anti-Semitism' of Pavel Florensky, a New Martyr," *Logos: A Journal of Eastern Christian Studies* 53, no. 1–2 (2012): 43–61; and Dominic Rubin, *Holy Russia, Sacred Israel: Jewish-Christian Encounters in Russian Religious Thought* (Academic Studies Press, 2010), 294–334. Slesinski seeks to downplay the severity of Florensky's anti-Semitic writings, but Rubin demonstrates that Florensky's views contain harmful stereotypes and baseless conspiracy theories.

13 Pavel Florensky, *The Pillar and Ground of the Truth: An Essay in Orthodoxy Theodicy in Twelve Letters*, trans. Boris Jakim (Princeton University Press, 1997), 283.

Florensky notes, "The mystical unity that is revealed in . . . friends permeates all the aspects of their life, makes even the everyday golden."[14] He compares Christianity's sanctification of friendship as the most essential unit of social life with paganism's reverence for family and kinship.[15] This distinction might not be obvious, but think of how virginity and monasticism clashed with the Roman concept of a paterfamilias. Indeed, Jesus told His disciples, "everyone who has left houses or brothers or sisters or father or mother or wife or children or lands, for My name's sake, shall receive a hundredfold, and inherit eternal life" (Matt. 19:29). God created the family to be good, but the Gospel does not portray it as the most perfect community. Only in the Church, where friends of Christ become "brethren," can family find its fulfillment, acting as a "sophic" window into Paradise. Thus, for Florensky, we must distinguish friendship from familial relations, even if close friends become a sort of second family or brotherhood. Drawing again on economist Kenneth Boulding's terminology,[16] we might say that as a "fuzzy set," friendship contains integrative, familial dynamics while remaining its own social system.

In connection with its theological grounding in Sophia, friendship constitutes a mystery of its own: "Friendship," says Florensky, "is the last word of the *properly human element of the Church*. . . . As long as man remains man, he seeks friendship."[17] Because the Church is the world becoming the Kingdom of God, the Church can be seen as the truest meeting point between divine Wisdom and its "echo" in creation. Thus, it must contain friendship. In friendship, we "bear one another's burdens, and so fulfill the law of Christ" (Gal. 6:2). Florensky even notes how, on this basis, obedient service to others finds a transfigured place in friendship: "Every friendship . . . is in this sense monasticism. Each of the friends uncomplainingly humbles himself before his life-companion, in the same manner as a servant before his master. . . . This is what the obedience of friendship, the bearing of one's Friend's cross, consists in."[18]

---

14  Florensky, *Pillar and Ground*, 297.
15  Florensky, 301.
16  Kenneth E. Boulding, *Three Faces of Power* (Sage Publications, 1989).
17  Florensky, *Pillar and Ground*, 317.
18  Florensky, 318.

Thus, the imitation of Christ, taking up one's cross (Mark 8:34), becomes something else through bearing the cross of others in friendship. But what?

According to St. Maria Skobtsova, suffering alongside others constitutes "the imitation of the Mother of God."[19] We'll examine this and more in the next chapter on sobornost'. In the meantime, however, we can summarize by saying that Bulgakov's and Florensky's sophiology helps us see the spiritual nature of work as a fulfillment of the command God gave us to spread His image and Kingdom over all creation. And this same revelation of divinity, this self-overcoming love, manifests itself through friendship, which transcends economic, familial, and civil social systems, finding its truest fulfillment in the Church.

## One Body, Many Members

ACCORDING TO ST. JOHN CHRYSOSTOM, "If in worldly matters no man lives for himself, but artisan, and soldier, and husbandman, and merchant, all of them contribute to the common good, and to their neighbor's advantage; much more ought we to do this in things spiritual."[20] Adam Smith and the Christian classical economists insisted that the division of labor, including even international trade, testifies to the work of divine Wisdom in orchestrating our daily activities to provide for each other's needs. Chrysostom, by analogy, insists that this same Wisdom ought to be at work in our spiritual lives. In our parishes, some are priests and deacons, some are parish council members, some are Sunday school teachers, some volunteer to cook and clean for events, and others contribute just by showing up, which, as a father of young children, I can testify is an accomplishment in itself. But we are not all just atoms buzzing around in a social void. We are the Body of Christ, and each member has irreplaceable value and dignity. "God has set the members, each one of them, in the body just as He pleased," writes St. Paul. "And if they were all one member, where would the body be?" (1 Cor. 12:18–19) Rather, "if one

---

19    Maria Skobtsova, "On the Imitation of the Mother of God," in *Mother Maria Skobtsova: Essential Writings,* trans. Richard Pevear and Larissa Volokhonsky (Orbis Books, 2003), 61–74.

20    John Chrysostom, *Homilies on Matthew,* 77, in *NPNF*[1] 10:451.

member suffers, all the members suffer with it; or if one member is honored, all the members rejoice with it" (1 Cor. 12:26).

It was the Church that first saw the Wisdom of God in the division of labor, and because of it everyone found a dignified existence. Women, children, slaves, foreigners—all were welcome in the Church, "for you are all one in Christ Jesus" (Gal. 3:28). We are all one Body, though many different members. Indeed, we commonly conceive of other social institutions in analogy to this: As citizens we belong to a "body politic," and we refer to businesses and non-profit organizations as "corporations," from the Latin *corpus*, meaning "body."

For example, I remember years ago working for a plastics injection molding factory. Basically, we made little plastic tubes, doodads, and widgets—some long, some short, some hard, some bendy. But these were medical devices, so they had high quality standards. We had to inspect every part for imperfections. If a machine started producing tainted parts, we had to call a technician to fix it right away. If quality assurance discovered that improperly molded parts had escaped the operators' notice, everyone would have to sort through the bags of little tubes or whatever and find the bad ones that had been missed, delaying the company's ability to fulfill its customers' orders.

It was easy to think about my work at the factory as "just a job." I gave them my work. They gave me a paycheck. Of course, that is part of every job, but every now and then I'd remember that the little tubes, widgets, and gadgets I was making would be used for lifesaving blood transfusions or open-heart surgery. What I did amounted to a very small component of a much larger process, but I wasn't just a cog in a machine (nor should any such workers be treated that way). Somewhere, even today, people are praying for loved ones who need a medical procedure as a matter of life or death. Often, God answers those prayers not by a stunning, supernatural miracle, but through the wise employment of little tubes, widgets, and doodads manufactured by workers who are just as essential as the doctors who use the things they make.

But perhaps readers might think, "Okay, that works for medical devices, but what about other jobs?" Well, just as essential as the people who produced those medical devices are the people who shipped them to where they needed to go. That means the auto mechanics and auto manufacturers were essential, too, since those parts are shipped in trucks and other vehicles. And so on. Economies, *as a whole,* produce these everyday miracles through the Wisdom of God, whether it be lifesaving medical procedures or simply putting food on our tables for our next meal. The Orthodox concept of divine Sophia reminds us not to lose the spiritual forest for the material trees, so to speak. Though some people claim that modern economies run on greed and injustice—and it is true that our economies, just like the rest of life, are not immune from sin—they don't *depend* on those vices. With the right perspective, in our economies we can see a glimpse, despite our sin, of the harmony and communion God created us for in the beginning.

So, too, consider how few people work alone. Most of us have coworkers, and while everyone has had the experience of getting annoyed by coworkers, many people today report forming lasting friendships on the job. These relationships often extend beyond playful chats about common likes or dislikes by the watercooler. We get lunch together or hang out after work. We go to each other's kids' birthday parties and graduations. We attend each other's weddings. We grieve with our coworkers at the death of someone they love. Just as at Church, so also at work, "if one member suffers, all the members suffer with it; or if one member is honored, all the members rejoice with it" (1 Cor. 12:26) . . . at least ideally.

We spend forty hours (or more) a week at work, and our faith better matter there, and for those people, too. Indeed, work may be the only place, through us, that our coworkers encounter the body of Christ. And in the spiritual connection of our friendships, we might all catch a clearer glimpse of that divine Wisdom through which the world was made and through which, even today, God sustains all creation. So, too, we might gain a better understanding of the catholicity at the heart of Orthodox social thought. The next chapter will explore that further in the Orthodox concept of sobornost'.

CHAPTER 35

# Sobornost'

THE EVANGELIST ST. LUKE IS known for his Gospel and its sequel,
the Acts of the Apostles. In Holy Tradition, he is also known for his
closeness to Mary, the Mother of God, and for painting the first icon of her.
His connection to her can be seen in his Gospel, in which he notes twice
that "Mary kept all these things and pondered them in her heart" (Luke 2:19;
see Luke 2:51). That statement could only be written by someone who knew
her personally or had special revelation from the Holy Spirit concerning her
inner life, for only "the LORD looks at the heart" (1 Kin./1 Sam. 16:7). We
should not be surprised, then, that the Church, following St. Luke's lead, has
specially venerated the Theotokos, the birthgiver of God, as an image of the
Church herself.

In fact, this connection is thoroughly biblical, thanks to St. Luke, among
others. At the Annunciation, he records in the beginning of his Gospel, the
Archangel Gabriel informed Mary, "The Holy Spirit will come upon you, and
the power of the Highest will overshadow you" (Luke 1:35). Then, at Christ's
Ascension, right at the beginning of the Acts of the Apostles, he records some
of the Lord's final words to His disciples, "You shall receive power when the
Holy Spirit has come upon you" (Acts 1:8). It is as if Jesus had said, "Wait in
Jerusalem until you are made like Mary." The Holy Spirit descended upon
Mary and empowered her, making her the Mother of God. At Pentecost, the
Holy Spirit descended upon and empowered Jesus' disciples, making them
His Catholic Church.

As we already saw earlier in this book, St. Ignatius of Antioch first coined the phrase "the Catholic Church."[1] Catholicity serves as a linchpin for understanding the earliest Christians' social thought. By the grace of the Incarnation, Cross, and Resurrection of Christ, manifest through the Church hierarchy and the Holy Eucharist, we are empowered to care for the poor and marginalized among us through self-giving asceticism, reconciling all the divisions of our lives—rich and poor, neighbor and foreigner, flesh and spirit, earthly and heavenly, human and divine. So, too, in both the Church and the Theotokos, we see the reconciliation of virginity and motherhood: We bear Christ in our hearts and are reborn through Baptism as children of God. And in the rediscovery of catholicity in the principle of sobornost', through the imitation of the Mother of God, we see in the works of S. L. Frank and St. Maria Skobtsova a path to overcoming all such divisions today.

## Internal and External

ONE OF MANY INTELLECTUALS EXPELLED from Russia by the Soviets in 1922, Semyon Lyudvigovich Frank (commonly just "S. L. Frank") was born in 1877 to a Jewish family in Moscow. Enchanted by revolutionary ideas at a young age, he came back to faith, like Fr. Sergei Bulgakov, in the first decade of the twentieth century, writing a critique of Karl Marx's labor theory of value in 1900 and also contributing his own essay to the 1909 volume *Vekhi*, criticizing the radical Russian intelligentsia. In 1912, he joined the Orthodox Church, seeing Christianity as the fulfillment of his Jewish upbringing.[2] After his exile, Frank unfortunately settled in Berlin, where he had previously studied decades before. But with Adolf Hitler's rise to power he had to flee again, moving to Paris in 1937, and once more had to escape the Nazis after the fall of France in 1940, hiding out near Grenoble. His children fled to Britain, and he

---

1    Ignatius of Antioch, To the Smyrnaeans, 6.2–8.2, in *Early Christian Fathers*, ed. Cyril C. Richardson (Westminster Press, 1953), 114–115.
2    On Frank's relation to his Jewish heritage, see Dominic Rubin, *Holy Russia, Sacred Israel: Jewish-Christian Encounters in Russian Religious Thought* (Academic Studies Press, 2010), 447–510.

and his wife followed them after World War II ended. He died there, far from home and three times a refugee, in 1950.

Frank's 1930 work *The Spiritual Foundations of Society* expounds the Orthodox principle of sobornost' as the "living, inner, organic unity of society."[3] Frank contrasted sobornost' with *obshchestvennost'* or "mechanically external"[4] social unity. What he meant by that was that a group of strangers isn't a community. It is not enough for people to have an outward appearance of unity (obshchestvennost') without any inner bond between them. Through sobornost', "he," "she," and "they" become "I," "you," and "we"—living communion rather than radical individualism. "All human relationships without exception . . . involve . . . one and the same inner spiritual connection, without which communion of any kind is inconceivable," says Frank. "It is precisely for this reason that the law of love of one's neighbor can and must be the genuinely universal law, to which our entire life must be subordinated."[5] As his translator Boris Jakim put it, for Frank, "All human rights are ultimately grounded in one 'innate' right: the right of man to demand that he be given the opportunity to fulfill his obligation, i.e., the opportunity to serve."[6] Frank did not, however, *oppose* each principle to the other. He describes them as the soul (sobornost') and body (obshchestvennost') of society. Thus, like our own soul and body, they can be rightly or wrongly related. Intriguingly, he relates them in a way that resonates strongly with the "new" social map we developed in chapter 33, and he even does so with reference to the economic aspect of our lives.

For example, Frank notes:

The relation between seller and buyer or between capitalist and worker in contemporary society is usually represented as an example of coldly utilitarian, purely external intercourse in which one man serves . . . only as a source of profit, and does not exist at all as [a] "neighbor," as a human being with whom

---

3    S. L. Frank, *The Spiritual Foundations of Society*, trans. Boris Jakim (Ohio University Press, 1987), 57.
4    Frank, 58.
5    Frank, 58–59.
6    Boris Jakim, "Translator's Preface," in Frank, *Spiritual Foundations*, viii–ix.

one associates feelings of respect, love, solidarity. But . . . without the elementary trust that the buyer is an honest man, the seller would not let him into his shop for fear of being robbed. Without trust in the conscientiousness of the worker, a trust that no control could replace, the capitalist would not entrust the worker with any work. . . . A difference only in degree . . . distinguishes these contemporary relations from more patriarchal relations, in which the apprentice is a member of the master-artisan's family or the buyer is a friend of the seller.[7]

In this long quote, we see several elements we covered before: the difference between the personal economy of families and friendship and the impersonal economy of states and markets, as well as their natures as "fuzzy sets," containing dynamics of the others. So, too, we see that Frank understands—as we saw in Part 4—that commerce does *not* require selfishness and that it *does* at least require some minimal trust and regard for others.

Thus, with reference to our map in chapter 33, sobornost' corresponds to the systems and dynamics of the personal economy. It is precisely personal social systems that Frank associates with the most basic manifestation of sobornost': "The primary and fundamental form of sobornost' is the unity of *marriage* and *family*. . . . The fact that man is not simply man, but precisely man or woman . . . and that man is the child of his parents, the fruit of their union—this self-evident, but mysterious fact is evidence of that eternal cosmic sobornost', which lies at the base of even our physical being."[8] He also equally relates sobornost' to our fundamental religious feeling. Frank writes that "the religious feeling in its most profound and purest form is the feeling of kinship between man and God (God as the Father). And on the other hand, reverence for one's parents, the cult of ancestors and of the family, the hearth as altar, are the primordial forms of religious faith."[9] Last, he relates sobornost' to the impersonal economy inasmuch as it expresses "the *common fate and life* of every united group of people."[10] After family and religion, he

---

7    Frank, *Spiritual Foundations*, 58–59.
8    Frank, 60.
9    Frank, 61.
10   Frank, 61, italics original.

notes the essential, personal dynamics of impersonal systems: "Workers in a common enterprise are bonded together by a feeling of camaraderie, an inner closeness. Soldiers who participate together in missions and battles become brothers forever."[11] But if sobornost' is just another word for catholicity, how does it relate to the Church?

## The Church as Sobornost'

FRANK SUMMARIZES THAT "A KIND of mystical, supranatural total unity lies at the bases of society. . . . This organism is *Godmanhood, the merging of human souls in God.* This organism is what we mean by the *church,* in the most profound and general sense of this word. We thus arrive at the affirmation that *every society is necessarily grounded in the church* as the nucleus and life-giving principle of society."[12] As St. Paul put it, the Church is "the pillar and ground of the truth" (1 Tim. 3:15). Frank distinguishes the "church" as the "one holy, catholic, apostolic Church"[13] from the merely external "union of believers, one of many social organizations."[14] He then distinguishes both of these from a third aspect: "The 'visible' church as the unity of believers now living is based on the 'invisible' church . . . not only because it encompasses its living members as well as those who are dead and those who are not yet born, but also because, in the wise words of a Russian bishop, 'the divisions between our faiths do not reach heaven.'"[15]

While this might sound either too radically ecumenical to some readers or else too similar to Protestant distinctions between the "visible" and "invisible" church, Frank's meaning seems closer to the early apologists' belief that there are seeds of the Logos in all peoples, nations, and cultures: "Every unity of people in faith, every merging of human souls in holiness in which their life is grounded, however illusory and deceptive this holiness, contains . . . the superhuman principle, the reflection—even if faint, distorted, or even

---

11    Frank, 62.
12    Frank, 106, emphasis original.
13    Frank, 106.
14    Frank, 107.
15    Frank, 107. Frank unfortunately does not name the bishop.

completely perverted—of Divinity in human hearts."[16] The one, true Church thus represents the fulfillment of this universal, free, and organic human unity—i.e., sobornost'. And "the world" relates to "church" in this third sense in the same way as merely external to inner unity or sobornost'. He similarly adds, "The fundamental . . . relationship between the church and the world" corresponds "to the relationship between grace and law,"[17] the former fulfilling and surpassing the latter, as we saw in this book's chapters on the Gospel.

According to Frank, confusing grace and law, internal and external power, leads to corruption: "All attempts at the external, artificial, mechanical organizational absorption of the world (the state, economic life, law, etc.) by the church are not only destined to fail, but lead to a result directly contrary to their goal: namely the secularization (i.e., the distortion and death) of the church, this inner holiness by which society lives."[18] Instead, the holiness of sobornost' can only enliven the world when we properly distinguish the Church from the world and understand the world as it really is.[19] Thus, I would add, we cannot hope to transform our economic life if we do not understand how it works and respect it for what it is, as we attempted to do in Part 4 of this book. To deny this requires a social Gnosticism that should be as unthinkable to us today as it was to St. Ignatius of Antioch on the road to martyrdom.

Rather, in an interesting variation of both sphere sovereignty and subsidiarity, Frank writes, "The world of social life is a kind of hierarchy of levels or spheres, differing in the degree of their categorial closeness to the element of holiness that inspirits them."[20] He gives an example of how this works: "The state is formally more distant than the family from the church as the spiritual unity of people in holiness, while the family, in turn, is formally more distant from the church than empirical moral and religious life. But this does not prevent a state official or any servant of the state . . . in his actions and relations with people from being at times more permeated by the pure holiness of the

---

16    Frank, 108.
17    Frank, 110.
18    Frank, 112.
19    Frank, 113.
20    Frank, 114.

good . . . than a father in relation to his children or a priest in relation to his flock."[21] We could say the same about the business world.

Put simply, while outlining a spectrum of social spheres from most to least holy, Frank acknowledges the reality of imperfection and sin, which tragically sometimes even infects what should be the most grace-filled spheres of life. "In this respect," he concludes, "the dividing line between the Divine and the human, between the church and the world, passes only through the depths of the human heart."[22] For the sake of discernment, then, we need that sword (the Logos of God) that pierces "even to the division of soul and spirit, and of joints and marrow, and is a discerner of the thoughts and intents of the heart" (Heb. 4:12). Like Mary, this "sword" must "pierce through [our] own soul, so that the deliberations of many hearts may be revealed" (Luke 2:35, my translation).

## *Mother and Martyr*

FOR DEEPER REFLECTION ON THIS dynamic, St. Maria Skobtsova can be our guide. Born Elizaveta ("Liza") Pilenko, like so many Russian Orthodox intellectuals, in early adulthood she, too, had rejected her faith and embraced revolutionary ideals. But Christ had different plans for Liza. Despite her rejection of religion, she could not escape an attraction to Jesus, whose radical love so sharply contrasted with the cheap talk of her fellow Bolsheviks. As Jim Forest put it, "It seemed to her that the real need of the people was not for revolutionary theories but for Christ."[23] She read the Gospel and lives of the saints regularly, eventually returning to prayer and to the Church. Of course, her renewed faith pushed against the winds of change in Russia. Like so many others, she, too, was forced to flee with her family, eventually settling in Paris, where Fr. Sergei Bulgakov became her confessor, and she taught and served other Russian émigrés there.

---

21 Frank, 114.
22 Frank, 114.
23 Jim Forest, "Introduction: Mother Maria of Paris," in *Mother Maria Skobtsova: Essential Writings*, trans. Richard Pevear and Larissa Volokhonsky (Orbis Books, 2003), 16.

"In the hard winter of 1926," Forest wrote, "each person in the family came down with influenza. All recovered except Nastia"—St. Maria's daughter—"who became thinner with each passing day."[24] After a month of the best medical care available, Nastia died with her mother at her side. The pain of losing her child pierced St. Maria's heart: "When someone you love has died, she wrote, 'the gates have suddenly opened onto eternity, all natural life has trembled and collapsed, yesterday's laws have been abolished, desires have faded, meaning has become meaningless, and another incomprehensible Meaning has grown wings on their backs.'"[25] Forest continued, "After her daughter's burial, Liza became 'aware of a new and special, broad and all-embracing motherhood.'"[26] When her second marriage collapsed, she took on a new monastic habit—and the name "Maria"—inspired by her newfound memento mori, actively serving the poor, neglected, and forgotten of Paris out of kenotic love rather than retreating to a monastery.

Later, when the Nazis took France in 1940, she worked tirelessly to protect Jewish families. On February 10, 1943, she was arrested by the Gestapo and sent to several concentration camps, where she continued her dedicated service to others despite her own deteriorating health. In turn, the other prisoners protected her, helping her stand to avoid execution for her infirmity. Yet according to at least one account, she ended her life by taking the place of another prisoner in the gas chamber on March 30, 1945, at Ravensbrück concentration camp, just a month before its liberation. In any case, taking account of the whole of her life and ministry, we can call her a new martyr for the love of Christ. But what was this "new and special, broad and all-embracing motherhood" that drove her kenotic love?

## *Imitating the Mother of God*

COMMENTING ON HOW OFTEN OUR private prayers use "we," "our," and "us," such as in "Our Father" and "have mercy on us," St. Maria notes, "Thus what is most personal, what is most intimate in an Orthodox person's life, is

---

24 Forest, "Introduction," 19.
25 Forest, 19.
26 Forest, 20.

thoroughly pervaded by this sense of being united with everyone, the sense of the principle of *sobornost'*, characteristic of the Orthodox Church."[27] Elsewhere, she elaborates, "I think that the fullest understanding of Christ's giving Himself to the world, creating the one Body of Christ, Godmanhood, is contained in the Orthodox idea of *sobornost'*."[28]

Reflecting on how the imitation of Christ too often becomes a sort of spiritual individualism, St. Maria sees a too Protestant spirit behind this distortion of it: "In so far as the world now lives the mystical life, it is for the most part infected by this isolating and individualistic Protestant mysticism. In it there is, of course, no place for the Church, for the principle of sobornost', for the God-manly perception of the whole Christian process."[29] Contrary to this, she insists that "the human soul unites in itself two images—the image of the Son of God and the image of the Mother of God—and thereby should participate not only in the destiny of the Son, but also in her destiny. . . . The cross of the Son of Man on Golgotha should pierce every Christian soul like a sword, should be experienced by it as a co-participation, a co-suffering with Him. Besides that, it should also accept the swords of its brothers' crosses."[30] With the sword of this imitation of the Mother of God, our failure to co-suffer with others serves as the measure of our sin.

Paradoxically, however, St. Maria does not envision this as an unbearable burden, and her own life attests to it: "Our relation to man should not be like a sort of extra burden that increases the burden of our own crosses, not like a pious exercise, a duty, the development of a virtue." She continues, "Only one single law exists here. Our relation is determined only by seeing the image of God in him, and, on the other hand, in adopting him as a son. Here duty, virtue, pious exercise—it all fades away."[31] She summarizes that "just as the only proper bearing of the cross in the world was Christ's bearing of the cross, so the only proper acceptance of the piercing sword was the acceptance of

---

27    Maria Skobtsova, "The Second Gospel Commandment," in *Mother Maria Skobtsova*, 47.
28    Skobtsova, "The Mysticism of Human Communion," in *Mother Maria Skobtsova*, 79.
29    Skobtsova, "On the Imitation of the Mother of God," in *Mother Maria Skobtsova*, 65.
30    Skobtsova, "Imitation of the Mother of God," 70.
31    Skobtsova, 71.

the Mother who stood by the cross on Golgotha."[32] Thus, much more than an intellectual principle, sobornost' finds its fulfillment in our own self-emptying love for others, co-suffering with them in this life, "bear[ing] one another's burdens, and so fulfill[ing] the law of Christ" (Gal. 6:2).

Mother Maria's unwavering commitment to the Gospel sometimes sounds like a rejection of natural law, but I think it fits better with the warning of St. Isaac the Syrian: "If thou settest up as thy aim to practice mercy, train thyself not to pursue justice in other fields, lest thou appear to work with one hand and to spill with the other."[33] So, too, it fits perfectly with Frank's warnings about confusing grace and the law. The world needs justice, but Christians can never be satisfied with mere justice barren of mercy. As we encounter others and their hardships and grief, we must take on—as we do every Holy Saturday—the vision of the Theotokos beholding her Son: "The Maiden pierced to the heart, cried out in her fervent weeping. / O Light of my eyes, my beloved Child, how are Thou now hidden in the grave?"[34]

Indeed, St. Maria's perspective contains a further, liturgical dimension: "During a service, the priest does not only cense the icons of the Savior, the Mother of God, and the saints. He also censes the icon-people, the image of God in the people who are present. And as they leave the church precincts, these people remain as much the images of God, worthy of being censed and venerated."[35] In this context, we return to Frank's understanding of the ecclesial nature of sobornost' in Maria's concept of the "churching" of life: "The whole world as one church, adorned with icons that should be venerated, that should be honored and loved, because these icons are true images of God that have the holiness of the Living God upon them."[36] As the Fathers teach, the honor paid to an image passes on to the original. The honor—or dishonor—paid to the image of God in everyone we meet passes on to God.

---

32   Skobtsova, 72.

33   Isaac the Syrian, "Treatise IV," in *Mystic Treatises by Isaac of Nineveh*, trans. A. J. Wensinck (Koninklijke Akademie Van Wetenschappen, 1923), 30.

34   George L. Papadeas, ed., *Greek Orthodox Holy Week & Easter Services* (Patmos Press, 1981), 393.

35   Maria Skobtsova, "Mysticism of Human Communion," 80.

36   Skobtsova, 81.

The next chapter on liturgical theology will further explore this "churching" of life, but we can see here in the work of S. L. Frank and St. Maria Skobtsova how sobornost' and the imitation of the Mother of God point us to a path of social reconciliation fully adaptable to our contemporary economies. To that end, I will give Mother Maria the final word: "Authentic, God-manly, integral, *sobornoe*"—i.e., catholic—"Christianity calls us in the Paschal song: 'Let us embrace one another, that with one mind we may confess.' Let us love—meaning not only one mind, but also one activity, meaning a common life."[37]

---

37  Skobtsova, 83.

CHAPTER 36

# Liturgical Theology

IF THERE'S ONE CONTRIBUTION TO Christian social thought the Orthodox Church is known for, both among clergy and laity, and even among Western Christians, it's our "liturgical theology." Yet in his 1914 book *The Pillar and Ground of the Truth*, Fr. Pavel Florensky observed that "liturgical theology awaits its creator."[1] Father Andrew Louth describes Florensky's friend Fr. Sergei Bulgakov as "a *liturgical* theologian, not in the sense that he writes *about* the liturgy, but that he writes *out of* the liturgy."[2] Yet Bulgakov's controversial teachings on divine Sophia have often overshadowed this aspect of his theology. How did Orthodox liturgical theology go from Florensky's aspiration, to Bulgakov's obscurity, to mainstream?

According to Louth, "'Liturgical theology' is a relatively new concept and it is, I think, pretty well universally agreed that the very notion of 'liturgical theology' is closely associated with the name of Fr. Alexander Schmemann." In fact, Schmemann studied under Bulgakov at the St. Sergius Orthodox Theological Institute in Paris, so perhaps its roots do stretch back to Fr. Sergei— as we'll see, there is something "sophic" about liturgical theology, even if it doesn't explicitly depend on sophiology. In any case, Louth continues, "Liturgical theology is theology that springs from the liturgy, that is implicit in the

---

1    Pavel Florensky, *The Pillar and Ground of the Truth*, trans. Boris Jakim (Princeton University Press, 1997), 218.

2    Andrew Louth, *Modern Orthodox Thinkers: From the* Philokalia *to the Present Day* (IVP Academic, 2015), 52.

liturgical worship of the Church, above all the celebration of the Eucharist, but stretching beyond that to encompass the daily offices of the Church, the sacramental rites, and also the structure of the liturgical day, week, year."[3]

Orthodox "eucharistic ecclesiology" developed out of liturgical theology. Once again, Louth provides a clear summary: "It is the Eucharist that makes the Church, for the Church is, in essence, the eucharistic assembly, gathered together, under the bishop, to proclaim Christ's death and rejoice in his risen presence with his people. In each eucharistic assembly the whole church is present, is instantiated in the celebration of the Eucharist under the bishop."[4] In this description, we find every element of St. Ignatius of Antioch's understanding of "the Catholic Church," except for one: "Concern for widows or orphans, for the oppressed, for those in prison or released, for the hungry or the thirsty."[5]

While I'm not an expert in liturgical theology, I have a theory that might explain this neglect: the separation of the sacramental aspect of liturgy from asceticism. If one only reads Schmemann's *For the Life of the World*, one might be tempted to blame him. However, as we'll see, Schmemann does duly attend to the connection between the Sacraments and asceticism in his *Great Lent*, and together with *For the Life of the World*—along with some "mysteriological piety"—we will see how the necessarily sacramental *and* ascetic nature of Orthodox liturgical life constitutes one last great contribution toward modern Orthodox Christian social thought today, highlighting the necessity of the Kingdom of God for the common good.

## *A Eucharistic Worldview*

SCHMEMANN WROTE *FOR THE LIFE of the World* for students, in order to explain "the Christian 'world view' . . . that stems from the liturgical

---

3    Louth, *Modern Orthodox Thinkers*, 194.
4    Louth, 221.
5    Ignatius of Antioch, To the Smyrnaeans, 6.2, in *Early Christian Fathers*, ed. Cyril C. Richardson (Westminster Press, 1953), 114. For an illustration of this general neglect of the necessary economic implications of catholicity, see John Romanides, "The Ecclesiology of St. Ignatius of Antioch," *The Greek Orthodox Theological Review* 7, no. 1–2 (1961–1962): 53–77.

experience of the Orthodox Church."[6] He contrasted the liturgical world-view of Orthodoxy with activists "who reduce the Church to the world and its problems" and those who focus exclusively on individual piety, "who simply equate the world with evil." But, he contends, "Both attitudes distort . . . the wholeness, the *catholicity* of the genuine Orthodox tradition which has always affirmed both the *goodness* of the world for whose life God has given his only-begotten Son, and the *wickedness* in which the world lies."[7] These alternative errors both wrongly separate the sacred from the secular. By contrast, "*Honesty* to the Gospel, to the whole Christian tradition, to the experience of every saint and every word of Christian liturgy *demands* . . . to live in the world seeing *everything* in it as a revelation of God, a sign of His presence, the joy of His coming, the call to communion with Him, the hope for fulfillment in Him."[8] As St. Justin the Philosopher put it, "To God nothing is secular, not even the world itself, for it is His workmanship."[9]

As for the details of this Orthodox liturgical worldview, drawing on the story of Paradise in Genesis 2, Schmemann focuses on eating: "Man is a hungry being. But he is hungry for God. Behind all the hunger of our life is God. All desire is finally a desire for Him."[10] As St. Augustine prayed, "Thou hast formed us for Thyself, and our hearts are restless till they find rest in Thee."[11] For Schmemann, all the world thus has a potentially sacramental quality: "By filling the world with this eucharist, [man] transforms his life, the one that he receives from the world, into life in God, into communion with Him. The world was created as the 'matter,' the material of one all-embracing eucharist, and man was created as the priest of this cosmic sacrament."[12] As God said to St. Augustine, "I am the food of strong men; grow, and thou shalt feed upon

6    Alexander Schmemann, *For the Life of the World: Sacraments and Orthodoxy*, rev. and expanded ed. (SVS Press, 1979), 7.

7    Schmemann, *For the Life of the World*, 8.

8    Schmemann, 112, emphasis original.

9    Justin Martyr, *On the Resurrection of the Dead* in ANF 1:296. Scholars disagree about whether this work is authentically attributed to St. Justin, but it certainly fits with the tone and content of his other known works. It is both ancient and Orthodox, whatever the case.

10   Schmemann, *For the Life of the World*, 14.

11   Augustine of Hippo, *Confessions*, 1.1, in NPNF[1] 1:45.

12   Schmemann, *For the Life of the World*, 15.

me; nor shall thou convert me, like the food of thy flesh, into thee, but thou shall be converted into me."[13] Through liturgy, the world once again becomes what God created it to be in the beginning: the means of our deification, the wedding feast of the Lamb.

So how does this relate to our economic life? Well, first of all, it guards us against Gnosticism, which claims the material world, and thus material wealth, is inherently evil. Second, however, it also guards against hedonism and greed, as it reshapes how we use and understand the world's resources. "It is not accidental," writes Schmemann, "that the biblical story of the Fall is centered again on food. . . . Not given, not blessed by God, it was food whose eating was condemned to be communion with itself alone, and not with God. It is the image of the world loved for itself, and eating it is the image of life understood as an end in itself."[14] By seeing the true, sacramental nature of God's creation, the liturgical worldview rejects both condemnation of and overindulgence in the world. It suggests a positive role for our work, business, and commerce, so long as they are offered to God in thanksgiving.

## Sacramental and Ascetic

BUT IN SCHMEMANN'S *GREAT LENT*, we see clearly that Sacraments are not the whole story: "Eucharist is always preceded by [a] total fast . . . which for the Church constitutes *a necessary condition* for Holy Communion."[15] As he put it in *For the Life of the World*, "The [eucharistic] journey begins when Christians leave their homes and beds. . . . They have been individuals, some white, some black, some poor, some rich, they have been the 'natural' world and a natural community. And now they have been called to 'come together in one place,' to bring their lives, their very 'world' with them and to be more than what they were: a *new* community with a new life."[16] What are we doing when we "leave [our] homes and beds"? Fasting, of course.

---

13    Augustine of Hippo, *Confessions*, 7.10, in *NPNF*[1] 1:109.
14    Schmemann, *For the Life of the World*, 16.
15    Alexander Schmemann, *Great Lent: Journey to Pascha* (SVS Press, 2001), 50, italics added.
16    Schmemann, *For the Life of the World*, 27.

Paul Evdokimov, like Schmemann another former student at St. Sergius in Paris, writes of asceticism in ways that perfectly dovetail with Schmemann's account of the Sacraments: "From the time of Clement of Alexandria and Origen the spiritual life bears the name of asceticism. This signifies diligence, training, practice. The negative asceticism of suppression is allied to the positive asceticism of acquisition and growth."[17] Orthodox asceticism is not purely negative. To misunderstand this robs Lent—and all ascetic labors throughout the year—of that "bright sadness" about which Schmemann so eloquently spoke. "Everyone who has practiced it," he writes, "knows that [an] ascetical fast"—reduction and limitation of consumption—"rather than weakening us makes us light, concentrated, sober, joyful, pure."[18]

All the ascetic disciplines, including fasting, have as their goal the flourishing within us of the grace we receive in the Sacraments through the cultivation of virtue, which in turn prepares us to receive the Sacraments again. The relationship between sacrament and asceticism is reciprocal. As Baptism, the Eucharist, and all the other Sacraments are rooted in Christ, so also asceticism means dying *and rising* with Christ daily. "Or do you not know," asked St. Paul, "that as many of us as were baptized into Christ Jesus were baptized into His death? Therefore we were buried with Him through baptism into death, that just as Christ was raised from the dead by the glory of the Father, even so we also should walk in newness of life" (Rom. 6:3–4). The ascetic aspect of liturgy is precisely *how* we "walk in newness of life." In that walk, we may stumble and fall. As Schmemann warned, "True fasting . . . will be a real fight and probably we shall fail many times."[19] But each time we get up and continue again down the narrow road of repentance that leads to life, we experience a new resurrection. When we look back at the broad road that leads to death and see how far we've come, despite our failures, we find true joy in the presence of God that surpasses all the pleasures of the world and can be the only foundation of true thanksgiving, i.e., Eucharist.

---

17   Paul Evdokimov, *Ages of the Spiritual Life*, trans. Michael Plekon and Alexis Vinogradov (SVS Press, 1998), 65.
18   Schmemann, *Great Lent*, 98.
19   Schmemann, 98.

When we include asceticism in our sacramental worldview like this, we see a spiritual and moral foundation for how best to use the scarce resources of the world for the sake not just of producing material wealth, but of offering it to God in service to our neighbors rather than being captivated by it. Asceticism connects the common good of worldly commerce with our spiritual destiny in the Kingdom of God.

## *Holy Altars*

IN ADDITION TO SCHMEMANN'S INSIGHTS, we should further note the importance of sacred places as an extension of liturgical theology. According to St. Luke, after Pentecost the first Christians "continu[ed] daily with one accord in the temple" (Acts 2:46). So, too, it likely wasn't merely coincidence that in the second century Emperor Hadrian built a pagan temple over the Holy Sepulchre. It was probably to dissuade Christians from gathering there. And in Rome, early Christians met in the catacombs, partly for safety but partly to be among the holy relics of the martyrs, which transfigured those places of death into places of life. I vividly saw this same phenomenon when I visited the prison at Pitesti in Romania in 2014, which is now a museum commemorating those tortured there for their faith under Communism, and where the main torture room has since been converted into a chapel.[20] The revolutionary worldview of Christianity demonstrates that God's blessing can reverse the curse of sin anyplace in the world, perhaps most especially through the consecration of new holy altars, without which there can be no Eucharist. As a result, we do care about specific holy places, precisely because anyplace can become holy through the martyric witness of the saints.

We even see this in every Orthodox parish. Saint Nicholas Cabasilas unites the sacramental and ascetic aspect of liturgy in his explanation of the consecration of an altar, which is "the basis or root . . . of the Mysteries,"[21] i.e.,

---

20 For a fuller account of my experience in Pitesti, see Dylan Pahman, "What I Saw in Pitesti," *Everyday Asceticism*, November 22, 2024, https://everydayasceticism.com/2024/11/22/what-i-saw-in-pitesti/.

21 Nicholas Cabasilas, *The Life in Christ*, trans. Carmino J. de Catazanaro (SVS Press, 1974), 149.

the Sacraments (Greek: *mysteria*). According to Cabasilas, "The hierarch approaching the sacred rite in his white linen garments is a vested type and image of the altar, which is man himself. If a man, as David says, 'wash away all wickedness and become whiter than snow' (Ps. [50:7]), and recollects himself and bends in on himself and bows down, that makes God truly dwell in the soul and makes the heart an altar."[22] Indeed, this is the goal of Orthodox hesychasm—inner stillness through watchful prayer—for the mind to enter the heart and there to offer to God the sacrifice of praise through the words of the Jesus Prayer: "Lord Jesus Christ, Son of God, have mercy on me, a sinner." Asceticism, then, is the liturgy of the heart, the sanctification of the rhythm of our breath and heartbeat, and it is no less a liturgy "for the life of the world" than that performed in our holy places. As St. Seraphim of Sarov is known to have said, "Acquire the Spirit of Peace, and thousands around you shall be saved."[23] In this way, asceticism transforms all of our relationships into an encounter with the Holy Spirit, whether among friends, family, workplaces, or elsewhere.

A beautiful illustration of this connection between the altar, the Liturgy, and our human nature comes from the Soviet era in Russia. In his book *Everyday Saints*, Archimandrite Tikhon recounts a story told to him by a priest about life in the Gulag: "Many priests knew the text of the Liturgy by heart. . . . Instead of the altar with the relics of the martyr on which Church rules require us to serve the Liturgy, we would get the fellow convict-priest among us who had the broadest shoulders to help us. He would strip to his waist, lie down, and then we would say the Divine Liturgy upon his chest."[24] In extreme circumstances, a man himself can literally be Christ's holy altar. This altar, too, contained holy relics—the bones of the "convict-priest." Through enduring suffering, whether the voluntary struggle of asceticism or the hardship of persecution, Christians become martyrs, i.e., *witnesses* to the

---

22 Cabasilas, *The Life in Christ*, 151.

23 See Evdokimov, *Ages of the Spiritual Life*, 207, for an alternate version of this quote: "Acquire interior peace, and many around you will find their salvation." The saying exists in several forms and, to my knowledge, does not occur in a specific primary source text but has rather been transmitted orally.

24 Archimandrite Tikhon (Shevkunov), *Everyday Saints and Other Stories*, trans. Julian Henry Lowenfeld (Pokrov Publications, 2012), 253.

invincible joy of Christ's Resurrection, just as much from the time of the apostles to the present day.

And what better way to witness to that joy than to give oneself to others, as Christ did for us? Since at least the time of Isaiah, whose prophecy we read on weekdays during Lent, fasting has been understood, especially during the great fasts of the liturgical year, as an act of conserving one's resources *in order to give alms* and care for the marginalized (see Is. 58:6–8). Schmemann claims that "nowhere in the New Testament, in fact, is Christianity presented as a cult or as a religion," in the mistaken sense of presuming "a wall of separation between God and man."[25] But St. James the Just, just once, actually does refer to the Christian life as "religion": "Pure and undefiled religion before God and the Father is this: to visit orphans and widows in their trouble, and to keep oneself unspotted from the world" (James 1:27). We cannot reduce "religion" here to a mere metaphor unless we fall into the error of dividing, rather than merely distinguishing, the sacred from the secular—ironically precisely what Schmemann worries we might do. But considering the positive role of asceticism, we can see how this "undefiled religion" does not require strictly secularized activism but rather necessarily grows out of our liturgical life.

## Interior Monasticism

INDEED, IT IS THROUGH THE everyday asceticism of what Evdokimov called *"interiorized monasticism,"*[26] the concept—in substance shared by both S. L. Frank and St. Maria Skobtsova[27]—that even those of us living "in the world" can monastically face our unique challenges today. "The monasticism that was entirely centered on the last things formerly changed the face of the world," he writes. "Today it makes an appeal to all, to the laity as well as to the monastics, and it points out a universal vocation. For each, it is a question of

---

25  Schmemann, *For the Life of the World*, 19–20.
26  Evdokimov, *Ages of the Spiritual Life*, 135.
27  See S. L. Frank, *The Light Shineth in the Darkness*, trans. Boris Jakim (Ohio University Press, 1989), 140–152; Maria Skobtsova, "Toward a New Monasticism I: At the Heart of the World," in *Mother Maria Skobtsova: Essential Writings*, trans. Richard Pevear and Larissa Volokhonsky (Orbis Books, 2003), 90–95; and "Toward a New Monasticism II: Love without Limits," in *Mother Maria Skobtsova*, 96–103.

adaptation, of a personal equivalent of the monastic vows."[28] He intriguingly recommends that everyone appropriate the disciplines of poverty, chastity, and obedience, which he labels "a great charter of human liberty."[29] Perhaps we might more clearly call them simplicity, purity, and service. Evdokimov sees these disciplines in Christ's answers to the devil's three temptations in the desert after Theophany. Particularly, with regard to the first temptation, he notes, "To transform stones into bread is to solve the *economic problem*, to suppress 'the sweat of one's brow,' to eliminate all ascetic efforts, and creation itself."[30] What he means by that is that we should not seek purely external substitutes or magical, utopian plans for what can only be accomplished through ascetic effort or love, and we absolutely *should* ascetically transform our labor and economic consumption from the inside out.

Unfortunately, Evdokimov goes on to claim that "only an economy based on need and not on profit has any chance of succeeding."[31] This is economically confused. What he should have said is not "profit" but "greed." The former, as nearly every economist since Adam Smith has pointed out, thankfully does not require the latter. Without profit, no one can provide for anyone's needs, businesses fail, and poverty abounds. As Clement of Alexandria asked, "If no one had anything, what room would be left among men for giving?"[32] *Only* an economy based on profit "has any chance of succeeding." Rather, as the principle of marginal utility shows, absent any unfair legal privileges, in modern market economies profit communicates to businesses, through uncontrolled prices, whether their products successfully fulfill human needs—or at least human wants. And therein lies the need for asceticism.

Asceticism is the means by which we put to death our selfish and greedy desires and transform them into a hunger for communion with God and each other. At their best, good laws can only restrain evil. No economic system can do that for us either. Only the grace of God, received through the Sacraments and cultivated through ascetic disciplines, can change people's hearts.

---

28   Evdokimov, *Ages of the Spiritual Life*, 139.
29   Evdokimov, 139.
30   Evdokimov, 141.
31   Evdokimov, 146.
32   Clement of Alexandria, *Who Is the Rich Man That Shall Be Saved?*, 13, in ANF 2:594.

In this way, both Schmemann and Evdokimov reveal, at their best, that rightly understood there can be no common good without the Kingdom of God. Yes, we should want our neighbors—even those who aren't Christians of any tradition—to flourish in their relationships and be freed from material hardship. But our efforts to alleviate their suffering must flow from the eucharistic life we've received from Christ in His Catholic Church, always directing them to the one in whom, through asceticism, we can say with St. Paul, "Everywhere and in all things I have learned both to be full and to be hungry, both to abound and to suffer need. I can do all things through Christ who strengthens me" (Phil. 4:12–13). After all, Christ asks us, "What will it profit a man if he gains the whole world, and loses his own soul?" (Mark 8:36)

With that in mind, now that we've surveyed modern Orthodox Christian social thought along with Scripture, Church history, and the history of economics, we can better evaluate recent official and unofficial statements from various Orthodox Churches that touch on economic matters. Do they provide an adequate basis for understanding modern society? Do they wisely guide Orthodox Christians to live their lives liturgically "for the life of the world" (John 6:51)? Could the Church do better? If so, should it? In my next chapter, I will attempt to answer these questions, offering up to God the "widow's mite" of my own intellectual labors, as a scribe of His Kingdom, for the common good of our communities, nations, and economies today.

CHAPTER 37

# Orthodox Church Documents

I N THE MIDST OF THE COVID-19 pandemic in 2020, I remember going for a walk, pushing two of my children in a stroller and seeing a "Black Lives Matter" sign in a yard at the end of a cul-de-sac. Surely the resident meant well, but what good did that statement really do? A person would have to be aware of the stream of stories like George Floyd's that flooded social media that year, and that same person would, like me, have to walk close enough to this house on a dead-end street in a quiet neighborhood to see the sign in the first place. The answer, of course, is that the sign didn't do anything to fight racial injustice or police brutality, just as signs in support of police also did nothing to relieve the stresses of their jobs that contributed to such tragic encounters. These signs only consoled the people who had put them in their yards with the notion that at least they had done *something*. After all, so another meme proclaimed, "Silence Is Violence."

I don't write this to criticize that consolation. It's relatable. But the Fathers teach that we must carefully watch and evaluate our thoughts and passions, and on reflection, I've decided silence isn't violence. Silence is the sound of listening. Moreover, the cultivation of spiritual silence through prayer is an ascetic discipline. Holy Tradition has a more meaningful perspective than memes. Silence can be a powerful tool for peace, reconciliation, and understanding. Though there is "a time to speak," there is also "a time to keep silence" (Eccl. 3:7) and listen—to God, to each other, to our own hearts. This gives me something better to console myself in my helplessness. I can listen, learn, and pray.

The Orthodox Church similarly practiced silence with regard to official statements on social issues, outside of isolated topics. All the insights we've so far covered in Part 5, from Sophia to sobornost' to liturgical theology, came from priests and lay intellectuals. For the Moscow Patriarchate, that changed in the year 2000 with the publication of *The Basis of the Social Concept* (BSC) of the Russian Orthodox Church. And in 2016, representatives from most autocephalous Orthodox Churches—though not Moscow, Sophia, or Antioch—met in Crete for a council to address issues facing the Church in the contemporary world. The Council issued an encyclical calling for further work, including on social and economic issues, and a commission published a document in 2020 to that end: *For the Life of the World* (FLW). The editors of this technically unofficial-but-still-important statement took the same title as Fr. Alexander Schmemann did for his well-known book on liturgical theology, though strangely they didn't reference him at all.

What guidance do these statements offer for the sake of a political economy informed by both Holy Tradition and economic science? What principles and frameworks do they employ to help us understand how to live our faith in our world of unprecedented abundance? In light of all that has preceded this final chapter, my answer regrettably must be "little to nothing," and in some cases worse than nothing. I understand the impulse to write such statements, to want to have done *something*, but sometimes silence—and listening—is a better witness. In this chapter, I will briefly review what these documents say specifically with regards to political economy, explain my criticisms, and point to a better alternative in the work of Ecumenical Patriarch Bartholomew.

## *The Good of the BSC*

To be fair, I will do my best to highlight the good—or at least "not bad"—in each document before explaining its problems, starting with the BSC, which does well to acknowledge that "it is the divine-human nature of the Church that makes possible the grace-giving transformation and purification of the world."[1] Additionally, it states that "the Church should go through the process of historical kenosis. . . . The Church is called to act in the world in the image of Christ, to bear witness to Him and His Kingdom."[2] Indeed, the Church should embody the kenotic, self-emptying humility of Christ in its service to the world, acting as a bridge between God and humanity. Kenoticism—the act of humbling oneself below the lowest member of society—characterized the chief contribution of the medieval Rus' to Orthodox social thought, as we saw in chapter 23. So, too, we ought to care for the less fortunate because "the members of the Church encounter Christ as the One Who assumed all sins and suffering of the world when they welcome the hungry, homeless, sick or prisoners."[3] Admitting that due to sin this work will always be imperfect, the BSC states that "the common service of the Church [is] performed on the basis of not one but many various gifts,"[4] acknowledging a variety of charisms and earthly vocations in this task. It also distinguishes between a few general social spheres: "It is inadmissible to shun the surrounding world in a Manichean way," because "the world, socium and state are objects of God's love."

Later, the BSC rightly notes, "Holy Scripture recognises the human right to property and deplores any encroachment on it."[5] Moreover, "The Church urges Christians to see in property . . . God's gift given to be used for their own and their neighbours' benefit."[6] Additionally, "The Church recognises the existence of various forms of ownership. Public, corporate, private and mixed forms of property."[7] It even touches, but does not elaborate, on intellectual property: "The Church . . . deplores the violation of copyright."[8] Also, mindful of the horrors of the Russian Revolution, it warns that "the Church cannot

1    *The Basis of the Social Concept* (Moscow: Department of External Church Relations, 2000), 1.1, retrieved from https://old.mospat.ru/en/documents/social-concepts/. Henceforth BSC.

2    BSC, 1.2.

3    BSC, 1.2.

4    BSC, 1.3.

5    BSC, 7.2, original bold.

6    BSC, 7.2, original bold.

7    BSC, 7.3, original bold.

8    BSC, 7.3, original bold.

approve the alienation and re-distribution of property with violations of the rights of its legitimate owners."[9] It correctly emphasizes that "the repudiation of private property in the early apostolic community (Acts 4:32) and later in coenobite monasteries was exclusively a voluntary affair and a personal spiritual option."[10] Nevertheless, it warns that not all products and industries are moral: "Modern times, however, have seen the emergence of a whole industry intended to propagate vice and sin and satisfy such baneful passions and addictions as drinking, drug-addiction, fornication and adultery."[11]

We saw in chapter 16 that the Edict of Milan understood religious freedom to require private property, and later in chapter 18 that monastic liberty also required it, and in general that the freedom of the Church is essential for Christian political economy. So, too, we can note here that the BSC elsewhere affirms, "The Christian socio-public ethics demanded that a certain autonomous sphere should be reserved for man, in which his conscience might remain the 'autocratic' master, for it is the free will that determines ultimately the salvation or death, the way to Christ or the way away from Christ."[12] Additionally, though it does not credit him, it directly quotes Vladimir Soloviev in acknowledging the limited scope of law: "The secular law has as its task not to turn the world lying in evil into the Kingdom of God, but to prevent it from turning into hell. The fundamental principle of law is: 'do not do to others what you would not want to be done to yourself.' "[13] This last sentence is also without attribution, but we can say that it summarizes the "Silver Rule" as found in Tobit 4:15, which Adam Smith saw to be the essence of legal justice.[14]

---

9    BSC, 7.3, first sentence bold.

10   BSC, 7.3, original bold.

11   BSC, 6.5.

12   BSC, 4.6.

13   BSC, 4.2, first sentence bold. Compare with Vladimir Solovyov, *The Justification of the Good*, rev. ed., ed. Boris Jakim, trans. Natalie A. Duddington (Eerdmans, 2005), 324.

14   Adam Smith, *The Theory of Moral Sentiments*, 6th ed., 2.2.1, in *The Theory of Moral Sentiments; Or; An Essay towards an Analysis of the Principles by Which Men Naturally Judge Concerning the Conduct and Character, First of Their Neighbours, and Afterwards of Themselves. To Which Is Added, A Dissertation on the Origin of Languages*, new ed. (Henry G. Bohn, 1853), 117, discussed in chapter 27.

## The Bad of the BSC

UNFORTUNATELY, THE BSC'S CONCEPTION OF society is vague. It speaks of various social spheres, but other than the Church, state, and nation, they are not well defined or differentiated. As for social principles, kenoticism is the only one mentioned, and it isn't well-employed. There's no mention of catholicity or sobornost'. Liturgical theology is only minimally referenced. There's no evidence that the positive contributions of sophiology have been incorporated. Its understanding of economics is basic, though perhaps better than nothing. Nevertheless, it claims, "The Church raises the question concerning the need to establish comprehensive control over transnational corporations and the processes taking place in the financial sector of economy. This control, aimed to subject any entrepreneurial and financial activity to the interests of man and people, should be exercised through all mechanisms available in society and state."[15] But we have seen that "comprehensive control" is incompatible with "entrepreneurial and financial activity," as F. A. Hayek demonstrated in *The Road to Serfdom*.[16] The BSC statement is also shaky on the question of natural law, as demonstrated by its other statements on freedom of conscience: "The adoption of the freedom of conscience as legal principle points to the fact that society has lost religious goals and values and become massively apostate and actually indifferent to the task of the Church and to the overcoming of sin."[17] Thus, despite later praising freedom of conscience, the BSC would here consign the early Christian apologists and the Edict of Milan to advocating for society to "become massively apostate," which, of course, is ridiculous. Either freedom of conscience is or isn't a human right. The BSC authors seem to want to have it both ways—it is a human right when they like it, but not when they don't.

Indeed, contradictory statements plague this text on a wide range of issues, especially related to fundamental human rights rooted in natural law. Perhaps that is why Moscow issued a follow-up statement in their *Basic Teaching on*

---

15   BSC, 16.1.
16   See F. A. Hayek, *The Road to Serfdom* (George Routledge & Sons, 1944), discussed in chapter 31 of this book.
17   BSC, 3.6.

*Human Dignity, Freedom and Rights* eight years later.[18] However, while intriguingly drawing upon the Orthodox distinction between the image and likeness of God and helpfully noting the importance of education, among other concerns, it still blurs rather than clarifies the line of inviolable rights and the limits of state power.

Not only that, but contradictory and hypocritical action also characterizes the application of even some of Moscow's better teachings. For example, despite its later condemnation of industries that promote addiction in the BSC, Andrei Zolotov reported in 1998 that "since 1994, when the government granted the Moscow Patriarchate the right to import thousands of tons of tobacco—duty free—as humanitarian aid, 10,000 tons of cigarettes have been imported by the church. According to estimates, that works out at about 8 billion cigarettes—10 percent of Russia's total tobacco imports."[19] While I do believe that prohibition of industries "intended to propagate vice and sin" is often imprudent and impossible—as Prohibition in the United States demonstrated—the Church should not *participate* in "vice and sin," since, as the BSC itself states, "being involved in such activities . . . corrupt[s] not only workers, but also society as a whole."[20] For these and many more reasons, I find the BSC's contributions to Orthodox social thought to be minimal at best and alarmingly harmful at worst.

## The Good of FLW

WHAT ABOUT FLW? THE ENCYCLICAL of the Council of Crete touches on liturgical theology—helpfully including both sacramentalism and asceticism.[21] It also mentions catholicity, but only in the context of conciliar

---

18    *The Russian Orthodox Church's Basic Teaching on Human Dignity, Freedom and Rights* (Moscow: Department of External Church Relations, 2008), retrieved from https://old.mospat.ru/en/documents/dignity-freedom-rights/.

19    Andrei Zolotov, "Orthodoxy, Oil, Tobacco, and Wine: Do They Mix?" *East-West Church Ministry Report* 5, no. 1 (Winter 1997): 7, retrieved from http://www.eastwestreport.org/articles/ewo5108.htm.

20    BSC, 6.5.

21    Encyclical of the Holy and Great Council of the Orthodox Church (Crete 2016), 5.13, retrieved from https://www.holycouncil.org/encyclical-holy-council.

authority and seemingly used synonymously with it.[22] It more than once affirms a form of the personalist principle of morality that human dignity is inviolable and that one cannot without sin use other people as a mere means rather than treating them as ends in themselves.[23] It emphasizes the importance of freedom of conscience[24] and highlights the challenge of secularism.[25] On economics, it recommends "not only repentance . . . but also asceticism as an antidote to consumerism, the deification of needs and the acquisitive attitude."[26] It furthermore—and perhaps more problematically—"proposes *a viable economy founded on the principles of the Gospel.*"[27] I say this is problematic not because the Gospel shouldn't, through the catholicity of the Church, enliven our economies, as S. L. Frank outlined with regard to sobornost'. Rather, it is problematic because the external structure of the impersonal economy should not be confused with the internal and personal spirit and holiness that alone can give it life. Indeed, as we'll see, failing to carefully distinguish between the Law and the Gospel, justice and mercy, plagues the FLW document produced in response to this Encyclical's call for the Orthodox Church to say *something* about a wide range of social issues, including economics.

But first, back to the good: "Our service to God is fundamentally doxological in nature and essentially Eucharist in character,"[28] says FLW, clearly evoking Schmemann's work of the same name, though again without crediting him. It continues, "Communion with Christ in the face of our neighbor . . . lies behind the first and great commandment of the Law to love God with one's whole heart and one's neighbor as oneself."[29] Furthermore, "Being made in the image and likeness of God, each person is unique and infinitely precious, and each is a special object of God's love."[30] It also acknowledges the importance

---

22  Encyclical, 1.3, 1.5.
23  Encyclical, 5.11, 5.12.
24  Encyclical, 6.16
25  Encyclical, 5.10.
26  Encyclical, 5.14.
27  Encyclical, 6.15, italics original.
28  David Bentley Hart and John Chryssavgis, eds., *For the Life of the World: Toward a Social Ethos of the Orthodox Church* (Holy Cross Orthodox Press, 2020), 1.1, 2. Henceforth, FLW.
29  FLW, 1.2, 2.
30  FLW, 1.3, 2.

of asceticism,[31] correctly connecting it with the Eucharist.[32] And it insists, "Christ's teachings confirm, while making even more urgent, the largest and most universal moral demands made by the Law and the Prophets of Israel: provision for the destitute, care for the stranger, justice for the wronged, mercy for all."[33] Though the term *catholicity* is only used in the context of ecumenical relations,[34] we can charitably see at least an intuition that Eucharist, asceticism, and care for the poor and marginalized should form a seamless garment for any Orthodox social ethos. Additionally, it at least acknowledges the importance of natural law and does repeatedly emphasize the inviolability of human dignity, from conception to natural death.

Furthermore, Archdeacon John Chryssavgis and philosopher David Bentley Hart make clear in their editorial preface that the commission "endeavored to steer well clear of simplistic, pietistic, or legalistic pronouncements"[35] and that they "sought to abstain altogether from the language and intonations of judgment or condemnation"[36] and that "its critiques [are] strictly constructive."[37] On several issues the document strikes that tone well. For example, it acknowledges the great benefits of modern medicine while warning of bioethical challenges, likely benefitting from the expertise of commission member Gayle Wooloschak, an expert in radiobiology and bionanotechnology at Northwestern University. Its ecological perspective no doubt benefited from Archdeacon Chryssavgis's expertise in environmental theology as well. It also praises the many blessings of modern democracy, while nevertheless warning of nationalism, secularism, and politicization, likely benefitting from the expertise of commission member Aristotle Papanikolaou, an expert in Orthodox political theology. Indeed, much better than Moscow, the document deserves commendation for its clear and unambiguous support for freedom of conscience. Charitably, we can also credit FLW with a creative spirit reminiscent of Social Gospel theologian Walter Rauschenbusch.

---

31   FLW, 1.4, 4.
32   FLW, 1.5, 5.
33   FLW, 1.6, 6.
34   FLW, 6.50, 68–69.
35   Hart and Chryssavgis, "Preface," in FLW, xviii.
36   Hart and Chryssavgis, xix.
37   Hart and Chryssavgis, xix.

## The Bad of FLW

UNFORTUNATELY, THE COMMISSION DID NOT include any Orthodox economists, businesspeople, or other scholars of related topics, and
it shows. Its section on wealth and poverty is devoid of any praise or gratitude whatsoever for the unprecedented abundance of the world we live in or
the economic arrangements and entrepreneurial endeavors that have made
that abundance possible. This abundance has led to the most drastic—and
ongoing—reduction of poverty in human history. Doesn't it deserve mention in a statement like this? Indeed, despite the editors' foreswearing of
judgmentalism, the section on wealth and poverty contains nine instances
of the word "condemn." It correctly notes, as we saw earlier in this book, that
"all creation's plenty comes from God and is the common birthright of all
persons; anything the rich man possesses has been entrusted to him for the
common good, and all he has belongs to all others."[38] But without understanding this—as the Fathers did—within the context of the proper ends of
one's stewardship of private property, the statement starts to sound nearly
communist, in the sense of condemning private ownership. Indeed, despite
its praise for human rights, it never once even acknowledges private property
to be among them, which according to the Edict of Milan and St. Nicholas
Cabasilas would unintentionally undermine its support for freedom of conscience as well.

Far more troubling, the FLW actually employs Marxist language, such
as "wage slavery"[39] and "the late capitalist world."[40] To be clear, I'm not
calling anyone on the commission a Marxist. They clearly are not, given
that they are not atheists and do not appeal to a deterministic social-
historical dialectic, which characterize the Marxist worldview, as we saw
in chapter 29. However, these terms are Marxist in their origin, as we saw
in chapter 30, and it is only Marxist analysis that makes them comprehen-
sible. As John Maynard Keynes put it, "Practical men, who believe themselves to be quite exempt from any intellectual influences, are usually the

---

38    FLW, 4.34, 45.
39    FLW, 4.36, 48.
40    FLW, 3.30, 39.

slaves of some defunct economist."[41] In the case of FLW, that economist is Karl Marx.

The term "wage slavery" depends on the debunked ideas of the labor theory of value and equality in exchange. Thus, it presumes that all profit comes from the exploitation of workers. "Late capitalism" refers to the belief that the class conflict caused by this alleged exploitation will lead to a crisis and collapse of modern market economies, and that we are very close to such a tipping point. These phrases make for effective memes on social media, but from the perspective of modern economics, they are pseudoscientific.

Rather, prices reflect the subjective marginal utility of products, not "congealed labour-time,"[42] to use Marx's term. Profit comes from producing and exchanging goods that people want and that they are willing to pay more than the costs of production to get. And Marxists have been talking about "late capitalism" for over a century now but the supposedly imminent crisis and collapse remains yet to come. Why? Because Marxist analysis does not accurately describe social or economic reality and thus cannot help us better understand or improve it. Exploitation only happens when labor contracts result not from freedom but from force or fraud, in which case, to be clear, the Church certainly should denounce it.

Unfortunately, Marxist memes are not the only problem with FLW. It is furthermore plagued by factual inaccuracies. For example, it asserts that economic globalization has increased poverty and inequality. This is an empirical claim that therefore requires empirical evidence to support it, which FLW does not provide. Thank God, according to Oxford's Our World in Data project, the opposite is the case.[43] Indeed, to cite just one remarkable example, in 2024, according to the World Bank, India completely eliminated extreme poverty

---

41 John Maynard Keynes, *The General Theory of Employment, Interest, and Money* (Harcourt, Brace and Company, 1935), 384.

42 Karl Marx, *Capital: A Critical Analysis of Capitalist Production*, trans. Samuel Moore and Edward Aveling, ed. Friedrich Engels, vol. 1 (Swan Sonnenschein, 1904), 6.

43 See Joe Hasell, Bertha Rohenkohl, Pablo Arriagada, Esteban Ortiz-Ospina, and Max Roser, "Economic Inequality," *Our World in Data* (2023), https://ourworldindata.org /economic-inequality; Joe Hasell et al., "Poverty," *Our World in Data* (2022), https:// ourworldindata.org/poverty; Max Roser, "Extreme Poverty: How Far Have We Come, and How Far Do We Still Have to Go?" *Our World in Data*, August 27, 2023, https:// ourworldindata.org/extreme-poverty-in-brief.

through international trade, economic liberalization (which includes private property and the rule of law), infrastructure improvements, and educational initiatives[44]—basically everything involved in Adam Smith's "obvious and simple system of natural liberty."[45] India still has a long way to go, but it continues to improve. And when over a billion people no longer face the harshest poverty in the world, those of us concerned with feeding the hungry, clothing the naked, and sheltering the homeless ought to listen and learn from how it happened.

Instead, FLW adds more inaccuracies, claiming, "Whole schools of economics arose in the twentieth century at the service of [extreme] inequality, arguing that it is a necessary concomitant of any functioning economy. Without fail, however, the arguments employed by these schools are tautologous at best, and proof of how impoverished the human moral imagination can make itself in servitude to ideology."[46] To which twentieth-century schools of economics do they refer? Not the Keynesian, Austrian, Ordoliberal, or Chicago schools discussed in chapters 31 and 32 of this book. Nor does this accurately describe any I wasn't able to cover, such as the Institutional, Experimental, or Behavioral schools. The supposedly tautological arguments of these unnamed schools are not discussed, and so the document asserts as "proof" a statement it has not proved.

This way of speaking shows a disappointing lack of intellectual charity and humility, a failure to first listen to economists and businesspeople before moralizing about their vocational areas of expertise. In light of this, when FLW then suggests that "new economic models" are needed, one must wonder, what is problematic about the current models? I tried my best to answer that question in Part 4 of this book, particularly in chapter 32. There is an opportunity not so much for new models but for fuller models that also account for spiritual, moral, and other noneconomic aspects of life, to which end I sought to "map" society in chapter 33. But FLW doesn't even identify this opportunity, nor does it encourage its readers to do so. In fact, it discourages them from doing so with its dismissive rhetoric.

---

44  "The World Bank in India," *World Bank Group*, last updated September 16, 2024. Amazingly, the benefits of basic education and other skills training for poverty alleviation are not mentioned by FLW either.

45  Adam Smith, *An Inquiry into the Nature and Causes of the Wealth of Nations*, 5th ed., 2 vols. (Methuen & Co., 1904), 2.4.9, 184, discussed in chapter 27.

46  FLW, 4.41, 56–57.

The inaccuracies continue when FLW claims, "The poor of most societies are victims of unprincipled credit institutions, and as a rule enjoy little protection from creditors who have exploited their need to place them in a condition of perpetual debt."[47] In fact, the poor in most societies cannot get loans at all because they have no credit or bad credit. Furthermore, the evaluation of credit scores as a prerequisite to lending is one way that modern lending largely is *not* usurious. The other way it avoids this sin is through modern bankruptcy laws, which allow people to renegotiate or cancel their debts if they become unable to pay, rather than being thrown into debtors' prisons or sold into slavery, as was the case in the ancient, medieval, and early modern eras. Moreover, Bangladeshi economist Muhammad Yunus received the Nobel Peace Prize in 2006 precisely for his work in microlending, which extends the benefits of credit to the poor through very small loans, because lending is a key means to *alleviating* poverty, *not* its cause.[48]

Holy Tradition has the tools we can use, along with modern economics, to enable our Orthodox Tradition to speak into concerns like this in our world today.[49] Unfortunately, FLW simply does not properly draw from the wisdom of either when it comes to its treatment of wealth and poverty. Indeed, its exhortations seem to imagine that we still live in the mid-nineteenth century, before things like bankruptcy laws, the forty-hour work week, mandatory holidays, and the social safety nets every developed nation provides today, as do even many developing ones.

## An Orthodox Assessment of FLW

I'VE FOUND FR. ALEXIS TORRANCE's evaluation of FLW to be an accurate distillation of the key problem: "At times, such as during the protracted

---

47 FLW, 4.39, 53.

48 Muhammad Yunus, "Nobel Prize Lecture," *Nobel Prize*, December 10, 2006, https://www.nobelprize.org/prizes/peace/2006/yunus/lecture/.

49 For example, with economist James Caton I have argued that student loans in the United States, which do not consider creditworthiness and are uniquely difficult to discharge in bankruptcy, in some cases qualify as usury according to the standards of the Scriptures and Church Fathers. See James Caton and Dylan Pahman, "Student Loans and the Sin of Usury," *Religion & Liberty Online*, September 6, 2023, https://rlo.acton.org/archives/124841-student-loans-and-the-sin-of-usury.html.

critique of unfettered capitalism, one senses an optimism that simply with the correct governmental policies and taxation models in place, the Gospel ideal as portrayed in Acts 2 might be, if not reached, at least approximated. Thus the document does not hesitate to call on the Church to 'require' and 'insist upon' certain governmental policies, including the active coercion of the wealthy to 'contribute as much as they can to the welfare of society as a whole.' "[50]

Indeed, though FLW acknowledges natural law, it claims that the Gospel merely "enlarges its range and makes its demands upon us absolute."[51] This misses the key distinction, discussed in chapter 12, that the justice of the Law is necessarily impersonal while the mercy of the Gospel is necessarily personal, thus falling into the sort of legalism the editors' sought to avoid. As illustrative of this, FLW quotes St. Maria Skobtsova's exhortation to *personal* charity as a support for national-level, *impersonal* state action.[52]

Alas, in this and many other areas, FLW could have been more helpful if it had even listened to Roman Catholic or Protestant social thought, from which it could have at least borrowed principles like subsidiarity or sphere sovereignty. Too often, issues that could better be addressed by institutions on a more personal and local level are harmfully elevated to the national and international levels and limited to state action, which blurs the boundaries between the spheres of social life. At the same time, national and transnational issues are either not mentioned at all—like inflation—or are badly misrepresented—like international trade.[53] Once again, Holy Tradition does have a vital voice to add to these conversations, but I'm afraid it truly would have been better for FLW to stay silent on economics. Though it wishes to be a prophetic "voice . . . crying in the wilderness" (Is. 40:3), its lack of charity

---

50  Alexis Torrance, "To Live is Christ: Exploring the Promise and Limits of *For the Life of the World*," *Studies in Christian Ethics* 35, no. 2 (2022): 229.

51  FLW, 1.7, 8.

52  FLW, 4.41, 57

53  With economist Alexander Salter, I've been able to write about how inflationary monetary policy falls short of "a perfect and just measure" (Deut. 25:15), as well as how international trade allows people to serve their neighbors across the world, getting the words of Nicaea II and St. John Chrysostom published in the *Wall Street Journal*. See Dylan Pahman and Alexander William Salter, "In God—and Sound Money—We Trust," *Wall Street Journal*, July 15, 2022; "Jesus Saves, but He's No Protectionist," *Wall Street Journal*, October 21, 2022.

and understanding of economic issues makes it more like "sounding brass or a clanging cymbal" (1 Cor. 13:1).

To be fair, as Torrance points out, "This is a text that calls its readers to go further and does not arrogate any special binding authority to itself. It would be a mistake either to treat the document as a last word on the matter, or as an ethical programme sufficient unto itself."[54] Torrance suggests, in line with the Council of Crete's encyclical, that future work should focus more on the transformation of the heart through repentance, since the heart is the source of sin. I second that. The heart should be an altar of prayer out of which we eucharistically offer the world back to God in all our vocations. In addition, I hope this book will be regarded as a further resource first to listen, and then to speak, more responsibly about issues of wealth and poverty in our economies today.

## Ecumenical Patriarch Bartholomew

I'LL CLOSE WITH A BETTER alternative to both the BSC and FLW: Ecumenical Patriarch Bartholomew's book *Encountering the Mystery*. Bartholomew's perspective on economic globalization is not without its own inaccuracies,[55] but his tone in this work at least evinces an effort to listen in charity, and his eyes aren't blind to the blessings we've received alongside the novel challenges of our world today, especially environmental concerns. "The globalization of the world's economy," writes His All-Holiness, "is . . . a continuous process, which cannot be understood even minimally without patient, careful analysis."[56] He notes that "its consequences are both positive and negative," and thus "it would not be correct simply to say that globalization is detrimental in all circumstances. . . . On the contrary, it is worth reflecting on how much has been achieved in recent years, in particular for the 800 million people in Asia—especially in India and China—whose poverty has been alleviated and whose quality of life has improved through education, health, and technology."[57] All the more so, I

---

54 Torrance, "To Live is Christ," 224.
55 See, e.g., Bartholomew I of Constantinople, *Encountering the Mystery: Perennial Values of the Orthodox Church* (Doubleday, 2008), 157, 164.
56 Bartholomew, *Encountering the Mystery*, 153.
57 Bartholomew, 153.

would add, we should reflect on the progress that has been made in Asia—as well as Africa and elsewhere—since he wrote this in 2008.

Bartholomew additionally articulates the Stoic and patristic[58] distinction between good, evil, and indifferent things, writing, "It is true, of course, that many people are uncomfortable speaking about money and wealth; this is perhaps more true of religious people, who will either denounce money as demonic (see Matt. 6:24) or silently idolize wealth as a blessing. Theologically and spiritually, however, the significance of money depends very much on what we do with it."[59] This perspective is so necessary and helpful for responsible Orthodox Christian social thought.

For example, in 2015 I had the opportunity to visit Greece to present a paper at a conference in Delphi. Afterward, I traveled to Thessaloniki to interview two priests about the work of their parishes in the midst of the Greek financial crisis. At Panagia Acheiropoietos, Fr. Spyridon told me how seeing the struggles of businesspeople in his parish changed his perspective: "There were many years in the history of Greece when there was confusion regarding body and soul. We took donations but we were against any kind of business. Money was black." Reflecting on those years in light of his present work to help those who had lost their businesses and jobs, he admirably admitted, "we were wrong."[60] Voices like his need to be heard to give a clearer representation of Holy Tradition in the broader conversation of modern Christian social thought today.

Bartholomew furthermore draws out the principle of ecumenicity in a way that echoes catholicity and sobornost': "The ecumenicity of the Orthodox Church, differs substantially from the recent phenomenon of economic globalization. The former is based on love for all people and respects the human person, whom it serves in its totality. The latter is primarily motivated by the

---

58  See John Chrysostom, *Against Publishing the Errors of the Brethren*, 2, in NPNF[1] 9:236; John Cassian, *Conferences*, 21.14, in NPNF[2] 11:508–09; Gregory Nazianzen, *Orations*, 2.22, in NPNF[1] 7:209; Basil of Caesarea, *Letters*, 236.7, in NPNF[2] 8:278. See also the discussion in chapter 11 of this book.

59  Bartholomew, *Encountering the Mystery*, 157.

60  Dylan Pahman, "'Crucified Love': The Human Side of the Greek Crisis," *Acton Commentary*, June 24, 2015, https://www.acton.org/pub/commentary/2015/06/24/crucified-love-human-side-greek-crisis.

desire to enlarge the economy."[61] Combining this with S. L. Frank's perspective, we can see how that ecumenicity might truly fulfill, rather than abolish, that global economic order. How so?

"Western societies have not really found any more beneficial economic mechanism than the markets to regulate the activities of labor and capital," writes Bartholomew. He then continues in a way that echoes Ordoliberal economist Wilhelm Röpke: "The Western system of capitalism forever seeks new ways of reducing costs and increasing gains. Nevertheless, not even the strongest advocates of capitalism would claim that it can serve as a basis for human society unless its activity is underpinned and regulated in the light of moral and spiritual values, which recognize the ultimate value of human beings," citing concerns such as care for the environment and upholding a moral culture.[62]

Indeed, Bartholomew makes clear, "I am by no means advocating sharing of wealth or eradication of poverty through some abstract dogma or Marxist formula for the redistribution of wealth."[63] Commenting on how ineffective international aid often is, he writes, "The kind of aid that is required is such that the recipient will be enabled to produce and empowered to thrive as a particular and unique nation in a global market. Then the act of giving—which is transformed into the art of communion and encounter—becomes an enrichment and blessing for all."[64]

If any council or patriarchate of the Orthodox Church should choose to make another statement—official or otherwise—on economic issues in the future, I suggest it take His All-Holiness's balanced approach here as a better baseline. Bartholomew both listens and speaks in a way that witnesses to, rather than detracts from, the Gospel of the Kingdom and its essential role in advancing the common good of our economies and communities today.

---

61    Bartholomew, *Encountering the Mystery*, 159.
62    Bartholomew, 170. Wilhelm Röpke and Ordoliberal political economy are discussed in chapter 31 of this book.
63    Bartholomew, 170.
64    Bartholomew, 168.

# Part 5 Summary and Discussion Questions

## Summary

TRADITIONALLY, ALL CHRISTIANS—PROTESTANT, ROMAN CATHO-LIC, and even Orthodox—thought about society in terms of family, state, and Church. Seeing that this social map was inadequate for the industrial era, figures such as Vladimir Soloviev saw the need to add "culture" or "economics." But even this sometimes falls short. Alternatively, Adam Smith understood society in terms of the state, the market, and beneficent relations or "civil society," which happen to correspond perfectly with the ascetic states of the servant, steward, and child of God in Holy Tradition. The economist Kenneth Boulding more precisely distinguished between threat, exchange, and integrative systems and dynamics. Augmenting his schema with a fourth system and dynamic also drawn from Holy Tradition—friendship—yielded four different "economies": the grants economy (consisting of threat and integrative systems) that is hierarchical and materially zero-sum; the exchange economy (consisting of market and friendship systems) that is egalitarian and materially positive-sum; the impersonal economy (consisting of threat and market systems); and the personal economy (consisting of integrative and friendship systems). This new map serves as a way to integrate insights of Christian social thought and modern economics to evaluate and incorporate more recent Orthodox contributions.

Although the idea of divine Sophia or Wisdom being reflected in creation, or "sophiology," has generated controversy, the reflections of Fr. Sergei

Bulgakov and Fr. Pavel Florensky on the role of divine Wisdom in economics and friendship can inform Orthodox social thought today. Together, they offer an image of the revelatory nature of the exchange economy, as well as of friendship and market dynamics in other social systems. Just as the Church is one body with many members, so also the division of labor in other social bodies to which we belong reflects God's Wisdom in ordering our social life for the good of our neighbors. Everyday miracles come about by the unplanned coordination of entire economies, offering us a revelation of God's wise and continuing care for His creation. And in these relationships, we form friendships that enrich our whole lives beyond these contexts.

Through the work of S. L. Frank, we discovered the distinction between the internal, personal, and spiritual unity of sobornost' or catholicity, on the one hand, and the external unity of mechanical or impersonal orders on the other. These respectively correspond to the distinction between grace and the law, mercy and justice, as proper to the personal and impersonal economies. Understood as the basis of sobornost' in society, Frank speaks of the "church" (lowercase) as the underlying holiness that gives even mechanical social orders, such as states and markets, true life and vitality. Building upon her own experiences of losing her daughter and caring for the poor—and later persecuted Jews—in Paris, St. Maria Skobtsova developed her concept of the imitation of the Mother of God. Through following the example of the Theotokos, we come to embody the sobornost' that turns our relations to others from "he," "she," and "they," to "I," "you," and "we," co-suffering with our neighbors and seeing them as living icons of Christ.

Though well-known today, Orthodox liturgical theology owes much of its origin to the work of Fr. Alexander Schmemann. His book *For the Life of the World* outlines a eucharistic worldview, arguing that living liturgically and sacramentally allows us to overcome social binaries, such as between fundamentalism and secularism. Furthermore, in the light of his *Great Lent* and the work of Paul Evdokimov, we see that liturgical theology also necessarily includes asceticism. Nevertheless, modern Orthodox liturgical theology can also be augmented by "mysteriological piety," for example in the work of St. Nicholas Cabasilas, which highlights the importance of holy places and of holy altars in particular, for there can be no Sacraments, no liturgy, without the altar. But the archetype of the altar is our human nature itself, thus reinforcing the ascetic dimension of our liturgical life, as demonstrated by Orthodox priests in the Soviet Gulag who celebrated the Divine Liturgy on the chest of a fellow convict-priest. So, too, through hesychasm, the mind enters the altar of the heart to offer sacrifices of praise to God through the words of the Jesus Prayer: "Lord Jesus Christ, Son of God, have mercy on me, a sinner." In so doing, we cultivate what Evdokimov called "interior monasticism," appropriating the spirit of traditional monastic vows into our own everyday asceticism, conforming our vocations and relationships to the ideal of Christ.

At the end of the twentieth century, the Orthodox Church still had no official statements on Christian social thought. That changed with the *Basis of the Social Concept* (BSC) of the Russian Orthodox Church in 2000 and the (technically unofficial) document *For the Life of the World* (FLW) in 2020, written in response to the Encyclical of the Council of Crete in 2016. First, while the BSC has some highlights in terms of affirming the right to private property and framing Orthodox social engagement in terms of kenosis, it also has shortcomings. In particular, it repeatedly contradicts itself, and the actions of the Moscow Patriarchate unfortunately have even proved hypocritical compared to its own standards in the BSC, such as how it sold eight billion cigarettes in the mid-1990s despite decrying addictive products as vice and sin. Second, FLW helpfully emphasizes some of the insights of liturgical theology, and the document tends to be most balanced in areas of the commission members' expertise. However, FLW is plagued with problems when it comes to wealth and poverty. It never even acknowledges the right to private property, instead invoking Marxist memes to support economically imprudent and impossible exhortations. Indeed, many of its economic claims are factually incorrect. It claims the world is getting poorer and more unequal, when thankfully the opposite is the case. It never expresses any gratitude for the abundance we live in today, nor any praise for the economic arrangements and entrepreneurial creativity responsible for it. At the end of the day, it would have been better to be silent on economics. A better alternative to both the BSC and FLW can be seen, however, in the work of Ecumenical Patriarch Bartholomew. While his book *Encountering the Mystery* does contain some factual inaccuracies, too, he nevertheless does not fall into the grave errors of either the BSC or FLW, and future official statements, should there be any, could be improved by following his example.

## Discussion Questions

- What do you think of the new social map drawn up in chapter 33? Are there any missing dimensions? Where might the Church fit into this social schema?
- Have you ever done any job or creative work that revealed something of Paradise?
- How do your closest friendships reveal the Wisdom of God in the goodness of creation and God's purposes for its transfiguration?
- According to S. L. Frank, how does distinguishing between internal and external unity help us relate the holiness of Christian life and the abundance of our modern economies?
- How does the imitation of the Mother of God differ from the imitation of Christ, according to St. Maria Skobtsova?
- How does Fr. Alexander Schmemann relate the Eucharist to our lives in the world?
- How does asceticism relate to the way we use scarce resources in our economies?
- What does it look like to cultivate Paul Evdokimov's "interior monasticism" in our economies today?
- Is silence in the face of injustice really violence? What does Holy Tradition teach us about silence?
- What are the strengths and weaknesses of the *Basis of the Social Concept* of the Russian Orthodox Church regarding wealth, poverty, and economics?
- What are the strengths and weaknesses of the *For the Life of the World* document of the Ecumenical Patriarchate regarding wealth, poverty, and economics?
- How does Ecumenical Patriarch Bartholomew's approach to economic globalization differ from the *Basis of the Social Concept* and the *For the Life of the World* document?

# A Vision, Not a Platform

As a member of the Greek Orthodox Church in America, whenever I travel, if I'm away on a Sunday, I go to Liturgy at a Greek parish if I can. In the summer months, I often hear announcements and advertisements for each parish's upcoming Greek festival. In these wonderful community events, which combine commerce and culture in order to raise funds to continue the work of the Church, I see an icon, however imperfect, of Paradise. Orthodox families and individuals, regardless of earthly political preferences, come together and volunteer in order to extend hospitality and provide products and services for their neighbors, all for the glory of God. Traveling bands of Greek musicians play strange songs in odd time signatures while children miraculously dance to them in antiquated outfits. Priests and lay educators give tours of the nave and teach visitors about our funny, foreign faith. And of course, parishes of other archdioceses have their own ethnic festivals, too. Perhaps someday, when "all nations shall come and worship before" the Lord (Rev. 15:4), there will even be an Orthodox Oktoberfest or Irish festival. This Celtic and German American can hope, at least.

## *Seeing the Kingdom Within Us*

Astute readers will have noticed by this point that I have failed to outline the One-and-Only-Orthodox™ political platform. Like F. D. Maurice,

"I am only a digger,"[1] excavating down to the foundation so that others can build upon it. I have endeavored to provide in one book an introduction to all the resources—including impressive ecumenical insights, timeless biblical wisdom, challenging historical episodes, counterintuitive economic science, and overlooked theological principles—that might help us see even in our new and strange economies today the Kingdom of God that is at once "within you" (Luke 17:21), "at hand" (Matt. 3:2), and yet to come (see Matt. 6:10; Luke 11:2). My hope is that as a result, whatever someone's earthly vocation, he or she might better follow our one universal calling—as members of the Orthodox and Catholic Church and citizens of the Kingdom of heaven—to deny ourselves, take up our crosses daily, and follow Jesus Christ (see Luke 9:23). In that Orthodox Christian spirit, I hope to see more friendships, schools, businesses, ministries, institutes, and associations in the years to come.

## Seeing the Kingdom at Hand

ORTHODOX SOCIAL THOUGHT MAY HAVE been undertheorized in recent times, but it has always existed. Moreover, Orthodox social action continues in all ages despite persecutions, hardships, crises, and sins. In my own parish, Holy Trinity, I have seen lavish generosity, often hidden and unheralded. The priests, imitating St. Nicholas, have at least once donated their services—and the parish donated its hall—to a young couple who otherwise could not afford a wedding. Parishioners have doted upon new parents and their children. The dead have been buried and memorialized. Care packages have been distributed to the homeless. Once a young man with no place to go found shelter in a family's summer cottage and avoided homelessness. And church members have volunteered more than once to renovate houses in our communities to be sold at an affordable price to lower-income families. I've seen coffee hours of abundant and delicious food amount to full meals for all who came, with only a basket set out for freewill donations. Again and again, strangers and refugees have been welcomed with love and hospitality. The lonely have found friends.

---

1 F. D. Maurice, To a Dear Friend [J. M. Ludlow], Rodington Rectory, Shrewsbury, September 8, 1852, in *The Life of Frederick Denison Maurice: Chiefly Told in His Own Letters*, ed. [John] F. Maurice, 2 vols. (Charles Scribner's Sons, 1884), 2:132.

The fatherless, orphaned, and estranged have gained godfamilies, father confessors, and God himself as their Father. The jobless have found employment through businessowners willing to take a risk and invest in them. Those struggling financially received help paying their bills. More than one autistic youth has been welcomed and integrated by his young peers into Greek Orthodox Youth of America (GOYA) events and teams. Parish council and endowment board members have worked without pay to ensure the continual functioning of our community life.

We've supported missionaries preaching the Gospel, caring for orphans, and bringing medicine and healing to the sick in far-off lands, as well as working to expand domestic ministries. We've worked through organizations like Philoptochos, International Orthodox Christian Charities (IOCC), Orthodox Christian Mission Center (OCMC), and FOCUS North America. Indeed, the unending generosity of our communities demonstrates the observation of economist John Bates Clark: "That which costs millions of dollars is, in this way, offered without reserve to whoever will take it."[2] We are students, factory workers, insurance agents, lawyers, doctors, nurses, nannies, reporters, politicians, entrepreneurs, accountants, therapists, restauranteurs, salespeople, retail workers, writers, artists, musicians, poets, teachers, coaches, and parents, even editors and academics. Most of all, we are Orthodox Christians. Of course, we have our faults and shortcomings, but those shadows recede whenever I just look, with gratitude, at what great light the love of God has shone upon us. I know that catholicity still exists in the Orthodox Church today, because I see it all around me.

If Christ can do all this among us, without any sophisticated intellectual frameworks, how much more might he do with the five loaves and two fishes offered herein? My goal has not been to convince my readers to sign on to another partisan program, but rather to help them more clearly see what talents and heavenly treasures our Lord has already entrusted them to creatively invest—and which in many cases they are already investing—so that they will yield interest when he returns. All of us—rich or poor, young or old, women or men, able-bodied or disabled, and so on—can see the Lord in the

---

2    John B. Clark, *The Philosophy of Wealth: Economic Principles Newly Formulated* (Ginn and Company, 1886), 228.

eyes of our neighbors, through serving their needs in our families, friendships, jobs, civic roles, and in any other sphere of life. For through the Eucharist, "we, though many, are one bread and one body; for we all partake of that one bread" (1 Cor. 10:17).

## Seeing Christ in Our Bishops

I HOPE MORE AND MORE of us will also be able to look each to our own bishop—not just patriarchs or international councils—and once again see "the protector of all those in need,"[3] as St. Justin the Philosopher once did. Indeed, one last time, as St. Ignatius of Antioch put it, "Where the bishop is present, there let the congregation gather, just as where Jesus Christ is, there is the Catholic Church."[4] Some economic problems truly arise at a global or national level, but just as many are regional or local matters. The Church wisely has developed its episcopal structure to offer guidance on a more personal, subsidiary level, through homilies, encyclicals, initiatives, and yes, when appropriate and necessary, even political advocacy. Sometimes state policy and privilege exclude people from market access or otherwise impede healthy economic mobility. Sometimes programs intended to help the poor fall short or even worsen the problem. In these cases bishops can—and perhaps already do—privately intercede with those officials who have the power to reverse course, elevating the personal stories of those among their flocks adversely affected by them before resorting to public statements. So, too, I'd love to see our bishops lead the way to lock arms with those of other churches in principled cooperation to spread the justice and mercy of the Lord to the poor and marginalized in our communities, through charitable work and thoughtful, responsible advocacy. "For he who is not against us is on our side" (Mark 9:40). Moreover, the Church still has her canon law, administered by our bishops, as a code of mercy to help us on the road of repentance and set an example of the rule of law for whatever polities we may inhabit. Perhaps bishops could also follow the example of early Celtic abbots, issuing

3    Justin Martyr, "First Apology," 67, in *Early Christian Fathers*, ed. Cyril C. Richardson (Westminster Press, 1953), 287.
4    Ignatius of Antioch, To the Smyrnaeans, 8.1–2, in *Early Christian Fathers*, 115.

social and moral guidebooks for their flocks—monastic and lay—in their specific contexts.

## Seeing Monks in Our Cities

I HOPE ALONGSIDE THE PROLIFERATION of Athonite monasteries across our countrysides that has so enriched and demonstrated our Orthodox Faith in non-Orthodox lands, someday we'll see more urban monasteries, too, after the model of St. Basil, founded in the hearts of our busy cities, as I've seen, for example, in Bucharest, Athens, and Thessaloniki. Population-dense urban centers so dearly need the example of those who order their whole lives toward the acquisition of the Spirit of Peace, that thousands around them might be saved. So, too, in our epidemic of loneliness, people need not only external services but to see the transcendent joy of a virginal life, showing how, just as they are, they too are not only "loved, but . . . lovely; or . . . that thing which is the natural and proper object of love,"[5] as Adam Smith put it. Both the rich and poor in our cities need to see those who have taken vows of material poverty for the sake of spiritual riches. Those worn down by demanding work need to see those who daily labor to maintain a holy hostel and regularly rest to observe the commemorations of the liturgical year. The sleep-deprived need to see those who keep prayerful vigil into the night as they wait for the coming of our Bridegroom. Those consumed by chasing the latest trend and luxury need to see the glories of fasting . . . and perhaps also consider purchasing candles, prayer books, incense, icons, or other devotional items while they are out shopping. The ringing of chapel bells should echo against skyscraper walls, and Orthodox crosses atop domes and spires should be seen from high rise windows as both a revelation of what the world could be and as a sign of contradiction, witnessing to what it fails to attain.

---

5   Adam Smith, *The Theory of Moral Sentiments*, 6th ed., 3.2, in *The Theory of Moral Sentiments; Or, An Essay towards an Analysis of the Principles by Which Men Naturally Judge Concerning the Conduct and Character, First of Their Neighbours, and Afterwards of Themselves. To Which Is Added, A Dissertation on the Origin of Languages*, new ed. (Henry G. Bohn, 1853), 166.

## Seeing the Resurrection

WHATEVER OUR VOCATIONS, I HOPE we continue to grow in understanding of the mystery of Jesus Christ, "who, being in the form of God, did not consider it robbery to be equal with God, but made Himself of no reputation, taking the form of a bondservant, and coming in the likeness of men. And [who] being found in appearance as a man . . . humbled Himself and became obedient to the point of death, even the death of the cross" (Phil. 2:6–8). The more we do that, the more we will acquire the mind of Christ and ascetically imitate His extreme humility in our service of others, "look[ing] out not only for [our] own interests, but also for the interests of others" (Phil. 2:4). For if our world needs healing—and it does—we need only remember that central insight of Byzantine humanism, as St. Gregory the Theologian put it, "That which [Christ] has not assumed He has not healed; but that which is united to His Godhead is also saved."[6]

Though our economies today scarcely resemble those of times past, though social arrangements, innovations, industries, nations, and empires have passed away, I hope we will see glimpses of Pascha in all the new and wonderful blessings we enjoy today. Though we face challenges in novel forms—whether secularism, consumerism, new addictive substances and technologies, world economic crises, or anything else—we struggle against the same sins and the same "principalities," "powers," and "rulers of the darkness of this age" (Eph. 6:12). I hope we will see how the solution to these problems, our victory in that struggle, is the same eternal Gospel first proclaimed at a garden tomb to sorrowful, myrrhbearing women: "You seek Jesus who was crucified . . . He is risen, as He said. Come [and] see" (Matt. 28:5–6). When it comes to Orthodox Christian social thought, in the wisdom of Christ's Catholic Church, where the world becomes the Kingdom of God through the bright light of lives reborn through Baptism and lived together in repentance, there is no clearer summary than that of the Creed: "I look for the resurrection of the dead and the life of the age to come." My hope is full of resurrection. Can you see it, too?

---

6   Gregory Nazianzen, Epistle 101: To Cledonius the Priest against Apollinaris, in *NPNF*[2] 7:440.

# Scripture Index

## Old Testament

Genesis: 1:1, 50; 1:27–28, 51; 1:28, 233, 237, 278, 313; 1:31, 51; 2:4, 51; 2:5, 51; 2:15, 51; 2:17, 51; 2:18, 15; 2:20, 51; 3:15, 52, 69; 3:19, 313; 9:6, 246; 25:29–34, 261

Exodus: 18:17–18, 52; 18:21–22, 52; 20:2, 53; 20:12, 185, 300n1; 20:15, 55, 120, 185, 300; 21:24, 257

Leviticus: 12:8, 71; 19:9–10, 300; 19:11, 55; 19:13, 55; 19:15, 55; 19:18, 12, 35, 76, 225; 19:34–36, 55; 19:36, 120; 23:42–43, 79

Deuteronomy: 4:6–8, 56; 8:3, 132, 276, 303; 23:20, 178; 24:17, 178; 25:15, 210, 352n53; 26:5, 161, 171; 26:12, 161; 30:19, 55–56

Judges: 17:6, 58–59

1 Kingdoms/1 Samuel: 1, 148; 4:1–11, 236n20; 8:5, 59; 8:7, 59; 8:18, 60; 13:14, 122; 16:7, 319

2 Kingdoms/2 Samuel: 10:12, 236n20; 11–12, 122

3 Kingdoms/1 Kings: 21, 61, 120

4 Kingdoms/2 Kings: 5:1–19, 61

1 Chronicles: 22:7–8, 122

Tobit: 4:15, 223, 343

Judith: 5:13–19, 58

Esther: 4:14, 111

Psalms: 15/14:5, 67; 18/19:4, 147; 19/18:1, 67; 24/23:1, 191; 50/51:1, 122; 50/51:7, 336; 82/81:6–7, 68; 103/104:23–24, 311; 111/110:10, 85; 138/139:14, 238–39

Job: 2:10, 65; 28:12–13, 67; 28:15, 67

Proverbs: 3:18, 68; 8:12, 203; 8:23, 66; 8:27, 66; 8:31, 67; 18:24, 305; 20:3, 64; 22:6, 32; 30:8–9, 67

Ecclesiastes: 1:9, 4; 3:3, 179; 3:7, 340; 3:12–13, 67

Song of Songs: 3:5, 94; 8:7, 94

Wisdom of Solomon: 7:26, 67; 8:7, 203

Ecclesiasticus (Wisdom of Sirach): 1:9, 66; 3:30, 67; 29:20, 67

Hosea: 6:6, 61

Micah: 4:2, 62; 4:7, 62; 4:9, 62

Zechariah: 8:4–5, 96

Malachi: 4:5–6, 72

Isaiah: 2:4, 172–73; 6:9, 75; 40:3, 352; 56:6–8, 81; 58:3, 61; 58:6–7, 61; 58:6–8, 337; 61:1, 72, 73

Jeremiah: 7:11, 81; 29:7, 2–3, 115

367

# Subject Index

love, 36, 48, 85, 88, 113
Ludlow, J. M., 246, 247–48
Luke, 319
Luther, Martin, 19–20, 22, 45, 179
Lutheran social thought, 18–25; about,
    18–19, 41; Bonhoeffer, 22–23; four
    divine mandates, 22–23, 24, 41;
    Luther, 19–20; Orthodox assess-
    ment, 24–25; three creational
    estates, 20–21, 41, 249; on vocation,
    20–21, 83

# M
Macarius III, Patriarch of Antioch, 170
Maccabees, 58, 62
MacCulloch, Diarmaid, 143, 152–53,
    156–57, 158–59, 162, 163, 168–69,
    169n31
MacIntyre, Alasdair, 140, 150
macroeconomics, 268
Magic (The Gathering), 255, 259, 261
Magness, Phillip W., 269, 272
Malthus, Thomas Robert, 233–35, 237,
    239, 240, 241–42, 242n41, 293
mandates, four divine, 22–23, 24, 41
Marcion, 76
Marcus Aurelius, 109
Marginal Revolution, 255–67; about,
    205–6, 255–56, 294–95; marginal
    utility, 258–62, 338, 349; morality
    and, 262–65; Orthodox assessment,
    265–67
Mariana, Juan de, 210, 211, 216
mark of the beast, 95, 100
market price, 228–29
markets, 229, 293, 303, 304–5, 307
marriage, 23, 234, 235. See also family
Marsh, Christopher, 312

Marshall, Alfred, 258, 259, 260, 261,
    264–65, 266, 277
Martensen, Hans Lassen, 21, 24, 28,
    29, 31
Martin I (pope), 154, 155
Martin of Tours, 146
Marx, Karl (Marxism): about, 205, 243,
    294; on economics, 256–57; *For the
    Life of the World* (social ethos doc-
    ument) and, 348–49; vs. marginal
    analysis, 258–61; modifications to,
    267; Orthodox assessment, 253, 265;
    on "practical and violent action,"
    281; worldview, 244–46
Mary, Mother of God (Theotokos), 94,
    316, 319–20, 325, 327–28, 357
Matson, Erik, 225
Maurice, F. D., 28, 205, 243, 246–50,
    248n23, 253, 294, 301
Maximus the Confessor, 51, 65, 154,
    155–56
McGuckin, John Anthony, 128, 129–30
McVickar, John, 238
Melkites. *See* Middle Eastern
    Christians
memento mori, 68, 279, 290, 326
Menger, Carl, 255, 260, 261, 272
mercantilism, 219–20, 224, 225
mercy, vs. justice, 82, 164–65, 352
Meyendorff, John: on barbarian con-
    quest of Western Europe, 143–44;
    on Boethius, 145; on Byzantine
    Church-state relations, 154–55; on
    Carolingian renaissance, 156; on
    English Church, 152, 153; on Greg-
    ory the Great, 151, 152, 153–54; on
    Middle Eastern Christians, 162–63;
    on monasticism, 135; on social

# About the Author

**D**YLAN PAHMAN IS FOUNDER AND president of the St. Nicholas Cabasilas Institute for Orthodoxy & Liberty, and a research fellow at the Acton Institute, where he serves as executive editor of the *Journal of Markets & Morality*. He is also the author of *Foundations of a Free & Virtuous Society* (Acton Institute, 2017). In 2025, he completed his PhD in theology from St. Mary's University, Twickenham, London, on the basis of his published works on Orthodox Christian social thought and asceticism. He is husband to Kelly and father to four children.

We hope you have enjoyed and benefited from this book. Your financial support makes it possible to continue our nonprofit ministry both in print and online. Because the proceeds from our book sales only partially cover the costs of operating **Ancient Faith Publishing** and **Ancient Faith Radio**, we greatly appreciate the generosity of our readers and listeners. Donations are tax deductible and can be made at **www.ancientfaith.com.**

To view our other publications, please visit our website:
**store.ancientfaith.com**

ANCIENT FAITH
RADIO

Bringing you Orthodox Christian music, readings, prayers, teaching, and podcasts 24 hours a day since 2004 at
**www.ancientfaith.com**

www.ingramcontent.com/pod-product-compliance
Lightning Source LLC
Chambersburg PA
CBHW021210130626
46554CB00004B/1166